I0798779

German Assault Troops of World War I

German Assault Troops of World War I

Organization • Tactics • Weapons Equipment • Orders of Battle • Uniforms

Thomas Wictor

Schiffer Military History
Atglen, PA

Acknowledgements
My deepest gratitude is extended to Thierry Ehret, Maurice Sublet, Chris Boonzaier, Chip Minx, Naxos, and Jean-Claude Laparra, whose contributions were indispensible. Thank you also to Bob Biondi for suggesting I write this book and for making it a reality.

Dedication
For the men and women of the United States armed forces.

All photos from the author's collection unless otherwise credited.

Book design by Robert Biondi.

Copyright © 2012 by Thomas Wictor.
Library of Congress Catalog Number: 2012930220.

All rights reserved. No part of this work may be reproduced or used in any forms or by any means – graphic, electronic or mechanical, including photocopying or information storage and retrieval systems – without written permission from the publisher.

The scanning, uploading and distribution of this book or any part thereof via the Internet or via any other means without the permission of the publisher is illegal and punishable by law. Please purchase only authorized editions and do not participate in or encourage the electronic piracy of copyrighted materials.

"Schiffer," "Schiffer Publishing Ltd. & Design," and the "Design of pen and ink well" are registered trademarks of Schiffer Publishing, Ltd.

Printed in China.
ISBN: 978-0-7643-4036-9

We are always looking for people to write books on new and related subjects. If you have an idea for a book, please contact us at the address below.

Published by Schiffer Publishing Ltd.
4880 Lower Valley Road
Atglen, PA 19310
Phone: (610) 593-1777
FAX: (610) 593-2002
E-mail: Info@schifferbooks.com.
Visit our web site at: www.schifferbooks.com
Please write for a free catalog.
This book may be purchased from the publisher.
Please include $5.00 postage.
Try your bookstore first.

In Europe, Schiffer books are distributed by:
Bushwood Books
6 Marksbury Ave.
Kew Gardens, Surrey TW9 4JF
England
Phone: 44 (0)20 8392-8585
FAX: 44 (0)20 8392-9876
E-mail: info@bushwoodbooks.co.uk
www.bushwoodbooks.co.uk
Free postage in the UK. Europe: air mail at cost.
Try your bookstore first.

Contents

Introduction

Several outstanding, seminal books have been produced on the history of German assault troops of World War I. This work is more a study of the organization, tactics, weapons, equipment, orders of battle, and uniforms of assault units. Several German primary documents are presented in their entirety, translated into English. A few descriptions of specific actions are included in order to illustrate German assault tactics and Allied countermeasures.

Major battles such as Verdun, the Somme, Riga, Cambrai, and so on are not covered in great detail, as countless volumes have already been written about them; a certain level of historical and military knowledge is presumed in the reader.

It should also be noted that the men credited with originating or improving assault tactics left records that contradict each other and fail to mention the contributions of "competitors." Only a limited amount of space in this book will be devoted to the question of who devised shock-troop tactics, and no firm conclusions will be drawn. The purpose of this work is instead to present factual information in one convenient volume.

To avoid confusion over British and American usage, German ranks are not translated, and German terms such as *Leib* and *Jäger* are retained in unit names. The German term *Ersatz* is retained when applied to divisions but translated as "replacement" when used for training formations. When German unit names are placed in parentheses, brackets replace the parentheses in the original name. For example, *Jäger- (Sturm-) Bataillon Nr.3* is rendered *(Jäger- [Sturm-] Bataillon Nr.3)*.

Finally, it appears from records, unit stamps, and handwritten messages on the backs of wartime postcards that the terms "shock troop" *(Stosstrupp)* and "assault detachment" *(Sturmabteilung)* were virtually interchangeable and were applied to units ranging in size from a nine-man squad to a company. Offical definitions of the words apparently did not exist.

CHAPTER 1

Early Assault Troops

Mobilization

When Kaiser Wilhelm II issued his decree of mobilization on August 1, 1914, there were no dedicated German assault units. However, the terms "assault troops" *(Sturmtruppen)* and "assault detachment" *(Sturmabteilung)* had already been in use for several years. *The Fighting by German Troops in Southwest Africa,* by Military-Historical Detachment I of the General Staff, provides an example from 1906:

> Major von Estrorff had contributed all the forces he had at hand, and they were joined with the assault detachment *[Sturmabteilung]*.[1]

In 1910 the War Ministry *(Kriegsministerium)* published *Instructions for Combat against Fortresses (Anleitung für den Kampf um Festungen),* which laid out guidelines for the use of assault troops.

> The assault positions and the nearest approach trenches must provide sufficient space for the assault troops *[Sturmtruppen]* and their assault devices to be brought in and protected from enemy fire, and so that congestion can be avoided and the enemy reached quickly.

Three Seesoldaten of the 3rd Marine Infantry Battalion (III. Seebataillon) in Peking during the China Relief Expedition of August 1900. They wear the assault order (Sturmanzug) adopted before the war and later modified by shock troops. Uniformed in the dark blue (Dunkelblau) M1893 Litewka, they are armed with Gew 98 rifles and S/98 bayonets. Equipment consists of M1895 ammunition pouches, rolled M1892 tent square, M1850 mess kit, M1893 water bottle, and M1887 haversack.

Pionier of the Pioneer Experimental Company (Pionier-Versuchs-Kompagnie) in full marching order. His M1907/10 field jacket (Feldrock) has Guard lace (Garde Litzen) and black piping on the collar and Swedish cuffs. The helmet cover (Überzug) lacks a number, while the shoulder straps feature piping and a "V" in red. Equipment consists of M1907/13 knapsack (Tornister), M.1887/88 ammunition pouches, Gew 98 rifle, and pioneer shovel (Pionierspaten) held in a leather carrier.

This Grenadier of Grenadier Regiment No.4 (Königen Augusta Garde-Grenadier Regiment Nr.4) wears the white brassard adopted by assault troops early in the war to differentiate themselves from the enemy in the smoke and confusion of battle. His M1907/10 field jacket – also called the service jacket (Waffenrock) – is decorated with white Guard lace on the collar and Brandenburg cuffs.

> The assault orders are to be explained by sketches; information on the furnishings of the works and positions, about the obstacle lanes, etc., is to be added as attachments.
>
> The assault troops move into their assault positions while maintaining the utmost caution against discovery, guided by officers with knowledge of the locality, and if necessary even during the dark, so that no additional movement into the area is required. If artillery fire or the throwing of explosive charges is expected, the assault troops are to limit their stay in the assault positions to the shortest period possible.
>
> The assault positions remain occupied in the meantime by machine guns and riflemen. Each enemy who appears is fired on. The machine guns thereby engage the armored observation posts as their targets and set their aim on the assault-defense cannons in order to bring them down.[2]

Wartime instructions for the use of assault troops were not significantly different; it would therefore appear that what became known as shock-troop tactics *(Stosstrupptaktik)* were less a ground-breaking innovation than an extension of accepted German military doctrine.

Infantry Divisions

At the start of the war German infantry divisions were normally "square." The combat units consisted of:

> Two infantry brigades (two regiments of three battalions each, 12 battalions in total);
> four regimental machine-gun companies (six heavy weapons each, 24 in total);
> one cavalry regiment (three or four squadrons);
> one or two pioneer companies;
> one field-artillery brigade (two regiments of two detachments each; three six-gun batteries per detachment, for a total of 72 guns).[3]

A battalion contained four infantry companies of 240 rifles each. One division in each Corps also contained one *Jäger* battalion with one machine-gun company, one bicycle company, and one motorized-vehicle column.

Reserve divisions often lacked the machine-gun companies and sometimes included regiments comprised of only two battalions. They also had only one artillery regiment with six batteries, a cavalry regiment with three squadrons, and only one medical company.

Ersatz divisions were made up of three mixed *Ersatz* brigades with a total of 13-15 infantry battalions, six machine-gun companies, three cavalry squadrons, 12 field-artillery batteries (72 guns), and two pioneer companies.

Landwehr divisions generally contained 12 infantry battalions with no machine-gun companies, three or seven cavalry squadrons, two artillery batteries (12 guns), and one pioneer company.

The first 12 reserve divisions raised in wartime were square, containing two infantry brigades of two regiments each, one cavalry squadron, one field-artillery regiment with three detachments, and one or two pioneer companies. Each detachment of field artillery contained three four-gun batteries, for a total of 36 guns per division.

Wartime reserve divisions raised after the first 12 were "triangular," composed of one infantry brigade of three regiments. In addition, each of

Opposite
Top: Landwehr assault troops attending a religious service before a mission. They are equipped with assault packs (Sturmgepäcke) consisting of greatcoat and tent section rolled into a tube and worn across the body; the mess tin is strapped to the tube, the ends of which are tied together either on the shoulder or the hip. Most of the men have shaved their heads, and they are armed with obsolete Gew 88 rifles and S71 bayonets.

Bottom: Heavy machine-gun squad of Saxon Landwehr Grenadier Regiment No.100. The 7.92mm MG08 with its sled mounting (Schlitten) weighed 126 lb. This weapon has been fitted with a circular flash hider and trench armor consisting of barrel protection and a facial shield for the gunner; note the rubber hose connecting the water jacket to the condensation can. Fed by 250-round cloth belts, the MG08 had a maximum range of 4800 yd.

226/572.

The Fourth Squad (IV. Gruppe) of a platoon of the Bavarian 16th Infantry Regiment. Nine-man squads were basis for assault tactics; Roman numerals were often used to identify assault squads and shock troops. These men wear the M1907 field jacket with Brandenburg cuffs, the Bavarian M1915 simplified service jacket with plain turn-up cuffs, and the M1907 field cap (Feldmütze or Kratschen).

these reserve divisions had one field-artillery brigade of two regiments; a field-artillery regiment was comprised of three detachments of three four-gun batteries each, for a total of 72 guns per division.

Infantry divisions of the 50s series, raised after March of 1915, were also triangular, comprised of one brigade of three regiments (nine infantry battalions), three regimental machine-gun companies (six heavy weapons in each, for a total of 18), one field-artillery brigade (two regiments of three detachments each; two four-gun batteries per detachment, for a total of 48 guns), and one foot-artillery battalion (two four-gun batteries, for a total of eight guns).

Infantry Divisions 101-123 were also formed in March of 1915; they were each a triangular formation of one brigade of three regiments, one field-artillery regiment of two detachments, and one foot-artillery regiment of two battalions. Each artillery detachment and battalion contained two batteries of four guns each.

By the end of 1915, most active, reserve, *Landwehr,* and *Ersatz* divisions were organized in the same way:

> one infantry brigade of three regiments (nine battalions of four companies each, for a total of 36 infantry companies);
> nine machine-gun companies (one per battalion);
> one cavalry squadron;
> one field-artillery regiment of two detachments, soon increased to three detachments (three six-gun batteries per detachment);
> one or two pioneer companies;
> one trench-mortar detachment.

A rifle company was comprised of three platoons *(Züge)* of four sections *(Korporalschaften)* each; a section had two squads *(Gruppen)* of one *Gefreiter* and eight men each. The nine-man squad formed the basis for most small assault units during the war. In November of 1916 the Austro-Hungarian army also adopted the nine-man assault squad, which it dubbed the "assault patrol" *(Sturmpatrouille).*

Pioneer Assault Tactics

On mobilization each peacetime pioneer battalion was divided into two battalions of three companies each, becoming the 1st and 2nd Battalion (*I.* and *II. Bataillon*) of Pioneer Battalion No.1, the 1st and 2nd Battalion of Pioneer Battalion No.2, and so on.[4] The 1st Battalion had the 1st, 2nd, and 3rd Companies, while the 2nd Battalion had the 4th Company and 1st and 2nd Reserve Companies. One or two pioneer companies, Reserve pioneer companies, *Landwehr* pioneer companies, *Landsturm* pioneer companies, or *Ersatz* pioneer companies were assigned to each division. Each pioneer company consisted of six officers and 264 NCOs and men, while pioneer companies of cavalry divisions had two officers and 46 NCOs and men. There was a total of 218 pioneer companies available to the field army when the war began.

During 1914 the Supreme Army Command (*Oberste Heeresleitung* or *OHL*) created 109 additional pioneer companies. Ten pioneer regiments with siege trains were also formed in order to assault fortresses. Each pioneer regiment was comprised of two pioneer battalions.

The pioneer arm was trained in assaulting fortified positions with explosives and hand grenades. *Pioneer Assault Instructions (Pionier-Sturmanleitung)* was published by the War Ministry in 1904, more than a decade before the Germans established their first official assault formations:

> Pioneer squads are at the head of the assault detachments which arrive first at the trench. After the assault equipment has been set up, these pioneers will provide the necessary assistance in mopping up, putting armored turrets out of action, and opening entrances.

Assault squad of Reserve Infantry Regiment No.201. The caption reads, "Our fiendish enemy. Showing German strong post with troops." Weapons include Gew 98 rifles, stick grenades, and wooden clubs studded with nails.

Every now and then it is advisable to form single assault detachments entirely from pioneers or to put pioneer platoons or half-platoons at their heads, in order to take advantage of the greater skill of the pioneers in overcoming obstacles under particularly difficult conditions.

The advance from the assault position takes place noiselessly as long as it remains unnoticed. If the defender recognizes that the operation is underway and begins to fire, then the only consideration is the task of bringing the assault equipment to the position under all circumstances. In addition loud commands, shouts, and ruthless procedures are used to create the quickest pace at the site.

After taking the positions, the pioneer squads following the assault detachments will search out explosive charges set by the enemy and destroy the fuses.[5]

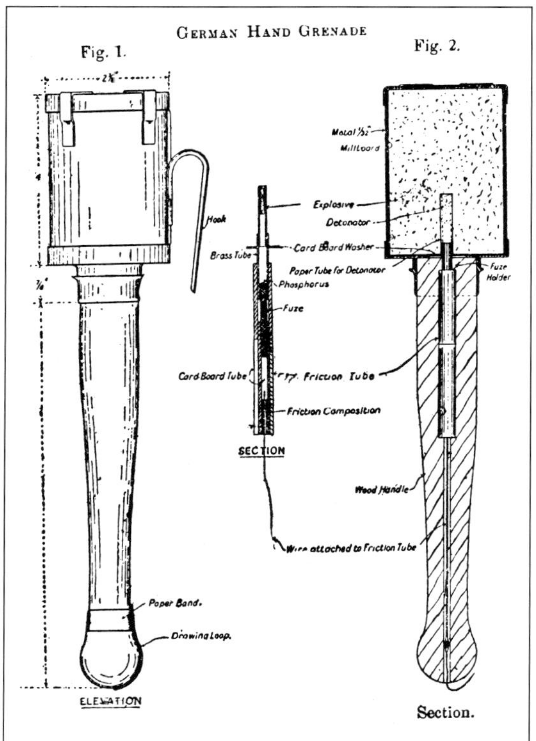

The M1915 stick grenade, which had a time fuse activated by pulling the lanyard taped to the ball-end handle. This arrangement was very dangerous, as the grenade could be accidentally set off if the lanyard caught on a projection. Note the belt hook on the grenade head.

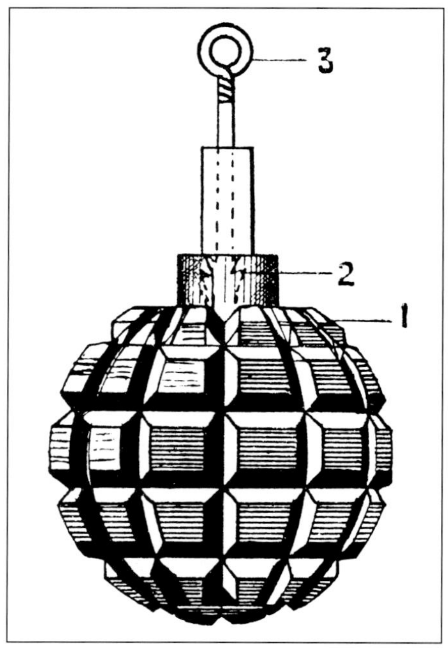

Above: The M1913 ball grenade (Kugelhandgranate). It had a friction fuse with a five- or seven-second delay, activated by pulling the wire ring. The grenade weighed 2.2 pounds and could be thrown about 16 yd by the average soldier; the segmented cast-iron shell produced 70 to 80 fragments.

Right: Pannier for M1913 ball grenade. It was hung on the belt, the chain attached to the pull ring of the grenade. Removing the grenade from the pannier activated the fuse.

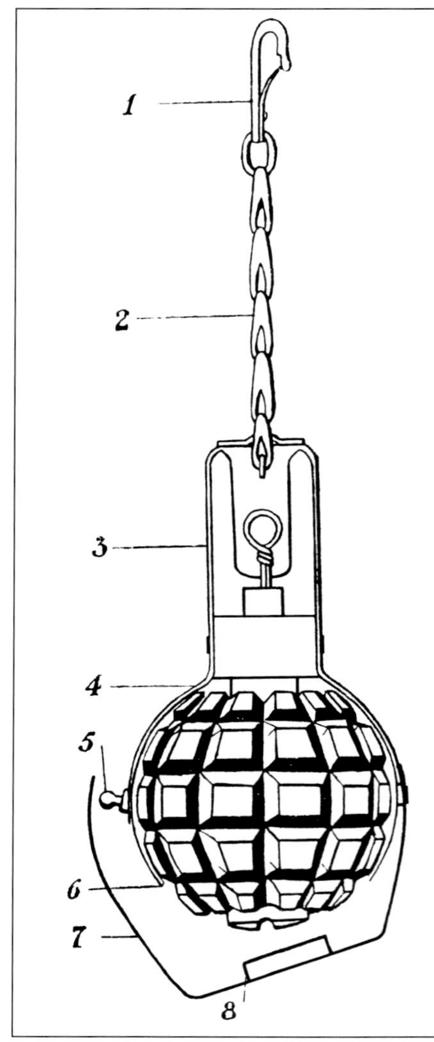

New weapons and tactics were tested in combat by the Pioneer Experimental Company *(Pionier-Versuchs-Kompagnie),* the de facto 5th Company of the Guard Pioneer Battalion *(Garde-Pionier-Bataillon).* Although the records of the outfit were destroyed during World War II, it appears that the Pioneer Experimental Company fought at Antwerp, Ypres, Lille, Rheims, and Verdun.[6] The unit conducted clandestine missions behind enemy lines and developed flamethrowers, fresh-water diving equipment, river-crossing

Squad of the Pioneer Experimental Company attached to the 26th Infantry Division in April of 1916. Officially the company researched and developed weapons and equipment, but in practice it was an assault unit. A handwritten message on the back of the postcard identifies the men as "the veterans of the gunpowder smoke in Reau, the warriors of the Pioneer Experimental Company."

techniques, hand grenades, and explosives. Its members refused to describe their experiences even decades after the war.

Hand Grenades and Steel Shields

In the fall of 1914 the Germans began organizing unofficial assault units in the Argonne.[7] *Leutnant* Walter Beumelberg, commander of the 2nd Company, Pioneer Battalion No.30, invented the technique of rolling up trenches *(Aufrollen)* with hand grenades, which was more effective and safer for the assault troops than storming the position with rifles and bayonets. Initially the infantry was not trained in the use of hand grenades; this often required that pioneers be temporarily attached to infantry regiments specifically to throw the new weapons at the enemy.

The infantry was not long in adopting pioneer assault tactics. In late September of 1914 the head of the Prussian Engineer Committee *(preussisches Ingenieur-Komitee), General* Oskar Hauffe, asked the Krupp firm to manufacture portable shields for assault troops to use during trench raids.[8] Prince Oskar of Prussia, commander of Grenadier Regiment No.7

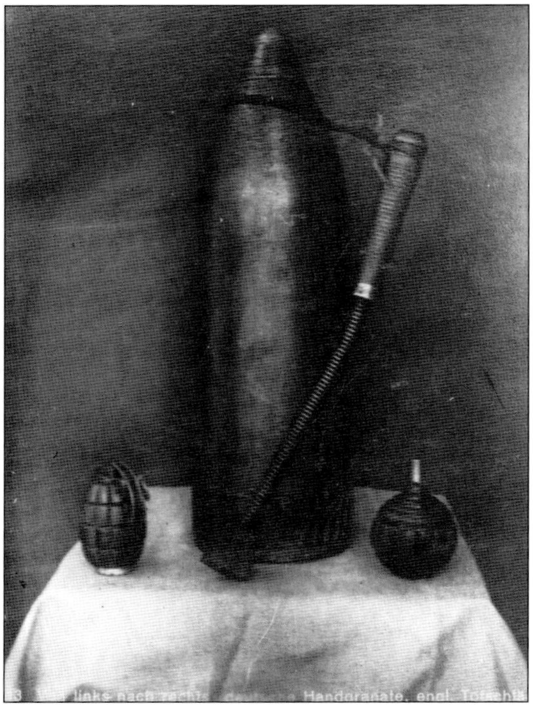

German M1915 ball grenade (right), an improvement of the 1913 model. Also pictured are a British Mills grenade on the left and a 15 cm shell in the center. Hanging from the shell is a spring-loaded British trench club consisting of a turned wooden handle, steel spring, and cast-iron head. The Germans called this weapon a "death club" (Totschläger).

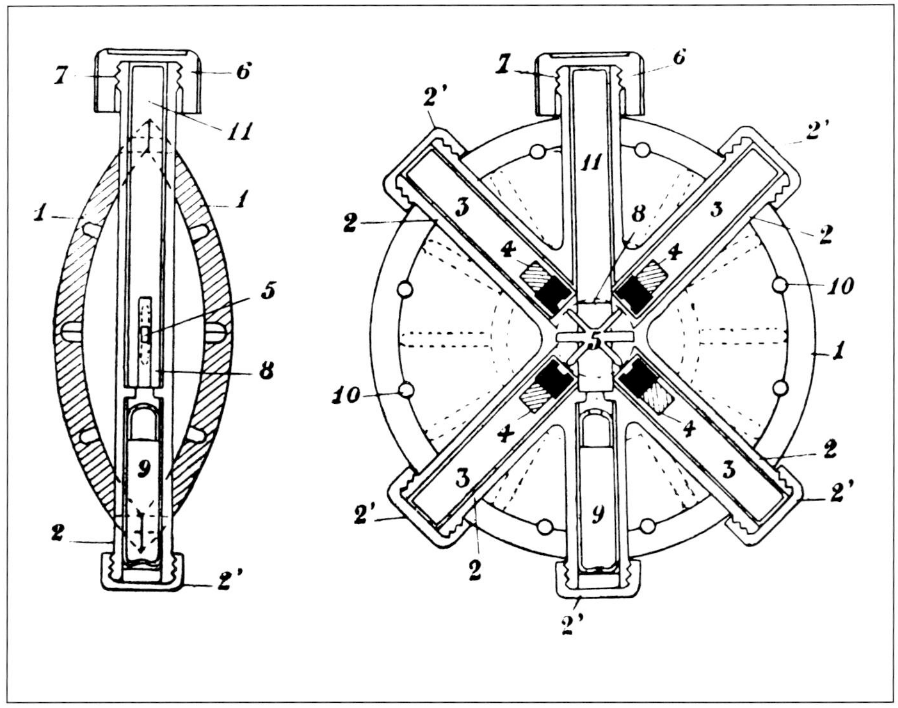

The M1913 disk grenade (Diskushandgranate), also called the oyster or turtle grenade. To use it, the soldier removed the safety cap (6) and flung the grenade like a discus, causing a rod (11) to fall out in flight. This allowed one to four primers (4) to hit firing pins (5) when the grenade struck the target, setting off the detonator (9), which was inserted before use. The cast-iron body consisted of two halves riveted together.

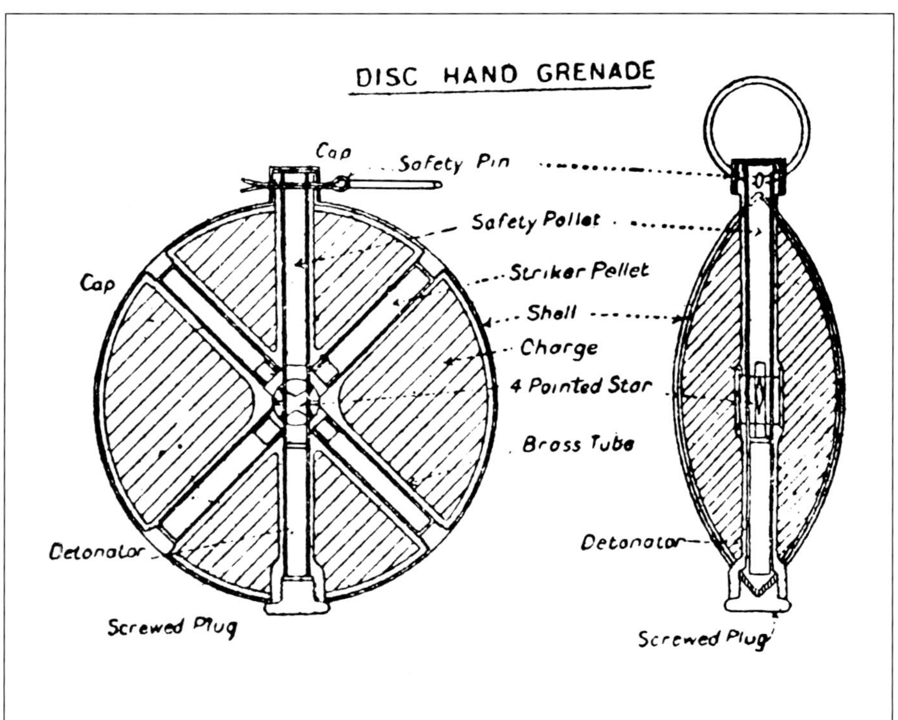

The M1915 disk grenade, an improvement of the M1913 model that included a safety pin rather than a cap. Like its predecessor, it was very dangerous for the man who threw it.

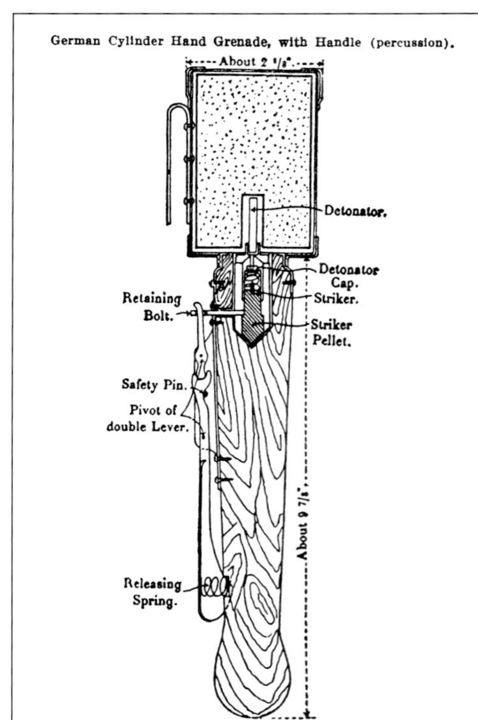

The M1915 percussion or impact grenade. Before throwing the grenade, the user pulled the safety pin; the spring released the lever in flight and freed the striker, which hit the detonator cap on impact with the target, exploding the grenade.

The three six-man hand-grenade squads (Handgranatentrupps) of the 7th Company, Infantry Regiment No.383, 1915. They are armed with M1915 stick grenades, M1915 ball grenades, and improvized "jam tin" grenades.

(Grenadier-Regiment König Wilhelm I. [2. westpreussisches] Nr.7), wrote a vivid account of infantrymen rolling up trenches in the Champagne:

> In another regiment three men cooperated as a trio during such trench attacks. The man in the middle, the strongest, carried two machine-gun shields connected together in his left hand and a pickaxe in his right. Following close behind him were the right and left men, one carrying a large number of hand grenades and the other armed with a bayonet. Thus this odd trio moved – striking, throwing, and thrusting its bloody way – to the fright of the French, and it has carried out excellent service for us.[9]

Soon every infantry platoon formed a hand-grenade squad *(Handgranatentrupp)* of six men each.[10] Chosen for their courage and expertise in throwing, these grenadiers wore special badges and fought offensively and defensively. In action two men and the commander took the lead with pistols while the rest of the squad bore daggers and slung rifles with fixed bayonets. All carried as many hand grenades as possible.

In early 1915 Army Detachment Gaede *(Armee-Abteilung Gaede),* commanded by *General der Infanterie* Hans Emil Alexander Gaede, held positions in the Vosges Mountains. The men suffered a disproportionately high number of head wounds from shell and rock splinters. Chief of Staff *Oberstleutnant* Hesse therefore supervised the fabrication of experimental

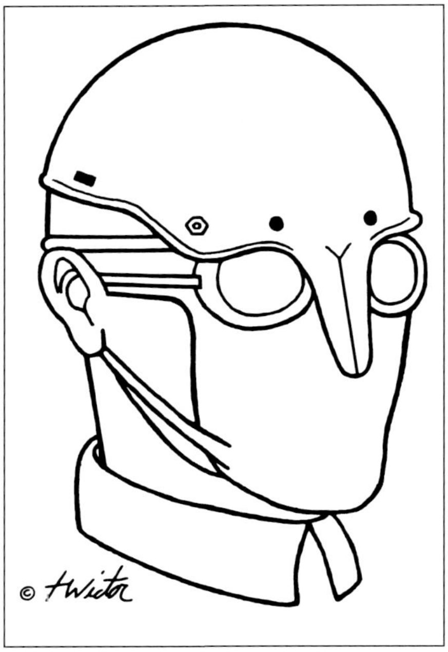

Helmet developed by Army Detachment Gaede (Armee-Abteilung Gaede) in the Vosges, early 1915. Also depicted are a Riechpäckchen respirator and antigas goggles. Issued in April of 1915, the mask consisted of a pad soaked in a hyposulphite solution. It was stored in a rubberized bag attached to the front of the uniform.

steel helmets at the Detachment artillery workshop in Mulhausen. The final design was a steel bowl that covered the forehead and the top of the head and included a nosepiece. Weighing about 4.5 lb, the helmet was worn over a cloth-and-leather cap. About 1500 examples were manufactured.[11]

General Gaede also ordered steel assault shields for his men, which they used in April of 1915. Gaede wrote a secret report on June 5, 1915, titled "Some Experiences Drawn from the Attacks on the Hartmannsweilerkopf":[12]

> **First Advance of the Infantry:**
> Even after the heaviest bombardment some enemy infantry and machine-gun positions will remain. This occurs especially in the case of steep slopes and additional defenses that obstruct a rapid infantry assault and allow the enemy time to return to his positions prior to our advance.
>
> During the attack of Column North on April 25, this surprise was avoided through the use of shields.
>
> **Method of proceeding:**
> Infantrymen carrying shields in the left hand leave the attack position on a wide front and try to cover as much ground as possible without stopping, as long as the enemy does not open effective fire on them.
>
> They then lie prone while sheltering behind the shields and returning fire through the shield loophole, aiming at the enemy ramparts.
>
> Protected as much as possible by shots fired from the attack position and from perches in trees (rifles with scopes, machine guns), and protected equally by the shields, the assault column is constantly reinforced and makes an effort to crawl toward the enemy position.
>
> In most cases the remaining ground to be crossed will not be considerable.
>
> When the men reach the wire entanglements, it is necessary that the enemy already be driven from his ramparts.
>
> This process allows for a fight on equal footing. Both adversaries have cover.
>
> The artillery of both sides is destroyed.
>
> The skillful shooting of our infantry and our superior numbers will determine the outcome.

Soldiers practice crawling with the steel trench shield (Grabenschild) produced by Krupp for use in the Argonne in late 1914. It featured a loophole with a swiveling cover. The shield in the foreground has a false loophole painted on it to deceive snipers.

A small-scale operation such as raiding or rolling up a trench was known as an "attack with limited objectives" *(Angriff mit begrenzten Ziele).* It was intended to capture a particular area rather than to destroy a particular enemy force.[13]

Special Weapons of the Pioneers

Early in the war the pioneer arsenal included many weapons not available to the infantry. In late 1914 most of the 1st Reserve Company of Württemberg Pioneer Battalion No.13 was attached to the 55th Reserve Brigade, 28th Reserve Division, XIV Reserve Corps, near Mametz.[14] The 18 NCOs and 161 men of the company were divided into subunits assigned specific weapons and tasks:

one rifle-grenade squad - one NCO and eight men;
one trench-mortar battery - one NCO and 12 men;
four mining squads - four NCOs and 32 men;
three sapper squads - three NCOs and 24 men;
three construction squads for shelters - three NCOs and 24 men;
four hand-grenade squads - four NCOs and 32 men;
one squad for constructing brigade shelters - one NCO and six men;
two depot squads for supply depots - eight men;
one searchlight platoon - one NCO and 13 men;
one flamethrower squad - two men.

Cartoon postcard depicting a pioneer laden with the specialized accoutrements of his branch, including shovel, assault ladder, serrated bayonet, barbed wire, rope, an anchor, an oar, a mallet, a saw, and a small wagon full of explosives.

Troops in the Argonne, early 1915; the caption reads "Enemy wire entanglements assaulted by our Field Grays." The soldiers carry minimal equipment of rifle, ammunition pouches, water bottle, bayonet, and wire cutters. Note the gray cloth "masking band" (Verdeckband) worn over the red cap band, adopted March 29, 1915.

The pioneers were under the command of a pioneer officer and two *Vizefeldwebel;* these three were responsible for the construction and technical work done in the sector. Pioneer officers in the front-line position, in agreement with the regimental and battalion infantry commanders, formulated orders for the trench-mortar battery, hand-grenade squads, searchlight platoon, and flamethrower squad.

An order titled "Requirement of Pioneer Spare Equipment for Dispatch in the Field," dated November 11, 1914, stated that special weapons of the pioneers such as trench mortars and ammunition, flamethrowers, hand grenades, rifle grenades, and smoke charges were exclusively at the disposal of the *OHL.*[15] With the exception of flamethrowers, the weapons were to be held for use in the west by Pioneer Replacement Battalion No.24 in Cologne, and for use in the east by Pioneer Replacement Battalion No.29 in Posen. Flamethrowers and accessories were to be held by the Acting Engineer Committee *(stellvertretendes Ingenieur-Komitee)* in Berlin.

Gefreiter of Infantry Regiment No.176 (westpreußisches Infanterie-Regiment Nr.176), 35th Infantry Division, outfitted as a trench raider. He wears light assault order of M1895 ammunition pouches, slung Gew 88 rifle, and water bottle. The numerals on his M1914 helmet cover are green instead of red to reduce visibility; soon they were omitted altogether.

Another weapon used by pioneers was the fire tube *(M.95 Brandröhre),* adopted in 1895. It was attached to a long pole in order to attack fortified positions:

> The Germans employ the Brandrohr*[sic],* or firestick, for the purpose of cleaning out the defenders of dugouts by subjecting them to a literal bath of fire. This firestick consists of a sheet iron cylinder, found in two sizes, 20 inches long and 4 in diameter, or 16x2. In both cases the metal is about one-twenty-fifth of an inch thick. The cylinder is closed at bottom by a two-ply disk of lead and iron and is filled with compressed thermite. At the top it is sealed by a celluloid plate one-sixth of an inch think, with six vents and a central orifice for the insertion of a stopper. The contents, thermite, is a close mixture of powdered aluminum and iron oxide. The flame is started by the extraction of the stopper, and continues for about a minute, playing at a distance of two yards from the mouth of the cylinder. Because of the heat, the soldier is obliged to throw the cylinder as a grenade, or better, to fasten it to the end of a long pole and sweep out the concealed corners. For cleaning up captured trenches it has no rival, the victims must surrender or die.[16]

The fire tube was operated by a five- or six-man squad *(Brandröhrentrupp)* consisting of two men to carry the long pole to which the device was attached, three men each carrying a fused fire tube to throw, and one squad leader.

Fire tubes were used to great effect during the taking of Fort Camp des Romains on September 25, 1914. In preparation for the operation, the Bavarian 6th and 11th Infantry Regiments and the 2nd Battalion of Pioneer Battalion No.16 formed eight assault detachments that moved close to the fort on the night of September 24.[17] Each detachment included infantrymen as well as specialists such as pioneer patrols *(Pionierpatrouille),* assault-ladder squads *(Sturmleitertrupps),* wire-cutting squads *(Scherentrupps),* carrying squads *(Trägertrupps),* scouting squads *(Erkundungstrupps),* hand-grenade squads, and fire-tube squads. An intense artillery bombardment that included Austrian 305mm mortars began at 4:00 A.M., at which time the assault detachments began cutting assault lanes *(Sturmgassen)* through the wire.

The attack itself was launched at 5:30 A.M., the eight assault detachments covered by heavy machine guns brought so far forward that the gunners were able to engage the French with hand grenades. Pioneers leading the assault detachments used hand grenades and concentrated charges

Assault on Fort Camp des Romains, September 25, 1914. After a short artillery bombardment, eight assault detachments of the Bavarian 6th and 11th Infantry Regiments and Pioneer Battalion No.16 used machine guns, fire tubes, and hand grenades to take the fort in three hours.

(geballte Ladung) to blow holes in the brickwork, which had been weakened by the Austrian mortars. Fire-tube squads were thus able to throw their weapons into the fort. After just three hours, the surviving French garrison surrendered, "half suffocated"[18] from the smoke.

Flamethrowers

In August of 1914 *kleine Flammenwerfer (Kleif) M.1912* portable flamethrowers were assigned to pioneer siege trains as weapons for reducing fortresses. At the beginning of position warfare the devices were issued to an unknown number of pioneer formations as offensive weapons. Each platoon received one portable flamethrower operated by a two-man squad. The first combat use of flamethrowers was by the 4th Company of Pioneer Battalion No.29 at Bagatelle-Pavillon on October 4 or 5, 1914.[19]

Note 32, titled "Means available to the pioneers for close combat: Projectors of flame and smoke-producing liquids," was published by the Second Army on October 16, 1914. The French Eleventh Army captured the note and distributed it in early 1915:

> The commander-in-chief will place these arms at the disposal of the army corps according to their needs. At the same time, the corps will receive the absolutely essential personnel educated in the use of these devices, who will have to be reinforced by pioneers of the field companies after they receive the necessary instruction for this purpose.
>
> The flame projectors are used by pioneers especially trained for this purpose; they are apparatuses similar to portable fire extinguishers, which project a liquid that immediately ignites spontaneously. The waves of flame have a working length and width of 20 meters. They have an immediate deadly effect and they force the enemy a long way back because of the heat that they produce. As they burn from one and a half to two minutes and can be stopped at will, short individual bursts are advisable in order to engage several objectives with only one filling of the tank. The flame projectors will be used mainly in house and street fighting and will be held ready at the position from where the assault will be launched.[20]

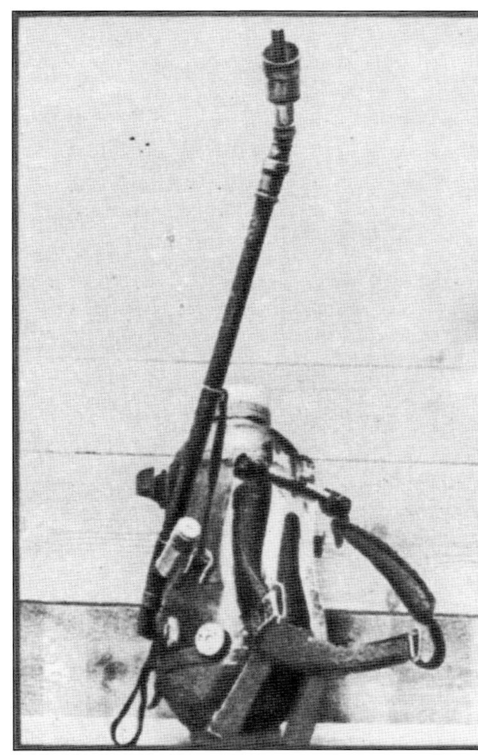

Kleine Flammenwerfer (Kleif) M.1912, one of which was issued to each platoon of line-pioneer formations in 1914. The Kleif M.1912 weighed about 70 lb when full and was operated by a two-man squad. One man wore the device and aimed the telescoping lance, while the assistant opened the propellant-release valve and block valve that sprayed the burning jet. Capacity was 4.2 gal of oil; duration was about 15 seconds; and maximum range was 60 ft.

Unteroffizier of Pioneer Battalion No.11 (kurhessisches Pionier-Bataillon Nr.11), which carried out several flamethrower assaults at Rawa, Poland, in early 1915. He wears the M1907/10 service jacket with yellow NCO braid on his collar and cuffs, and his M1910 service cap (Dienstmütze) has a black band piped in red.

The experience of Kurhessian Pioneer Battalion No.11 *(kurhessische Pionier-Bataillon Nr.11)*[21] illustrates how early in the war pioneers served as lethal assault troops armed with state-of-the art weaponry. Based in Hannover-Münden, Pioneer Battalion No.11 was sent to Poland with the XI Army Corps in late 1914. The 1st and 2nd Companies of the battalion took part in the fighting at Hill 10 in Rawa, a town 76 miles southeast of Warsaw.

On March 6, 1915, the Germans at Rawa observed that the Russians were massing infantry in their trenches and their artillery fire had intensified.[22] At 3:30 on the morning of March 8, the artillery fire increased to a crescendo. Most of it was concentrated on Hill 10, which was held by the 8th Company of Infantry Regiment No.83 *(Infanterie-Regiment von Wittich [3. kurhessisches] Nr.83)*.

At 4:30 A.M. the Russian infantry attacked in closely packed lines. Part of the assault broke down in front of the German trenches, but at 5:00 A.M. the Russians reached Hill 10 and fell on the 8th Company of Infantry Regiment No.83. A vicious close combat with sharpened spades and stick grenades raged throughout the trenches. In the midst of the battle, the German infantrymen were rescued by a flamethrower squad from the 2nd Company of Pioneer Battalion No.11, which entered the trench and sprayed the Russians at pointblank range. Later in the morning the Russians retreated, leaving 400 dead and wounded, while Infantry Regiment No.83 suffered casualties of 20 dead and 40 wounded.

When the Russian artillery fire increased on the night of March 7-8, the 1st Company of Pioneer Battalion No.11 was given the alarm and made available to Infantry Regiment No.82 *(2. kurhessisches Infanterie-Regiment Nr.82)*.[23] These pioneers, armed with portable flamethrowers, were put in the reserve position at Indomice, further back from Hill 10. The Russian attack began at 5:30 A.M. and concentrated on Hill 10. It was partially repelled by the heavy fire of German infantrymen and bombardment from light and medium trench mortars.

The Russians who assaulted the first German trench on Hill 10 encountered two defensive flamethrower posts under the command of an *Unteroffizier*. He ordered the flamethrowers ignited, causing a German pioneer to lose an eye. Most of the Russians fled from this unknown weapon. The rest were dealt with by the wave of Infantry Regiment No.82 counterattacking behind the flamethrowers.

After Hill 10 was back in German hands, a second Russian attack barely made it beyond its own trenches. The only Russians who arrived at the German lines were deserters, frantically racing ahead of their artillery barrage. They were captured and told to march unaccompanied to Rawa. One German *Unteroffizier* and eight pioneers at the Rawka Bridge had collected approximately 1000 Russians by the morning of March 8.

On March 10 Petrograd reported that the Germans were using new methods of fighting, "throwing boiling pitch or some other liquid on our infantry."[24] Russian assaults ceased, and on March 11 the 1st Company of Pioneer Battalion No.11 was pulled out of Rawa. One small command stayed to operate the trench mortars and flamethrowers.

From April 7 to July 17, 1915, the 1st Company of Pioneer Battalion No.11 engaged the Russians in mine warfare *(Minenkrieg)* at Rawa. One platoon of pioneers was given the task of mining under Hill 10; one platoon was assigned trench mortars and flamethrowers; and one platoon served as assault troops to take the hill itself.[25] On June 1 it was decided that since neither mining nor direct assaults had been successful, poison gas would be tried. A *Major* from Army Command 9 *(AOK 9)*, headquartered in Lodz, was sent to organize the

Austrian sailors posing with several varieties of smoke helmet, gas mask, and breathing device. The Dräger Company produced the Model 1903 self-contained breathing apparatus (second from left) and the Model 1914 Selbstretter re-breathing apparatus (fifth from left). One or both of these were issued to the pioneers and cavalrymen who sprayed poison gas at Rawa on June 6, 1915.

attack. Cavalrymen of an unidentified unit were transferred to the sector and trained in the use of flamethrowers as gas sprayers.

It is not clear if the devices were to spray liquefied gas only, or flame oil mixed with toxic chemicals and ignited. In either case, the flamethrowers required no modification; during training the Germans often sprayed water with flamethrowers in order to save on oil and igniters. These flamethrowers were never again used for combat, as there was always a possibility that moisture would remain and cause firing irregularities. Any flamethrower that sprayed water would thereafter be used only for training purposes or as a fire extinguisher.[26]

Chemists and meteorologists made an extensive study of Hill 10 and recommended a new gas, likely the choking agent diphosgene (trichloromethylchloroformate). The wind was determined to be favorable on June 6; at 8:20 P.M. the cavalrymen and pioneers donned firefighters' oxygen masks and released the gas from their flamethrowers. As the cloud drifted over the Russian line, the sporadic rifle fire directed at the Germans immediately ceased. A German patrol in oxygen masks later crawled out and found the enemy trenches full of dead and dying. The next day Russian deserters reported that the gas had killed 600 men.

Italian postcard depicting the Louis Raemaekers cartoon "The Ex-convict," captioned "Now I am a soldier and will spread Kultur among our neighbors in France." He is equipped with a bag of incendiary pastils, a flask of "poison for wells," and a portable flamethrower labeled "asphyxiating gas."

Postwar photo of a flamethrower squad of Hussar Regiment No.14 (Husar-Regiment Landgraf Friedrich II von Hessen [2. kurhessisches] Nr.14). This unit may have supplied the cavalrymen trained to operate the flamethrowers used as poison-gas sprayers at Rawa. These men wear the M1910 hussar Atila and M1916 steel helmet. They are armed with the Wechselapparat (Wex) M.1917 and M1917 lance with a self-closing valve that shut off the jet of oil if the operator were wounded or killed.

During the reconnaissance conducted after the attack, the oxygen mask of one of the German patrol came loose as he crawled across No Man's Land, causing him to instantly lose consciousness. He survived only because a comrade quickly replaced his mask. A June 7 newspaper article painted a grim picture of the Russian situation:

> The reports received state that when the terrible fumes swept down the valleys every living thing suffered. Appalling scenes are described, and it is admitted at headquarters that the Russian operations have been considerably hampered in consequence of the use of the gas.[27]

To date no other accounts of German flamethrowers used as poison-gas sprayers have been found.

Endnotes

[1] Kriegsgeschichtlichen Abteilung I des Grossen Generalstabes, *Die Kämpfe der deutschen Truppen in Südwestafrika,* Volumes I and II (Berlin: Ernst Siegfried Mittler und Sohn, 1906), p. 78.

[2] Kriegsministerium, *Anleitung für den Kampf um Festungen (K. u. F.)* (Berlin: Ernst Siegfried Mittler und Sohn, 1910), pp. 49-52.

[3] Hermann Cron, *Imperial Germany Army 1914-18: Organisation, Structure, Orders-of-Battle* (Solihull, West Midlands, England: Helion and Company, 2002), pp. 96-99.

[4] Ibid., pp. 155-156.

[5] Kriegsministerium, *Pionier-Sturmanleitung (P. St.) vom 10 Marz 1904* (Berlin: Reichdruckerie, 1904), pp. 57-61.

[6] Hans Schmidt, e-mail to the author, June 15, 2006. Information about the combat experience of *Pionier* Hermann Schmidt, of the Pioneer Experimental Company.

[7] Jean-Louis Larcade, *Deutsche Sturmtruppen: Troupes d'assaut allemandes (1914-1918)* (Les Jonquerets de Livet, France: Editions des Argonautes, 2002), p. 10, and Bruce Gudmundsson, *Stormtroop Tactics: Innovation in the German Army, 1914-1918* (Westport, Connecticut: Praeger, 1989), p. 35.

[8] Ibid.

[9] Oskar Charles Gustavus Adolphus, *Die Winterschlacht in der Champagne (16. Februar bis 18. Marz 1915).* (Oldenberg, Germany: Druck und Verlag von Gerhard Stalling, 1915), p. 12.

[10] Adrien Gay, *Grenade Warfare* (Atlanta: E. W. Allen and Company, 1918), pp. 73-74.

[11] Floyd R. Tubbs and Robert W. Clawson, *Stahlhelm: Evolution of the German Steel Helmet: Revised and Expanded Edition* (Kent, Ohio: Kent State University Press, 2000), pp. 8-9.

[12] Larcade, p. 18.

[13] Gudmundsson, p. 28.

[14] Records of Württembergisches Pionier-Bataillon Nr.13, Hauptstaatarchiv Stuttgart M 209 Bü. 17.

[15] Although this document, Order No.365/11, is found in the German Bundesarchiv-Militärarchiv, the file number is not known. It cannot be easily traced because there are no precise lists for the contents of each file in the archive.

[16] "Sweeping Out Captured Dugouts with a Broom of Fire," *Scientific American* (September 8, 1917).

[17] General Haenichen, "Die Erstürmung des Sperrforts Camp des Romains am 25. September 1914," in *Das Ehrenbuch der deutschen Pioniere,* edited by Paul Heinrici (Berlin: Verlag Tradition Wilhelm Rolf, 1931), pp. 106-114.

[18] *The Americans in the Great War, Volume II: The Battle of St. Mihiel* (Clermont-Ferrand, France: Michelin and Cie, 1920) p. 70.

[19] Hans Tröbst and Artur Leipold, *Das posensche Pionier-Bataillon Nr.29 und seine Kriegsformationen* (Berlin: Kolk, 1932), p. 56, and Jean-Joseph Rouquerol, *La Guerre en Argonne* (Paris: Payot, 1937), p. 53.

[20] Ministère des Affaires Étrangères, *Les Violations des Lois de la Guerre par l'Allemagne* (Paris/Nancy: Librairie Berger-Levrault, 1915), pp. 171-172.

[21] The adjective *kurhessisches* is derived from Kurhessen, or "Electoral Principality of Hessia."

[22] Information on this part of the attack is found in Oberstleutnant Clausius, *Erinnerungsblätter deutscher Regimenter, Band 176: Infanterie-Regiment von Wittich (3.kurhessiches) Nr.83* (Oldenburg iO/Berlin: Verlag Georg Stalling, 1926), pp. 50-52.

[23] Information on this part of the attack is found in Prof. Dr. Hartenstein, *Das kurhessische Pionier-Bataillon Nr.11 im Weltkriege 1914-1918* (Zeulenroda in Thüringen, Germany: Verlag Bernhard Sporn, 1936), p. 26.

[24] "Germans Use Liquid Fire in Attack on Russians," *The Syracuse Herald* (March 10, 1915), p. 2, col. 6.

[25] Hartenstein, pp. 34-36.

[26] Charles Theune, *Sturmtruppen und Flammenwerfer* (Berlin: Landes-Verlag, 1921), pp. 97-98.

[27] "Germans Using Gas," *Fairbanks Daily Times* (June 8, 1915), p. 1, col. 2.

CHAPTER 2

The First Official Assault Units

Oberst Max Bauer

Oberst der Artillerie Max Bauer of the General Staff claimed to have created three "front-line experimental units of the Supreme Army Command" *(Front Versuchstruppen der OHL)* in early 1915. These were an assault detachment, which would test the Krupp 37mm assault cannon; a flamethrower detachment led by *Hauptmann* Bernhard Reddemann; and Trench Mortar Battalion I *(Minenwerfer-Bataillon I),* commanded by *Major* Lothes.[1]

While it is possible that the assault detachment was indeed Bauer's idea, Bernhard Reddemann wrote in his history of the flamethrower arm that he himself originated the idea of a dedicated flamethrower unit.[2] Flamethrower Detachment Reddemann *(Flammenwerfer-Abteilung Reddemann)* was established on January 18, 1915. The unit was comprised of an *Offizier-Stellvertreter* from the Posen Fire Brigade and 48 Posen firefighters and war volunteers who worked with Reddemann to create entirely new tactics. Assigned to the Fifth Army, the Flamethrower Detachment traveled to Aachen on February 1, 1915, and first saw action on February 26 at Malancourt. Another officer and 22 more men were added to the Detachment, and a second flamethrower attack was carried out at Vauquois.

Nowhere in his records did Reddemann acknowledge Bauer. The only individuals he mentioned as having aided in the development of the flamethrower arm were the Kaiser and Crown Prince Wilhelm, whom he described as the unit's "highest friends and patrons."[3] Based on the tone and claims of his writings, however, Reddemann was clearly not a man given to sharing credit with anyone, and he may have been prone to exaggeration. He described the weapons built by his workshops as "sinister, perfect flamethrowers"[4] that were better than the original weapons provided to the army by the Fiedler Flame Apparatus Company (Fiedler Flammenapparate G.m.b.H.) since 1912. *Oberleutnant* Ludwig Charles Theune, commander

Major Bernhard Reddemann (left), commander of the Flamethrower Detachment and later flamethrower battalions and regiment. He is pictured here in about 1917, having tea with an infantry officer (right) and two officers of the Guard Reserve Pioneer Regiment, one of whom displays the death's head sleeve badge embroidered in silver bullion. The infantry officer and the pioneer officer in the center wear the undress smock (Litewka) and "small jacket" (kleiner Rock) respectively.

The Krupp 37mm "assault accompanying cannon" (Sturmbegleitkanone) used by Assault Detachment Calsow. This gun was photographed in the Vosges, Upper Alsace, in late 1915 or early 1916. It was fitted with a steel shield to protect the four- or five-man crew. Courtesy Thierry Ehret.

of the 10th Company of the later flamethrower regiment and author of the comprehensive *Sturmtruppen und Flammenwerfer,* challenged this notion:

> [T]he apparatus which the Flame Projector Regiment (Flammenwerfer regiment) manufactured in its own workshop in the field, in order to make itself independent of the industry in Germany, naturally did not have the good qualities and the efficiency of apparatus made in the workshop of the inventor who had had many years experience.[5]

Complicating matters, Theune himself was given to grandiose claims, having identified himself after the war as the inventor of the flamethrower.[6] The actual inventor was mechanical engineer Richard Fiedler, who filed his first flamethrower patent in 1900.[7]

Bauer's claim that he organized the trench-mortar arm is not persuasive. Trench Mortar Battalion I was established on April 16, 1915, but every Army Corps and Reserve Corps had been armed with heavy and medium trench mortars since December of 1914, and every pioneer company had received six light weapons in January of 1915.[8] In addition, seven Trench Mortar Detachments had already been created, as well as a large number of autonomous light, medium, and heavy trench-mortar detachments. Other than Bauer's own word, there is no evidence that he was deeply involved in the development of the trench-mortar service. The lack of proof may not be conclusive, as most of the records of the Imperial German Army were destroyed during World War II. There is no doubt that Bauer was an influential, visionary officer; how influential may never be known.

It is equally unclear if Bauer or Reddemann was the man who first suggested to the *OHL* that a flamethrower unit be established. Regardless, the portable flamethrower had been mostly recalled from service at the end of 1914, due to design flaws and a lack of specialized training among the pioneers assigned the weapon.

A comprehensive report on the shortcomings of the *Kleif M.1912* was filed by *Leutnant der Landwehr* Schenck of the 3rd Company, Bavarian 4th (Fortress) Pioneer Replacement Battalion *(königlich bayerisches 4.*

Assault squad (Sturmgruppe) of Bavarian 4th (Fortress) Pioneer Replacement Battalion (königlich bayerisches 4. [Festungs-] Pionier-Ersatz-Bataillon) posing with their two trainers (center). They are all uniformed in Bavarian M1907 field jackets and trousers with leather reinforcement patches on the knees. Pioneer shovels with shortened handles, dummy grenades painted red, rolled assault packs, and M1915 Pickelhauben with the spikes removed complete the assault order. In late 1914 this unit was trained in the use of flamethrowers.

[Festungs-] Pionier-Ersatz-Bataillon), on December 6, 1914. This secret document, sent from Ingolstadt, was titled "Remarks on the Training of Flamethrower Operators":

> The armatures are poorly designed, presumably out of the intention that the apparatus be carried as easily as possible. It is therefore feared that the apparatuses will soon become useless in the field and/or require many spare parts.
>
> Filling the gas tanks with air instead of Number 16 Fl.W., which consists of nitrogen or carbonic acid, appears dangerous because the flame oil absorbs air and the apparatus leaks, creating an explosive mixture of air and flame oil. Since the propellant bottles are transported containing neither nitrogen nor carbonic acid, constant caution is required on site.
>
> A disadvantage in handling the apparatuses is the fact that the lance is connected to the flame-oil tank by a swiveling elbow joint. It can be foreseen that handling the apparatus in its current form will not be particularly comfortable, and there is a danger that through an inadvertent movement of the carrier the elbow joint or lance will be bent, thereby rendering the entire apparatus nearly useless.
>
> It may have to be considered whether or not it would be better to replace the swiveling elbow joint with a flexible hose. The weapon rarely achieves an effect of 18 meters *[20 yards];* the longest ranges are observed only in the first individual spray.

Apart from the direct influence on living targets, no particularly outstanding effects were observed. Only easily inflammable materials (straw, dry sticks, and such) immediately caught fire. In drills, individual flame bursts did not burn new wood at all, except in connection with the previously mentioned materials. To burn new wood, a continuous stream of flame must be thrown.

Of the enemy nothing much can be seen at short distances (about 50 paces in front of the flamethrower) because the burning flame oil produces a very intensive smoke cloud which goes into action very disturbingly and covers everything.

The applicability of the portable light flamethrower will therefore be quite limited.[9]

The Assault Detachment

On March 2, 1915, the Acting General Command of the VIII Army Corps *(stellvertretende Generalkommando VIII A.K.)* accepted from the War Ministry the mission of forming an Assault Detachment which would initially remain in Germany for its training and the development of new combat techniques.[10] Coincidentally, March 2, 1915, was also the day the Guard *Schützen* Battalion *(Garde-Schützen-Bataillon)* created an assault company of hand-picked volunteers in the Champagne, close to Somme-Py. The men of this assault company were "the first ones used if especially dangerous or difficult missions were to be carried out."[11]

A Schütze of the Guard Schützen Battalion in heavy assault order. His gray-green simplified field jacket displays shortened yellow Guard lace on the collar, while his leather shako is missing the imperial cockade. The Guard Schützen Battalion formed an all-volunteer assault company in the Argonne on March 3, 1915, the same day that the Assault Detachment was established.

Three young Kanoniere of a field-artillery regiment. They wear M1907/10 service jackets, corduroy trousers (Manchesterhose), and ball-topped Pickelhauben. Note the Mauser C96 pistols and S98/02 saw-backed pioneer bayonet. Artillerymen were used as assault troops early in the war, hauling field guns close to enemy positions to engage in direct fire.

Umzug zum neuen Geschützstand
Infanterie hilft

Kriegsjahr 1915
Max Goetze Nachf.
Berlin, Langestr. 110.
9992

One requirement for a successful assault was that the artillery identify and destroy targets as soon as the infantry broke into the first enemy trench. At this point in the war artillery was often moved forward in order to engage machine-gun nests, flanking installations, points of resistance, and enemy field guns, but the 77mm Field Gun M1896, new pattern *(7,7 cm Feldkanone 96 n/A),* was far too heavy and cumbersome for these missions. A much lighter gun was needed.

The Assault Detachment would be comprised of one staff, two pioneer companies equipped with steel shields *(Panzerschilden)*, and one cannon detachment *(Kanonen-Abteilung)* armed with 37mm guns. *Major* Calsow, of Pioneer Battalion No.18, was made commander. The 1st Pioneer Company was formed of men from the Recruit Depot of Pioneer Replacement Battalion No.3 *(Pionier-Ersatz-Bataillon von Rauch [1. brandenburgisches] Nr.3),* while the 2nd Pioneer Company drew on the Recruit Depot of Pioneer Replacement Battalion No.10 *(hannoverisches Pionier-Ersatz-Bataillon Nr.10).* The men of the Cannon Detachment were combat-experienced volunteers from artillery regiments fighting on the eastern front.

In March of 1915, Assault Detachment Calsow was brought together near Cologne; its live-fire training ground was at Wahn. The weaponry of assault pioneers designated "shield carriers" *(Schildträgers)* was defined for the initial tests as the *Kar 98AZ* carbine and hand grenades.

The pioneers were issued different models of portable steel shields, ranging from a large, man-sized version to one that protected only the head *(Kopfschild).* For the sake of mobility, each assault company was the size of a

Opposite
***Top:** Artillerymen and infantrymen moving a 77mm Field Gun M1896, new pattern (7,7 cm Feldkanone 96 n/A, or "neue Art"). This gun was used in assaults in the heavily wooded Argonne in early 1915, but it was far too heavy, leading to the development of lighter "assault cannons" (Sturmkanone) of 37mm and 76.2mm.*

***Bottom:** Five pioneers of Pioneer Replacement Battalion No.3 (Pionier-Ersatz-Bataillon von Rauch [1. brandenburgisches] Nr.3). This unit formed the 1st Assault Company (also called 1st Pioneer Company) of Assault Detachment Calsow (Sturmabteilung Calsow), established on March 3, 1915. The men wear privately purchased summer tunics in field-gray cotton; the material faded quickly, leading to the different shades shown here.*

Pioneers of the 2nd Detachment, 3rd Recruit Depot, Pioneer Replacement Battalion No.10 (hannoverisches Pionier-Ersatz-Bataillon Nr.10). This pioneer formation provided the men of the 2nd Assault Company (or 2nd Pioneer Company) of Assault Detachment Calsow.

Left: Krupp assault shield (Sturmschild) on the left. Measuring 55 in tall by 18 in wide, it weighed 62 lb. On the right is the infantry shield (Infanterieschild) and head shield (Kopfschild), which together weighed 40 lb. Assault Detachment Calsow tested several models of armor; only the infantry shield was adopted. Courtesy Thiery Ehret.

Right: Assault squad of Pioneer Battalion No.21 early in the war. They are armed with the Mauser Kar 98AZ, the standard weapon of the Assault Detachment. Introduced in 1908, the Kar 98AZ was a 7.92mm weapon fed by five-round clips. It was 42.9 in long, weighed 8.18 lb, and had a muzzle velocity of 2755 ft-lb.

peacetime pioneer company, about six officers and 264 NCOs and men. This average strength was retained for assault companies throughout the war.

The Assault Detachment trained with its shields at Wahn for several weeks. Following these tests, the officers and experienced soldiers of the Detachment concluded that these cumbersome and heavy devices would be much more hindrance than benefit in combat.

Development of Tactics

Both German and enemy positions were reconstructed on the training grounds. During a simulated attack, the artillery fired live rounds on the enemy positions the same way it would in actual combat. Where necessary, the 37mm guns and trench mortars also destroyed obstacles blocking the assault troops. At the moment of the attack, the 37mm guns were pushed out of the German positions and brought as close as possible to the enemy line, maintaining an interval of 55 to 80 yards between each assault gun. On both wings, well-dispersed guns followed. The forward guns prepared the way for the first wave of pioneers by firing from their positions. When the guns arrived at the enemy positions, the pioneer patrols carrying shields advanced and removed the remaining obstacles.

Infantrymen and pioneers followed the initial wave of assault pioneers with shields. Both waves advanced in alignment in the intervals between the assault guns. The mission of the assault guns then became to protect the assault troops, particularly from enemy machine-gun nest and artillery. The flanking positions of the enemy were identified and destroyed by the 37mm guns in order to protect the insertion of reserves.

If the attack on the first line was successful, the same methods were used to take the other enemy lines.

The Successful Assault

A successful assault was broken up into four simple steps:

Left: Men of Grenadier Regiment No.110 (badisches Grenadier-Regiment Kaiser Wilhelm I. Nr.110) prepare for an assault. The soldier in the rear wears an improvised gas mask consisting of a cotton pad soaked in a chemical solution, while the other two are equipped with Atemschützer respirators issued in late 1915. Grenadier Regiment No.110 developed assault tactics independently of Assault Detachment Calsow and Bernhard Reddemann.

Bottom left: Musketier of Infantry Regiment No.76 (Infanterie-Regiment Hamburg [2. hanseatisches] Nr.76), 111th Infantry Division, wearing two field jackets. The pockets of the outer tunic are likely stuffed with ball grenades, and he is equipped with a size 3 M1915 Gummimaske in a cloth carrier. He has draped a 70-round cotton bandolier (Patronentragegurte) around his neck; assault troops often wore the bandolier in place of the leather ammunition pouches.

Below: Undated photo of Reservist Augustin Tacherting, Bavarian 1st Reserve Infantry Regiment. He has a serious wound on his right thigh; under the blood-soaked trouser leg a bulky bandage can be seen, and his face is clearly wracked with pain. Below the "I" on his shoulder straps he wears an uppercase "H," possibly an unofficial badge standing for "hand-grenade squad" (Handgranatentrupp).

Men of Landwehr Infantry Regiment No.111 armed with M1913 rifle grenades (Gewehrgranaten). Fired with a blank cartridge, the grenade had a range of up to 400 yd. These Gew 98 rifles have been mounted on metal stands fitted with heavy recoil springs; note the wire lanyards attached to the rifle triggers.

1. Leave own trench and cross to the enemy position.
2. Enter the enemy position and fight the garrison.
3. Clear and eliminate obstacles.
4. Advance against the enemy rear lines through communication trenches or outside of them.

The 37mm gun detachment had six basic rules:

1. Bring the guns up to own positions.
2. While firing, clear the ground well before advancing. Carefully observe the effects of the fire.
3. Move the guns forward of own positions.
4. Use high-explosive shells to engage the enemy machine guns and artillery behind and on the flanks of the position.
5. Use canister rounds to engage the enemy infantry.
6. Advance and overcome the subsequent enemy lines of defense.

While Assault Detachment Calsow trained, the flamethrower battalion was established.

The 3rd Guard Pioneer Battalion

On March 15, 1915, the *OHL* ordered that a flamethrower battalion be established. Raised in Berlin around a core of men from the Guard Pioneer Replacement Battalion *(Garde-Pionier-Ersatz-Bataillon),*[12] it was the second officially sanctioned pioneer assault unit.

On mobilization the peacetime Guard Pioneer Battalion had been divided into the 1st Battalion (1st, 2nd, and 3rd Companies) and 2nd Battalion (4th, 1st Reserve, and 2nd Reserve Companies). In early 1915 each peacetime pioneer battalion received the 5th Company, which brought the total number of Guard Pioneer companies – including the Pioneer Experimental Company – to eight. The new flamethrower battalion was therefore designated the 3rd Guard Pioneer Battalion *(III. Garde-Pionier-Bataillon),* comprised of the 9th through 12th Companies and its own Experimental Company *(Versuchs-Kompagnie).* On June 1, 1915, the Replacement Company *(Ersatz-Kompagnie)* was added.[13]

The all-volunteer 3rd Guard Pioneer Battalion had an initial strength of 800.[14] Its noncommissioned officers and men were drawn not only from the Guard Pioneer Replacement Battalion but also fire brigades, 16 different pioneer battalions,[15] and most other branches of the service.[16] Men from

Four-man attack squad (Angriffstrupp) of a municipal fire brigade; their Feldwebel stands on the right. Bernhard Reddemann modeled his flamethrower squads on the fire-brigade attack squad. Flamethrower shock troops also used modified firefighting tactics when taking fortified enemy positions.

Pionier Wolfram Schwarz, of the 8th Section (Korporalschaft), Replacement Company, 3rd Guard Pioneer Battalion (III. Garde-Pionier-Bataillon). Dated June 26, 1915, the card depicts Pionier Schwarz (called "Schwarz II" by his unit to differentiate him from other soldiers named Schwarz) in full marching order. Flamethrower pioneers were armed with the Kar 98AZ carbine instead of the Gew 98 rifle.

all over the empire were recruited. *Hauptmann der Landwehr* Bernhard Reddemann, soon to be known by his men as the "Prince of Hades,"[17] was the commander of the battalion.

The 3rd Guard Pioneer was under the direct control of the *OHL,* to which Reddemann addressed all of his proposals. He was also ordered to present written reports every two or three months, describing the state of the unit, its engagements, its practical experiences, and any new experiments and equipment. Finally, he delivered a monthly oral report to the Operations Detachment *(Operationsabteilung)* of the *OHL.*

Individual flamethrower companies or the battalion as a whole were put at the disposal of the various armies and army groups for specific objectives. The technical details of the flamethrowers' employment were left to Reddemann. Flamethrowers were to be employed offensively; continuous use for defensive purposes in the front line was prohibited.

Absolutely vital to the development of the 3rd Guard Pioneer Battalion was the support of Crown Prince Wilhelm, who lobbied for the new flamethrower unit and bankrolled it to an unknown extent.

Each 139-man field company of the 3rd Guard Pioneer Battalion was armed with 12 large flamethrowers (*grosse Flammenwerfer M.1912* or *Grof*), each of which was operated by a five-man squad. Each field company was also armed with 18 small flamethrowers *(Kleif).* Two models were issued to the 3rd Guard Pioneer Battalion, both operated by four-man attack squads *(Angriffstrupps)* modeled on those of the fire brigades.[18]

The battalion experimental company generated its own ideas and took input from the flamethrower pioneers in the field. Improvements in the weaponry were made quickly because the workshop was located at headquarters, and technical advancements had high priority. The hands-on experience of the troops was reported directly to the engineers of the research staff. Prototypes were designed, tested, manufactured, and fielded more rapidly than many present-day armies, partly because office-bound bureaucrats had been entirely eliminated from the process.[19]

Each field company of the 3rd Guard Pioneer Battalion was comprised in part of three combat platoons *(Kampfzüge);* there may have been replacement and ordnance detachments as well. In late 1915 the number of *Grof* in each field company was increased from 12 to 20.

Flame Tactics

Reddemann determined from the outset that flamethrowers were not suitable for every attack because they could only be used under the right circumstances; the formulation of proper tactics was imperative.[20] Every deployment brought new experience and new concepts. The battalion staff collated and improved upon these by talking to the participants and interviewing as many members of the unit as possible.

The first tactic was very simple: "shock" the enemy positions with large flamethrowers installed in intervals of 55 yards. This was known as the "stationary attack" *(stehenden Angriff),* and it was successful on only a few occasions. When small flamethrowers were added so that the operators could leave their own positions and carry the assault all the way to the enemy's rear, this became the "combined stationary and pouncing attack" *(vereinten stehenden und springenden Angriff).* Later on the "pouncing attack" *(springenden Angriff)* with small flamethrowers alone was the tactic most often used.

At the training center in Berlin, officers and men were instructed in all three methods of frontal attack. Another tactic was rolling up *(Aufrollen),*

whereby small flamethrowers were introduced into enemy trenches in flanking attacks, usually in conjunction with hand-grenade throwers.

A fifth tactic was tunneling, used when the enemy trench was more than 44 yards distant. Long underground tunnels were dug out into No Man's Land, ending in camouflaged vertical shafts in front of the target. Large flamethrowers were moved into the tunnels and placed at the base of the shafts. At zero hour flamethrower operators popped out of the ground and sprayed the enemy at pointblank range. If the tunnel could not be dug far enough because of time constraints, the lance operators were trained to leap into the open and fire the flamethrower on the run, while assistants carried the hose behind. Reddemann claimed that because of the element of surprise, this tactic resulted in far fewer casualties than expected among his men.[21]

On May 15, 1915, the 9th Company of the 3rd Guard Pioneer Battalion was sent to Douai to reinforce Flamethrower Detachment Reddemann; the three remaining companies followed soon after. When the Battalion was fielded, each company received seven two-ton trucks.

***Above:** Squad of the 14th Company, 3rd Guard Pioneer Battalion. All wear the simplified field jacket with the shortened Guard collar lace mandated by the AKO of March 3, 1915. The bayonets all appear to be Ersatz models, and some of the men have thick mittens hanging from their belts. Many of these pioneers are older men; they were likely firefighters in civilian life.*

***Right:** Gefreiter of the 12th Company, 3rd Guard Pioneer Battalion (right), photographed with a member of a Prussian state railway. The flamethrower pioneer has removed the shoulder straps of his M1907/10 field jacket and is armed with an S98/05 bayonet.*

The First Large-scale Flamethrower Assault

The 3rd Guard Pioneer Battalion first saw action on May 22 at Neuville, north of Douai. Large flamethrowers fired first, followed by an attack of pioneers carrying portable flamethrowers, a combined stationary and pouncing attack. The pioneers had been trained to approach the enemy positions stealthily, using the cover of trenches. However, at Neuville the flamethrower pioneers were ordered by infantry commanders – against Reddemann's will – to escort the infantrymen as they crossed the open ground in the traditional

Infantry assault troops training for a flamethrower attack. They wear light assault order of rolled pack, bread bag, water bottle, entrenching tool, Gew 98 rifle, and Pickelhaube with the spike removed.

Shock troop (Stosstrupp) of the 7th Company of an unidentified Saxon infantry regiment. All except the Unteroffizier with the bandaged hand wear the M1907/10 field jacket with Saxon cuffs; the NCO is uniformed in the M1915 blouse (Bluse). He also displays a shock-troop badge on his upper left sleeve, consisting of an oval patch in field gray with a red "S" in the shape of a snake, the head at the bottom.

skirmish line. As a result the 3rd Guard Pioneer Battalion suffered what Reddemann regarded as heavy casualties.

Neuville prompted a debate in the German officer corps over the usefulness of the flamethrower. Reddemann pledged to retrain and reform his battalion to prove the worth of his men.[22]

The first step in the retraining program was to adopt the principle that flamethrower pioneers would not escort or support the infantry but would instead go in ahead of them as shock troops *(Stosstrupps),* a term Reddemann himself coined.[23] Shock troops would penetrate deeply into the enemy line and bypass or silence points of resistance such as blockhouses and machine-gun nests.

For assaults, the tactical unit was the 12-man small-flamethrower shock troop *(Kleifstosstrupp)* consisting of two flamethrower squads, four hand-grenade throwers, and two squad leaders. To cross wide expanses of ground, the flamethrower pioneers developed the tactic of "Indian-style forward stalking" *(indianermässigen Vorpirschen).*[24] The men would approach the target indirectly, as individuals instead of a unified force. They would describe wide arcs and move forward in short leaps and bounds, staying within shouting distance of each other, constantly varying their intervals and taking cover in natural features of the terrain.

The flamethrower pioneers were to hold their fire in order to not reveal themselves. If they were seen, they would be perceived as a spectacle "that the enemy often considers crazy, chaps hopping aimlessly from cover to cover."[25] When they had approached to within 70 to 90 yards, one flamethrower squad would release a "covering jet" *(Deckungsstrahl),* which provided enough

Flamethrower shock troops training in France. They wear Pickelhauben – some without cloth covers – and are armed with hand grenades and pistols. The large black cloud of smoke was called a "covering jet" (Deckungstrahl).

smoke and flames to allow the remainder of the group to sprint the final distance to the target.

Infantry machine-gun, trench-mortar, and grenade-launcher squads would provide cover for the flamethrower shock troops during their entire approach. This cooperation led Reddemann to develop another tactic. During an assault the machine gunners went forward with the flamethrower shock troops to provide close-range suppressing fire from the flanks. Grenade-launcher squads would either accompany the shock troops or lay down covering fire from the jumping-off point. Since the target was squeezed between machine guns, grenade launchers, and flamethrowers, Reddemann called it the "Pincers Tactic" *(Zangen-Taktik.)*[26]

After a month of retraining, the 3rd Guard Pioneer Battalion resumed large-scale flame assaults in July of 1915. The most famous and successful of these was the attack at Hooge on July 30, the first time British troops experienced flamethrowers. The Germans used nine *Grof* and 11 *Kleif* in a combined stationary and pouncing attack, which drove the British out of their forward trenches. Over the next nine days, however, the British retook all the lost ground.

In early February of 1916 the 4th Guard Pioneer Battalion *(IV. Garde-Pionier-Bataillon)* was created as a second official flamethrower unit. Comprised of a staff, the 1st and 2nd Companies, and a workshop detachment, it existed for only two months before being absorbed into the flamethrower regiment established on April 20, 1916.

Assault Detachment Calsow in Combat

On May 16, 1915, Assault Detachment Calsow was sent from the Wahn training ground to Douai, France.[27] The Detachment demonstrated its techniques to Army Group von Lochow on May 18; after two demonstrations the infantry commanders were highly critical of the steel shields carried by the pioneers.

Under pressure from *General* von Lochow and his staff, Calsow decided that only the final assault wave would carry shields.

The Assault Detachment carried out several days of reconnaissance in the area held by Army Group von Lochow and was then ordered to the Loretto front in the sector of the 31st Infantry Brigade, 16th Division, VIII Army Corps. From June 5 to 15 the two pioneer companies of the Detachment were put to work building infantry shelters and artillery positions. They were sent into action on June 16 and 17 without being given a rest period to recuperate from the labor of the previous 10 days. Employed as infantry rather than assault pioneers in two counterattacks, they suffered extremely high casualties. From July 22 to 25, the assault cannons were used in the sector held by the 1st Bavarian Reserve Infantry Regiment. As soon as the guns opened fire, they were located by French counterbatteries and fired upon. They relocated quickly but were then prohibited from firing by the sector commander, since the French fire was causing casualties to the infantry and the 37mm guns could not respond effectively.

Eberhard Graf von Schwerin served as adjutant of the Assault Detachment and later Assault Battalion. In his history of the unit he devoted only a paragraph to Loretto:

> When the Assault Detachment was used on Loretto Hill in its first major engagement, it lost half its strength in only one day. The 1st Pioneer Company was sent into battle with one officer, one deputy officer, one *Vizefeldwebel,* 13 NCOs, and 119 pioneers. Six NCOs and 40 men returned. The failure was due to the fact that the experimental devices had not worked satisfactorily when employed and the assault

Assault squad engaging in hand-grenade combat. Each man is armed with two stick grenades and carries his rifle slung. Equipment includes field caps instead of Pickelhauben and gas masks in cloth carriers. At Loretto, the Assault Detachment fought as infantry, with hand grenades and carbines.

An improved 37mm assault accompanying cannon in action on the eastern front. This model was also called a "trench cannon" (Grabenkanone). The large shield was fitted when the gun was used in the open. Note that the man on the right holds a shell and kneels on an ammunition box.

troops had performed haphazardly in a night and dawn attack, with neither a briefing on the area nor an investigation of the enemy positions taking place beforehand. Of course, the necessary lessons were learned from these failed enterprises. The next time these assault companies were used, which was in the Vosges, they were successful.[28]

Endnotes

[1] Stephen Bull, *German Assault Troops of the First World War. Stosstrupptaktik: The First Stormtroopers* (Stroud, Gloucestershire: Spellmount Publishers, Ltd, 2007), p. 44.

[2] Bernhard Reddemann, *Geschichte der deutschen Flammenwerfer-Truppe* (Berlin: Verein ehem. Angehöriger der Garde-Reserve-Pionier-Regiments, 1933), pp. 10-13.

[3] Bernhard Reddemann, "Die Totenkopf Pioniere," in *Das Ehrenbuch der deutschen Pioniere,* p. 516.

[4] Reddemann, *Geschichte,* p. 25.

[5] Charles Theune, "The Flame Thrower," *Artilleristiche Monatschafte* (January-February, 1921). Translated by the Military Intelligence Division of the U.S. War Department. Records of the Chief, Chemical Warfare Service, Record Group 175, File #470.71/1164, U.S. National Archives, pp. 4-5.

[6] Military Attaché, the Hague, to Director of Military Intelligence Division, General Staff, War Department, April 18, 1921. Records of the Chief, Chemical Warfare Service, Record Group 175, File #470.71/1164, U.S. National Archives.

[7] German Patent No.134348.

[8] Cron, p. 161.

[9] Records of Württembergisches Pionier-Bataillon Nr.13, M 200 Bü. 80.

[10] The information on the development of the Assault Battalion is found in Larcade, p. 10-16.

[11] Oskar Charles Gustavus Adolphus, page 12.

[12] Cron, *Imperial Germany Army,* p. 168.

[13] *Dem Andenken unserer gefallenen Kameraden: Garde-Reserve-Pionier-Regiment (Flammenwerfer)* (Berlin: Kameradschaft der Flammenwerfer im NS.-Reichskriegerbund, 1931), p. 32.

[14] Bernhard Reddemann to Brigadier General Amos A. Fries, Chief, Chemical Warfare Service, Thru: Major Herman H. Zornig, U.S. Army, Military Attache, U.S. Embassy, Berlin, February 29, 1928, Record Group 175, File #470.71/32, U.S. National Archives, p. 5.

[15] Reddemann, *Geschichte,* p. 14.

[16] Cron, *Imperial Germany Army,* p. 168.

[17] Victor Lefebure, *The Riddle of the Rhine: Chemical Strategy in Peace and War* (New York: E. P. Dutton and Company, 1923), p. 73.

[18] Reddemann, "Die Flammenwerfer," *Unsere Pioniere im Weltkriege,* edited by Otto Riebicke (Berlin: Kyffhäuser Verlag, 1925), p. 197.

[19] Bruce I. Gudmundsson, *Stormtroop Tactics,* p. 53; and "These Hideous Weapons," in *The Great War: Perspectives on the First World War,* edited by Robert Cowley (New York: Random House, 2003), pp. 312-313.

[20] Most of the information on flame tactics is found in Reddemann, "Die Totenkopf Pioniere," pp. 516-524.

[21] Reddemann, *Geschichte,* pp. 16-17.

[22] Ibid., p. 17.

[23] Reddemann, "Die Totenkopf Pioniere," p. 250.

[24] Ibid.

[25] Ibid.

[26] Reddemann, *Geschichte,* p. 18.

[27] The information on the first attack by Assault Detachment Calsow is found in Larcade, pp. 16-18.

[28] Eberhard Graf von Schwerin, *Königliches preussisches Sturm-Bataillon Nr.5 (Rohr)* (Zeulenroda in Thüringen, Germany: Drud und Verlag von Bernhard Sporn, 1939), p. 107.

CHAPTER 3

The Further Development of Assault Tactics

Reservist of Bavarian 15th Reserve Infantry Regiment, Bavarian Ersatz Division. He wears the Bavarian M1915 simplified field jacket with plain cuffs, the M1907 field cap with a Landwehr cross on the state cockade, and an S98/05 bayonet. Interestingly, his belt buckle is Prussian, with the motto "God is with Us" (Gott mit Uns).

Infantry Assault Troops

While the two new pioneer assault formations – Assault Detachment Calsow and the 3rd Guard Pioneer Battalion – struggled to find their tactical footing, the infantry began improvising assault tactics that mirrored those of the pioneers. The Bavarian *Ersatz* Division was one formation that created and used assault squads relatively early in the war:

> The stubborn French defense from pill-boxes and dugouts located in woods and the failure of the attack under the fire positions arranged for close defense but unknown to and unobserved by the attackers, compelled the employment of "assault groups" *[Sturmtrupps in the original German, ed.]* of a strength of 1 to 3 infantry squads in conjunction with a pioneer squad, machine guns, minenwerfers, and flame throwers. The "assault groups" were specially trained; and in the attack remained in the rear of the front line at the disposal of the company commanders. In place of the rigid skirmish line which was too easily stopped by organized resistance, the employment of a series of small assault detachments was considered, in which the personality of the leader, on which everything depended, was brought into greater use. Adopting this method, on July 7, 1915, the Bavarian *Ersatz* Division captured a position of 1800 meters front to the 4th line within twenty-five minutes after an artillery preparation of only seventy-five minutes, the same procedure having had satisfactory results on May 5th and 14th.[1]

As the composition, weapons, tactics, and use of the "assault groups" are virtually identical to the shock troops that came later, it is likely that no one man can be credited with originating infiltration techniques. What seems to have actually occurred is that several innovative thinkers faced with the same problem – how to break through the enemy line with the fewest number of casualties – came up with similar solutions at the same time. One such innovative thinker was the officer most military historians identify as the inventor of shock-troop tactics.

A New Commander for the Assault Detachment

On August 5, 1915, the Assault Detachment was assigned to Army Detachment Gaede, and *Major* Calsow was relieved of command.[2]

His replacement, who took charge of the Assault Detachment on September 13, was *Hauptmann* Willy Martin Rohr of the Guard *Schützen* Battalion. He was ordered to retrain the unit based on his experiences on the front line. It is not clear if Rohr fought with the all-volunteer Assault Company of the Guard *Schützen* Battalion, created on March 3, 1915, in the Champagne.

When Rohr became commander, the Assault Detachment was comprised of a staff, two pioneer companies, a park company, and the cannon detachment. *General* Gaede soon provided Rohr with Machine Gun Platoon

Opposite

Top: German weapons captured by the French. These are the same arms used by the ad hoc assault squads (Sturmtrupps) of the Bavarian Ersatz Division in the spring and summer of 1915. Pictured are three Lanz 91.5mm light mortars, an MG08 heavy machine gun, and a Kleif M.1912 portable flamethrower.

Bottom: Reservists of the Bavarian 4th Reserve Infantry Regiment, Bavarian Ersatz Division. The soldier second from the left wears an "M" beneath the "4" on his shoulder strap. It may be an unofficial badge that signifies "Trench-mortar Squad" (Minenwerfertrupp).

ND.
Visé Paris N° 122 CAMPAGNE DE 1914-1915
Matériel allemand. Crapouillots, mitrailleuse, réservoir pour liquide inflammable.

Men of the Replacement Battalion, Bavarian 16th Infantry Regiment. The chalkboard reads, "15th Section. In memory of the encampment-assault training during the World War, 1914-15, Passau." An archaic term, "encampment-assault" (Lagersturm) describes attacks that Germanic tribes carried out on Roman bases. In this case it means assaults on any fortified position.

250, armed with two MG08; a trench-mortar platoon armed with four light weapons; and a flamethrower platoon armed with six small devices.[3] Even more powerful weapons were to come.

While the Assault Detachment was being reorganized, the 3rd Guard Pioneer Battalion continued garnering combat experience.

Flamethrower Assaults in the Vosges

On September 9, 1915, the 3rd Guard Pioneer Battalion launched two assaults in the Vosges Mountains in northeastern France. One was in the area known as the Schratzmännele; Reddemann himself directed the combined stationary and pouncing attack and described it in his book:

> Attack of Company Kempf under the Battalion Commander by the Steinbruch on the Schratzmännele in the Vosges on September 9, 1915, with 10 *Grof* and 13 *Kleif*. After the panicked evacuation of the first positions, the ones behind were taken in close combat with *Kleif*. Many machine guns were silenced. Trenches were rolled up. The ordered objective was greatly exceeded.[4]

Opposite: Pionier uniformed in the simplified field jacket and armed with a Gew 98 rifle and saw-backed S98/05 bayonet. The cloth cover of his M1915 Pickelhaube has the crudely painted notation "St" on the front, which could be an abbreviation for "shock troop," "assault squad," or "assault detachment" (Sturmabteilung).

Above: A patrol of Jäger Battalion No.14 (großherzoglich mecklenburgisches Jäger-Bataillon Nr.14) in mountainous terrain. Their M1895 shakos have cloth covers that include squares of white cloth on the rear to make the men more visible during nocturnal operations. Jäger Battalion No.14 provided two companies for the attack at the Hartmannsweilerkopf on September 9, 1915.

Below: Men of a motor-transport (Kraftwagen) unit demonstrating a fire-brigade hand pump. Many motor-transport troops were trained as firefighters, which made them familiar with spraying equipment. They also worked with the combustion of gasoline, which could explain why a motor-transport officer designed the five gasoline-spraying flamethrowers used at the Hartmannsweilerkopf on September 9, 1915.

The second assault took place in the Hartmannsweilerkopf, a rocky, heavily wooded ridge where elite German and French alpine troops clashed. Flamethrower squads from the 9th and 10th Companies of the 3rd Guard Pioneer Battalion carried out the combined stationary and pouncing attack,[5] but Reddemann failed to note the mission. This omission is puzzling given the scale of the operation and the deployment of five "gasoline sprayers" used in addition to Reddemann's flamethrowers. The devices were ordered built after artillery bombardments were deemed ineffective.[6]

Opposing front lines at the Hartmannsweilerkopf were close, creating a No Man's Land no wider than 35 yards on the summit. Accordingly, *Leutnant der Reserve* Schlayer of Cavalry Motor Transport Column 24 *(Kavallerie Kraftwagen-Kolonne 24)* was appointed on May 13 to design a device that could spray flammable liquid across this short divide. It is not clear why a cavalry motor-transport officer was chosen to design a flamethrower, but the rationale may have been that the central focus of his branch of service was machinery and the combustion of gasoline. In addition, some motor-transport personnel are known to have trained as firefighters, allowing them to become familiar with spraying equipment.

Research into the feasibility of the project was approved by the general staff of the 12th *Landwehr* Division, and the general of pioneers of Army Detachment Gaede agreed to bear the costs of manufacturing.

The resulting construction consisted of one tank that held 69 gallons of gasoline connected to two propellant tanks containing carbon dioxide pressurized to 147 psi. (10 atmospheres). Pressure inside the gasoline tank was 73.4 psi. (5 atmospheres), resulting in a range of 115 feet. Beginning May 31 two days of trials were carried out at a training field near Westhalten. The observers were high-ranking officers, among them *General der Infantry* Mengelbier, commander of the 12th *Landwehr* Division.

Spraying ignited gasoline proved insufficient to burn trenches and blockhouses, and it was also very dangerous for the personnel. A safer and more efficient process was to spray unlit gasoline and ignite it by throwing fire tubes. The months of June and July were dedicated to improving the device and finding the best mixture of gasoline. On August 7, 1915, the Schlayer

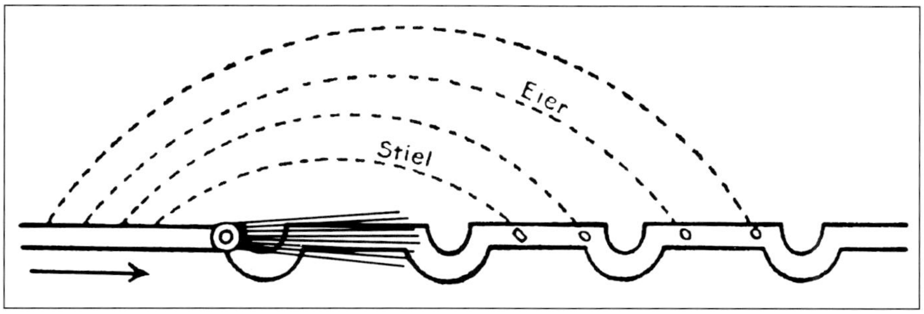

Rolling up a trench (Aufrollen) with hand grenades and a portable flamethrower. The flamethrower operator sprays burning oil across the open ground between traverses, driving the enemy out of his position, while other members of the shock troop throw stick grenades (Stiel) and smaller, lighter egg grenades (Eier) that could travel longer distances and force the enemy even further back.

sprayer was demonstrated to *General* Gaede and the commanding officers of the 12th *Landwehr* Division, and the decision was made to proceed with a flame attack. The target was the first French trench line on the summit of the Hartmannsweilerkopf.

On September 8 Reddemann observed the Schlayer sprayer in action and judged it wanting. He said that the ignition took place too late, and the flame would not be effective against shelters.[7] Nevertheless, preparation for the assault continued, and pioneers of the 1st *Landwehr* Pioneer Company, XIV Army Corps *(1. Landwehr-Pionier-Kompagnie XIV. Armee Korps)* adapted five positions in the foremost German lines where Schlayer's equipment would be installed.

The attack was planned for the late afternoon of September 9. Two companies of Mecklenburger *Jäger* Battalion No.14 *(großherzoglich mecklenburgisches Jäger Bataillon Nr.14)* would lead, accompanied by pioneers of the 1st *Landwehr* Pioneer Company armed with hand grenades. Troops of the 3rd Guard Pioneer Battalion would bring two portable army-issue flamethrowers *(Heeresflammenwerfern)*.[8] Since pioneers from two companies of the flamethrower battalion took part in the attack, it appears that Reddemann's men also operated the Schlayer sprayers.

After a one-hour artillery bombardment, the French lines were attacked at three points. One Schlayer sprayer on the southern flank was damaged and could not be fired. The remaining four joined Reddemann's flamethrowers in driving the French out of their positions. At the end of the day, the Germans had gained a section of trench 98 yards wide. Three officers and 82 men of the French 213th Infantry Regiment were taken prisoner, and three machine guns and two trench mortars were captured. The newly won trench gave the Germans an unobstructed view of the open terrain in front. German losses were 10 dead, including one officer and one ensign, and 44 wounded.[9]

Leutnant Schlayer was also wounded in the attack, but neither the nature nor the extent of his injuries are clear.[10] Despite the Schlayer sprayer being judged a success,[11] it is not known if it was used again.

Hauptmann Willy Rohr Retrains the Assault Detachment

Rohr abandoned the steel shields carried by the assault pioneers and replaced the skirmish line with surprise assaults launched by squad-sized shock troops deployed in depth.[12] He coordinated the supporting arms of machine guns, assault cannons, trench mortars, indirect artillery, and flamethrowers at the lowest possible level, and he adopted the tactic of rolling up trenches with hand-grenade throwers. The intention of *General* Gaede and *Hauptmann* Rohr was to create new methods of using all the weapons available to a regiment or division. In the process they also developed an entirely new concept of how infantry battalions could be armed and organized, and how they could engage in combat.

Pionier of the 3rd Guard Pioneer Battalion in heavy assault order. Men of the battalion's 9th and 10th Companies used portable flamethrowers and Schlayer gasoline sprayers against French positions at the Hartmannsweilerkopf on September 9, 1915.

In place of the 37mm guns, Rohr would use captured Russian 76.2mm field pieces, powerful and accurate weapons that could engage in close-range suppressive fire. The Assault Detachment would no longer have to rely as much on indirect artillery fire, which could fall disastrously short, had to be coordinated before the assault, required an artillery liaison officer and field telephones, and could not be quickly shifted to new targets.

The 76.2mm Putilov M1902 field guns had originally armed Fort Kowno but had been converted by the Russians into trench guns. They lacked a modern sighting system, which made Rohr initially refuse them. However, after much testing a method of sighting by eye was developed, sufficient for the short ranges at which the weapons would be used.[13]

These cannons went by many names, including "assault defense gun" (*Sturmabwehrgeschütz),* "assault accompanying cannon" *(Sturmbegleitkanone),* "infantry accompanying gun" *(Infanteriebegleitgeschütz),* and "infantry gun" *(Infanteriegeschütz).* Rohr had the barrel shortened and the carriage lightened to save weight, and the gun was rechambered to take German 77mm shells.

A memo from the Staff Officer of the Pioneers of Army Detachment Gaede to Army Command Ib, dated January 4, 1916, listed the weapons of Assault Detachment Rohr in October of 1915:

> The Assault Detachment of Army Detachment Gaede possesses the following close-combat weapons:
>
> 1. In accordance with War Ministry 355/10.15 A 6 II of October 15, 1915, there were transfers made in the budget for:
>
> six small flamethrowers
> four light rifled trench mortars.
>
> 2. According to the information put forth in the army order of November 1, 1915, there were transferred from the Supreme Army Command:
>
> four Russian 7.62cm assault defense cannons.
>
> 3. In addition there were transferred by the Staff Officer of Pioneers, in accordance with verbal permission by the Army Command:
>
> four heavy charge throwers *[Ladungswerfer]* (No. 79, 99, 108, and 91)
> two medium charge throwers (No. 4 and 5)
> one grenade launcher Priester (No. 311).[14]

Assault Detachment Rohr carried out its first attack on October 12, 1915, which was followed by another on October 15. On October 17 a flamethrower platoon of one officer and 23 men armed with six portable devices was assigned to the Assault Detachment.[15] These flamethrower operators may have been transferred from the 3rd Guard Pioneer Battalion, which worked together with Assault Detachment Rohr on several missions. However, the origin of Rohr's first flamethrower troops is not certain. The confusion

Opposite
***Top:** Hauptmann Willy Rohr (front row, center), posing with assault troops of a grenadier regiment late in the war. The photo was likely taken at the training ground of Assault Battalion No.5 (Rohr) in Beuville. Courtesy Maurice Sublet.*

***Bottom:** Cigarette card showing Russian Putilov 76.2mm Divisional Gun Model 1902. Hauptmann Willy Rohr had several of these weapons converted to infantry guns by shortening the barrel, lightening the carriage, and rechambering them to accept the German 77mm shell. Prior to its modification by the Germans the gun had a combat weight of 2976 lb and a range of 9296 yd.*

Ehrhardt heavy charge thrower (schwerer Ladungswerfer). A smoothbore 250mm trench mortar issued to Assault Detachment Rohr, it fired a 220-lb shell with a 110-lb explosive charge. Maximum range was about 460 yd.

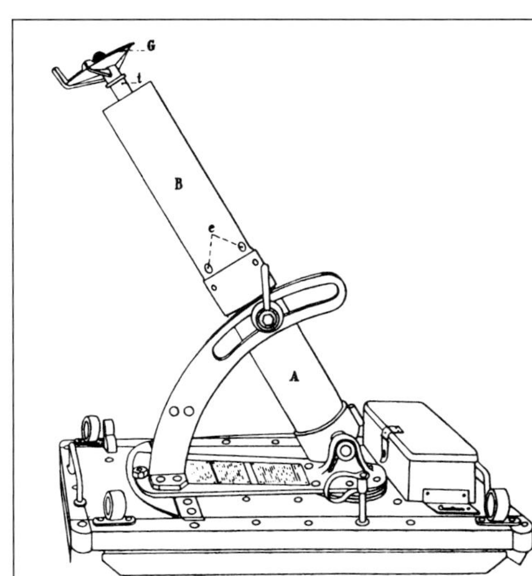

Ehrhardt 91.3mm light charge thrower (leichte Ladungswerfer), an auxiliary (behelfmässigen) trench mortar supplied to Assault Detachment Rohr in late 1915. Propellant was loaded into the firing chamber (A); an explosive charge of 5.5 to 9.9 lb was placed on the platform (G); and the propellant was detonated electrically, driving the piston (T) and hurling the charge. The weapon weighed 109 lb and had a range of 55 to 110 yd.

Above: Saxon grenadiers armed with a Granatenwerfer 15, also known as the "Priesterwerfer" or "Priestwerfer." This light spigot mortar weighed about 30 lb, while the bedplate weighed 48 lb. The grenade – fired by the pull of a lanyard – weighed 5.5 lb, had a maximum range of 275 yd, and created a fragmentation spread 3-5 yd wide and 30-50 yd long.

Left: Trench-mortar Pionier equipped with the M1907/13 knapsack, M1909 ammunition pouches, a long-handled pioneer shovel, and a Kar 98AZ carbine. The tunic is the M1915 blouse with black shoulder straps and slip-on covers to conceal the unit number. Trench-mortar personnel were transferred into Assault Detachment Rohr to operate the rifled weapons and smoothbore charge throwers.

about the background of the flamethrower platoon is significant as it leads to the broader question of whether or not *Hauptmann* Rohr was in fact the originator of German shock-troop tactics. The answer may never be known, although the issue will be addressed below.

The First Combat Operations of Assault Detachment Rohr

On October 12, 1915, an assault detachment of the 3rd Guard Pioneer Battalion and the 2nd Assault Company of the Assault Detachment assisted Infantry Regiment No.187 in clearing about 110 yards of enemy trench in the Vosges at the ridge called the Schrätzmannele.[16] No artillery preparation was used in order to maintain the element of surprise. At 5:29 P.M. the assault detachment of the 3rd Guard Pioneer Battalion shocked the French forward trenches with six *Grof* in a stationary attack. From behind each flamethrower came a squad of assault pioneers assigned a specific section of enemy trench, which it cleared with hand grenades. French artillery and machine guns were dealt with by German counterbattery fire and trench mortars; once the six trench sections were taken, the positions were consolidated by pioneers and infantrymen equipped with sandbags, pickaxes, and shovels. (See Appendix 1 for "Instructions for the Employment of Flame Projectors," a detailed description of this type of assault.) Casualties of the 2nd Assault Company were four men killed and 11 wounded.

Kanonier of the howitzer battery of the later Assault Battalion No.5. He wears the M1907/10 service jacket and M1907 field cap; the shoulder straps are field gray with the exploding grenade of the field artillery and the number "5," both in red. The bayonet is the serrated S98/05 pioneer model, while the leather gaiters (Gamaschen) are standard for field artillery.

Musketier Lindman, a Swede serving in the 8th Company of Infantry Regiment No.187, of the 187th Brigade and later 187th Infantry Division. He wears full marching order, including an extremely large, nonregulation blanket folded and strapped to his M1907/13 knapsack.

The assault troops of the 3rd Guard Pioneer Battalion and Assault Detachment Rohr were withdrawn, while the 5th Company of Infantry Regiment No.187 and the line pioneers remained in the newly won trench to fight off the inevitable counterattacks. A former captain of the regiment, Wolf Jan Dose, did not mince words when comparing these new, specialized assault troops to the regular infantry of his regiment:

> As always in such cases, the main burden of the fight was carried not so much by the matadors of the assault detachment – whose gumption is entitled to the highest regard – but instead by the ones who again squeezed the lifeblood out of the target, the men of the 187th.[17]

On October 15, 1915, 10 assault squads from the 1st Assault Company of Assault Detachment Rohr assisted the 82nd *Landwehr* Brigade of the 12th *Landwehr* Division in an attack on French positions in the Hartmannsweilerkopf.[18] Flamethrower pioneers also carried out a combined stationary and pouncing attack, in which large flamethrowers were fired first and then squads armed with portable flamethrowers advanced with the infantry from the German trenches to drive the enemy further back from his position.

A large-flamethrower squad (Groftrupp) of the 3rd Guard Pioneer Battalion at Sivry, northeastern France, firing an M1912 double Grof (Doppelgrof). The 3rd Guard Pioneer Battalion used six large flamethrowers during the first combat operation of Assault Detachment Rohr on October 12, 1915. This model of double Grof held 52 gal of oil; duration was about a minute and maximum range was 130 ft.

Trench raider armed with M1916 stick grenades and a P08 pistol attached to a lanyard and tucked into his belt. He wears the M1915 blouse with shoulder straps removed; his field cap displays the yellow-red-yellow Baden state cockade. Courtesy Maurice Sublet.

The attack presented serious difficulties, particularly the inability of German artillery to bombard the foremost French positions that were the target of the operation. German gunners would therefore lay down barrages in front of the peak to prevent the arrival of enemy reserves during the assault.

Only a short time was allowed for preparations, the most important of which was installing the assault units in their sectors. The Guard *Jäger* Battalion was placed on the right wing. Four *Jäger* assault groups assisted by pioneers and flamethrowers were to seize the support points of the enemy positions and pave the way for the assault columns. On the same peak the Guard *Schützen* Battalion formed a continuous line. The companies of the Guard *Schützen* Battalion were distributed as follows:

1st Company - Sap D, trench "Emma," and north in trench "Johann-Albrecht";
2nd Company - near sap "Moss";
3rd Company - sap "Dora";
4th Company - part of it south of "Johann-Albrecht" up to the Dortmund trench.

In sap "Rohr" the 1st Company of the Guard *Jäger* Battalion was held in readiness for the advance. The six heavy machine guns of the Guard *Schützen* were distributed among all the attacking units. Two companies of bicyclists were maintained in reserve. *Leutnant* Hoffmann of Assault Detachment Rohr had distributed his 10 assault squads and four consolidation squads *(Bautrupps)* in the sectors of the Reserve *Jägers* and the Guard *Schützen,* keeping his four construction squads *(Verbindungstrupps)* with him.

Once the Guard *Schützen* and *Jäger* Battalions were ready, the 1st Company of *Landwehr* Pioneer Battalion No.14 arrived and took its place in the German line. Two large and six small flamethrowers of the 9th Company, 3rd Guard Pioneer Battalion, were brought to the front by funicular the day before the assault. The *Grof* were installed on the left of "Dora" under the supervision of the flamethrower company commander, while the *Kleif* were to advance with the Reserve *Jäger* and Guard *Schützen.* The 9th Company of *Landwehr* Infantry Regiment No.56 was extended around the "Untere Rehfelsen." *Oberleutnant* Neumann-Hofer placed Detachment Panke at the *"Hexenküche"* (Witch's Kitchen) and Detachment Willke at the *"Gabel-Sappe"* (Fork Sap).

In front of the German line, pioneers cut openings in the wire and all patrols were stopped; cases of ammunition and hand grenades were piled up in shelters. Runners formed chains of communication while the final telephone wires were laid. The medical service was organized, and supply depots were filled. All the preparations were carried out under heavy French bombardment. Every soldier – rifleman, pioneer, grenadier, machine gunner, artilleryman, trench-mortar operator – knew his station, his mission, and the goal he must achieve.

At 6:00 A.M. a massive barrage of light trench mortars signaled the beginning of the attack. An enormous tongue of flame from sap "Dora" covered the advance of the 3rd Company of the Guard *Schützen* Battalion. Rapid rifle fire and flurries of hand grenades came from both sides. As the Germans continued their harassing fire with small mortars, the French responded with artillery. The flamethrowers illuminated the 4th Company of the Guard *Schützen* Battalion, making them easy targets. German casualties were heavy in this sector.

Signalist E. Soosten of Fortress Telephone Signal Detachment Metz (Festungs-Fernsprech-Signal-Abteilung Metz) in heavy assault order that includes a Russian M1891 Moisin Nagant rifle and bayonet. Signalers and telephonists accompanied assault troops into action and were thus trained in shock-troop tactics.

The violence of the assault was remarkable even by the standards of the First World War. *Leutnant* Schneider of the Baden pioneers threw five concentrated charges in the trench networks and sapheads, blowing them up to clear the way for the 2nd Company of the Guard *Schützen* Battalion. In spite of this effort the assault troops of the 2nd Company took half an hour to penetrate the enemy position. They succeeded only after portable flamethrowers eliminated the French machine guns installed on the German flanks. The two assault columns of the 9th Company of *Landwehr* Infantry Regiment No.56 advanced close behind the rolling German barrage and captured two French machine guns and 41 prisoners. In the *Jägertanne* sector the assault squads of Reserve *Jäger* Battalion No.8 – three from the 2nd Company and one from the 1st – penetrated the French line under such a storm of machine-gun fire that the entire right-hand element was mowed down. The 7th and 8th Companies of *Landwehr* Infantry Regiment No.56, following behind the assault troops of Reserve *Jäger* Battalion No.8, were pounded by 220mm mortar shells that stopped them in their tracks and prevented them from either advancing or retreating.

Wire-cutting squad (Scherentrupp) leading an assault early in the war.

Although the Germans managed to take their objectives, at 5:00 P.M. they were ordered to abandon the ground they had gained and fill in the communication trenches of sap "Moss." French counterattacks led to a German barrage at 6:00 P.M.; by nightfall the 82nd *Landwehr* Brigade occupied the positions it had held before the operation. The German view was that the sacrifices of their troops had not been in vain, since the assault tied up several elite French units.

The operation cost the Germans 32 dead, 203 wounded, and 63 missing.

Shock-troop Tactics: Willy Rohr versus Bernhard Reddemann

The flamethrower platoon of one officer and 23 men assigned to the Assault Detachment on October 17, 1915, did not take orders from Rohr or Army Detachment Gaede.[19] Instead, like the 3rd Guard Pioneer Battalion, it was directly subordinate to the *OHL*. The Replacement Company of the 3rd Guard Pioneer Battalion supplied replacements for the flamethrower platoon; however, the origin of the initial flamethrower pioneers to serve under Rohr is confusing. While Rohr's former adjutant, von Schwerin, wrote that they came from "Flamethrower Regiment Pioneer Battalion 36" *(Flammenwerfer-Regiment Pionier-Bataillon 36),*[20] no such unit existed. Von Schwerin also claimed that the first time the flamethrower platoon was used in combat on December 24, 1915, at the *Jägertanne,* the men were utterly incompetent: "The flamethrower troops of the flamethrower regiment had never cooperated with infantry and had no idea how to behave with our people."[21]

Addressing von Schwerin's accusation leads inevitably to speculation on the roles played by *Hauptmann* Rohr and *Major* Bernhard Reddemann in the creation of German shock-troop tactics.

The inability of the flamethrower platoon to cooperate with assault troops could be explained if the platoon had been transferred into the Assault Battalion without having had experience with incendiary weapons. Instead of belonging to the fictitious Flamethrower Regiment Pioneer Battalion 36, they may have come from Pioneer Replacement Battalion No.36 *(Pionier-Ersatz-Bataillon Nr.36),* the replacement battalion of the two poison-gas units, Pioneer Regiments 35 and 36. As poison-gas specialists, they would not have been trained in how to use flamethrowers during infantry assaults. Another possibility is that von Schwerin misremembered unit numbers and dates. He may have been referring to Pioneer Replacement Battalion No.35, which provided replacements for the Assault Battalion after March 11, 1916.

There is no good reason why gas troops would be transformed into flamethrower pioneers, except that perhaps both arms of the chemical-warfare effort were so new and technically advanced that higher command did not differentiate between them. Staff officers may have thought that since both services involved spraying pressurized liquids, they were interchangeable. An alternative explanation is that Reddemann, a man whose writings reveal him to be a somewhat belligerent, self-serving individual, may have balked at providing a flamethrower platoon for a man he saw as a rival.

In April of 1916, when Assault Detachment Rohr became Assault Battalion Rohr, two more assault companies were formed from Pioneer Replacement Battalion No.7 and the Replacement Battalion of Pioneer Regiment No.35.[22] The connection between Rohr's assault troops and poison gas is therefore genuine but still puzzling. One possibility is that it was a question of simple convenience and proximity, as the Replacement Battalion of Pioneer Regiment No.35 had its barracks on the training ground at Wahn, where the Assault Detachment was established. After September 1, 1917, the replacements for Assault Battalion No.5 (Rohr) may have come from Pioneer Replacement Battalion No.35.

There is no question, however, that if the flamethrower platoon transferred to the Assault Detachment on October 17, 1915, had been trained by Bernhard Reddemann, the men would have known how to cooperate with infantry during an assault. By that date the 3rd Guard Pioneer Battalion had already carried out many successful attacks with infantry, including those at the Bolante and near St. Hubert in the Argonne, at Hooge, and in the Vosges. As noted previously the Assault Detachment had carried out two successful

Pionier of Pioneer Replacement Battalion No.36, the replacement battalion of the two gas regiments. The Flamethrower Platoon of Assault Detachment Rohr may initially have been comprised of men from Pioneer Replacement Battalion No.36. Perhaps coincidentally, the photographer who produced this carte-de-visite, Otto Hoeffke of Berlin, was a favorite of flamethrower pioneers.

1916.
Die lustige
Korp. VIII

operations with the 3rd Guard Pioneer Battalion before the flamethrower platoon had been assigned to Rohr's unit. On October 6, 1915, the *OHL* ordered that the 3rd Guard Pioneer Battalion be expanded from four to six companies, due to the overwhelming requests of infantry commanders for flamethrowers.[23]

The *OHL* had published "Instructions for the Employment of Flame Projectors" on December 12, 1915, two weeks before Rohr's attack on the *Jägertanne*. The document describes in precise detail how flamethrower troops must cooperate with the infantry. It reads, in fact, as a manual for such attacks. It would seem that in December of 1915 Reddemann was actually more proficient in carrying out shock-troop attacks than Rohr.

Captain G. C. Wynne's 1939 book *If Germany Attacks: The Battle in Depth in the West* was the first English-language book to cover shock-troop tactics. Wynne stated that in the summer of 1915 Rohr and Reddemann collaborated to create the first assault battalion, under the supervision of *Oberst* Bauer of the *OHL* Operations Detachment.[24] According to Bauer, Rohr and Reddemann were "to be regarded as the authors of the shock-troop concept *(Stosstruppgedanke),*"[25] which was ready for testing a few weeks after Rohr became commander of the Assault Detachment in September of 1915.[26] No less an authority on shock-troop tactics than *Oberleutnant* Ludwig Charles Theune, commander of the 10th Company of the Guard Reserve Pioneer Regiment and author of *Sturmtruppen und Flammenwerfer,* gave Reddemann most of the credit:

> The flamethrower regiment produced the first assault battalion Rohr (Fifth Army). The newly emerging assault battalions adopted the pioneer shock-troop tactics of the flamethrower and developed them.[27]

As mentioned previously, Theune had a less-than-stellar record of truth telling, having claimed to have invented the flamethrower himself.

The patronage of Crown Prince Wilhelm may have played a role in the apparent rivalry between Rohr and Reddemann. Wilhelm was said to refer to the later Assault Battalion as his favorite unit *(Lieblingstruppe);*[28] from February 18, 1918, the men of Assault Battalion No.5 (Rohr) wore a badge on their lower left sleeve consisting of an oval of field-gray cloth to which was attached a white-metal "W" surmounted by a crown. This sleeve badge was unofficial, having never received approval by the Kaiser. Reddemann's men also had a special relationship with the Crown Prince, who called them his Body Guard *(Leibgarde)* and encouraged them to address him in an informal manner.[29] Unlike Assault Battalion No.5 (Rohr), the men of the Guard Reserve Pioneer Regiment were awarded an officially sanctioned sleeve badge in the form of a death's head, which the Crown Prince announced in a letter to the regiment on July 28, 1916:

> His Majesty the Kaiser and King has, at my recommendation, decreed that the Guard Reserve Pioneer Regiment, which has been developed under my eyes, should wear during the war on the left sleeve of its uniform an insignia in the form of a death's head. In recognition of its outstanding achievements I wish to congratulate the flame projector regiment on the award of this insignia.
>
> Always placed into action in the most difficult places, both officers and men everywhere brought their arm into play both effectively and quickly, and became one of the most fearful opponents in close combat the French had.

Opposite
Top: Pioneers of the Replacement Battalion, Pioneer Regiment No.35; the chalkboard reads "1916: The merry Section VIII." This unit provided replacements for both Pioneer Regiment No.35 and the Assault Battalion. In April of 1916 the Assault Battalion created two additional assault companies comprised of men from the Replacement Battalion of Pioneer Regiment No.35.

Bottom: Kleif M.1914, a modification of the Kleif M.1912. It weighed about 70 lb when full; duration was 15 seconds and maximum range 60 ft. This lance operator (Strahlrohrführer) and Kleif carrier (Kleifträger) wear the uniform shared by the 3rd Guard Pioneer Battalion and the Flamethrower Platoon of Assault Detachment Rohr.

Pionier of the Flamethrower Platoon, Assault Detachment Rohr, in the parade uniform of the Guard Pioneers. The M1897 Pickelhaube has a black horsehair plume and fittings in "pioneer silver"; the M1895 service jacket is dark blue with black collar and cuffs piped in red; and the peacetime overcoat (Mantel) is dove gray with black "coat patches" (Mantelpatten).

Flamethrower platoon of Assault Battalion No.14. Standing on the right is a former member of the flamethrower platoon of Assault Battalion No.5 (Rohr), as indicated by the position of the death's-head sleeve badge. Rohr's men displayed their badge below the left elbow, while all other flamethrower pioneers wore the death's head on or directly above the cuff, depending on the type of jacket.

> I am convinced that the outer insignia of the young arm will always be an exhortation to continue to develop in the spirit of death-defying joy of combat.[30]

Despite the internecine squabbles, by late 1915 Rohr received his flamethrower pioneers from Reddemann's formations. However, unique among flamethrower pioneers attached to assault units these men were considered full members of the Assault Detachment and later Assault Battalion. When they were killed in action or died of wounds, accident, or disease, their names were not recorded in the death book of the Guard Reserve Pioneer Regiment. Instead, they appeared in the honor rolls included in the history of Assault Battalion No.5 (Rohr) written by von Schwerin.

Although flamethrower pioneers were often transferred out of Rohr's unit into Reddemann's flamethrower battalion and later regiment, the transfers did not operate in the other direction. As members of Rohr's unit, they wore Guard Pioneer uniforms, but with a red "5" on the shoulder strap. Photographs show that after Reddemann's flamethrower pioneers were awarded the death's head, the flamethrower pioneers serving with Rohr displayed an identical badge, except theirs were worn directly below the left elbow instead of on or above the cuff. This position was clearly an effort to differentiate Rohr's men from Reddemann's. If Rohr's flamethrower pioneers were transferred into Reddemann's regiment, they were required to move the badge lower, onto the cuff. Thus Rohr and Reddemann staked out their territories and enforced their own regulations.

Endnotes

[1] Wilhelm Balck, *Development of Tactics – World War* (Fort Leavenworth, Kansas: The General Service School Press, 1922), pp. 69-70.

[2] Cron, p. 119.

[3] Gudmundsson, pp. 47-48.

[4] Reddemann, *Geschichte,* p. 19.

[5] War diary of the General of Pioneers of Armee-Abteilung Gaede, Genrerallandesarchiv Karlsruhe 456 EV 105/57.

[6] Most of the information on the Schlayer gasoline sprayer is found in the War Diary of 1. Landwehr-Pionier-Kompagnie XIV. Armee Korps, Generallandesarchiv Karlsruhe 456 EV 105/98.

[7] War Diary of the Commander of Pioneers of Landwehr Division Nr.12, Genrerallandesarchiv Karlsruhe 456 EV 105/69.

[8] War Diary of the General of Pioneers of Armee-Abteilung Gaede.

[9] War Diary of Landwehr Division Nr.12, Genrerallandesarchiv Karlsruhe 456 EV 142/1.

[10] Gustav Goes, *Hartmannsweiler Kopf: das Schicksal eines Berges im Weltkriege* (Berlin: Traditionsverlag Kolk, 1930), p. 101.

[11] War Diary of Landwehr Division Nr.12.

[12] Gudmundsson, pp. 48-49.

[13] Larcade, pp. 24-25.

[14] Although this document, Order No.l No.237/16, signed by "Salzenberg," is found in the German Bundesarchiv-Militärarchiv, the file number is not known. It cannot be easily traced because there are no precise lists for the contents of each file in the archive.

[15] Generallandesarchiv Karlsruhe 456 F3/966.

[16] Gudmundsson, pp. 49-50.

[17] Wolf Jan Dose, *Die 187er im Felde* (Hamburg: Eigenverlag, 1922), p. 16.

[18] Gustav Goes, *Hartmannswillerkopf.* French translation by P. Waechter (Paris: Payot, 1934), pp. 130-149.

[19] von Schwerin, p. 18.

[20] Ibid.

[21] Ibid., p. 7.

[22] Larcade, p. 26.

[23] Reddemann, *Geschichte,* p. 15.

[24] G. C. Wynne, *If Germany Attacks: The Battle in Depth in the West* (Westport, Connecticut: Greenwood Press, 1976), p. 147.

[25] Helmuth Gruss, *Die deutschen Sturmbataillone im Weltkrieg: Aufbau und Verwendung* (Berlin: Junker und Dünnhaupt, 1939), pp. 24-25.

[26] Martin Samuels, *Command or Control? Command, Training and Tactics in the German and British Armies, 1888-1918* (London: Frank Cass, 1995), p. 88.

[27] Theune, *Sturmtruppen und Flammenwerfer,* p. 248.

[28] Gudmundsson, pp. 83, 89.

[29] Reddemann, *Geschichte,* pp. 48-49.

[30] Bernhard Reddemann to Brigadier General Amos A. Fries, Chief, Chemical Warfare Service, Thru: Major Herman H. Zornig, U.S. Army, Military Attache, U.S. Embassy, Berlin, February 29, 1928, Record Group 175, File #470.71/32, U.S. National Archives, p. 21.

CHAPTER 4

Assault Battalion Rohr, Mountain Troops, and Jäger

Pionier of the 2nd Assault Company, Assault Battalion Rohr, uniformed in a privately purchased M1907/10 field jacket with the high collar usually worn by officers. The Assault Detachment was transformed into a battalion on April 1, 1916.

Assault Battalion Rohr

Following several more attacks, Assault Detachment Rohr was transferred to the Fifth Army in March of 1916. On April 1, 1916, the War Ministry added two more assault companies, transforming the detachment into a battalion. The new Assault Battalion was composed of:

one battalion staff;
four assault companies (210 assault pioneers in each);
one machine-gun company;
one trench-mortar detachment;
one flamethrower platoon;
one assault-gun detachment;
one pioneer park company.[1]

Soon afterward the Assault Battalion added a second machine-gun company and expanded the trench-mortar detachment into a full company armed with eight light mortars. The pioneer park company became a fifth assault company, while the assault-gun detachment was reorganized as a howitzer battery, its eight Russian 76.2mm guns replaced with four Krupp 105mm mountain howitzers *(10,5 cm Gebirgshaubitz L/12).*

In April of 1916 the Assault Battalion built a training ground in the ruins of the village of Doncourt. German and Austrian officers and noncommissioned officers were trained in assault tactics at Doncourt until the end of the war.

According to French intelligence, Assault Battalion Rohr achieved most of its success during the Battle of Verdun through the element of surprise. Rather than attacking in lines of riflemen, the battalion sent in small groups of men who advanced in open formation to break into the French positions at specific points. The assault was very methodical and consisted of three detachments advancing in three waves.

The first detachment, formed of several shock troops, was followed by three to four infantry squads. The number of troops in the first wave was kept low to avoid the risk of the men obstructing each other.

Krupp 105mm mountain howitzer L/12 (10,5 cm Gebirgshaubitz L/12) with short carriage. In April the infantry-gun detachment of the Assault Battalion was reorganized as a howitzer battery, its eight Russian 76.2mm infantry guns replaced with four Krupp 105mm mountain howitzers. Courtesy Thierry Ehret.

The second detachment followed the first at an interval of approximately one minute and penetrated the French line through the same breaches. The second detachment served as reinforcements.

The third detachment carried ammunition and a small amount of matériel.

Each attack unrolled minute by minute according to a previously determined schedule regulated by the clock. The signals agreed upon for the advance and the expectations of the events which might take place during combat were battle tested and not in any way expedient or stopgap in nature. The assault troops leapt forward the moment the artillery barrage began to taper off.

Assault Battalion Rohr was able to organize counterattacks against French assaults in as short a time as 20 minutes.

Unteroffizier of Grenadier Regiment No.110 posing with a captured Hotchkiss M1872 37mm revolving cannon of the type advocated by André Laffargue for destroying machine-gun nests at close range. A five-barreled weapon fed by 10-round magazines, it had a range of 2000 yards.

André Laffargue

In the summer or fall of 1915 Captain André Laffargue, of the French 153rd Infantry Regiment, published a pamphlet titled *Étude sur l'attaque dans la période actuelle de la guerre, impressions d'un commandant de compagnie,* rendered in English as *The Attack in Trench Warfare.* In his pamphlet Laffargue described infiltration tactics that in many ways resembled the assault tactics developed by Rohr and Reddemann in early to mid 1915. A copy of the pamphlet was captured by the Germans in the summer of 1916, translated into German, and distributed to an unknown number of German units.[2]

A German officer, Arnold Friedrich Vieth von Golssenau, writing under the pseudonym Ludwig Renn, asserted that in 1916 German infantry regiments were trained according to the theories of Laffargue. Von Golssenau also claimed that Laffargue's pamphlet was used as a tactical manual for infantry operations.[3]

Oberleutnant Karl Bruno Hock, commander of the 1st Company of the Bavarian 2nd *Jäger* Battalion, wrote that in May of 1916 his unit was thoroughly trained in Laffargue's tactics:

> There is nothing like German thoroughness. A year ago the French captain Laffargue used a new method of attack, which had worked well during the May offensive at Arras. Only a benevolent Providence saved us when it was tested on us. German organization had taken up the procedure and with its spirit brought the French form into fulfillment. Now we held in our hands the booklet of the competent captain, which he had written at his leisure during a holiday at a seaside resort, and we strove to adopt the procedures which we had first embraced in theory. We practiced on a large training ground in the Ardennes, with the conditions of Verdun recreated true to life, and we were taught on smaller training grounds close to our accommodations.[4]

Comparing Laffargue's assault tactics with those developed by the Germans reveals some similarities, such as the use of sudden barrages, 37mm assault guns, and small patrols of trench raiders armed with grenades and pistols.[5] However, *Oberleutnant* Hock was mistaken when he claimed that the French had applied Laffargue's tactics at Arras in May of 1915. In fact Laffargue did not write his pamphlet until May or June of that year. By that time the Bavarian *Ersatz* Division and Württemberg Infantry Regiment No.124 had already created their own infiltration tactics and used them successfully in combat (see below). The 3rd Guard Pioneer Battalion and Assault Detachment

Cavalrymen of Bavarian 2nd Schwere Reiter Regiment (2. [königlich bayerisches] Schweres Reiter-Regiment Erzherzog Franz Ferdinand von Österreich-Este) training as dismounted assault troops. The M1886 Pickelhaube for mounted troops has a square visor and a very tall spike. Equipment consists of dummy grenades, M1907/13 knapsacks, and M1887 haversacks.

Opposite
Left: Infanterist of the Bavarian Infantry Leib Regiment uniformed in the M1907 wartime tunic with Brandenburg cuffs. His shoulder straps display an uppercase "P," an unofficial badge possibly signifying "Patrol Squad" (Patrouillentrupp). The Bavarian Leib Regiment was initially not permitted to wear Guard lace on the wartime service jacket. After the men protested, they were allowed to buy their own lace. Note the corduroy trousers with reinforced knees.

Right: Infanterist Bonifaz Maiberger, Bavarian Infantry Leib Regiment, photographed in May of 1918. He is outfitted in a privately purchased M1907 peacetime service jacket with Guard lace and Swedish cuffs, M1907 trousers, and an M1910 officer's cap. Gloves and an S98/05 bayonet complete the elegant picture. Comparison to the wartime uniform in the previous image is instructive.

Calsow had developed similar tactics even earlier in 1915, but both units had been forced by higher command to fight as conventional infantry rather than shock troops the first time they took to the battlefield.

Although the Germans clearly studied Laffargue, and although the Bavarian 2nd *Jäger* Battalion may have been trained in the "French form" of attack, there is no question that German officers invented shock-troop tactics and used them before any Allied army.

Mountain Troops

At the beginning of hostilities the German army had no mountain troops. *Jäger* battalions and the 82nd Infantry Brigade had some experience in mountain warfare due to peacetime exercises in the Alsatian village of Colmar. However, the first dedicated ski formations were not established until December of 1914. Mountain warfare was much more difficult and dangerous than fighting in lowlands. Not only did troops contend with snow, fog, sleet, avalanches, falling rocks, and specialized equipment such as climbing gear, skis, and snow shoes, the simple act of advancing required a high level of training.

Mountain troops generally marched in single file on narrow pathways; this made issuing orders nearly impossible, as runners could not make their way past their fellow soldiers. The single file created a column of surprising depth, 1 to 1.2 miles per battalion of 800 men.[7] Deploying more than one battalion at any one place was inadvisable unless the men had been carefully trained in mountain warfare. The use of pack animals, the launching of

Bavarian Jäger of the Alpine Corps uniformed in a field-gray M1907 jacket and an M1910 officer's cap with the Alpine Corps badge, a metal Edelweiss awarded by Austria-Hungary to German troops who served in the Tyrol between July and October of 1915. The badge was approved by Kaiser Wilhelm II in September of 1915 and worn on the left side of the cap.

counterattacks, and the bringing in of reinforcements all required such a high level of skill that mountain troops were by definition an elite before they ever faced combat:

> In comparison with earlier wars the development of the use of high explosives, the service of communication (wireless stations, visual signal means of all kinds) and methods of bringing up supplies has made the conduct of mountain warfare easier, but all our fights have merely confirmed the old rule that in mountain fighting the value of and not the number of troops is decisive.[8]

The Alpine Corps

Formed on May 21, 1915, the Alpine Corps *(Alpenkorps)* was a division-sized mountain formation.[9] At its establishment the order of battle was:

Bavarian 1st *Jäger* Brigade.
Bavarian Infantry *Leib* Regiment;
Bavarian 1st *Jäger* Regiment:
a) Bavarian 1st *Jäger* Battalion;
b) Bavarian 2nd *Jäger* Battalion;
c) Bavarian 2nd Reserve *Jäger* Battalion.

2nd *Jäger* Brigade.
Jäger Regiment No.2:
a) *Jäger* Battalion No.10;
b) Reserve *Jäger* Battalion No.10;
c) Reserve *Jäger* Battalion No.14.

Jäger Regiment No.3:
a) Bavarian Ski Battalion I;
b) Baden Ski Battalion II;
c) Prussian Ski Battalion III;
d) Bavarian Ski Battalion IV.

Additional Units.
3rd Squadron, Bavarian 4th *Chevauleger* Regiment König;
Mountain Machine Gun Detachments 201 to 205, 210;
Bavarian Mountain Machine Gun Detachments 206 to 209;
Reserve Machine Gun Detachment 4;
Field Artillery Detachments 203 and 204;
Mountain Artillery Detachments 1 and 2;
Foot Artillery Batteries 101 and 102;
Pioneer Company 101;
Bavarian 102nd Pioneer Company;
Mountain Trench Mortar Detachments 269 and 270.

Opposite
Left: Pionier of Bavarian Pioneer Company 101, Alpine Corps, in full marching order that includes M1907/10 knapsack, M1887/88 ammunition pouches, long-handled pioneer shovel, flashlight, M1888 haversack, Gew 98 with saw-backed S98/05 bayonet, puttees, and cleated mountain boots. He wears his Alpine Corps badge on his collar, against regulations.

Right: Mountain Jäger (Gebirgsjäger) of a Bavarian Ski (Schneeschuh) Battalion. He wears the M1914 ski Litewka with green "S" badges on collar, the M1914 mountain cap (Bergmütze), mountain breeches, a rucksack, and cleated mountain boots. Equipment includes a hiking staff and Kar 98AZ carbine. Mountain troops developed tactics very similar to those used by assault troops in the lowlands.

The composition of the Alpine Corps changed several times throughout the war, as units were withdrawn and added. By August of 1918 the Alpine Corps was comprised of the following:

Bavarian 1st *Jäger* Brigade.
a) Bavarian Infantry *Leib* Regiment;
b) Bavarian 1st *Jäger* Regiment.
c) *Jäger* Regiment No.2;

***Left:** Two Bavarian alpine Landwehr infantrymen and a Bavarian Mountain Jäger on ski patrol. Both Wehrmänner are armed with Kar 88 carbines. The Mountain Jäger is uniformed in the M1914 ski Litewka and M1908 service cap for enlisted men.*

***Right:** Bavarian alpine infantry. The man in the center wears an M1910 officer's style service cap with the metal badge of the Carpathian Corps (Karpatenkorps), the 1st and 200th Infantry Divisions. Awarded by Austria-Hungary to Germans who fought with the Austrian Seventh Army, the badge represented a set of stag's antlers. It was officially approved by German high command in December of 1916.*

d) Machine Gun Marksman Detachment 24;
e) Mountain Machine Gun Detachments 204 and 205.
3rd Squadron, Bavarian 4th *Chevauleger* Regiment König.

Bavarian Artillery Commander 7.
a) Field Artillery Detachment No.204;
b) Mountain Artillery Detachment 6;
c) 1st Battalion, Bavarian 1st Reserve Foot Artillery Regiment.

Headquarters Bavarian 9th Pioneer Battalion.
a) Bavarian 102nd Pioneer Company;
b) Pioneer Company 283;
c) Mountain Trench Mortar Company 175.
Division Communications Commander 622.

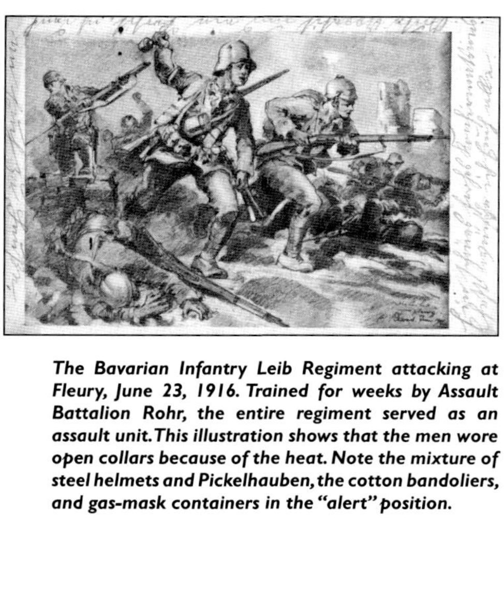

The Bavarian Infantry Leib Regiment attacking at Fleury, June 23, 1916. Trained for weeks by Assault Battalion Rohr, the entire regiment served as an assault unit. This illustration shows that the men wore open collars because of the heat. Note the mixture of steel helmets and Pickelhauben, the cotton bandoliers, and gas-mask containers in the "alert" position.

The Bavarian *Leib* Regiment as an Assault Unit

In the first year of its existence the Alpine Corps fought on the Italian front, in Serbia, and in France.[10] Attached to the Fifth Army in May of 1916, it served as an assault division at Verdun.

In preparation for Verdun, Assault Battalion Rohr trained the Bavarian *Leib* Regiment for several weeks. The Bavarian infantrymen practiced throwing hand grenades, rolling up trenches, taking strong points from the flanks and rear, and consolidating and transforming captured trenches.

On June 23, 1916, the Bavarian *Leib* Regiment assaulted Fleury after a heavy bombardment of high-explosive and Green Cross (disphosgene) gas shells. The attack took place at 8:00 A.M; the 2nd and 3rd Battalions of the *Leib* Regiment and an attached *Jäger* battalion led the way, while the 1st Battalion remained in reserve. In the center of the first line, the 2nd Battalion was reinforced by two shock troops from Assault Battalion Rohr and 20 pioneers. The 3rd Battalion and the *Jäger* battalion were each reinforced with one shock troop from Assault Battalion Rohr and 20 pioneers. In the rear, a pioneer platoon and a light trench-mortar detachment with four weapons were attached to the 1st Battalion.

There were approximately 24 machine guns available from the *Jäger* machine-gun company, the machine-gun company of the *Leib* Regiment, and an independent machine-gun detachment attached to the *Leib* Regiment. About six were kept with the reserve battalion, while the rest were distributed among the companies of the assault troops.

The Bavarian Infantry *Leib* Regiment took Fleury by about 10:30. However, the unit suffered heavy casualties in the house-to-house fighting and from French machine guns and artillery. In addition, other German units were unable to push as far forward as the *Leib* Regiment, leaving the latter to fight a costly hilltop defensive battle over the next three weeks.

Unteroffizier of the Bavarian Infantry Leib Regiment in 1916. He is uniformed in the M1907 field jacket, mountaineering breeches (Gebirgsstiefelhose) with leather knees patches, puttees, and cleated mountain boots. The regiment was considered one of the most effective assault formations of the German army.

Four Schützen of "Forward-shock Troop No.18" (Vorstoss Trupp Nr.18), 2nd Machine Gun Company, Reserve Jäger Bataillon No.14, Alpine Corps. The handwritten message on the postcard reads "In memory of the Romanian campaign." Note the two styles of Guard lace on the collars, leather knee reinforcement, and Alpine Corps cap badge worn by the man on the right. "Vorstoss" was an early term replaced by "Stoss."

This young soldier of the Alpine Corps (right) wears a Prussian M1908 peaked cap for enlisted men, a Prussian belt with trench dagger, a Bavarian M1915 simplified field jacket, and leather-reinforced trousers for mounted troops. It is not known if men from the different German kingdoms served in each other's armed forces, or if this soldier was simply issued uniform items from the stocks at hand.

Schütze of the 1st Company, Württemburg Mountain Machine Gun Detachment 250. He is uniformed in the gray-green M1915 field jacket, and his face is deeply scarred on cheeks and chin. The state cockade of his M1910 officer's service cap is Bavarian, possibly indicating that he was temporarily attached to the Bavarian 1st Jäger Brigade of the Alpine Corps.

Mountain Machine Gun Detachments

The fighting in the Vosges and on the eastern front showed the need for machine-gun units able to perform in mountainous terrain.[11] On August 21, 1915, the War Ministry therefore ordered the formation of Mountain Machine Gun Detachments (*Gebirgs-Maschinengewehr-Abteilungen*) 201 to 251. Of these, 250 was raised in Württemberg; 249 was raised in Saxony; 206 to 209 and 248 were raised in Bavaria; and the remainder were raised in Prussia. A Mountain Machine Gun Detachment had a compliment of four officers, 175 enlisted men, 85 horses, and seven vehicles organized into two platoons armed with three heavy weapons each. Uniforms were of the gray-green cloth worn by machine-gun troops, but with three-button Brandenburg cuffs instead of Swedish cuffs. An experimental helmet of felt with a neck flap was also issued.

Detachments 201 through 209 were formed primarily from cavalrymen fighting on the western front. The units were trained in Döberitz; 40 of them were ready for duty in only one month.

In March of 1916 Detachments 207, 235-238, 243-246, and 248 were reorganized as machine-gun companies and attached to infantry regiments. The remaining Mountain Machine Gun Detachments were each strengthened with 21 men, 20 horses, and three wagons. In July each detachment received three more heavy weapons, increasing its armament to nine machine guns. A field recruitment depot *(Feldrekrutendepot für Gebirgs-Maschinengewehr-Abteilungen der Heeresgruppe Scholtz)* was established in Alexinac for units fighting in Serbia. It consisted of a staff, trainers, a detachment of riflemen, a carriage-animal unit, and a surgical unit. The total personnel of the depot was 16 officers and 827 men.

On May 7, 1917, the Mountain Machine Gun Detachments were reorganized. Each unit would now consist of four officers, 247 men, 139 horses, and 21 vehicles. Machine guns remained at nine per detachment. In 1917 Detachments 252 to 255 were added, as well as Bavarian Detachments 1 and 2.

In 1918 Mountain Machine Gun Detachments 260 to 265 were established, each comprised of three companies. The existing Mountain Machine Gun Detachments were transformed into the companies of the new detachments:

Two Unteroffiziere of the shock troop, 7th Company, Landsturm Infantry Regiment No. 38, 48th Landwehr Division, photographed in Lorraine. Mountaineering gear includes leather-reinforced breeches, cleated boots, and the woolen socks worn by the man on the left. As theirs was a quiet sector, these middle-aged soldiers of the shock troop saw no action during the war.

Maschinengewehr-Abteilung auf dem Marsche (Neue Uniform)

Men of a Mountain Machine Gun Detachment, Alpine Corps. They wear gray green instead of field gray; the original M1915 field jacket had Brandenburg cuffs instead of the Swedish cuffs of other machine-gun troops. Along with the infantry-style jacket the company-sized (later battalion-sized) units received an experimental lightweight Pickelhaube with a neck flap. The men in this photo are armed with Kar 98AZ carbines.

Mountain Machine Gun Detachment 260 (Detachments 206, 208, and 209);
Mountain Machine Gun Detachment 261 (Detachments 213, 215, and 218);
Mountain Machine Gun Detachment 262 (Detachments 221, 223, and 226);
Mountain Machine Gun Detachment 263 (Detachments 227, 233, and 234);
Mountain Machine Gun Detachment 264 (Detachments 240, 247, and 252);
Mountain Machine Gun Detachment 265 (Detachments 253, 254, and 255).[12]

Württemberg Mountain Battalion

Another important unit was the all-volunteer Württemberg Mountain Battalion *(württembergisches Gebirgs-Bataillon)*. The Württemberg Ski Company *(württembergisches Schneeschuh-Kompagnie)* was formed on November 25, 1914, to answer a need for highly trained specialist troops in the Vosges mountains.[13] On March 31, 1915, the Ski Company was renamed the Württemberg Mountain Company *(württembergisches Gebirgs-Kompagnie)*, and then on October 1 it was expanded into the Württemberg Mountain Battalion. At its formation the battalion was comprised of six mountain companies of five officers and 212 men each, and six mountain machine-gun platoons *(Gebirgs-Maschinengewehr-Züge)* of one officer

Squad of the Württemberg Mountain Battalion in 1916, led by an Oberjäger (third from left). The Württemberg Mountain Battalion wore the M1914 ski Litewka with green collar patches and green padded rolls on the shoulder seams for enlisted men, green shoulder-board underlay for officers.

A 77mm mountain gun (Rheinmetall 7,7cm Gebirgskanone L/17 M.1915) of the 1st Platoon, Württemberg Mountain Battery No.6. The artillerymen wear the M1914 ski Litewka with field-gray shoulder straps that display the red exploding grenade of the field artillery and the number "6." Note the map case hanging around the neck of the squad leader kneeling in the foreground. Courtesy Maurice Sublet.

and 57 men each. Soon after its establishment the Battalion merged its six machine-gun platoons into three machine-gun companies. By the time the Battalion took part in the Battle of Caporetto in November of 1917, it consisted of six rifle companies, each armed with three light machine guns; three machine-gun companies armed with 12 heavy weapons each; and a trench-mortar company armed with four light weapons and six grenade launchers.[14]

Since the Württemberg Mountain Battalion could not request heavy artillery support in the steep mountain passes, the unit became skilled at using mountain guns, mortars, and machine guns. On May 3, 1918, it was expanded into the Württemberg Mountain Regiment, with two battalions (three mountain companies each) and three machine-gun companies. It spent the remainder of the war as an infantry regiment on the western front.[15]

Württemberg Infantry Regiment No.124

The most famous member of the Württemberg Mountain Battalion was *Leutnant* (later *Hauptmann*) Erwin Rommel, the Desert Fox of World War II. Before he joined the Mountain Battalion, he served in Württemberg Infantry Regiment No.124 *(Infanterie-Regiment Köning Wilhelm I [6. württembergisches] Nr.124)*. In his book *Infanterie greift an* (published in English as *Attacks*), Rommel described the assault tactics of Infantry

Poor-quality but interesting photo of a trench raider in the Vosges mountains, 1915. He is armed with a P08 pistol, two M.1915 stick grenades, and a trench dagger (Nahkampfmesser) clipped to the front of his jacket.

Regiment No.124.[16] Although they were identical to those attributed to Willy Rohr, Rommel's unit had first used them in June of 1915, a full two months before Rohr was even given command of the Assault Detachment. According to Rommel Infantry Regiment No.124 also benefited from the kind of artillery preparation generally said to have been created by *Oberstleutnant* Georg Bruchmüller on the eastern front in 1917 (see Chapter Twelve).

The first major assault Rommel described took place in June of 1915. The target was a French position called "Central"; the plan called for assault echelons to be organized by five companies of Infantry Regiment No.124. Following them would be infantrymen carrying grenades, ammunition, and entrenching equipment. Rommel himself was assigned to the assault echelon of the 9th Company.

On June 30, the German artillery opened fire at 5:15 A.M. Field guns and heavy and medium trench mortars destroyed the French front lines. One hour before the assault, the heavy and medium trench mortars targeted blockhouses, wire entanglements, and breastworks. The French shelled the German front lines in an attempt to eliminate the assault troops, but the Germans had anticipated this move and had already moved their troops back. In addition, the opposing trenches were too close together for the French tactic to be effective.

As zero hour approached, the German assault troops took cover in natural features of terrain outside the communication trenches, which were being heavily shelled. Lying side by side at their jumping-off points, the assault troops waited out the barrage.

At 8:45 A.M. the assault began. The company assault echelons led the way, followed by infantrymen carrying spades and sacks filled with hand grenades or ammunition. The assault troops moved in small squads, using

Men of the 6th Company, Infantry Regiment No.124 (Infanterie-Regiment König Wilhelm I. [6. württembergisches] Nr.124). They wear simplified field jackets and a mixture of puttees and ankle boot, jackboots, and leather gaiters. The Gefreiter and Musketier on the left also have unidentified circular insignia on the points of their collars.

shell holes and embankments for protection. French machine gunners engaged the Germans from positions in the rear, as the French front-line trenches, "Central I," had been smashed to pieces. Hand-grenade duels between the opposing forces took place all along the sector. During the advance Rommel assumed command of his company assault echelon after its leader was wounded.

German artillery shifted its fire to the second French line, "Central II," about 160 yards to the south. When the German artillery fire eased, Rommel's assault echelon attacked Central II with salvos of hand grenades and an explosive charge to breach the wire. The French garrison fled or surrendered. Leaving some men behind to widen the breach in the wire, Rommel led his assault echelon south, entering a 10-foot-deep communication trench and capturing a French battalion commander and his staff without a fight. After 100 yards the trench opened into a clearing in the woods, where French infantry was in the process of massing. Rommel's assault echelon opened fire, driving the French back into the trees. Rommel had lost contact on both flanks to the right; he reestablished contact with elements of the 1st Battalion of the 9th Company on his left and reorganized his command, deploying it in a defensive position 350 yards south of Central II.

Musketier of Infantry Regiment No.124, uniformed in the M1915 blouse with the ribbon for the Iron Cross, 2nd Class (Eiserne Kreuss or EKII). Although not officially a mountain formation, Infantry Regiment No.124 fought extensively in the Vosges region of northeastern France and developed assault tactics similar to those created by Willy Rohr and Bernhard Reddemann.

Due to his exposed flanks and a memory of once advancing so far that he lost all support, Rommel decided to halt. When a reconnaissance detachment reported that the Germans had been unable to clear Central I, Rommel ordered his men to build blocking positions against counterattacks from the west. Over the next few hours the French launched several counterattacks, each of which Rommel's men defeated. The Germans then began digging a new trench, achieving a depth of five feet by evening. Rommel kept one platoon of the 9th Company in reserve and ordered it to bring ammunition and hand grenades forward. Despite heavy French artillery fire that cut Rommel's single telephone wire, he was able to emplace a heavy machine-gun platoon in the 9th Company's sector.

To the call of bugles, the French attempted an assault from the woods; Rommel's men drove off the waves of enemy infantry with heavy fire. Hand-grenade duels continued throughout the night, but the Germans held their new positions. Over the next several days the 9th Company dug the trench to a depth of six feet, built wooden dugouts, installed steel trench shields, and made sandbagged firing ports. Due to French mortar fire and artillery, Rommel supervised the building of shellproof dugouts 26 feet underground. These reduced casualties considerably.

A Second Assault by Infantry Regiment No.124

In late August, Rommel was given temporary command of the 4th Company of Infantry Regiment No.124 and ordered to prepare his unit for an assault. Rommel personally conducted reconnaissance of the target area and directed several rehearsals of the assault before he was removed as acting company commander because he was too junior an officer.

On September 5 Rommel moved his platoon into a forward position in preparation for the assault. He and his men could hear the French tunneling beneath them but could do nothing except wait.

German artillery and mortars opened fire on the French positions at 8:00 A.M. on September 8, hitting targets only about 50 yards in front of Rommel's platoon. French counterbattery fire forced the assault troops to huddle in their three- and four-man dugouts, waiting for the storm to pass as the trenches were torn to pieces.

At 10:45 A.M. the three assault detachments of the 9th Company emerged from their dugouts and assembled at the jumping-off points. The men synchronized their watches, preparing to attack at exactly 11:00. In the 15 minutes before the assault, the pioneer squads, hand-grenade squads, ammunition carriers, and matériel parties assembled with the assault troops. Rommel described the objectives to each squad leader and stressed that it was vital that the pioneers and carrying parties keep up with the assault troops. The second wave of attacking infantry would deal with pockets of resistance; the objectives were about 25 yards behind the enemy line. If the attack was successful, the pioneers, carrying parties, and subsequent waves of infantry would consolidate the positions gained, establish contact with friendly forces, and block off sectors taken.

At 11:00 A.M. the final German shells hit the French positions and the three German assault detachments attacked on a front 280 yards wide, following the procedures carefully rehearsed over the past few days. The assault squads ignored surrendering French soldiers and ran toward their objectives. Behind them, the second wave gathered up the prisoners. Rommel advanced with the assault detachment on the right; pioneers, hand-grenade squads, and entrenching squads kept up with the assault troops, all refraining from the usual cheers and shouts in order to maintain the element of surprise. Reaching their objective in minutes, Rommel and his men established contact with the center and left assault detachments, as well as the adjacent 2nd Company, and began to consolidate their position. The trenches leading back to the French rear were blocked off with sandbags, and hand-grenade and ammunition dumps were set up.

French artillery opened fire and the French attempted several counterattacks on Rommel's' position, which Rommel's assault detachment easily defeated with hand grenades. German hand grenades could be thrown further than the French versions, giving the Germans a distinct advantage. As French machine guns made resupply difficult, Rommel ordered that a trench 100 yards long and six feet deep be dug from the newly won position back to the jumping-off point. The work was begun at 10:00 P.M. and was finished by dawn. The trench was lined with sandbags; when the sandbags ran out the men emplaced steel shields along a 200-foot gap and stood in a skirmish line, rifles and grenades at the ready as enemy bullets bounced off the armor plate.

During the assault the 2nd and 9th Companies of Infantry Regiment No.124 captured their assigned objective, along with over 140 French officers and men, 16 trench mortars, two machine guns, two drilling machines, and one electric motor. The 9th Company lost three dead and 15 wounded. Five of the wounded were members of an assault detachment who had been injured by a German hand grenade. Rommel had prohibited his men from throwing hand grenades during the attack, since advancing troops might run over them, which is precisely what had happened to the five wounded men of the assault detachment.

Jäger Battalions and Regiments

By virtue of their uniforms, weapons, and tactics, as well as the experience they garnered fighting in the Argonne, Vosges, and Carpathians early in the war, mountain troops and *Jäger* were essentially assault units indistinguishable from the shock troops raised by the regular infantry.[17]

Jäger units were quasi-independent forces attached to cavalry divisions, infantry divisions, and inexperienced divisions. At the start of the war they were each comprised of four rifle companies and one machine-gun company

Opposite
***Top:** Assault Detachment 27 (Sturmabteilung 27) of Infantry Regiment No.124. The cardboard sign is decorated with drawings of hand grenades and pistols, the favored weapons of assault troops. Uniforms are the M1907/10 field jacket and M1915 blouse.*

***Bottom:** Four Musketiere of Württemberg Infantry Regiment No.124 in light assault order consisting of M1909 ammunition pouches, bayonets, M1915 Gummimasken in the "alert" position, and Gew 98 rifles with 20-round trench magazines, which increased the weapon's capacity to 25 rounds.*

Jäger of the Württemberg Mountain Regiment. Attached to the Alpine Corps in 1917, the Württemberg Mountain Battalion was not formally awarded the Edelweiss badge. Many Württemberg veterans of the Battle of Caporetto therefore purchased the decoration and wore it on the right side of the cap, as shown in this photo. The Prussian belt buckle and M1915 blouse indicate late-war service on the western front.

Above: Squad of Westphalian Jäger Battalion No.7 (westfälisches Jäger-Bataillon Nr.7) in full marching order. Uniforms are the M1907/10 field jacket and simplified jacket, both in gray green. Equipment includes knapsack, M1895 or M1909 ammunition pouches, S98/05 bayonets, and Gew 98 rifles.

Below: Crown Prince Wilhelm and his father the Kaiser inspect an assault company of Jäger (Assault) Battalion No.3 (Jäger- [Sturm-] Bataillon Nr.3). The Crown Prince wears an M1915 Jäger uniform including shako with cloth cover. In late 1917 Assault Battalion No.5 (Rohr) returned to combat, and Jäger (Assault) Battalion No.3 became the main training unit for shock-troop tactics.

of 12 heavy weapons. The *Jäger* had been quick to adopt the tactics used by Boer irregulars against the British. Instead of attacking in massed infantry formations, they advanced in small groups or as individuals, taking cover in the natural features of the terrain. Traditionally *Jäger* units had higher physical standards than the regular infantry. They recruited hunters and foresters, men with a sense of self-reliance and a more individualized approach to warfare.

From May 21, 1915, *Jäger* regiments of three or four battalions were formed, while the *Jäger* engaging in mountain warfare were organized into the Alpine Corps, the 200th Infantry Division, and the *Jäger* Division. Each *Jäger* battalion contained a bicycle company (three officers and 124 NCOs and men) and a motor-transport column of 10 vehicles. Joining the 18 *Jäger* battalions that existed at mobilization was *Jäger* Battalion No.27, raised to train Finnish volunteers; 12 additional Reserve *Jäger* Battalions (15-26) were added to the 18 that went to war in 1914.

Each active *Jäger* battalion received a second bicycle company in 1915. In 1917 the *OHL* transferred 21 of these 36 companies into the regular infantry to form bicycle battalions.

In April of 1916 the War Ministry decided to convert four *Jäger* battalions into assault battalions. The conversion would be relatively straightforward, requiring only the addition of mortar platoons, infantry-gun batteries, and flamethrower platoons. Officers and NCOs of the four *Jäger* battalions attended a two-week course given by Assault Battalion Rohr at Beuville but had to cut their training short when Romania entered the war on the Allied side. Three of the four *Jäger* battalions were sent to the Romanian front immediately, leaving only *brandenburgische Jäger-Bataillon Nr.3* to complete the program. On July 8, 1916, it was redesignated *Jäger* (Assault) Battalion No.3 *(Jäger- [Sturm-] Bataillon Nr.3)*.

Jäger in Macedonia, 1917. The Gefreiter (left) has been issued the M1915 blouse and cleated mountain boots; the Oberjäger wears the M1907/10 field jacket with green piping on all seams. Both M1910 officers' field caps have green bands and piping.

As the second assault Battalion, *Jäger* (Assault) Battalion No.3 was comprised of four assault companies, one machine-gun company, one infantry-gun battery of six captured Russian 76.2mm field pieces, one trench-mortar company armed with eight light trench mortars, and one flamethrower platoon armed with six small devices. On July 25 the flamethrower platoon was strengthened with an additional officer and 25 NCOs and men from the 2nd Guard Pioneer Replacement Battalion.

In August of 1916, every *Jäger* battalion received a second machine-gun company and a trench-mortar company of eight light weapons. Since mountain-gun batteries were usually attached to *Jäger* battalions, the units were now assault battalions in everything but name. By the end of the war *Jäger* (Assault) Battalion No.3 had become the main training unit for shock tactics, as Assault Battalion No.5 (Rohr) had returned to combat full time.

Endnotes

[1] Larcade, pp. 27-28, 36.

[2] Gudmundsson, p. 195.

[3] Wynne, p. 58.

[4] Fritz Gollwitzer and Karl Bruno Hock, *"Jäger vor!" Erinnerungs- und Gedenkbuch der Aschaffenburger Jäger (2. Bayr. Jäger-Batl., bayr. Res. Jäger Batl. Nr.2, Radfahrer und Ersatz Radfahrer-Komp.)* (Münchberg: A Dreschler, 1936), pp. 127-128.

[5] André Laffargue, *The Attack in Trench Warfare* (New York: D. Van Nostrand Company, 1917),. pp. 6-55.

[6] André Laffargue, "Advice to the Infantry Soldier," *The Infantry Journal,* Volume 13, Part 2, November 1916-June 1917 (Washington, D.C.: The United States Infantry Association, 1917), pp. 271-272.

[7] Balck, p. 124.

[8] Ibid.

[9] David Gregory, "Alpenkorps 1915-1918," http://www.militaerpass.net/alpenkorps.htm (accessed August 2, 2010).

[10] Gudmundsson, pp. 67-68.

[11] Joe Robinson, "Scroll Helmets," http://www.pickelhauben.net/articles/Scroll_helmets.html (accessed August 3, 2010).

[12] Cron, p. 368.

[13] Ibid., p. 117.

[14] Gudmundsson, p. 130.

[15] Cron, p. 118.

[16] Erwin Rommel, *Attacks* (Provo, Utah: Athena Press, 1979), pp. 76-78, 84-89.

[17] The information on *Jäger* is found in Gudmundsson, pp. 24-25, 77-80, 130; and Cron, pp. 116-117, 365-366.

CHAPTER 5

Verdun and the Somme

Infantry Divisions

The Battle of Verdun began on February 22, 1916. At the opening of the battle the combat units of a German infantry division were:

One infantry brigade (three regiments);
two cavalry squadrons;
one or two pioneer companies;
one mortar company;
one field-artillery regiment.[1]

Each infantry regiment was comprised of three battalions.

A battalion was comprised of four infantry companies (240 rifles each) and one machine-gun company armed with six heavy weapons.

Each pioneer company was armed with six smooth-bore light trench mortars.

The mortar company was armed with two heavy, four medium, and six (then 12) light weapons.

The field-artillery regiment was comprised of three detachments of three batteries each; three batteries were armed with four 105mm howitzers each, six batteries were armed with four 77mm field guns each.

Kleif squad using a small flamethrower to fire signal jets. Such squads were assigned to assault units that had not been issued flare guns, which were always in short supply. The number of jets had a specific meaning, such to halt an artillery barrage or warn of shells falling short.

Composition of Infantry Shock Troops at Verdun

"Pamphlet Ia No.491, Use of the Flamethrowers," February 6, 1916.[2]

A. Organization

1. Each company in the front line forms a shock troop. It usually remains behind the first swarm line *[Schwarmlinie]* (exception Number 5). Especially courageous and adroit men are now selected from each company and, together with the necessary pioneers, flamethrowers, and machine-gun troops, are immediately trained for their special task.

2. Each infantry battalion proceeding to the front line receives three flamethrower squads for the shock troops of the foremost companies.

3. Each shock troop receives a prudent infantry officer as leader and a specially selected deputy (officer or deputy officer).

Each shock troop consists of:

(a) 16 to 20 infantrymen (rifle, three hand grenades each);
(b) one squad of pioneers (axes, hatchets, saws, wire cutters, concentrated and elongated charges);
Task: Clear the way for the shock troop through the forest, undergrowth, obstacles.
(c) Flamethrower squad (with reserve apparatus, flame balls, hand grenades);
Task I: Proceed against blockhouses, machine-gun nests, etc., from general line or immediately together with shock troop.
Task II: Roll up trenches.
(d) Machine-gun squad.

Organization of Assault Troops at Verdun, February 22, 1916

<table>
<tr><td colspan="2">Army Corps</td><td colspan="9">Sector A (right)
VII Army Corps</td></tr>
<tr><td colspan="2">Divisions</td><td colspan="6">14 Reserve Division</td><td colspan="3">13 Reserve Division</td></tr>
<tr><td colspan="2">Infantry Brigades</td><td colspan="2">77 Infantry Brigade</td><td colspan="4">27 Reserve Brigade</td><td colspan="3">28 Reserve Brigade</td></tr>
<tr><td colspan="2">Assault Regiments</td><td>Fus. Regt. No. 37</td><td>Regt. Major Freiherr v. Stotzingen</td><td colspan="2">R. I. R. 16</td><td colspan="2">I. R. 159</td><td>R. Jäger Bat. 7</td><td colspan="2">R. I. R. 39</td></tr>
<tr><td colspan="2">Battalions in Foremost Line</td><td></td><td>R. Jäger 5</td><td>III.</td><td>II.</td><td>I.</td><td>II.</td><td></td><td>III.</td><td>I.</td></tr>
<tr><td rowspan="4">Attack Com-panies</td><td>4th Line</td><td></td><td>3</td><td>9.</td><td>6.7.8.</td><td>1. 3.</td><td>6. 7.</td><td>3.</td><td>9. 10.</td><td>1. 2.</td></tr>
<tr><td>3rd Line</td><td></td><td></td><td></td><td></td><td></td><td></td><td>4.</td><td></td><td></td></tr>
<tr><td>2nd Line</td><td></td><td>1. 5. 4. 2</td><td>10.11. 12.</td><td>5.</td><td>2. 4.</td><td>8. 5.</td><td>1.</td><td>11.12.</td><td>3.</td></tr>
<tr><td>1st Line</td><td></td><td></td><td></td><td></td><td></td><td></td><td>2.</td><td></td><td>4.</td></tr>
<tr><td colspan="2" rowspan="2">Pioneers and Flame-throwers Assigned to Assault Troops</td><td rowspan="2">1/Pio. 5, 3 Lands.Pio. Co. X.</td><td rowspan="2">3/Pio. 18, 2 Lands.Pio. Co. XI., 12, 13/3rd G.P.</td><td rowspan="2">4/Pio 18</td><td>2 R.Pio. 18</td><td colspan="2">2. R/Pio. 7</td><td>2/Pio. 18</td><td>5/Pio. 18</td><td>1 R./Pio. 7</td></tr>
<tr><td colspan="3">10./3rd G.Pio.</td><td colspan="3">16./3rd G.Pio.</td></tr>
<tr><td colspan="2">Regimental Reserves</td><td>II. III. I. in Line of Departure</td><td>III./155 6./R. Jäger 5</td><td colspan="2">I.</td><td colspan="2">III. 4./Pi. 7</td><td></td><td colspan="2">II. 1. R/Pio.18</td></tr>
<tr><td colspan="2">Brigade Reserves</td><td colspan="2"></td><td colspan="4"></td><td colspan="3">R. I. R. 57 (w./o. II. Bat.)</td></tr>
<tr><td colspan="2">Div. Reserves, incl. Pioneers</td><td colspan="2"></td><td colspan="4">R. I. R. 53, Staff II. and 6/Pio. 18</td><td colspan="3">II./R. I. R. 57 Staff I./Pio. 18</td></tr>
<tr><td colspan="2">Corps Reserves, incl. Pioneers</td><td colspan="9">R. I. R. 13, Staff /Pio. Regt. 18 Staff II./Pio. 7, Pio. Co. 283, Pio. Co. 287</td></tr>
<tr><td colspan="2">Target of Attack</td><td colspan="2">Consenvoye Wood</td><td>Nameless Wood</td><td>Lines 53-59</td><td colspan="2">Haumont</td><td>Facility 74</td><td colspan="2">Haumont Wood</td></tr>
<tr><td colspan="2">Enemy</td><td colspan="4">351st Inf. Reg. 44th Territ. Inf. Reg.</td><td colspan="3">362nd Inf. Reg. 1 Batl./324th Inf. Reg.</td><td colspan="2">½ I./ 165th Inf. Reg.</td></tr>
</table>

<table>
<tr><td colspan="2">Army Corps</td><td colspan="4">Sector B (middle)
XVIII Army Corps</td></tr>
<tr><td colspan="2">Divisions</td><td colspan="2">21 Infantry Division</td><td colspan="2">25 Infantry Division</td></tr>
<tr><td colspan="2">Infantry Brigades</td><td colspan="2">42 Infantry Brigade</td><td colspan="2">49 Infantry Brigade</td></tr>
<tr><td colspan="2">Assault Regiments</td><td>I. R. 81</td><td>I. R. 87</td><td colspan="2">Leibgarde I. R. 115</td></tr>
<tr><td colspan="2">Battalions in Foremost Line</td><td>I., II.</td><td>1/2 III., I.</td><td>I.</td><td>II.</td></tr>
<tr><td rowspan="4">Attack Com-panies</td><td>4th Line</td><td>1. 4.</td><td>9. 12.</td><td></td><td></td></tr>
<tr><td>3rd Line</td><td>3. 2.</td><td></td><td>2.</td><td>8.</td></tr>
<tr><td>2nd Line</td><td>7.</td><td>3.</td><td></td><td></td></tr>
<tr><td>1st Line</td><td>6. 8. 5.</td><td>1. 4. 2.</td><td>Lehr, 3. 4.</td><td>6. 7. 5.</td></tr>
<tr><td colspan="2" rowspan="2">Pioneers and Flame-throwers Assigned to Assault Troops</td><td>3/Pio. 30</td><td>5/Pio. 21</td><td>R. Pio. Co. 89</td><td>3/ Pio. 21</td></tr>
<tr><td colspan="2">9./3rd G. Pio.</td><td colspan="2">R. Co./3rd G. Pio</td></tr>
<tr><td colspan="2">Regimental Reserves</td><td></td><td>11. 10.</td><td colspan="2">10. 11.</td></tr>
<tr><td colspan="2">Brigade Reserves</td><td colspan="2">III./81</td><td colspan="2">9. 12./115, I./117</td></tr>
<tr><td colspan="2">Div. Reserves, incl. Pioneers</td><td colspan="2">II./87, Staff I./Pio 21 1./Pio. 21, Pio. Co. 282</td><td colspan="2">I. R. 117 (w/o I.), Staff I./ Pio. 30, 2./Pio. 30, Pio. Co. 285</td></tr>
<tr><td colspan="2">Corps Reserves, incl. Pioneers</td><td colspan="2">Fus. R. 80 Staff/Pio. Reg. 30</td><td colspan="2">I. R. 116, Staff II./Pio. 20, 2. 3. and 1. R./Pio. 20, Pio. Co. 286</td></tr>
<tr><td colspan="2">Target of Attack</td><td colspan="4">Caures Wood</td></tr>
<tr><td colspan="2">Enemy</td><td colspan="4">½ I./165th Inf. Reg., 59th and 56th Chasseurs, 9./165th Inf. Reg., part of 233rd and 327th Inf. Reg.</td></tr>
</table>

<table>
<tr><td colspan="2">Army Corps</td><td colspan="6">Sector C (left)
III Army Corps</td></tr>
<tr><td colspan="2">Divisions</td><td colspan="2">5 Infantry Division</td><td colspan="4">6 Infantry Division</td></tr>
<tr><td colspan="2">Infantry Brigades</td><td colspan="2">10 Infantry Brigade</td><td colspan="4">12 Infantry Brigade</td></tr>
<tr><td colspan="2">Assault Regiments</td><td>Leib G. R. 8</td><td>Gren. R. 12</td><td colspan="2">I. R. 24</td><td colspan="2">I. R. 64</td></tr>
<tr><td colspan="2">Battalions in Foremost Line</td><td>II.</td><td>F.</td><td>III.</td><td>I.</td><td>III.</td><td>II.</td></tr>
<tr><td rowspan="4">Attack Com-panies</td><td>4th Line</td><td></td><td></td><td>11.</td><td></td><td>10.</td><td>⅔ 6.</td></tr>
<tr><td>3rd Line</td><td>8. 7.</td><td>12. 9.</td><td>9.</td><td>1.</td><td></td><td></td></tr>
<tr><td>2nd Line</td><td></td><td></td><td></td><td></td><td></td><td></td></tr>
<tr><td>1st Line</td><td>6. 5.</td><td>11. 10.</td><td>12. 10.</td><td>3.2. 4.</td><td>11.9. 12.</td><td>7. ⅓ 6.</td></tr>
<tr><td colspan="2" rowspan="2">Pioneers and Flame-throwers Assigned to Assault Troops</td><td>1./Pio. 3</td><td>2./Pio. 3</td><td colspan="2">4/Pio. 22</td><td colspan="2">1. R./ Pio. 22</td></tr>
<tr><td colspan="2">11./3rd G. Pio.</td><td colspan="4">14./3rd G. Pio.</td></tr>
<tr><td colspan="2">Regimental Reserves</td><td>I.</td><td>II.</td><td colspan="2">5. 7.</td><td colspan="2">I.</td></tr>
<tr><td colspan="2">Brigade Reserves</td><td colspan="2">F./1. L.Gr. 8 1. R./Pio. 23</td><td colspan="4">6. 8./24 5. 8./64 5./Pio. 3 Assault Detach. Rohr</td></tr>
<tr><td colspan="2">Div. Reserves, incl. Pioneers</td><td colspan="2">I./12, Staff I./Pio. 3 2./Pio. 23</td><td colspan="4">Jäg. 3, Staff II./Pio. 22, 3./Pio. 3</td></tr>
<tr><td colspan="2">Corps Reserves, incl. Pioneers</td><td colspan="2">I. R. 52 Staff/Pio. Reg. 23</td><td colspan="4">I. R. 20, Staff I./Pio. 23 2. R./Pio. 20, 1. 5./Pio. 23 Pio. Co. 284</td></tr>
<tr><td colspan="2">Target of Attack</td><td colspan="2">Bois de Ville</td><td colspan="4">Herbebois</td></tr>
<tr><td colspan="2" rowspan="2">Enemy</td><td colspan="2">½ I./164th Inf. Reg. part of 233rd Inf. Reg.</td><td colspan="4">½ I., II./164th Inf. Reg</td></tr>
<tr><td colspan="6">9./165th Inf. Reg., part of 233rd and 327th Inf. Reg.</td></tr>
</table>

B. Kinds of Procedures

4. Rule: as shown in the illustration. The shock troops advance spread out behind the foremost swarm line.

5. Facing resistance from hostile strong points, etc.

(a) Swarm line halts and draws fire upon itself from the strong point (use cunning).

(b) Next, the shock troop thrusts forward (with pioneers, flamethrowers, machine guns) in a spread-out surprise attack on the strong point, etc., launched from the side. One echelon of infantrymen moves forward under cover; the other echelon together with the flamethrowers attacks the strong point from the side or from the rear. Use cover, shell holes when advancing. When appropriate, machine guns can sometimes be set up in shell holes or such along the way. When the shock troop advances to within approximately 20 meters from the hostile strong point, the flamethrower is activated.

(c) Swarm line penetrates as soon as the fire from the strong point diminishes. Afterwards, the shock troop passes by and continues to penetrate in the same way as the prior unit.

6. It is often necessary for the shock troop to move sideways.

C. Force of Thrust

7. Second echelon overtakes the first echelon according to a certain time frame (also arranged). Third echelon overtakes the second echelon, and so on.

Opposite

Left: Musketier of Infantry Regiment No.87, which served as an assault regiment of the 21st Infantry Division at Verdun, February 22, 1916. He wears full marching order with a pair of heavy mittens on his left hip, and his weapons include a Gew 98 rifle and long S98 bayonet.

Right: Pioneer of the 5th Assault Company, Assault Battalion No.5. He is uniformed in the M1097/10 field jacket, M1916 steel helmet, mountaineering trousers with leather knee patches, and cleated mountain boots. Since his five M1916 stick grenades are his main weapons, he keeps his Kar 98AZ carbine slung. Ammunition is carried in jacket pockets. Courtesy Maurice Sublet.

Charcoal study by war artist Josef Correggio depicting a night attack by a German assault company on a French position in the woods of Verdun. Note the flamethrower squad on the right. The date of the sketch – February of 1916 – and the equipment depicted indicate that this is probably a pioneer company of Assault Detachment Rohr.

Opposite
Top: Postcard captioned "Assault on the Haumont Woods February 21, 1916, at 5:00 P.M., with flamethrowers." An infantryman follows a heavily laden flamethrower squad of the 16th Company, 3rd Guard Pioneer Battalion, through cheval-de-frise. In this assault German troops wore white brassards on their left arms to differentiate themselves from the French. The flamethrower is an early-model Kleif M.1915.

Bottom: Assault detachment of the Bavarian 2nd Reserve Infantry Regiment, in a postcard sent March 3, 1916. The mustached soldier in the center, the man on his right, and the Infanterist second from the right all wear badges on their upper left arms. The first two are embroidered chevrons in two different colors, while the third is a stick grenade mounted on a field-gray cloth oval.

Rolling up Trenches with Shock Troops

Sixty-two infantry battalions provided three companies each for the assault on Verdun; a total of 186 shock troops were thus formed. When clearing a trench, the shock troop advanced in the following order: shock-troop leader, first element *(Teil)* of grenadiers, pioneer squad, ensign bearer, second element of grenadiers, and the machine-gun squad.[3] The flamethrower squad would be positioned at either the front or the rear of the shock troop, depending on the circumstances.

The shock troops would arrive with the last shells and would spend about two minutes in each trench. Heavy fighting was left to following waves of infantry; shock troops constituted the assault wave *(Sturmwelle)* while regular infantry made up the clearing-out wave *(Aufraumungswelle)* and strengthening wave *(Verstärkungswelle.)*

On April 20, 1916, the 3rd and 4th Guard Pioneer Battalions were combined into the Guard Reserve Pioneer Regiment *(Garde-Reseve-Pioneer Regiment),* which was ultimately comprised of three staffs, 12 field companies organized into three battalions, one experimental company, three battalion workshop detachments, and one recruit depot, for a total of 3000 men. The 2nd Guard Pioneer Replacement Battalion *(II. Garde-Pionier-Ersatz-Bataillon)* provided replacements for both the flamethrower regiment and the flamethrower platoon of Assault Battalion Rohr.

Raid at La Boiselle

"Regimental Orders for a Raid on the Spion," April 11, 1916.[4]

1. The raid will probably take place at dusk on the 11th of April.

2. *Organization of the raiding party*:
In command. – Captain Wagener, assisted by Lieutenant Boening, Assistant-Surgeon Wisser, one bugler and six stretcher bearers.

Jäger of a shock troop, Reserve Jäger Battalion No. 8. The raiding party that attacked the Spion was similarly lightly equipped with pistols, rifles, hand grenades, wire cutters, and gas masks tucked into tunics.

Patrol commanders. – Lieutenants Stradtmann, Freund, Dumas, and Böhlefeld.
Raiding party – 50 men of the 110th Reserve Infantry Regiment and four Pioneers of the 1st Reserve Company, 13th Pioneer Battalion.

3. Upon the day fixed, *the raiding party* will be assembled in Dug-outs Nos. 1-10, on the right wing of the left-hand battalion. Dug-out No.9 will be used as advanced regimental command post.

Shortly after dusk the assaulting party will leave the Blaue Stellung by Sap No.3 with the object of breaking into the enemy's position in the neighborhood of the Süd Spion, from which point the enemy's trenches will be cleared northwards, if possible, as far as the Spion. Unless prevented by the enemy's fire, the raiding party will return to our Blaue Stellung by the same way.

4. For 25 minutes before the commencement of the raid, *the artillery* will prepare for the assault by shelling the enemy's trenches between Besenhecke and the Windmühle, and also the Weisse Steinmauer. During the raid the artillery will control by its fire all the enemy's trenches likely to prove a source of danger to the enterprise.

5. In order to draw the fire of the enemy's artillery away from the spot to be raided, a feint attack against the enemy's position just north of La Boiselle Cemetery will start 15 minutes after the artillery opens fire.

6. In order that the registration of the objective by the heavy artillery and Minenwerfer shall not be apparent, on the morning of the day before the raid – probably the 10th April – a feint bombardment of Target-sectors 76-79 will be carried out, combined with a mine explosion, *with the object of misleading the enemy.* The exact time will be fixed beforehand by the artillery commander, Officer Commanding Ersatz Abteilung, 76th Artillery Regiment.

7. *The machine-gun officer* will arrange that, during the whole time of the raid, the enemy's rear trenches in Target-sectors 76-81 are kept under a constant fire, with a view to causing him all possible loss, and, at the same time, to safeguarding our patrol against counter-attacks.

8. *The Officer commanding 1st Reserve Company, 13th Pioneer Battalion,* will arrange for a gallery of the left-hand minefield to be ready charged by the morning of the day before the raid, and for a gallery of the right-hand minefield to be ready charged by the evening of the raid. The former will be sprung at the conclusion of the feint bombardment, the latter as an introduction to the feint attack.

From today, the "earth mortars" *(Erdmörser)* will systematically cut the enemy's wire opposite the Blinddarm. On the day before the raid, they will coöperate with all other close-range weapons to assist in the feint bombardment of Target-sectors 76-78. On the evening of the raid, they will assist in the feint attack by bombarding Target-sectors 76 and 77 (*see* Appendices 3 and 4).

Throughout the raid, the "Albrecht-Mörser," in position on the Lehmgrubenhöhe, will heavily bombard the enemy's trenches in the Nordronell. Particular care will be taken that the enemy's machine guns do not interfere with the raid from that quarter (*see* Appendix 1).

Left: "Earth mortar" (Erdmörser), a wooden cylinder with an inside diameter of 9.82 in (25cm), reinforced with wire. It was fitted with a wooden racer 7 ft 10 in long and semi-circular in cross section. The mortar was buried in the parados of the trench while the racer rested on the parapet at an angle of 45 degrees; the electrically fired projectile slid along the racer. Known by the French as a "coal bucket," the projectile was a sheet-iron cylinder 15 in long, plugged with wood at both ends. One wooden plug featured a handle for transporting and loading, and the other had a hole for a Bickford fuse that was ignited by the flash of the charge.

Right: Albrecht 250mm mortar. The wooden barrel was 6 ft 8 in long and reinforced with steel wire. It fired the same 52-lb projectile as the earth mortar, but instead of being fixed in the ground the barrel could be elevated and depressed with a hand-wheel screw. Maximum range was 656 yd.

9. *The Officer Commanding 228th Minenwerfer Company* will register the enemy's wire at the point of entry with one heavy and two medium Minenwerfer in the course of the feint bombardment on the day before the raid. He will also take part in this bombardment and fire 30 medium Minenwerfer shells at the Weisse Steinmauer (*see* Appendix 4). On the afternoon of the same day, with both medium Minenwerfer mounted in the Minenwerfer Weg, he will cut the enemy's wire at 76y, and throughout the whole night and the following day will keep up a desultory fire.

On the evening of the raid, the wire in front of the point of entry of the raiding party will be cut on a width of 50 meters by the heavy and two medium Minenwerfer (*see* Appendix 1). Meanwhile, the two other medium Minenwerfer will take part in the feint attack against 76y (see Appendix 3). The light Minenwerfer at the disposal of the 228th Minenwerfer Company will take part in the feint attack, in accordance with the orders (para. 8) issued for the close-range weapons of the 1st Reserve Company, 13th Pioneer Battalion (*see* Appendices 3 and 4). The Officer Commanding 228th Minenwerfer Company will receive further detailed instructions from Captain Wagener.

10. On the evening of the raid, *battalions* will hold themselves in a state of readiness for an alarm. Arrangements will be made that, in the event of the

Trench raiders of the 11th Company, Reserve Infantry Regiment No.141, armed with three different types of pistol: the P08, the Mauser C96, and the 10.6mm M1879 Reichsrevolver.

enemy opening a barrage on our trenches, as well may happen, the number of sentries will be reduced to a minimum. Gas masks and other gas equipment must be ready for use.

11. I shall be at the regimental command post from the morning of the day before the raid. From 6 p.m. of the evening of the raid, I shall be in the advanced regimental command post in Dug-out No.9 on the right wing of the left-hand battalion. Captain Wagener will maintain constant communication with me. The artillery liaison officer will also be with me.

(signed) FRHR. V. VIETINGHOFF

Appendix 1
Special Orders for the Raid on the Spion

1. *Organization of the raiding party:*
Commander. – Captain Wagener; with him, Bugler Held.
Stradtmann's patrol. – Lieutenant Stradtmann and 10 men.
Supports, at my disposal – Lieutenant Freund and 24 men.

In addition to the latter party, at my disposal – Boening, and Assistant-Surgeon Wiser and six stretcher bearers.

2. *Dress and equipment.* – Attack order without greatcoat or cap, belts to be worn without pouches, gas masks to be slung and tucked into tunic.

The Stradtmann, Dumas, and Böhlefeld patrols will each be equipped, half with rifles and half with pistols and wire-cutters.

The supports will carry rifles, five men will carry pistols, each man will carry two grenades.

As a distinguishing mark each man will wear a triangle of white linen sewn on the breast and back.

3. *Time table. – The artillery* will open fire with gas shells on the enemy's trenches on both sides of the point of entry and on the objectives opposite the southwest corner of La Boiselle, where the feint attack is to take place.

For a quarter of an hour, all the enemy's trenches likely to prove of importance to the raiding party will be brought under fire. At the same time, the *close-range weapons of the 1st Reserve Company, 13th Pioneer Battalion,* with the two medium and the light Minenwerfer of the *228th Minenwerfer Company,* will fire with maximum rapidity on the enemy's trenches opposite the southwest corner of La Boiselle.

The one heavy and two medium Minenwerfer of the *228th Minenwerfer Company* will open fire with the object of cutting the wire in front of the point of entry.

On the right flank of the minefield a *shallow gallery will be fired.*

The artillery, which was firing on the southwest corner of La Boiselle, will increase its range and shell the trenches in rear.

The close-range weapons will cease fire.

The machine guns will sweep communications trenches in this sector and in the Galgen.

In the Blinddarm and just south of the same, isolated groups of *dummies* will be exposed in order to make the enemy think an attack is pending. From now on, *artillery and Minenwerfer* fire will increase to its maximum intensity on the real objective.

The "Albrecht-Mörser" of the *1st Reserve Company, 13th Pioneer Battalion,* in position on the Lehmgrubenhöhre, will bombard the Nordrondell with the utmost intensity.

The patrols will leave their dug-outs and take up their positions in readiness, in accordance with direct orders received from me, in the Holweg by Sap No.3.

Bavarian trench raiders from at least two different infantry companies pose at a French field bakery they have captured in Verdun, summer of 1916. Caked with mud, the men have stripped down to the bare essentials, including field caps, pistols, bayonets, wire cutters, and gas masks.

Stradtmann's patrol will leave the Hohlweg at "*a*" and crawl forward as far as "*b*."

Lieutenant Boening will post the *stretcher bearers* as connecting files between *Stradtmann's patrol* and myself.

The artillery will lift its fire from the objective between Besenhecke and the Windmüle to the targets in rear, and will open a barrage on those of the enemy's trenches which may prove a source of danger to the raid.

The Minenwerfer will cease fire.

The machine-guns will open fire on positions in rear and on the communication trenches which lead to the objective from both sides.

The "Albrecht-Mörser" of the *1st Reserve Company, 13th Pioneer Battalion,* on the Lehmgrubenhöhe, will continue to bombard the Nordrondell. *All close-range weapons and the artillery,* which from 0' to 15' had been bombarding the enemy's position opposite the southwest corner of La Boiselle, will reopen fire on these targets with renewed vigor.

Stradtmann's patrol will break into the enemy's trenches at the Süd Spion and, at point 1 (*see* Sketch No.1), will defend the point of entry from the direction of the enemy.

***Left:** Hornist of a Saxon infantry regiment. Shock troops used bugle calls to sound the advance, call a halt, gather leaders to one place for a conference, and separate troops from different units who had become intermingled during the fighting. This bugler wears the M1907/10 field jacket with slip-on covers for his shoulder straps. He is equipped with an M1918 steel helmet and an S98 bayonet.*

***Right:** Trench raider of the 7th Company, Infantry Regiment No.67 (left) with his French prisoner, April 16, 1916. The German has reduced his equipment to the absolute minimum of a trench dagger and a P08 pistol tucked into his belt.*

Shock troop of the 8th Company, West Prussian Infantry Regiment No.176, photographed during Christmas of 1916. On their upper left arms five wear unofficial badges consisting of a field-gray "S" on a dark cloth oval. The photographer has written "Sharp shooters (Scharf-Schützen)" on the top of the glass negative. However, the Musketier lying on the left suffers from strabismus in his left eye, an affliction that would obviously prevent him from becoming a sniper. Courtesy Mike Hibberd.

On orders received from me personally, *Dumas' patrol* will follow Stradtmann's patrol and advance southwards along the enemy's trench as far as point 2.

On orders received from me personally also, *Böhlefeld's patrol* will follow Dumas' patrol and, once in the enemy's trench, will push on toward the Spion.

The stretcher bearers will act as connecting files between Stradtmann's patrol and myself.

The supports will hold themselves in readiness at 4, so as to be able to push on after the other patrols immediately on receipt of an order from me.

If the enemy opens a barrage on our position and on the Holweg before the patrols come out of their dug-outs, I shall either lead the patrol to the enemy's position by another route, or cancel the raid.

4. *Duty of the patrols.* – As many of the enemy as possible must be made prisoners; in addition, rifles, machine guns, rifle grenade stands, trench mortars, etc., as well as filled packs are to be brought back. Should it be found impossible to carry back all the booty owing to the small numbers of the raiding party, but if, as far as regards the enemy's fire it could be done, report will be passed on to me by Stradtmann's patrol.

5. *Return.* – On a signal given by Lieutenant Stradtmann, or on the "Charge" being blown by my bugler, the raiding party will make its way back from the Süd Spion to the Hohlweg by the shortest way, and immediately make for the same dug-outs whence it started. In the dug-outs, I shall ascertain whether everyone has returned. Prisoners and booty will be taken into the dug-outs.

During the raid, if the enemy should open a heavy barrage on the trenches on the Schwabenhohle and on the Hohlweg, the raiding party will remain in the enemy's trench and acquaint me of the fact by firing a red flare. I shall then endeavor to reach the party and lead them back by some other way. Should I not arrive, the senior officer present will lead the entire party.

6. Assistant-Surgeon Wisser will organize No.1 Dug-out as a first aid post and will remain there until the conclusion of the raid.

7. Until the 15th minute I shall be in the advanced regimental command post; after that time in the Hohlweg, which will be connected by telephone with the advanced regimental command post.

(Signed) WAGENER,
Captain and Company Commander.
Verbally and in writing to participants in the raid.

The Assault on Fort Vaux

Assault troops played a critical role in the attack on Fort Vaux, the smallest of the defensive fortifications at Verdun. The fort was protected by a wide moat with large, detached concrete installations in the corners. These *coffres* (counterscarp or flanking galleries) were connected to the main body of the fort by underground tunnels. The flanking galleries were armed with cannons and machine guns to engage enemy troops crossing the moat.

At around dawn on June 2, men of Pioneer Battalion No.20 climbed on top of the double flanking gallery in the northwest corner of the fort to attack its revolving cannons. The Germans used rope to lower baskets of explosives

Postwar recreation of the assault on Fort Vaux, June 2, 1916. As artillery reduces much of the superstructure to rubble, a German heavy machine gun fires on a counterscarp gallery defending the moat.

and bundles of hand grenades that knocked out the guns, then they ignited fire tubes attached to long poles held down in front of the firing loopholes. The thick smoke and flames drove the French gun crews out of the gallery.[5]

By the afternoon the Germans had overrun the flanking galleries in the northwest and northeast corners of the moat, and they had established machine-gun positions on the fort's roof. Once inside the galleries, the Germans had access to the western and eastern tunnels. These led into the fort's central corridor, which lay near the barracks and branched off into tunnels connected to the two *casemates de Bourges* or bunkers in the southern corners, as well as the passageway to the commandant's observation turret where Colonel Sylvain-Eugène Raynal had holed up.

Inside the fort the Germans and French fought in the western and eastern tunnels for a day and a half. These brick corridors were often only 35 inches wide and 60 inches tall. The French set up sandbag barricades and defended them with machine guns and hand grenades; the Germans assaulted the barriers with grenades and demolition charges. When a barricade was breached, troops engaged in fierce hand-to-hand combat with rifle, bayonet, dagger, and club. Much of the fighting took place in pitch darkness filled with suffocating clouds of smoke, cordite fumes, and dust. The Germans requested flamethrowers to clean out the most stubborn pockets of French resistance, but the weapons did not arrive until the morning of June 4.

Ten *Kleif* squads from the 8th Company of the Guard Reserve Pioneer Regiment arrived from the rear.[6] Four apparatuses were destroyed by artillery fire on the way, leaving six to arrive intact. A *Leutnant* of Pioneer Battalion No.27 helped the flamethrower pioneers undertake a thorough reconnaissance inside the fort, and then the shock troops entered through the two flanking galleries in the northern corners of the moat.

In the western tunnel three flamethrower squads crept up to the first French barricade at 12:30 P.M., unnoticed by the defenders. The three apparatuses fired simultaneously, spraying burning oil through the embrasures and filling the passageway with smoke. Along the walls and the floor, the wooden planking caught fire. Men of Pioneer Battalion No.27 broke through the sandbag wall and raced up the narrow stairs, where they were confronted by another barricade. The French threw hand grenades and fired a machine gun, which forced the pioneers to throw themselves flat and burrow down between the sandbags lying in the passageway.[7]

Pionier of Pioneer Battalion No.20, which assaulted the northwestern double counterscarp gallery of Fort Vaux on June 2, 1916. Many historians identify the incendiary weapons used in the assault as flamethrowers on long booms, but in reality they were fire tubes. This pioneer wears a simplified field jacket and corduroy trousers.

As soon as the machine gun fell silent, the Germans established a breastwork of sandbags. They had taken 27 yards of corridor, including a stairway leading up to the surface. This provided the assault teams with a short, protected connection to German troops on the roof of the fort. The newly won position was strengthened with a second sandbag barricade behind the first. When they returned from their mission half of the pioneers were wounded, and all were ill from smoke poisoning, their faces blackened and their clothing scorched.

The fort filled with acrid black smoke that compelled the French to remove the armor plating from the barracks windows in order to get fresh air. As the flamethrower assault continued, the French retreated down the western tunnel into the main corridor and took refuge in the barracks, reluctantly closing the armor-plated windows again. The Germans tried to blow open the armor using sacks of explosives fitted with delayed-action fuses but the effort failed.[8] Smoke and fumes had extinguished the kerosene lamps, forcing the combatants to confront each other in complete darkness.

While the attack in the western tunnel took place, the Germans launched a second operation in the eastern tunnel.[9] A shock troop consisting of men from

Above: Fire tube (Brandröhre) on a boom. To ignite the weapon, the soldier yanked on a lanyard attached to the pull ring of a friction fuse. The fire tube burned for about 50 seconds, producing a seven-foot flame and clouds of choking smoke. A fire-tube squad (Brandröhrentrupp) consisted of an Unteroffizier as needed, two men to carry the boom, and three men armed with one fused fire-tube each.

Pioneer Battalion No.27 and the 9th Company of Infantry Regiment No.39 were accompanied by three flamethrower squads from the 8th Company of the Guard Reserve Pioneer Regiment. The shock troop entered the fort from the northeastern flanking gallery and traveled down the tunnel until it reached a stairway of 51 concrete steps, at the top of which was a sandbag barricade. At the head of the shock troop, one or more flamethrower squads climbed the stairs and directed their flame jets upward. Rags, sandbags, packs, and pieces of clothing lying around in the stairway caught fire, and thick smoke filled the narrow passageway, nearly overcoming the Germans.

The French continually threw hand grenades that rolled down the stairs and detonated among the attackers, who pushed ahead and left their wounded behind. Finally the Germans were able to breach at least one barricade and force the French back almost to the latrines.[10] Hours after the fires caused by the flamethrowers were extinguished, the smoke continued to pour out of the tunnel. Both the Germans and the French built sandbag barricades to keep out the fumes, and sentries wore their gas masks while on duty.

After this second assault the Germans decided to temporarily refrain from using flamethrowers inside the fort, having deemed the assaults ineffective. The French barricades blocking the corridors would be attacked with hand grenades and machine guns instead. It was only when the fort had fallen that the Germans learned how devastating the June 4 flamethrower attacks had been to French morale. Shouts of "Gas! Masks on!" had echoed down the

Opposite: Pioneer of a shock troop, identified by the red or green tags sewn to his shoulder straps, which also conceal his unit number. He wears an M1915 blouse and M1916 steel helmet and is armed with a Gew 98. Shock troops of Pioneer Battalion Nos. 15 and 27 played a vital role in the taking of Fort Vaux.

Below: In this postwar recreation of the assault on Fort Vaux, a German heavy machine-gun squad advances on the northeast counterscarp gallery. The MG08 has been removed from the sled (left), and most of the assistant gunners and ammunition carriers are armed with rifles, transforming the squad into a shock unit.

Postwar recreation of the German assault progressing through the tunnels of Fort Vaux on June 2, 1916. Troops of both sides wore gas masks due to the smoke and concrete dust. The French built sandbag barriers that the Germans attacked with hand grenades, machine guns, flamethrowers, and fire tubes. Most of the combat took place in pitch darkness.

main corridor, and the closely packed men panicked, some jumping out of the windows of the barracks and landing in the moat below.[11]

One account of the June 4 attacks claimed that the French killed at least two flamethrower squads at the southwestern casemate de Bourges, captured their weapons, and used them to hold off any further German advances into the southern moat.[12]

Raynal told a slightly different story; in his version, the Germans attempted to fire flamethrowers through the loopholes of the southeastern *casemate de Bourges,* not the southwestern. The operators of the "infernal devices"[13] were killed; the French machine gunners seized the flamethrowers and brought them to Raynal, who wrote nothing about using them on the Germans.

The Germans did not mention a flamethrower attack against either of the southern bunkers on June 4, nor did they provide any accounts of pioneers being killed and their weapons taken. In addition, the death book of the Guard Reserve Pioneer Regiment listed no names for June 4 at Vaux.

Raynal wrote that on June 5 there was a failed flamethrower assault that did more damage to the Germans than to the French:

> Around five o'clock in the morning, the barricade of the covered passageway close to the *casemate de Bourges* on the left jumps in a formidable explosion which knocks down a part of the masonry, and the enemy appears through the breach thus opened, projecting ignited liquids. Fortunately, the enormous draft which occurs opposes and cancels the action of the flames by rejecting them towards their source of emission. One surprised moment, and then our machine gunners and our grenadiers, led by Bazy and Girard, return and attack with grenade strikes. The enemy moves back.[14]

According to the German account of this operation, the men attacking the passageway to the bunker were five shock troops from Pioneer Battalion No.15 armed with concentrated charges and fire tubes instead of flamethrowers.[15] The explosives created only a small hole in the wall of the tunnel; the smoke and flames from the fire tubes were not able to penetrate and blew back because of the draft. On the roof of the fort, two more shock troops attacked the eastern tunnel. French sentries fired at the pioneers as they ran, but the

Infantry and pioneer shock troops training with a Kleif. Note the large grenade bags worn very high on the chest. The brightness of the flame may indicate the use of smokeless or "Yellow" oil, which produced significantly more heat than the standard "Blue" oil. It is difficult to image using this weapon within the narrow tunnels of Fort Vaux.

Germans reached their objective and ignited the charges. As before only a small breach was made in the tunnel, and the draft counteracted the fire tubes. All attempts to enter by blowing holes in the tunnels failed.

On June 5 an assault by the 1st Company of Pioneer Battalion No.15 was launched against the southwestern *casemate de Bourges* at 9:00 A.M. Four flamethrower squads accompanying the shock troop simultaneously sprayed the loopholes of the bunker. The pioneers reported that while smoke penetrated the structures, the flame jets did not, allowing the French to withstand the assault and repel the raiders with hand grenades and machine guns.[16]

In the German version of this event, Raynal wrote that the attack – though unsuccessful – caused him more losses because the smoke and dust aggravated the suffering brought about by lack of water. In Raynal's book, however, the incident was described as a failed assault by a single German pioneer carrying a "case" that emitted intense smoke and noxious fumes after the man was killed by French machine gunners.[17] The device in question was clearly a fire tube rather than a flamethrower.

Neither side reported flamethrower or fire-tube assaults after June 5. The weapons had made conditions inside the fort as intolerable for the Germans as they were for the French; the Germans would therefore rely on the smoke from bursting shells to "make the French miserable."[18] A *Hauptmann* of Pioneer Battalion No.20 said that in the end, using flamethrowers and fire tubes inside the fort was impossible because the smoke and gases blew back into the passageways occupied by the men igniting the weapons. Another reason flamethrowers were abandoned was that they caused panic among German troops.[19]

On June 7 Raynal surrendered the fort.

Young Soldat of a company shock troop, Saxon Infantry Regiment No.182, photographed in the Champagne in 1916. Note the trench dagger-bayonet, the "Grabendolch 16" produced by DEMAG.

The Somme

The report "Experience of the German First Army in the Somme Battle," by *General* Fritz von Below, was dated January 30, 1917. It covered the fighting that took place June 24 to November 26, 1916. At this date German commanders already contemplated transforming all regular infantry into specially trained assault troops who displayed a high level of individual initiative:

> Apart from the general regulations in force, the instructions laid down for assault formations form the best guide for the training of the infantry soldier.
>
> Physical fitness and confidence in his arms (rifle, hand grenades, spade, etc.) must be increased by constant practice. Self-confidence and resolute determination are a guarantee of success, even against a numerically superior opponent...
>
> The following are the most important branches of training –
>
> (a) The education of the group *[one NCO and eight men]* commander and of the individual private to the highest possible degree of self-reliance. (In positions which often consist of unconnected shell holes, control by platoon and company commanders is rendered extremely difficult.)
> (b) The training of every single man of the infantry in the use of all patterns of German hand grenades.
> (c) The training of the greatest possible number of men in the use of captured hand grenades.

Squad Reuder (Gruppe Reuder), an assault squad of Reserve Infantry Regiment No. 15; Unteroffizier Reuder sits in the center of the back row. Weapons include M1917 stick grenades, sharpened spades, and Gew 98 rifles. The M1916 steel helmets have been camouflaged in geometric shapes of several colors.

Unteroffizier Reuder, Reserve Infantry Regiment No.15. He wears his M1915 Gummimaske on his chest and is surrounded by weapons and equipment that include stick grenades, a Gew 98, binoculars, and M1917 steel trench armor (Grabenpanzer or Sappenpanzer). His pistol is an Austrian 9mm M1912 Steyr automatic.

(d) An increase in the personnel trained in the use of our own and of the enemy's machine guns. Every infantry officer must be able to work a German machine gun. The guns crews must be drilled until, when prepared for action, they can bring up an unloaded gun from the bottom of a dug-out and be ready to open fire within 30 seconds. Special practice is required in the use of improvised mountings and sandbag supports.
(e) Patrol work.
(f) Rapid counter-attack across open ground, launched on the initiative of a subordinate commander, down to a group commander or some stout hearted man.
(g) Methodical counter-attack, following an artillery preparation...

The attachment of "Flammenwerfer" to the assault troops is specially desirable when methodical counter-attacks are to be carried out. Consequently, one of the "Flammenwerfer" battalions allotted to the Army was combined with an Assault School, and, by means of small detachments, trained those divisions which were behind the front, waiting to act as reliefs, in the technical use of "Flammenwerfer."

The detailing of **assaulting parties** in an attack has proved very useful. Their chief advantage lay in the freshness of the specially selected personnel who had not been engaged in previous fighting. The careful training beforehand of the assaulting parties resulted in these troops proving themselves quite equal to all tasks which fell to their lot in village or wood fighting. They felt they were a body of élite troops, which indeed they proved themselves to be...

Every individual must be trained to the highest possible degree of self-reliance, so that he may know how to act during the critical periods of his own or the enemy's attacks, when he must generally be left to his own resources, and is beyond the control of his superiors.[20]

Opposite
Top: Men of the 5th Regiment of Foot Guards (Garde-Regiment zu Fuß Nr.5); a handwritten note on this postcard reads "At the shock-troop course in Bouillonville, near Fleury." While most of these soldiers wear camouflaged steel helmets, seven retain the Pickelhaube without spikes.

Bottom: Artillerymen attending a course taught by the Howitzer Battery of Assault Battalion No.5 (Rohr). A battalion instructor is seated on the right; with him are a Kanonier of a Prussian field-artillery regiment (marked with an X) and three members of a Saxon foot-artillery regiment. The field and foot artillery sent men to the assault battalion to learn the use of captured Russian light field howitzers.

After the Battle of the Somme, Chief of the General Staff Paul von Hindenburg ordered that all infantrymen and artillerymen be trained in hand-grenade combat. The best grenadiers were to be issued a badge, and those who proved themselves in combat would wear a special mark of distinction.[21]

Hand-grenade squad of Infantry Regiment No. 251. They wear the M1907/10 and simplified field jackets with guard lace, and their helmet covers display the number "251" in green. Weapons and equipment include M1916 grenades, Gew 98 rifles, S98/05 bayonets, and M1915 gas masks in cloth cases.

Endnotes

[1] Gudmundsson, p. 59.

[2] Bundesarchiv-Militärarchiv W10/51589. Issued by the Fifth Army.

[3] War Department, *German and Austrian Tactical Studies: Translations of Captured German and Austrian Documents and Information Obtained from German and Austrian Prisoners from the British, French and Italian Staffs* (Washington, D.C.: Government Printing Office, 1918), p. 109.

[4] William A. Ganoe, *The English of Military Communications* (Menasha, Wisconsin: George Banta Publishing Co., 1918), pp. 126-135, and Stephen Bull, *World War I Trench Warfare (1)* (Botley, Oxford: Osprey Publishing, 2002), pp. 61-62. The result of the raid was 29 British prisoners and more than 30 killed. Captured equipment included one Lewis gun, one sniper rifle, 20 infantry rifles, and assorted equipment. One German trench raider was wounded.

[5] Alexander Schwencke and Martin Reymann, *Die Tragödie von Verdun 1916. II. Teil: Das Ringen um Fort Vaux Reichsarchiv Band 14* (Oldenburg, Germany: Drud und Verlag von Gerhard Stalling, 1928) p. 97.

[6] Schwencke and Reymann, p. 108.

[7] Ibid., pp. 108-109.

[8] Henry Bordeaux, *The Last Days of Fort Vaux* (Paris: Thomas Nelson and Sons, 1919), pp. 203-204.

[9] Schwencke and Reymann, p. 109.

[10] Bordeaux, p. 204.

[11] Schwencke and Reymann, p. 110.

[12] Alistair Horne, *The Price of Glory: Verdun 1916* (London: Penguin Books, 1993), p. 258.

[13] Colonel Sylvain-Eugène Raynal, *Le Drame du Fort de Vaux* (Frémont, Verdun: Éditions Lorraines, 1949), p. 126.

[14] Ibid., p. 145.

[15] Schwencke and Reymann, p. 111.

[16] Ibid., pp. 111-112.

[17] Raynal, p. 164.

[18] Schwencke and Reymann, p. 112.

[19] Hauptmann Lindow, "Das II/Pi. 20 (bestehend aus 3 Pionierkompagnien: I.K./Pi. 20, 2./Pi. 20 und 3./Pi. 20) bei Vaux," in *Das Ehrenbuch Der deutschen Pioniere,* p. 239.

[20] Engineer School, United States Army, *Experience of the German 1st Army in the Somme Battle, by General von Bülow*[sic]. *Occasional Papers Number 56* (Washington Barracks, D.C.: Press of the Engineer School, 1917), pp. 11-12, 32, 75, 78.

[21] S. A. Dion, *Tanks, Gas, Bombing, Liquid Fire* (New York: George U. Harvey Publishing Company, 1917), p. 2.

CHAPTER 6

The Eastern and Balkan Fronts

Shock-troop Attack at Skrobowa

From July of 1916, the Germans and Austrians carried out seven failed assaults at Skrobowa, near Baranovichi in Brest. In late September Army Group Woyrsch was given the mission of taking the stubborn objective. The 5th Reserve Division and elements of the 201st Infantry Division would attack, this time in concert with flamethrowers.[1] Accordingly, the *OHL* placed the Guard Reserve Pioneer Regiment at the disposal of *Generalleutnant* von Woyra, commander of the 5th Reserve Division.

Located on a hillside near the Skrobowa Stream, the target area was 2.5 miles wide by 1000 yards deep. *Major* Bernhard Reddemann reconnoitered the trench system personally, describing it as fortresslike strong points, blockhouses, and flanking installations of concrete climbing up one behind the other, bristling with machine guns and served by as many as 100 soldiers per site. The Russian units occupying the positions were the 218th Gorbatovsky Infantry Regiment, the 217th Kovrov Infantry Regiment, and the 1st and 2nd battalions of the 322nd Soligalichskiy Infantry Regiment.

Detail of the illustration "Defeat of the Russians in bayonet and hand-grenade combat at Skrobowa-bach, August 9, 1916," by Professor Hans W. Schmidt. On the left is an assault accompanying gun (Sturmbegleitkanone) with a bullet -riddled shield; other assault troops carry steel trench shields.

Reservist of Reserve Infantry Regiment No. 12, 5th Reserve Division. The regiment formed shock troops for the assault on Skrobowa, November 9, 1916. This infantryman is equipped with a pickaxe (Beilpicke) instead of the more usual entrenching tool. Both the sharpened spade and pickaxe were brutally effective weapons in hand-to-hand combat.

An elaborate, interlocking close-defense network, the entrenchments at Skrobowa were carefully designed so that machine-gun, rifle, mortar, and artillery fire could sweep the intervals between the strong points. Flanking trenches and fighting shelters were intended to protect the garrisons from infantry assaults and all but the heaviest artillery fire. Despite the complex nature of the fortifications, some of the trenches were shallow and primitive, inexplicably left bare of barbed wire.

Reddemann decided that none of the tactics he had developed for frontal attacks would work at Skrobowa. He had to try something more audacious, an approach he christened the "Knife Tactic" *(Messertaktik)*. Reddemann, von Woyra, and the divisional general staff officer drew up a battle plan, which Reddemann presented orally to the Grand Headquarters in Pless. He

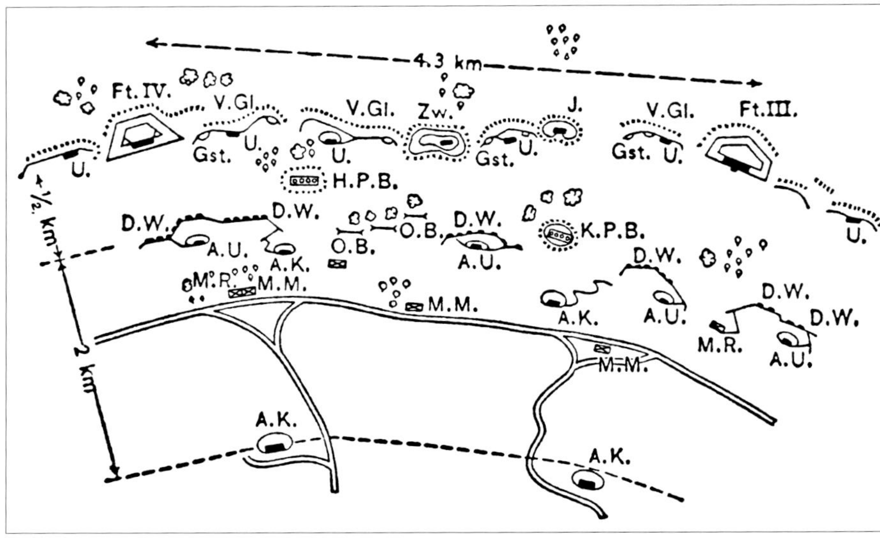

Layout of typical Russian defenses, such as those found at Skrobowa:

Ft. = concrete forts facing enemy line;
V. Gl. = trench with glacis foreground;
Zw. = closed infantry position;
Gst. = machine guns or light quick-firing guns for flank protection;
U. = concrete fighting shelter;
J. = barracks;
H.P.B., K.P.B. = armored batteries;
D.W. = field batteries or mortar positions;
M.R. = shelters;
A.U. = infantry detachments on duty;
A.K. = protected barracks for reinforcements;
O.B. = mobile reserve;
M.M. = main magazine.

received permission from *General der Infanterie* Erich Ludendorff to use the 4th, 5th, possibly the 6th, and the 7th Companies of the Guard Reserve Pioneer Regiment in the operation. Reddemann himself would command the flamethrower troops during the battle, a departure from his regular duties.

German assault troops advancing in "shock columns" (Stosskolonnen). At Skrobowa Bernhard Reddemann expanded the shock-column concept into the Knife Tactic (Messertaktik), lines of several dozen men armed with flamethrowers, hand grenades, light machine guns, and automatic rifles.

The Plan of Attack

The plan that Reddemann and Woyra conceived was ambitious and risky. First, 24 large flamethrowers *(Grof)* would be secretly positioned in the German front line over a period of several days. On the morning of the assault they would open fire after an extended artillery and trench-mortar barrage, "shocking" the Russian line with long tongues of flame and huge, boiling clouds of black smoke. At this moment pioneers armed with *Kleif* would emerge from the German trenches and pierce the enemy front line ahead of infantry shock troops and six infantry battalions advancing abreast. The portable flamethrowers were to be deployed in new formations called "flame shock troops" *(Flammenstosstrupps)*. A flame shock troop was composed of six *Kleif* troops, each of which contained two *Kleif* squads. Rounding out each flame shock troop were a hand-grenade squad from the flamethrower regiment and several infantry squads under the command of flamethrower officers and deputy officers.

Reddemann described the flame shock troops as serpentine, indicating long, thin formations, essentially an expansion of the shock column *(Stosskolonne)*. In some places they were to sprint across 330 to 550 yards

Assault squad of the Guard Reserve Pioneer Regiment. They wear light assault order and are armed with P08 pistols and Kar 98AZ carbines. Ammunition is carried in jacket pockets; all except one wear the M1915 blouse, while the pioneer standing second from right is uniformed in the M1907/10 field jacket. Note the death's head sleeve badge on the left cuff.

of open ground, moving side-by-side 220 to 330 yards apart and striking the Russian lines perpendicularly. Their speed and momentum, as well as their single-file formation, would allow them to cut the Russian line into "twitching pieces" by destroying every point of resistance in front and to the sides with flamethrowers, hand grenades, light machine guns, and automatic rifles. The specific routes the shock troops would take were precisely determined beforehand, based on large aerial photos that the men studied carefully.

As the flame shock troops punched through the Russian lines and raced up the communication trenches to take the heights, flamethrower and hand-grenade squads would turn to the sides and suppress the heavy flanking fire that was expected. These shutting-down *(schliessenden)* units would screen infantry shock troops that followed 55 to 110 yards behind the flame shock troops. Two *Kleif* squads were placed in the interval between each flame shock troop and infantry shock troop to neutralize any remaining or developing points of resistance. After the infantry shock troops poured through the holes in the Russian line, the six battalions of regular infantry would follow in four waves. Twelve flame shock troops would execute the frontal Knife Attack, followed by 12 infantry shock troops and 24 *Kleif* squads. Two flame shock troops would take important objectives on the left wing, and Reddemann would hold two in reserve. The 216 *Kleif* and 24 *Grof* made a total of 240 flamethrowers used in the attack.

At Skrobowa the massive scale of the flamethrower assault dwarfed later American operations in the Pacific. Dramatic newsreel footage notwithstanding, in reality American forces generally deployed no more

Opposite
Top: Shock troops of Reserve Infantry Regiment No.12 observe a Grof at Gorodishche, during training for the assault on Skrobowa, November 4, 1916. Cloth Pickelhaube covers have the letter "R" and the number "12" on the front and the designation "XIVS" on the left side, indicating "Shock Troop 14."

Bottom: Shock troops of Reserve Infantry Regiment No.12 observe a Kleif squad rolling up a trench during training at Gorodishche, November 4, 1916. The flamethrower is the late-model Kleif M.1915. Note that while the infantrymen retain the Pickelhaube, the flamethrower pioneers wear steel helmets.

Above: Shock troops of Reserve Infantry Regiment No.12 observing a Kleif squad during training at Gorodishche, November 4, 1916. The puff of white smoke rising from the flame jet is produced by the lance igniter, which lasted about two minutes. In the background, three members of a Grof squad stand over a large-flamethrower lance and hose lying on the ground.

Troops of Guard Grenadier Regiment No.4 display M1916 reinforcement plates called "brow armor" (Stirnpanzer) on their M1916 steel helmets. The additional armor was .2 in thick and weighed 5 lb. Although issued to assault troops, it was generally rejected or discarded on the battlefield.

than about 40 portable flamethrowers in any one mission. The Table of Equipment for the Marine Division allowed for 72 portable flamethrowers per engineer combat battalion, while the Infantry Division had 24 portable flamethrowers per engineer combat battalion. In comparison, each of the three battalions of the Guard Reserve Pioneer Regiment was armed with 216 portable and 24 static flamethrowers. A battalion's entire store of flamethrowers was therefore used at Skrobowa.

Preparations

Reddemann's operation was rehearsed for a week in a mockup of the Russian trench system built behind the German lines at Gorodishche. Russian intelligence officers observed the preparations and informed their commanders that a flamethrower attack would take place on November 9. It is not clear how they pinpointed the date, although it is likely that German prisoners or deserters were the source.

On the night of November 8, Russian officers alerted their men that the next day would see the introduction of a new German weapon, the flamethrower. The warnings were passed to the troops by word of mouth, an ineffective method that had mixed results. A few officers thoroughly explained the device to the lower ranks, using information gleaned from newspaper articles and drawings in periodicals. This thoroughness was hardly universal, however. Russian preparations were also haphazard. In one company of the 332nd Regiment some men were issued supplies of water to extinguish flames, while others were given no warning at all of the impending attack. In general, most Russian officers were ignorant of flamethrowers and methods to counteract their effects. A post-battle Russian commission concluded that as a result much of what the officers said merely frightened the men.

The Assault

German artillery and trench mortars opened fire at 0600 hours on November 9. The barrage continued for four hours, reaching "the level of a hurricane" and systematically destroying front-line entrenchments, shelters, communication trenches, and artillery positions. At 1000 hours the 24 *Grof* – arrayed in five groups – "shocked" their targets with flame and dense clouds of black smoke. According to Reddemann, the 12 flame shock troops left their jumping-off points, crossed No Man's Land, and bored into the Russian line as the artillery barrage and *Grof* assault continued. On the left wing, two more flame shock troops drove forward under the cover of smoke and fire. Behind these forces, the 12 infantry shock troops advanced, each preceded by two *Kleif* squads. The six battalions of regular infantry brought up the rear in four waves.

Contradicting Reddemann, the Russian report claimed that German infantry tried three times to leave their trenches between 1200 and 1400 hours, but were repulsed by rifle, machine-gun, and artillery fire. After each failed attempt, the German mortar fire increased; by 1500 hours the Russian barbed-wire entanglements had been mostly destroyed, and so many men in the front lines had been killed or evacuated that surveillance of the German movements was greatly diminished. It was only now, between 1400 and 1500 hours, that portable-flamethrower squads were sent against the Russian positions.

Young member of an infantry shock troop; note the embroidered "S" insignia on the inner left elbow of the M1915 blouse. Equipment includes M1909 ammunition pouches, Kar 98AZ carbine, and M1916 steel helmet.

As the advance of the flamethrower troops appeared no different from the day's three previous failed assaults, the Russians were initially unaware that the new weapon had been deployed. In the southern sector of the front, the 6th Company of the 217th Regiment was the first Russian unit to experience

Shock troops of Brunswick Infantry Regiment No.92 training at Olesky-Olasko, Galicia, May of 1917. They are armed with Kar 98AZ carbines and M1916 hand grenades in factory-made bags. Their helmets have been painted white to increase their visibility, either for safety or so that observers can gauge the progress of the assault.

the flame jets. Here there was no barbed wire, and the opposing trenches were only 33 yards apart. German flamethrower operators were therefore able to stand on their own parapets and fire into the Russian fortifications. The flame jets mostly failed to penetrate the loopholes; only one Russian soldier was slightly burned by a few drops of oil. Heavy Russian fire forced the flamethrower troops to retreat.

In the northern section of the front, the 3rd Company of the 218th Regiment was housed in fortifications only 27 yards from the German lines. The flamethrower operators leading the assault were able to set the entire Russian entrenchment ablaze.

Russian eyewitnesses reported that the German flamethrower troops were organized into squads of five, seven, or 10 men armed with one flamethrower, hand grenades, and light machine guns or automatic rifles. In some of these formations the hand-grenade throwers preceded the flamethrowers, while in others the grenadiers advanced beside or behind them. Infantry followed the flamethrower pioneers everywhere except for some areas held by the 217th Regiment.

When the distance between the trenches was around 165 yards or more, the flamethrower operators created smoke screens by directing their flame jets at the ground as soon as they left their trenches. Many Russian soldiers of the 217th Regiment mistook the smoke for gas and hurriedly put on their masks. They soon realized their mistake and tore off the masks, but during this panic the Germans had advanced considerably. Rather than march forward in a linear fashion, they zigzagged, using the natural features of the ground for cover. When the flamethrower pioneers reached the Russian trenches, they first ran along the parapet, dousing the defenders below. Once inside the trenches, the Germans rolled them up using flamethrowers and hand grenades.

Savage Close Combat

One unverifiable claim made by the Russians is that the Germans used flamethrowers to spray a caustic liquid such as sulfuric acid. Oil-spraying flamethrowers were deployed against the 218th Regiment, the right flank of the 217th Regiment, and against the 332nd Regiment, while the acid sprayers were used on the remaining front held by the 217th. No German reports of such weapons have ever been found, even though the British and French made the claim as well as the Russians. If the Germans sprayed acid with flamethrowers, they would have had to use either the *Kleif M.1912* or captured French late-model Schilt No.3 devices, both of which had metal swiveling lances attached to the oil tank instead of rubber hoses. The Russian description of the weapon could identify the weapon as a late-model Schilt No.3:

> [T]he small apparatuses are arranged thus: on the back of the flamethrower operator are placed two cylinders, one under another, the first about 23 inches tall and eight inches in diameter, the second under it and somewhat smaller, with a length of 20 inches and a diameter of four inches. The first cylinder is behind the shoulders and the second against the waist... Hoses for the spraying of liquid came from under the left arm of the flamethrower operator, and he worked it like a fire hose, moving it from side to side. Some witnesses saw that with the spraying of the jet, the flamethrower operators made some action with their right hands, as if pumping air into the tank that contained liquid.[2]

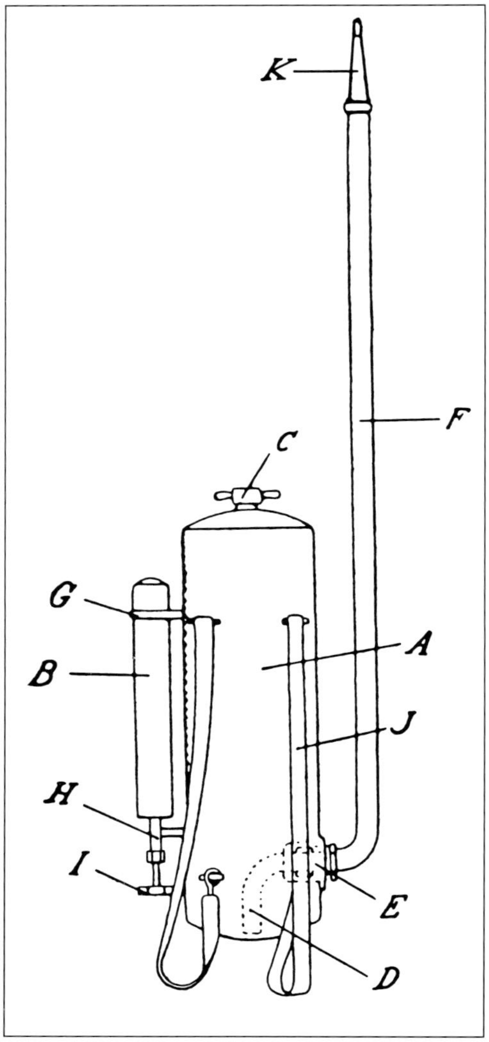

French late-model Schilt No.3, a flamethrower captured and used by the Germans. The description of the acid-sprayer allegedly deployed at Skrobowa is very similar to the late-model Schilt No.3. A) oil tank; B) propellant bottle; C) oil filler cap; D) oil-outflow pipe; E) rotating joint; F) lance; G) retaining ring; H) tap; I) handle; J) shoulder strap; K) nozzle.

Sulfuric acid in a concentration between 70 percent and 99.5 percent will not corrode unprotected steel at ambient temperature, as it forms a protective iron sulfate film on the metal. It would therefore be technically possible for the Germans to have used flamethrowers as acid sprayers.

Both Russian and German accounts of Skrobowa describe vicious, unrelenting combat. At one point Russians of the 217th Regiment discovered

PORTABLE APPARATUS USED BY GERMANS FOR FLAME-THROWING AND SQUIRTING CORROSIVE LIQUIDS.

Kleif M.1912 captured by the Russians. As the caption indicates, the Germans may have used this model flamethrower to spray acid. The angled nozzle allowed the pioneer to fire the weapon from a trench or shell crater without exposing himself. The block valve for releasing the pressurized oil or acid is visible behind the soldier's elbow.

that their rifles were full of earth from the shelling and would no longer fire. In desperation they attempted a bayonet attack against a line of shock troops but were driven back by jets of flame and caustic liquid. Reddemann wrote that he remained at his headquarters in the rear and kept track of the battle through airborne intelligence officers in observation aircraft equipped with two-way radios. They reported on the progress of individual flame shock troops and dropped message streamers containing fresh orders to the men on the ground, allowing Reddemann to save his reserves for the toughest points of resistance.

One such example was a concrete fortification on a commanding height occupied by a garrison of more than 100. Given the code name "Stronghold" *(Feste),* it was armed with dozens of machine guns that swept the glacis in front and threatened to halt the entire advance. Since the reinforced concrete withstood direct hits by artillery and heavy mortars, the decision was made to attack the fortress with Flame Shock Troops 5 and 6, one of which was commanded by a *Leutnant* Fredenhagen. During the ensuing frontal assault, Fredenhagen and a number of his men were killed, but the flame shock troops persevered in an "exceedingly death-defying fashion," in Reddemann's words. Despite the hail of bullets they moved in close enough to spray their weapons through the firing loopholes of the Stronghold, which persuaded the Russians to surrender.

After an hour the entire Russian trench system had been taken. Russian casualties were heavy, according to Reddemann, although he gave no numbers. In addition, 49 officers and 3380 men were captured, along with many machine guns, trench mortars, and other material. The flamethrower pioneers suffered 69 casualties, including two officers and 14 NCOs and

Shock troop of the 16th Company, Saxon Landwehr Infantry Regiment No.133, photographed on the Dvina River, Latvia, in 1916. They wear Pickelhauben with the spike removed and are armed with Gew 98 rifles and M.1916 stick grenades.

Below: German shock troops with three Russian prisoners after a trench raid, date and place unknown. The Germans are equipped with M1909 ammunition pouches, M1916 gas-mask canisters, and M1916 steel helmets; they are armed with Gew 98 rifles. Two of the Russians wear M1915 Adrian steel helmets.

Opposite
Top: Russian machine guns and trench mortars captured at Skrobowa on November 9, 1916. Three mortars are Russian copies of the German Lanz.

Bottom: German shock troops on parade in Galicia, May 18, 1917. The officer marching on the left wears a steel helmet with the visor removed. Most sources identify this helmet as an M1918 model intended for export to the Ottoman Empire but never delivered. Its presence in this photo is unexplained.

men dead, the worst single-day tally of the war. Reddemann described these numbers as very high in comparison with those of the infantry, a view shared by divisional commander *Generalleutnant* von Woyra, who wrote that the participation of the flame shock troops was of decisive importance in the outcome of the attack:

> These troops, who for three days had worked to move up during the artillery-fire preparation on the enemy positions, went forward with the greatest bravery... The success of the flamethrower units was certainly bought through considerable casualties that were much higher than among the infantry, for whom they had cleared the way for victory... A carefully selected and excellently organized and led elite unit.[3]

Based on statements from the participants in the battle, the Russian commission of inquiry concluded that the effects of flamethrowers were negligible in comparison with artillery, mortar, machine-gun, and rifle fire. Russian soldiers who survived the attack noted that the flame jets had a maximum range of about 25 yards and that the flamethrower operators could move only at a walk. Flamethrowers did not have a decisive influence on the success of the German attack; instead, artillery and mortar preparation was almost solely responsible. However, it was undeniable that flamethrowers had a significant negative effect on the degree of perseverance shown by the defenders of the Russian trenches and also on the immediate reserves. The wounded of the 218th Gorbatovsky Infantry Regiment streaming to the rear shouted, "The Germans are spraying fire! All the trenches are burning," which made the remaining men extremely nervous.

Erbeutete russische Maschinengewehre und Minenwerfer
9. 11. 16 Skrobowa

The Russians brought in reinforcements and launched several counterattacks at Skrobowa on November 10. Russian reports claimed that some of the trenches were taken back, but according to German communiqués all of the assaults failed.

Reddemann imported the Knife Tactic to the western front, where his men constantly adapted it. The elastic defense used by the enemy in the featureless, shell-cratered landscape required that the regiment modify its shock-troop tactics. Flame shock troops were split into two echelons, the second moving from cover to cover behind the first and eventually overtaking and relieving it. In addition, trenches and occupied lines of shell holes were rolled up from the inside using much heavier firepower.

This new form of assault was usually made against the most critical strong points, such as command blockhouses and machine-gun nests. Proper execution required that the flamethrower squads utilize blind spots for breaking through laterally in what Reddemann called "surprise flanking thrusts"; once inside the enemy line, the squads would then turn against the actual objective. For the tactic to succeed, the opposing trenches had to be relatively close, or there had to be enough cover for the flamethrower squads to approach undetected to within 110 yards.

New Flame Shock-troop Formations

Reddemann continued to modify the flame shock troop until the end of the war, introducing at least three more formations:

a) The reinforced *Kleif* shock troop *(verstärkter Kleifstosstrupp)*:

two shock-troop leaders;
three *Kleif* squads;
six hand-grenade throwers.

Three representative members of the German 52nd Special Corps, which consisted of the German 217th Infantry Division, the Ottoman 26th Infantry Division, and Bulgarian 1st and 12th Infantry Divisions. This photo was taken in Dobroudja, Romania, in 1916; the German soldier is a Wehrmann of Landwehr Infantry Regiment No.22. In the fall of 1916 the Germans began training their Turkish and Bulgarian allies in shock-troop tactics.

b) The shock unit in serpentine, columnar, or single-file form for rolling up a trench *(Stosseinheit in Schlangen-, Säulen-, oder Reihenform zum Aufrollen eines Schützengrabens)*:

two *Kleif* shock troops (four *Kleif* squads, eight hand-grenade throwers);
two light machine-gun squads;
two grenade-launcher squads;
one infantry squad.

c) The shock unit in the form of a flock or attacking wedge *(Stosseinheit in Rudelform oder in Form eines Angriffskeils)*:

three *Kleif* shock troops (six *Kleif* squads, 12 hand-grenade throwers);
four light machine-gun squads;
four grenade-launcher squads;
two infantry squads;
one squad of pioneers with explosives;
one infantry half-squad to carry machine-gun ammunition;
one infantry half-squad to carry grenade-launcher ammunition;
one infantry half-squad as hand-grenade throwers.

Two Turkish assault infantrymen and an Austrian machine gunner in Galicia, 1917. All would have been well versed in German assault techniques. The Ottoman soldiers wear the M1909 khaki uniform and "Enver Pasha helmet" (enverieh), while the Austrian is uniformed in the field-gray M1916 duty blouse (Einheitsbluse).

Bulgaria

On September 23, 1916, Germany sent a training command of two officers, four NCOs and 25 men of Assault Battalion Rohr to Bulgaria to create a pioneer *(pioner)* assault battalion *(Shturmova Druzhina)* in the Bulgarian First Army.[4] This formation would provide troops for operations and would train Bulgarian officers, NCOs, and men of the First and Second Armies, as well as Turkish officers, NCOs, and men.

In November Army Group Below intended to form an assault detachment in each of its armies. These units would be independent of the assault battalion in Sofia and would each consist of one German and one Bulgarian company, under the command of German officers.[5] The plan was not carried out. During the same month the Bulgarian Headquarters of the Standing Army issued a formal order that an assault battalion be established.[6] Assault Battalion No.5 (Rohr) trained the Bulgarian assault Battalion for five weeks, beginning in late November.[7]

Order No.653 of the Headquarters of the Standing Army, dated December 29, 1916, officially established a trench-mortar battalion and an assault battalion[8] of around 650 men. Order No.654 of the same day decreed that the assault battalion of the First Army would consist of:

two pioneer assault companies;
one trench-mortar detachment;
one howitzer battery;
one flamethrower detachment.

In Bulgarian, assault troops were called *shturmovatzi*. During the war, the Germans gave the Bulgarians a total of 3127 heavy machine guns, 284 light mortars, 162 medium mortars, 1932 grenade launchers, 528 artillery pieces, and eight flamethrowers.[9]

The First Army Assault Battalion never fought as a unified whole but instead sent detachments to divisions or brigades for particular operations. It was formed mainly for training purposes, as the Bulgarian army followed

Page 116
Top: Bulgarian officers of an assault formation, date and place unknown. Pioneers of Assault Battalion Rohr trained a 650-man assault battalion (Shturmova Druzhina) in the Bulgarian First Army. These officers are armed with pistols and bayonets and are equipped with alpine canes, Austrian M1915 Gummimasken, and German M1916 steel helmets.

Bottom: Assault troops of the Guard Jäger Battalion and Jäger Battalion No.9 photographed at Hill 1248 during the Battle of Monastir, May 18, 1917. Behind a rolling barrage, the Bulgarian First Army Assault Battalion attacked the heavily fortified French positions with flamethrowers and hand grenades. Of the two French infantry regiments, only 261 soldiers survived to be taken prisoner.

Page 117
Top: Bulgarian shock troops receiving awards; the caption reads, "After a successful assault on Seret." During the Romanian Campaign the Bulgarians reached the Seret River on January 15, 1917. In Bulgarian, assault troops were called "shturmovatzi." These soldiers are equipped with German M1916 steel helmets and Austrian 8mm Mannlicher M95 rifles.

Bottom: Bulgarian postcard titled "Prisoners and trophies at Seret," dating from early 1917. German shock troops of imposing stature and Bulgarian soldiers display Russian prisoners, a Maxim M1910 heavy machine gun, and a Russian hand grenade (second from left). Two of the Germans and all three Bulgarians wear the Bulgarian Medal for Military Merit.

Слѣдъ успѣшенъ щурмъ на Серетъ.

Плѣнници и трофея на Серетъ.

the early German practice of creating ad hoc assault units from regular infantry. The assault battalion, as a coherent unit, was under the command of the Engineer Corps *(Inzherni Voinski).*

On May 2, 1917, the German military plenipotentiary in Sofia asked the *OHL* on behalf of the Bulgarian War Ministry that the training command of Assault Battalion No.5 (Rohr) be allowed to remain in Sofia to continue its mission. Due to the heavy fighting on the western front that required the assistance of all German assault-troop instructors, the *OHL* rejected the request and the German trainers were withdrawn.[10]

Assault on Toboly

Another major assault on the eastern front took place at the Toboly bridgehead in the Ukraine on April 3, 1917. The 1st *Landwehr* Infantry Division, reinforced by elements of the 86th and 92nd Infantry Divisions, attacked with the 3rd, 4th, and 7th Companies of the Guard Reserve Pioneer Regiment.

The preparatory barrage from 300 artillery pieces and 100 trench mortars lasted five hours and 45 minutes.[11] The commander of artillery, *Oberstleutnant* Georg Bruchmüller (see Chapter Twelve), used a tactic of his own creation called "gas squares *(Gasvierecke)*. Each "square" was actually a rectangle 220-330 yards wide and 440-550 yards deep, which contained at least one known enemy battery. Bruchmüller used gas to cover the square

Assault squad of Mounted Jäger Regiment No.12 (Jäger-Regiment zu Pferde Nr.12) trains in rolling up trenches prior to the April 3, 1917, operation against the Toboly bridgehead. The men wear the M1915 blouse in gray-green, which replaced the cavalry tunic. Note that the Jäger in the center is placing his grenade bags over his shoulders. In the background a flamethrower sprays burning oil.

Opposite

Top: Shock troop of Landwehr Infantry Regiment No.61, 85th Landwehr Division, photographed in a Lithuanian swamp. They are armed with Gew 98 rifles and hand grenades, and their M1915 gas masks have been fitted with cloth inserts over the filter to block chloropicrin and Blue Cross particulates.

Bottom: Squad Frost (Gruppe Frost), Bavarian 10th Infantry Division, which includes soldiers of the Bavarian 6th Reserve Infantry Regiment, 8th Reserve Infantry Regiment, 16th Infantry Regiment, and Infantry Leib Regiment. This unit would almost certainly be an assault squad, with two experienced men of the Infantry Leib Regiment temporarily attached. From February to May of 1917 the Bavarian 10th Division served in Galicia, engaging in several shock-troop missions.

Assault Detachment of the 19th Reserve Division; all these soldiers are Unteroffiziere or Gefreitere of Infantry Regiment No. 78. They are likely squad leaders trained in shock tactics, which they would then pass along to their men. Weapons consist of hand grenades in bags and slung Gew 98 rifles.

so that his guns did not have to be registered for accuracy; in addition, the guns did not have to be eliminated, merely rendered inoperative during the German assault.[12]

After the preparatory barrage the assault troops attacked along a front 4400 yards wide.[13] They advanced about 55 yards behind a rolling barrage *(Feuerwaltz)* of shrapnel, high explosive, and gas shells, while box barrages prevented reinforcements from moving in and the defenders from retreating in an orderly fashion. The assault troops were required to stay as close as possible behind the rolling barrage for it to be effective; for their part the artillerymen had to adhere strictly to the predetermined schedule and work diligently to prevent the firing of short rounds that would fall among the assault troops.

The three flamethrower companies provided 10 flame shock troops and several flame-accompanying squads armed with a total of 64 portable devices half-filled with oil in order to lighten the load of the flamethrower pioneers and allow them to keep up with the assault troops. Although these "half-*Kleif* squads" *(Halbkleiftrupps)* could move quickly, the trade-off was that the lightened flamethrowers fired a drastically reduced number of one-second bursts.

Advancing behind the rolling barrage, the assault troops penetrated 1600 to 3300 yards and captured 10,000 prisoners, 15 cannons, and much war material.

Endnotes

[1]The account of the German shock-troop attack at Skrobowa is pieced together from several sources, including Reddemann, *Geschichte,* pp. 26-28; Reddemann, "Die Totenkopf Pioniere," pp. 522-524; *Dem Andenken unserer gefallenen Kameraden;* and Aleksandr Nikolaevich De-Lazari, *Khimicheskoe Oruzhie na Frontakh Mirovoĭ Voĭny 1914-1918 gg.* Editing and commentary by Dr. Mikhail Vasilyevich Supotnitskiy (Moscow: Vuzovskaya Kniga, 2008), pp. 132-134.

[2] "Report of the Commission for the Inspection of the Methods of Application by the Germans of Flamethrowers in Combat on November 9 in the Region of the Skrobowa Stream," http://supotnitskiy.ru/book/book5_prilogenie8.htm (accessed December 1, 2010).

[3] Reddemann, "Die Totenkopf Pioniere," p. 524.

[4] Gruss, p. 70. According to von Schwerin, p. 34, the German training command consisted of two officers and 40 NCOs and men.

[5] Gruss, p. 71.

[6] V. N. Krapchanski; D. D. Vazel; G. R. Hristov; and I. K. Skachokov, *Kratak Obzor na boynia sastav, organizatsiyata, popalvaneto i mobilizatsiyata na balgarskata armia ot 1878 do 1944g* (Sofia: Darzhavno voenno izdatelstvo, 1961), p. 106.

[7] Gruss, pp. 169-171.

[8] Interview with Dobrin Todorov Dobrinov, staff member of the National Museum of Military History, Sofia, conducted by Ventsislav Gramatski on May 26, 2008.

[9] Krapchanski, p. 118.

[10] Gruss p. 71.

[11] Gudmundsson, pp. 112-114.

[12] David T. Zabecki, *Steel Wind: Colonel Georg Bruchmüller and the Birth of Modern Artillery* (Westport, Connecticut: Praeger, 1994), p. 36.

[13] Reddemann, *Geschichte,* p. 35.

CHAPTER 7

Official Army Assault Battalions; Elastic Defense

The Training of Assault Squads

Enclosure 2a, "Instruction for the Training of Assault Squads," April 4, 1916:

> Each company of all battalions and regiments will form two or three assault squads of good, select people to be trained by specially qualified officers.
>
> Strength: One noncommissioned officer (as leader) and six to eight men.
>
> Task: Investigation of enemy positions.
> Elimination of own and enemy obstacles. Guidance of the individual assault column during the attack. Rolling up of enemy trenches and taking of blockhouses and bases.
>
> Equipment: Without pack or cartridge pouches (ammunition in jacket pockets or bread bag); if possible with steel helmet; rifle, or better yet carbine slung over the back or pistol; sandbags with three hand grenades in each worn around the neck over both shoulders; large wire cutters with wood grips hung around the neck. Pioneer tools (axe or hatchet) with half-length handle in case fastened to belt, handle upward.

Unidentified Brigade Assault Detachment in a postcard sent from the Vosges sector on November 28, 1916. Most are infantrymen, while those lying in front are pioneers. Weapons and equipment include Kar 98AZ carbines, grenade bags, wire cutters, small automatic pistols, trench daggers, and a Bangalore torpedo. These troops display the uniform and accoutrements adopted by assault battalions, which at this date were still in the process of being organized.

Grenadiers of Assault Battalion No. I in the Argonne Forest, 1918. The soldier on the right throws an egg grenade inside a sock, whirling it like a lariat over his head. It is not known if this technique was widespread.

Gas mask.

Small red or green (sandbag) tag for mutual recognition during trench fighting.

Use: As much as possible only for the attack, otherwise preserve (do not use for work, so that the troops remain fresh for the attack).

Men who particularly distinguish themselves (award Iron Cross and promotion).

(signed) Rohr
Hauptmann and Commander of the Assault Battalion.[1]

In May of 1916 the *OHL* ordered that officers and NCOs of armies on the western front be trained by Assault Battalion Rohr.[2] These men would then train their own units in assault tactics. By November of 1916 most divisions had an assault detachment or company, and most infantry companies had shock troops.

Army Assault Battalions

In August of 1916 *General* Erich Ludendorff visited the headquarters of Crown Prince Wilhelm at Montmedy, where he reviewed a company from Assault Battalion Rohr that served as an honor guard.[3] Ludendorff had spent the past two years on the eastern front and had not seen soldiers with steel helmets, leather patches on the knees and elbows, and puttees and ankle boots. The Crown Prince explained the purpose of the men; soon afterward Ludendorff decided that all German infantry should be trained as shock troops.

Opposite
Left: Grenadier of Assault Battalion No.2 uniformed in the M1915 blouse and M1908 officers' peaked cap. He wears a field-gray cloth sleeve badge above his left cuff, consisting of two crossed hand grenades in a circle, both in black. Note the trench dagger on his left hip.

Top right: Jäger Schillo, 1st Recruit Depot, Jäger Replacement Battalion No.3. This unit provided men for Jäger (Assault) Battalion No.3 and Assault Battalion No.1. Schillo wears the gray-green M1907/10 field jacket piped in green, the M1915 peaked cap with green band, and the all-green Jäger bayonet knot.

Bottom right: Classic image of a young Jäger of Jäger (Assault) Battalion No.3, taken during the Battle of the Somme, late 1916. He is equipped with small grenade bags, M1915 Gummimaske in M1916 metal carrier, pioneer shovel with shortened handle, Kar 98AZ carbine, and M1916 steel helmet.

On August 29, 1916, Ludendorff became *Generalquartiermeister* of the army, essentially an equal to Chief of Staff *General* Paul von Hindenburg. On October 23, 1916, Ludendorff authorized each army on the western front to form an assault battalion. A War Ministry order of December 4, 1916, formally established the organization of the assault battalions.[4] Assault companies had a compliment of 210-270; each machine-gun company of four officers and 85 men was armed with six MG08 heavy weapons, doubled to 12 guns operated by 135 men in September of 1917; and each trench-mortar company of two officers and 108 men was armed with eight 76mm mortars. Flamethrower platoons armed with six to 10 devices were permanently attached, and infantry-gun batteries of six pieces each were temporarily attached, depending on the mission.

Assault Battalion No.1

Established December 4, 1916, in the First Army, Somme; from April 1917 the Champagne.
Composed of one staff;
three assault companies (one dissolved May 16, 1918, and a second dissolved August 22, 1918);
one machine-gun company;
one trench-mortar company.

Replacement depots:
Staff and assault companies - *Jäger* Replacement Battalion No.3;
Machine Gun Company - 2nd Replacement Machine Gun Company, III Army Corps;
Trench Mortar Company - Pioneer Replacement Battalion No.28.

Assault Battalion No.2

Established November 2, 1916, in the Third Army, Champagne.
Composed of one staff;
four assault companies (3rd Company dissolved August 22, 1918);
one machine-gun company;
one trench-mortar company.

Replacement depots:
Staff and assault companies - Replacement Battalion, Infantry Regiment No.30;
Machine Gun Company - 3rd Replacement Machine Gun Company, XVI Army Corps;
Trench Mortar Company - Pioneer Replacement Battalion No.20.

Jäger (Assault) Battalion No.3

Transformed from *Jäger* Battalion No.3 on July 8, 1916. Assault battalion of the Second Army, Somme.
Composed of one staff;
four assault companies;
two machine-gun companies;
one trench-mortar company;
one flamethrower platoon;
Infantry Gun Battery 3.

Replacement depots:
Staff and assault companies - *Jäger* Replacement Battalion No.3;
Flamethrower Platoon - 2nd Guard Pioneer Replacement Battalion.

Leutnant (left) and Grenadier of the 1st Assault Company, Assault Battalion Nr.4 (Guard). The Leutnant wears the light-gray peacetime greatcoat (Paletot) with collar faced in dark blue; the Grenadier is outfitted in the troops' version of the garment with red shoulder straps and Guard lace and red panels on the collar.

Opposite: Three pioneers of Assault Battalion No.5 (Rohr). Each is equipped with a Kar 98AZ carbine, two grenade bags, four M1917 stick grenades clipped to the belt, and wire cutters. The two on the right wear M1918 steel helmets, while the pioneer on the left has been issued an M1916 helmet.

Assault Battalion No.4 (Guard)
Established December 9, 1916, in the Fourth Army, Flanders.
Composed of one staff;
two assault companies (both dissolved August 22, 1918);
one machine-gun company;
one trench-mortar company.

Replacement depots:
Staff and assault companies - Replacement Battalion, 1st Guard Reserve Regiment;
Machine Gun Company - 4th Replacement Machine Gun Company, Guard Corps;
Trench Mortar Company - Guard Pioneer Replacement Battalion.

Assault Battalion No.5 (Rohr)
Established as Assault Detachment March 3, 1915. In March of 1916 transferred to Crown Prince Wilhelm's Fifth Army, Verdun. Designated Assault Battalion April 1, 1916; became Assault Battalion No.5 on December 4, 1916. Renamed Assault Battalion No.5 (Rohr) on February 7, 1917.
Composed of one staff;
four assault companies, one pioneer park company later transformed to a fifth assault company;
two machine-gun companies;
one trench-mortar company;
one flamethrower platoon;
Howitzer Battery 5;
one transportation section.
Infantry Gun Battery 28 attached as an instruction unit.

Replacement depots:
Staff and assault companies - Pioneer Replacement Battalion No.7 and the Replacement Battalion of Pioneer Regiment No.35;
Machine Gun Companies - Commander of Machine Gun Replacement Troops, VIII Army Corps;
Trench Mortar Company - Trench Mortar Replacement Regiment Markendorf;
Flamethrower Platoon - 2nd Guard Pioneer Replacement Battalion;
Howitzer Battery - Replacement Detachment, Mountain Artillery Detachments 5 and 6.

Assault Battalion No.6 (Bavarian and Prussian)
Established December 4, 1916, in the Sixth Army, Northern France.
Composed of one Bavarian staff;
two assault companies (Prussian company dissolved September 11, 1918);
one machine-gun company;
one trench-mortar company.

Replacement depots:
Staff and 1st Assault Company - Replacement Battalion, Bavarian 19th Infantry Regiment;
2nd Assault Company - Replacement Battalion, Infantry Regiment No.23.
Machine Gun Company - 2nd Replacement Machine Gun Company, VI Army Corps;
Trench Mortar Company - Pioneer Replacement Battalion No.6.

Opposite
Top left: *Unteroffizier of the Flamethrower Platoon, Assault Battalion No.5 (Rohr). He wears the simplified field jacket with a death's-head sleeve badge at the left elbow, the position adopted by Rohr's men to differentiate themselves from the personnel of the Guard Reserve Pioneer Regiment.*

Top right: *Kanonier of the Howitzer Battery, Assault Battalion Nr.5 (Rohr). He is equipped with the M1915 Gummimaske, M1887/88 ammunition pouches, and a camouflaged M1918 steel helmet. His simplified field jacket is adorned with red field-artillery shoulder straps with a yellow exploding grenade and a yellow number "5." Note that his beard has been trimmed to allow the respirator to create an airtight seal.*

Bottom: *Grenade-launcher squad of Assault Battalion No.6. The two men on the left carry the Granatwerfer 16, while the two on the right carry the base plate. Those four Grenadiere are Bavarians, while the man in the center is a Prussian. Note the Wurfgranate 16 carried in bags. The lone Prussian is equipped with stick grenades to defend the squad.*

Assault Battalion No.7 (Badener)

Established December 4, 1916, in the Seventh Army, Aisne.
Composed of one staff;
two assault companies (one dissolved August 22, 1918);
one machine-gun company;
one trench-mortar company.
Men of the 1st Assault Company were called Grenadiers, while men of the 2nd Assault Company were called Fusiliers.

Replacement depots:
Staff and assault companies - 2nd Replacement Battalion, Infantry Regiment No.111 (3rd Badener);
Machine Gun Company - 2nd Replacement Machine Gun Company, XIV Army Corps;
Trench Mortar Company - Pioneer Replacement Battalion No.14.

Assault Battalion No.8

Established December 28, 1916, in Army South, eastern Galicia.
Composed of one staff;
two assault companies (one dissolved August 22, 1918);
one machine-gun company;
one trench-mortar company.

Replacement depots:
Staff and assault companies - 2nd Replacement Battalion, Infantry Regiment No.21;
Machine Gun Company - 4th Replacement Machine Gun Company, XVII Army Corps;
Trench Mortar Company - Pioneer Replacement Battalion No.17.

Assault Battalion No.9

Established December 18, 1916, in the Ninth Army, Romania; after June of 1918 in Soissons, France. Dissolved May 22, 1918, and its component units attached to Assault Battalion Nos. 5 and 12.
Composed of one staff;
two assault companies;
one light machine-gun section (later a machine-gun company);
one trench-mortar company.

Replacement depots:
Staff and assault companies - Replacement Battalion, Infantry Regiment No.50;
Light Machine Gun Section - 3rd Battalion, Machine Gun Instruction Course Döberitz;
Machine Gun Company - 3rd Replacement Machine Gun Company, V Army Corps;
Trench Mortar Company - Pioneer Replacement Battalion No.29.

Assault Battalion No.10

Established December 28, 1916, in Army Group Eichorn, Nieman.
Composed of one staff;
two assault companies (2nd Assault Company became garrison company on August 6, 1918);
one machine-gun company;
one trench-mortar company.

Extremely young Pionier of the Trench Mortar Company, Assault Battalion No.6. He wears the Bavarian M1916 blouse, which featured blue-and-white checkered collar lace. His black shoulder straps are piped in red and have the letters "MW" and the number "6" in red.

Opposite
Left: Pionier Alfred of Shock Troop 11, the Guard Pioneer Battalion. He is uniformed in the M1915 blouse with white Guard lace and plain black shoulder straps piped in red.

Right: The former Pionier Alfred is now Grenadier Alfred, having transferred into Assault Battalion No.7. Photographed in November of 1917, he wears a simplified field jacket with the ribbon of the Iron Cross Second Class.

Replacement depots:
Staff and assault companies - Pioneer Replacement Battalion No.30;
Machine Gun Company - Commander of the Machine Gun Replacement Troops VIII Army Corps;
Trench Mortar Company - Pioneer Replacement Battalion No.30.

Assault Battalion No.11
Established December 28, 1916, in Army Group Linsingen, Poland.
Composed of one staff;
two assault companies;
one machine-gun company;
one trench-mortar company.

Replacement depots:
Staff and assault companies - Replacement Battalion, Infantry Regiment No.149;
Machine Gun Company - 1st Replacement Machine Gun Company, II Army Corps;
Trench Mortar Company (soon reduced to a Trench Mortar Platoon) - first from Pioneer Replacement Battalion No.2; later Trench Mortar Replacement Regiment Markdorf.

Assault Battalion No.12
Established December 28, 1916, in Army Group Woyrsch, Poland. Dissolved October 10, 1918
Composed of one staff;
three assault companies (two companies dissolved August 22, 1918; 3rd Company assigned to Assault Battalion No.7 as 2nd Assault Company);
one machine-gun company;
one trench-mortar company.

Replacement depots:
Staff and assault companies - Replacement Battalion, Infantry Regiment No.46;
Machine Gun Company - 3rd Replacement Machine Gun Company, V Army Corps;
Trench Mortar Company - Pioneer Replacement Battalion No.29.

Assault Company No.13
Established December 28, 1916, in the I Army Corps.
Composed of one staff;
one assault company (dissolved March 26, 1918, and assigned to Assault Battalion No.12 as reinforcements);
one machine-gun platoon;
one trench-mortar platoon.

Replacement depots:
Staff and Assault Company - 2nd Replacement Battalion, Grenadier Regiment No.4;
Machine Gun Platoon - 4th Replacement Machine Gun Company, I Army Corps;
Trench Mortar Platoon - Pioneer Replacement Battalion No.18.

Assault Battalion No.14

Established January 1, 1917, in Army Detachment Stranz (Army Detachment C from February 2, 1917), hernie de Saint-Mihiel. Previously designated the "Assault Half-battalion of the Field Combat School" at Mouzon.
Composed of one staff;
two assault companies;
one machine-gun company;
one trench-mortar company.

Replacement depots:
Staff and assault companies - Replacement Battalion, Infantry Regiment No.88;
Machine Gun Company - 4th Replacement Machine Gun Company, XVIII Army Corps;
Trench Mortar Company - Pioneer Replacement Battalion No.25.

Assault Battalion No.15 (Bavarian and Württemberger)

Established December 23, 1916, in Army Detachment A, Lorraine.
Composed of one staff;
two assault companies;
one machine-gun company;
one trench-mortar company.

Below: Half-platoon of Assault Battalion No.8. Their weapons include a 76mm light mortar, new pattern; MG08 heavy machine gun; rifles; hand grenades; and two fire tubes attached to poles. Two grenadiers in the second row wear steel trench armor.

Opposite: Grenadier of Assault Battalion No.10 (right), uniformed for mountain warfare. Although young, his face shows strain and exhaustion. The man on the left is a member of the Alpine Corps. He wears the M1917 universal field cap with field-gray peak and the Edelweiss badge above the left ear.

M.W.K.
St.B.11.

Replacement depots:
Staff and 1st Assault Company - Replacement Battalion, Bavarian 15th Infantry Regiment;
2nd Assault Company - Replacement Battalion, Württemberger Infantry Regiment No.120;
Machine Gun Company - Replacement Battalion, Bavarian 15th Infantry Regiment;
Trench Mortar Company - Replacement Detachment, Bavarian 2nd Train Battalion.

Assault Battalion No.16 (Badener and Württemberger)
Established December 23, 1916, in Army Detachment B, Upper Alsace.
Composition:
one staff;
four assault companies (three dissolved August 22, 1918);
one machine-gun company;
one trench-mortar company.

Replacement depots:
Staff and 1st, 2nd, and 4th Assault Companies - 2nd Replacement Battalion, Infantry Regiment No.114;
3rd Assault Company - Replacement Battalion, Württemberger Infantry Regiment No.120;
Machine Gun Company - 2nd Replacement Machine Gun Company, XIV Army Corps;
Trench Mortar Company - Pioneer Replacement Battalion No.14.
(Unique among assault battalions, Assault Battalion No.16 experimented with aircraft-mounted portable flamethrowers.)

Opposite
Top: Two platoons of the Trench Mortar Company, Assault Battalion No.11. They display two 76mm light trench mortars, new pattern. The two pioneers standing on either side of the mortars are equipped as infantry assault troops, with steel helmets, grenade bags, and slung Kar 98AZ carbines. Their mission was to protect the mortar squads during the attack.

Bottom: Machine gunners of Assault Battalion No.12 during an assault course for Austro-Hungarian officers and NCOs in Nyárádszereda, Romania, May of 1917. The machine gun is a German Maxim MG08 fitted with the steel shield and wheeled carriage of the Russian Maxim M1910. The gunner on the left wears dragging straps and holds a rubber steam condensation hose in his right hand.

Below: Grenadiere of Assault Battalion No.14 pose with members of the battalion flamethrower platoon and French prisoners. The sign reads "The Assaulters of Ronveaux, August 9, 1918." Ronvaux is located in the Department of the Meuse, Lorraine. The Unteroffizier in the center wears an M1915 summer tunic with the shoulder straps of Infantry Gun Battery 51.

Grenadier of Bavarian Assault Battalion No.15 about to depart for the front, as indicated by the white rose on his chest. He has rolled up the shoulder straps of his Bavarian M1915 simplified field jacket in order to conceal his unit numbers. Note the sweater worn beneath the tunic.

Assault Battalion No.17 (German-Austrian)
Established January 19, 1917, by the Austrian Command of Army Front Erzherzog Karl, Russian front. Dissolved August 22, 1918.
Composed of one staff;
two assault companies (2nd Assault Company Austrian);
one light machine-gun section;
one trench-mortar company;
one mobile Flak platoon.

Replacement depots:
Staff and 1st Assault Company - 2nd Replacement Battalion, Grenadier Regiment No.4;
Light Machine Gun Section - 3rd Battalion, Machine Gun Instruction Course Döberitz; later 4th Replacement Machine-gun Company, I Army Corps;
Trench Mortar Company - Pioneer Replacement Battalion No.18.

Assault Company No.18 (Assault Battalion No.18 as of August 22, 1918)
Established August 7, 1917, in Army Group Eichorn; later transferred to the Eighth Army, eastern front.
Composed of one staff;
one assault company;
one machine-gun platoon;
one trench-mortar platoon.

Replacement depots:
Staff and Assault Company - Replacement Battalion, Infantry Regiment No.88;
Machine Gun Platoon - Commander of Replacement Machine Gun Troops, VIII Army Corps;
Trench Mortar Platoon - Pioneer Replacement Battalion No.30.

A proposal by Headquarters Mackensen *(Oberkommando Mackensen)*, dated March 12, 1917, recommended that, with the exception of *Jäger* (Assault) Battalion No.3 and Assault Battalion No.5, the troops of official army assault companies be designated "Grenadiers."[5] The men serving in the assault companies of *Jäger* (Assault) Battalion No.3 would be *Jäger*, while those of Assault Battalion No.5 would be pioneers. This proposal did not apply to members of infantry-gun batteries, trench-mortar companies, machine-gun companies, or divisional assault companies.

Other Assault Battalions

On October 29, 1916, Army Detachment B created an assault battalion on the Vosges front by merging the four respective assault detachments of the 6th Bavarian *Landwehr* Division, 7th Württemberger *Landwehr* Division, and the 8th and 12th *Landwehr* Divisions.[6] Each detachment had a compliment of 100 to 150 men and was armed with two machine guns, two to four charge throwers, and two to four grenade launchers. Two infantry guns from Infantry Gun Battery 9 were attached to the assault battalion, along with four *Grof* and 12 *Kleif* of the Guard Reserve Pioneer Regiment.

"Detachment Picht" *(Abteilung Picht)* was established in Romania by the 41st Infantry Division, November of 1916.[7] It was comprised of four assault companies, one machine-gun company, and an artillery section.

Detachment Picht was formed with the following German units:

Left: Wehrmann of Bavarian 1st Landwehr Infantry Regiment, 6th Bavarian Landwehr Division. In late 1916 the divisional assault detachment became part of the assault battalion of Army Detachment B in the Vosges region. This spectacularly mustached soldier wears the Bavarian M1915 simplified jacket.

Right: Two Musketiere of Infantry Regiment No.148, 41st Infantry Division, in Romania, December of 1916. In November of 1916 the 41st Infantry Division formed "Detachment Picht" (Abteilung Picht), an assault battalion comprised mainly of troops from Infantry Regiment No.148. Note the leather-reinforced trousers and M95 ammunition pouches worn by the soldier on the left.

a) the 1st Battalion of Infantry Regiment No.148;
b) one-half of the 1st Battery of Field Artillery Regiment No.79;
c) an "officer patrol" *[Offizierpatrouille]* of the 4th Squadron of Dragoon Regiment No.10 and the 5th Squadron of *Kürassier* Regiment No.2;
d) drivers of the 41st Infantry Division;
e) Light Radio Station *[leichten Funkenstation]* 1.

Detachment Picht later served as the assault battalion of Austro-Hungarian Group von Scivo, strengthened by these Austrian infantry and artillery units:

a) one-half of the 5th Battalion, Infantry Regiment No.76;
b) Batteries 5 and 6 of Field Howitzer Regiment No.16;
c) Battery 46 of Heavy Howitzer Division No.2;
d) the 5th Battalion of Bosnia-Herzegovinian Infantry Regiment No.3.

On September 9, 1917, Army Group Herzog Albrecht ordered the creation of a provisional assault battalion for use in the Battle of Caporetto.[8] The battalion staff, 2nd (Württemberger) Assault Company, and a flamethrower section of Assault Battalion No.16 were transferred from Army Detachment B and merged with an assault company, the machine-gun company, and the trench-mortar company of Assault Battalion No.14, provided by Army Detachment C; Infantry Gun Battery 9 was also attached. After the battalion was issued winter clothing it was transported to Metz for training. Designated the Assault Battalion of Army Group Herzog Albrecht *(Sturmbataillon der Heeresgruppe Herzog Albrecht),* the unit was sent to the Italian front in October, where it was reinforced with Austrian assault troops.[9] The battalion fought at Ortigara and was then inserted at the Isonzo as part of the offensive from Friaul to Monte Tomba. In December the battalion was returned to the western front and disbanded.

Elastic Defense; Defense in Depth

Increased artillery preparation before assaults meant that the front-line trenches were always lost.[10] If the defenders insisted on holding those trenches, they would lose much more in terms of soldiers and material, in addition to losing the terrain. To prevent the loss of men, the troops were distributed in depth. The goal of the defensive battle was no longer to retain possession of terrain. Instead, the defenders would inflict the highest possible losses on the enemy while preserving their own forces. If possible unfavorable terrain would be left in the possession of the enemy, since it was more advantageous to give up shell-torn positions rather than lose valuable men and material defending them.

The defenders would not be rigidly bound to one place. They would adopt the principle of mobility, advancing or giving way according to their needs. When they retreated under enemy fire, the line responded to the pressure and wrapped itself like an elastic band around the attacker. To support mobile defense, strong points were created in the intermediate zone, along with machine-gun nests and infantry groups. The strong points were carefully hidden from view to prevent them from being destroyed by artillery. Their mission was to stop the attackers after they breached the front lines, inflicting heavy casualties and disorganizing the enemy troops before they

Squad of Assault Battalion No.16, February of 1918. Some of these young Grenadiere retain the cap cockades of Baden and Württemberg. The soldier standing in the center rear wears the "swallows' nests" (Schwalbennester) of a musician.

Men of the 2nd Assault Company, Assault Battalion No.16, using wooden beams to improvise a bridge over a stream in June of 1918. The steel helmets are painted in disruptive lozenge camouflage, and the grenade bags are factory-made articles.

reached the defenders' rear. The reserves were made more mobile, which resulted in the battle moving all through a position. Horse artillery would also be brought up to participate. Thus the battle for possession of the front line became a battle in a depth zone.

The regular infantry evolved the elastic defense on its own, resulting in the same military skills that were developed and taught by the formal assault battalions.[11] By the end of 1917 riflemen standing in trenches had been replaced by a network of bunkers and strong posts that housed platoons, squads, and machine gunners. More squads, platoons, and companies were kept in larger shelters further from the front, ready to mount small counterattacks wherever the enemy broke through. NCOs were often required to make decisions without orders from their superiors. Tactics became much more individualized.

Fritz von Lossberg

Oberst Fritz von Lossberg, Chief of Staff of the First Army, is generally credited with developing elastic defense, even though initially he vehemently opposed the tactic. His evolution from opponent to innovator of elastic

Above: Assault Battalion No.17 training at Rohatyn, Galicia, summer of 1917. The 2nd Assault Company of the battalion was Austro-Hungarian; in this photo most of the steel-helmeted troops are German, while one is Austrian. Note the small size of the grenade bags worn by the grenadiers in the foreground.

Left: Men of Bavarian Landsturm Infantry Battalion Würzburg No.I, waiting in an underground shelter to carry out a counterattack. They are equipped with M1917 Rahmenmasken. the improved version of the M1915 Linienmaske. Cloth has been inserted over the filters of the masks to protect against particulates. Two of the men in the center wear steel body armor, while the soldier on the left carries a Dräger oxygen breathing apparatus in addition to his Rahmenmaske.

defense began when he discovered that it took eight to 10 hours for messages to travel from divisional headquarters to the front line.[12] Responses took the same amount of time. Lossberg gave battalion commanders control over their sector of the front, so that they did not need to consult with divisional headquarters before making a decision. Like battalion commanders, divisional commanders controlled specific sectors. They were responsible for controlling the conduct of the battle. In December the *OHL* made it official that divisional commanders were given control of all troops moving into their sector, regardless of the seniority of the officers involved. Both divisions on the line and counterattacking divisions were now under the undivided command of the officer in charge of the battle sector. The commander of the battle sector no longer had to wait for orders from the Army or Corps when managing the battle.

Independence of action on so many levels in the chain of command ensured that the Germans could react to enemy attacks in the shortest possible time. The German army had always relied on the initiative of small-unit commanders, but now entire divisions could make rapid decisions based on circumstances on the ground.

Two Jäger and an assault infantryman recover a Russian Maxim machine gun from a battlefield on the eastern front. The Jäger are equipped with rolled assault packs, shovels, M1916 gas-mask containers, and Gew 98 rifles with fixed bayonets, while the infantryman wears grenade bags and a steel helmet.

On December 1, 1916, the *OHL* published *Principles of Command in the Defensive Battle in Position Warfare (Grundsätze für die Abwehrschlacht im Stellungskrieg)*, which the Germans revised twice before the end of the war.[13] It officially rejected the idea of holding the forward line no matter the cost and refusing to retreat. The new objective was to force the enemy to expend his resources, while the defender preserved his own.

The most important aspects of the new defense were maintaining the initiative and using heavy firepower instead of masses of troops. *General* Ludendorff credited *Major* Max Bauer and *Hauptmann* Hermann Geyer with authoring the new manual.

Von Lossberg had rejected the notion of elastic defense when his subordinates, Bauer and Geyer, had conceived it in early 1915.[14] However, he changed his mind after viewing the battlefield at Arras and seeing how the British had placed so many artillery observers on Vimy Ridge overlooking the German defense zone that they had a massive advantage. Holding the front line would be very costly to the Germans. As a result, von Lossberg overcame his own long-held objections to elastic defense.

Elastic defense as von Lossberg conceived it consisted of three zones:[15]

1. Forward outpost zone - one to one and a half miles in depth, containing 10 to 12 percent of the forward troops located in a checkerboard pattern of mutually supporting pillboxes, strong points, and machine-gun bunkers called "nests of resistance" *(Weiderstandnester)*. The forward outpost zone was defended by squads and sections, which could withdraw at will. The rear of the forward outpost zone was situated on a reverse slope *(Hinterhang)* if possible, in order to defend artillery observation posts. This area was the objective of the German counterattack in the enemy penetrated the position.

2. Main battle zone - one and a half miles in depth, where the enemy was to be stopped. At the front of the main battle zone was a trench system deemed the main line of resistance, and at the rear was another trench system designated the artillery protection line, behind which were located the majority of the field guns and the counterattack forces. The main battle zone was defended at the front by companies garrisoned in large shelters, while at the rear it was defended by battalions of the divisional reserves.

3. Rear battle zone - three miles in depth. The front part was defended by battalions, while in the rearmost area were located the field guns and regiments of the counterattack divisions *(Eingreifdivisionen)*.

The Germans first used elastic defense at the Battle of Arras (April 9-May 16, 1917) and then at Passchendaele (July 31-November 6, 1917).

Counterattacks

The independence of action required by shock troops, assault battalions, and infantrymen engaging in elastic defense was also the primary factor that led to successful counterattacks, according to *General* von Below's report on the Battle of the Somme:

> An immediate counter-attack can scarcely ever be ordered by the Higher Commanders. It must be the result of the quick initiative of the commanders, subordinate commanders and men in the front line. Every man must be trained to eject, on his own initiative, an enemy who has penetrated our positions, and not to rest content until the foremost line has been entirely cleared. Quick, mobile bombing parties, moving rapidly over the open or along the trenches, vie with assault detachments specially distributed and allotted to special objectives. The commanders of the supports must take in the situation and make up their minds quickly and attack the enemy, distributing their groups, platoons and companies to meet the situation, allotting special tasks to detachments, and giving them short and precise instructions as to objectives. For this purpose, it is necessary that the quarters of supports and reserves, when the fighting develops its fully intensity, should be distributed over different points in the ground (in trenches and dug-outs, or on the slopes of hills)...
>
> It is very important that, in addition to the transmission of information from front to rear, communication should also be established from rear to front. Troops which wait for reports to reach them from the front will always come up too late for a counter-attack...
>
> Methodical attacks may either be carried out as surprise attacks without artillery preparation or with the employment of intense artillery preparation. A compromise between the two methods nearly always leads to failure...
>
> Machine guns should be brought up to the captured position as soon as the infantry has taken it. They must be dug in before a hostile counter-attack is delivered or the enemy's annihilating fire is opened against the captured position. To bring up machine guns from the lines in rear to the position from which the attack is to be made, and thence to the captured trenches, demands thorough reconnaissance and clear orders as to time, route, objective and duties.
>
> It is advisable to detail a few infantrymen to the machine guns, to act under the order of the section commander. Their duties are: to protect the machine gun, to defend it in hand-to-hand fighting (hand grenades), to help in digging in the gun in the captured trench, and to dig connecting trenches in shell hole positions...
>
> The detailing of special assault detachments, which are to deal entirely with machine guns which have not been put out of action, has proved to be very effective.[16]

Opposite

***Top:** Assault squad of Infantry Regiment No.116 (Infanterie-Regiment Kaiser Wilhelm [2.großherzoglich hessisches] Nr.116), 25th Infantry Division, armed with M1917 hand grenades, P08 pistols, and trench daggers. During the Battle of Passchendaele the 25th Infantry Division served as a counterattack division (Eingreifdivision).*

***Bottom left:** Assault troops blocking off a trench section with a steel shield, sand bags, and rubble. They are armed with hand grenades and Gew 98 rifles and have smeared mud on their helmets as camouflage. The soldier on the right carries his M1915 Gummimaske in a cloth bag on his belt; behind him a trench periscope on a wooden beam leans against the trench wall.*

***Bottom right:** A defensive position in a front-line trench. When engaging in defense in depth, German troops used shock-troop tactics in local areas. Note the Gew 88 rifles, the box of M1915 ball grenades, and M1915 Gummimasken. On the left is a sign that reads "To the 2nd Line."*

Endnotes

[1] Although this document is found in the German Bundesarchiv-Militärarchiv, the file number is not known. It cannot be easily traced because there are no precise lists for the contents of each file in the archive.

[2] Bull, *German Assault Troops of the First World War,* pp. 83-84.

[3] Gudmundsson, p. 84.

[4] The information on official army assault battalions is found in Larcade, pp. 42-63, and Cron, pp. 118-120.

[5] Gruss, p. 80.

[6] Werner Lacoste, *Deutsche Sturmbataillone 1915-1918: Der Kaiserstul und das Markgräflerland als Geburtsstätte und Standort deutscher Sturmbataillone des Ersten Weltkrieges* (Aachen, Germany: Helios Verlag, 2009), p. 22.

[7] Bernhard Bellin, *Sturmtruppe Picht: Ein Erinnerungsblatt aus dem Kriege gegen die Rumänen im Jahre 1916* (Berlin: Verlag Tradition Wilhelm Kolk, 1929), Forward.

[8] Lacoste, p. 70.

[9] Jean-Claude Laparra, *Les "Gladiateurs": Les Formations Offensives dans l'Armée Allemande 1914-1918* (Louviers Cedex, France: Ysec Éditions, 2007), p. 128.

[10] Balck, p. 153.

[11] Gudmundsson, pp. 93-94.

[12] Bradley J. Meyer, "Innovation and Expertise: Some Changes in German Tactical Doctrine during World War I" (Master of Art thesis, Ohio State University, 1981), pp. 54-60, 66-67.

[13] Timothy T. Lupfer, *The Dynamics of Doctrine: The Changes in German Tactical Doctrine During the First World War*. Leavenworth Papers No.4 (Fort Leavenworth, Kansas: Combat Studies Institute, U.S. Army Command and General Staff College, 1981), p. 12.

[14] Meyer, pp. 66-67.

[15] John A. English, *A Perspective on Infantry* (New York: Praeger Publishers, 1981), pp. 18-21.

[16] *Experience of the German 1st Army,* pp. 24-27.

CHAPTER 8

Mortars, Grenade Launchers, Assault Artillery, and Machine Guns

Mortars

At the start of the war the German army had no trench-mortar formations.[1] The weapons were assigned to pioneer siege trains, as were flamethrowers. When the conflict began, the Germans possessed only 70 heavy and 116 medium trench mortars; light mortars were still in development. Trench mortars were kept secret prior to the war. As a result the Germans were the only combatants who fielded the weapons in 1914.

Left: Medium 170mm trench mortar, old pattern (17 cm mittlerer Minenwerfer a/A). Weighing 1064 lb, the medium mortar required 17 men to move it and shot a 109.1-lb high-explosive or 92.6-lb gas shell a maximum of 1094 yd. It could fire 30-35 high-explosive shells per hour or 40-45 gas shells per hour.

Below: Medium 170mm trench mortar, new pattern (17 cm mittlerer Minenwerfer n/A), adopted in 1916. The new-pattern medium trench mortar had a longer barrel and hydraulic recoil cylinders, weighed 1232 lb, and required 21 men to move it. Shell size and rate of fire were the same as those of the old model but the range was increased to a maximum of 1258 yd. M1916 shells had either impact or delay fuses.

On December 18, 1914, Trench Mortar Detachments 1-7 *(Minenwerfer-Abteilungen 1-7)* were established, which were armed with two to six of the medium and heavy weapons held by pioneer siege trains. They would be known collectively as the Army Trench Mortar Reserve *(Armee Minenwerfer-Reseve).*

In January of 1915 the *OHL* ordered that each pioneer company would receive six light trench mortars; in addition, a large number of autonomous trench-mortar detachments armed with heavy, medium, or light weapons was established. On February 5, 1915, each army corps and reserve corps was assigned two heavy trench-mortar detachments armed with two weapons each and one medium trench-mortar detachment armed with six weapons each.

On April 16, 1915, the War Ministry created Trench Mortar Battalion I *(Minenwerfer-Bataillon I),* which joined the seven detachments of the Army Trench Mortar Reserve. Established on April 22 and commanded by *Major* Lothes, the battalion initially consisted of five detachments, each armed with four medium and two light trench mortars. Attempts were made to fire gas shells, but these were not successful because there were too few trench mortars to create an effective gas cloud. In addition this form of attack depended too much on wind direction. In 1915 the *OHL* established Trench Mortar Battalions II to IV.

Left: Heavy 250mm trench mortar, new pattern (25 cm schwerer Minenwerfer n/A), which was produced in 1916 and had a longer barrel and recoil cylinders. The new-pattern heavy trench mortar weighed 1680 lb, requiring 28 men to move it. Full-sized shells weighed 207.2 lb, compared to 134.4 lb for the half-sized shell. Rate of fire remained 20 rounds per hour, but maximum range was increased to 1094 yd.

Right: Lanz 91.5mm light trench mortar (9,15 cm leichter Minenwerfer System Lanz) of of Pioneer Battalion No.11. A smoothbore, auxiliary weapon (behelfsmässigen Minenwerfer or Behelfswerfer) adopted at the start of the war, the Lanz weighed 250 lb and fired an 8.4 lb shell a maximum of 490 yd. Each pioneer company was armed with six smoothbore light mortars. Note the trench periscope in the foreground.

Opposite
Top: Heavy 250mm trench mortar, old pattern (25 cm schwerer Minenwerfer a/A), captured by the French. Note the half- and full-sized shells, the latter in its wicker carrying case. The full-sized shell weighed 207.2 lb, while the half-sized weighed 134.4 lb. Twenty-one men were required to move the mortar, which together with its removable wheels weighed 1260 lb. It had a rate of fire of 20 rounds per hour, with a maximum range of 601 yd.

Bottom: These 76mm light trench mortars, old pattern (7,6 cm leichter Minenwerfer a/A), have had their rectangular steel bedplates embedded in concrete. As one pioneer loads a shell, the other holds the firing lanyard. This mortar weighed 224 lb and shot a 9.9-lb high explosive or gas shell a maximum of 1094 yd. Six men were required to move the weapon, which could fire up to 20 rounds per minute for short periods.

After a year of combat there were 86 heavy, 108 medium, and 114 light unofficial trench-mortar sections *(Abteilungen)* attached to units at the front, and 113 heavy, 169 medium, and 206 light official trench-mortar detachments (also *Abteilungen*). On September 22, 1915, all unofficial trench-mortar sections and official trench-mortar detachments were unified into divisional trench-mortar companies. Each trench-mortar company was to consist of one detachment armed with two heavy weapons, one detachment armed with four medium weapons, and one detachment armed with six light weapons. Trench-mortar surveying units worked with divisional topographical sections to create trench-mortar firing maps, artillery observation serving as the model.

At end of 1915, the trench-mortar arm consisted of the Inspectorate of Trench Mortars, four heavy trench-mortar battalions and eight heavy trench-mortar motorized vehicle sections in the Army Trench Mortar Reserve, 105 divisional trench-mortar companies, and six light trench mortars in every pioneer company.

In 1916 the number of trench-mortar companies was increased to 217 and the trench-mortar battalions to seven (I to VII). Each trench-mortar company was to be armed with three heavy, six medium, and 12 light weapons, for a total of 21 trench mortars per division. Mountain Trench Mortar Companies 170-175 were established (Company 176 was added in 1917), and each assault battalion and *Jäger* battalion in the west received one trench-mortar company armed with eight light weapons.

On November 16, 1916, in accordance with an order from the *OHL*, the War Ministry decreed that rifled light trench mortars were weapons of the infantry rather than the pioneers. Individual pioneer companies would retain six smooth-bore auxiliary mortars each as close-combat weapons, which along with two grenade launchers were carried in two Close Combat Equipment Wagons *(Nahkampfgerätwagen)*.

B—1505 L'Invasion des Barbares modernes
Canon de tranchée allemand, calibre de 250 mill., trouvé dans les ruines de Souchez
édit., Berck-Plage

Große u. kleine Minenwerfer

Each divisional trench-mortar company would now be armed with four heavy and eight medium weapons, and each trench-mortar battalion would consist of four such companies. The order of November 16 also discontinued gas gunnery by trench-mortar battalions. Originally the *OHL* wanted to add a second trench-mortar company to each division, but the pioneer arm could not provide enough men to fulfill the requirements. By shifting the light trench mortars to the infantry, this manpower shortage was addressed. Each of the nine infantry battalions in a division was now armed with four light trench mortars, for a total of 36, while each divisional trench-mortar company was armed with four heavy and eight medium weapons. Thus the number of rifled trench mortars per division rose from 21 to 48.

The War Ministry order of October 13, 1916, stated that Army Trench Mortar Schools would be opened behind the front to instruct infantrymen in the use of the weapon. One trench-mortar officer was assigned to every infantry regiment, and by the end of 1917 there were also four Trench Mortar Inspectorates. In 1917 39 more trench-mortar companies were added to the pioneers, bringing the total to 256.

In 1917 the *OHL* increased the number of trench-mortar battalions in the Army Trench Mortar Reserve from seven to 13 (I to XIII), in order to facilitate mass deployment of the weapons during breakthroughs. The *OHL* also took control of 40 trench-mortar companies, which it used on July 25, 1918, to form Trench Mortar Battalions XIV to XXIII. Each of these battalions was also equipped with 32 Rheinmetall 37mm antitank guns (*3,7 cm TAK Rheinmetall; TAK* stood for *Tankabwehrkanone*). Although 1020 antitank guns were ordered, only 600 had been produced by the end of the war.

On October 26, 1917, the War Ministry set up Army Reserve School Valenciennes to train trench-mortar commanders. Senior commanders and General Staff officers also took part in the courses.

For the Spring Offensives, the *OHL* issued directives that all trench-mortar battalions and companies, as well as the light trench-mortar platoons of infantry battalions, were to be considered part of the offensive artillery. They would all take part in preparatory fire, under the command of trench-mortar officers. To provide more personnel the War Ministry established Trench Mortar Field Recruit Depots 1-6 in the Army of the West on February 19, 1918.

On February 24 the four trench-mortar inspectorates were transformed into Trench Mortar Staff Officer Nos. 1 to 4, giving them the authority of regimental commanders. This was to create unity of command when several trench-mortar battalions were brought together in the field. At the same time Inspectorates of Trench Mortar Equipment No.1 and No.2 were created. They controlled the material state of the trench-mortar arm, while the Trench Mortar Staff Officers supervised the training and activities of the troops and served as their commanders in battle.

Due to a continuing shortage of pioneers to man the weapons, the *OHL* dissolved the divisional trench-mortar companies; the corresponding War Ministry order was issued on September 17, 1918. The medium trench mortars were assigned to the three infantry regiments of each division, while the heavy trench mortars were assigned to the 13 battalions of the Army Trench Mortar Reserve. Each infantry regiment was now to form a trench-mortar company – designated the 13th Company – armed with three medium and nine light weapons. The regimental trench-mortar officer of the regimental staff was discontinued. This reorganization had not been completed by the time the Armistice was declared.

Opposite
Top: Pioneers of the Trench Mortar Company, Assault Battalion No.2. They pose with a 76mm light trench mortar, new pattern (7,6 cm leichter Minenwerfer n/A), adopted in 1916. This improved model featured a longer barrel and a bedplate with a circular turntable, allowing the mortar to be fired in any direction. Weighing 312 lb, it fired a 9.9-lb high explosive or gas shell a maximum of 1422 yd. The rate of fire was 20 rounds per minute for short periods.

Bottom: Equipment depot of Trench Mortar Company 230. From the left, the weapons are the heavy 250mm trench mortar, old pattern; three light 76mm trench mortars, new pattern (including two late-model versions with steel wheels); and a medium 170mm trench mortar, old pattern. Hundreds of steel trench shields are stacked on the ground.

By the end of the war there was a total of 23 trench-mortar battalions, 250 pioneer trench-mortar companies, 580 infantry trench-mortar companies, six trench-mortar recruit depots, 11 trench-mortar replacement battalions, and three trench-mortar parks.

Grenade Launchers

The *Granatenwerfer 15,* also called *Priesterwerfer* or *Priestwerfer* because it was invented by a Hungarian priest named Vecer, was a small spigot mortar supplied to the pioneers; the War Ministry order of September 22, 1916, stipulated that each pioneer company would receive two. The improved *Granatwerfer 16* was issued to the infantry in 1917. Initially 12 were assigned to each regiment, organized in one platoon of two batteries per battalion, four weapons in each platoon.[2] In April of 1917 each infantry regiment was issued 24 grenade launchers: eight per battalion, two per company.[3]

The second edition of the *Training Manual for Foot Troops in War (Ausbildungsvorschrift für die Fusstruppen im Kriege),* dated January of 1918, contained instructions for the use of the grenade launcher by assault troops:

Heavy 240mm trench mortar "Iko" (Schwerer 24 cm Flügelminenwerfer "Iko"); "Iko" is an abbreviation of Engineer Committee (Ingenieur-Komitee), which designed the weapon as a copy of a French mortar. The "Iko" weighed 2800 lb, requiring 42 men to move it. Twenty of the 220.5-lb finned shells could be fired per hour, for a maximum range of 1312 yd. The mortar was mounted on a platform of wooden railroad ties and placed in a pit 6.5 ft long by 5 ft wide and 18 in deep.

> Each infantry company has two grenade launchers, which are carried along with their ammunition on the close-combat equipment wagons.
>
> Grenade launchers are used primarily against living targets which cannot be engaged by hand-grenade throwers. A major advantage of the grenade launcher is that the shooter cannot be easily seen by the enemy.
>
> The grenades are used on targets 60 to 300 meters *[65 to 330 yards]* away. The launcher is very accurate. Lateral dispersion is three to five meters *[3.3 to 5.5 yards];* horizontal dispersion is approximately 50 meters *[55 yards].* The rate of fire is six to eight shots per minute. The

Infantrymen being trained by pioneers in the use of the 76mm light mortar, new pattern. After November of 1916, the rifled light trench mortar became a weapon of the infantry rather than the pioneers, as the pioneer arm could not provide enough personnel to serve the weapons.

grenade fragments spread up to 200 meters *[220 yards]*. The explosive power of the grenade and its effect on barbed wire are small. It is fired in curved or flat trajectories. In addition, the grenade launcher may be used to fire signal or messenger grenades, the latter up to 600 meters *[656 yards]*.

As a rule, a grenade launcher in position is operated by a three-man squad of one leader and two men. The leader gives orders for the operation of the launcher according to the requirements of the mission.

Additional personnel may be necessary to carry ammunition or provide observers for the launcher.

Each platoon of the infantry company must include two grenade-launcher squads and one replacement grenade-launcher squad.

When advancing the foremost man carries the launcher and the next carries the base plate. The rest of the squad carry the grenades in backpacks or sandbags. The leader carries accessories and spare parts, including a carpenter's level, wrenches, the lanyard. the firing pin, and firing-pin spring.

Grenade-launcher personnel must be skilled at:

rapid and pouncing action in the area;

mutual support when overcoming a difficult area;

rapid setting up of the launcher without the base plate in shell holes and shot-up trenches and beside crumbled stone walls;

rapid preparation for firing;

firing under the direction of a distant observer.

During the attack the grenade launcher is used for the preparation and lateral isolation of the breakthrough points as well as for engaging recognized machine-gun and rifle-grenade nests and other suspicious positions. For these operations the grenade launcher is used with the base plate. Unobtrusive, precise shooting under the direction of an officer must take place shortly before the attack. Depending on the circumstances, grenade launchers are given to the individual infantry waves or shock troops for the attack, in order to defeat any resistance which may arise. In this way the assault troops will not be detained in

their advance. If feasible, grenade launchers not used in the preparatory fire are to be brought along. The inclusion of the base plate depends on the type of soil. If the base plate is not initially carried forward, it is to be brought up later as soon as possible. The allocation of ammunition carriers may be necessary. In the conquered position the grenade launcher is used for pursuit fire, combat in the rear lines, and in the defense against counterattacks.

In the defense the grenade launcher is used to engage machine-gun and rifle-grenade nests as well as to deliver disruptive and annihilating fire, usually as roving launchers *[Wanderwerfer]*.

To both increase defensive fire and engage important points in the enemy position several grenade launchers may be combined into grenade-launcher squads in or better yet behind the front line. Alternating stations for the launchers should be established.

If the enemy penetrates the position, grenade launchers are placed on the sides and behind the breakthrough point to support the counterattack.

When not being fired, the grenade launchers are always to be laid on defensive fire tasks and protected from the weather and aerial observation. It is often practical for grenade launchers to be used in cooperation with searchlights.

Security precautions: Firing must take place only from behind cover. Grenades that lodge on the launching rod are not to be fired, as this may cause premature detonation or rounds to fall short. During practice shooting the range is to be closed out to a radius of 400 meters *[437 yards]*. All personnel close to the firing point are to take cover. Those directly involved are to wear steel helmets. If the grenade is not fired, the safety pin is to be reinserted, the grenade is to be removed from the firing post and the detonator is to be removed. Storage of ammunition is subject to the same regulations that apply to hand grenades. Duds are not to be touched. They are to be blown up.[4]

Opposite
Top: Pionier (left) of Württemberger Pioneer Battalion No.13 and Musketier of Württemberger Infantry Regiment No.127; the infantryman wears an "S" insignia on his upper left arm, denoting "Stosstrupp." In the left foreground is an M1916 grenade launcher loaded with a Wurfgranate 16. Combined weight of the launcher and steel platform (not shown) was 88 lb. Maximum range of the 5.5-lb grenade was 328 yd.

Bottom: Demonstration of portable flamethrowers and grenade launcher. The Guard Reserve Pioneer Regiment cut off the edges of the launcher base plate (third from left) and built wooden knapsack-type carriers for the launcher (second from left). From the right, the flamethrowers are the Kleif M.1914, late-model Kleif M.1915, Wex M.1917 (behind the propellant bottle), and two Kleif M.1917.

Assault Artillery

Following the experience of Assault Battalion No.5 (Rohr), other assault batteries were formed from May of 1916.[5] Their mission was to support infantry with close-range fire. They were named Infantry Gun Batteries *(Infanteriegeschützbatterien)* or Assault Accompanying Batteries *(Sturmbegleitbatterien)*. Infantry Gun Battery 1 was armed with six 37mm guns abandoned by Assault Detachment Rohr. It was dissolved on May 2, 1917.

Infantry Accompanying Batteries *(Infanteriebegleitbatterien)* were divisional artillery attached to the infantry for the duration of one operation. Initially these were called "shock batteries" *(Stossbatterien)*.[6] From 1916 one four-gun battery was attached to each attacking regiment in the main penetration zone to follow the first wave at 1000 to 2000 yards. The guns were usually positioned on the flanks of infantry battalions in the second wave and advanced by echelons of two-gun detachments so that two guns were always ready for use. Infantry Accompanying Batteries were under the direct orders of the infantry battalion commander. Equipped most often with the 77mm Field Gun Model 96, New Pattern *(7,7 cm Feldkanone 96*

Right: Kanonier of the field artillery in heavy assault order, armed with a Kar 98AZ. He wears the M1907/10 field jacket with black piping on the collar and cuffs; his M1916 gas-mask carrier is in the "alert" position, and his steel helmet is the M1918 model. Men of assault-artillery units were identically uniformed and equipped.

Crew manhandling an Infantry Gun L/16.5 (7,62 cm Infanteriegeschütz Krupp L/16.5), originally the Russian Putilov 76.2mm M/13. Krupp rechambered the gun to 77mm and added a shield, two seats, and a wheeled carriage. The Infantry Gun L/16.5 weighed 1338 lb emplaced and had an effective range of 4374 yd for high explosive and 656 yd for canister shot.

n/A.), they fired high explosive and Blue Cross gas shells in close support of the infantry. The crews of the guns were trained as infantrymen (some also underwent specialized training as infantry shock troops),[7] while the infantrymen in the second wave did everything possible to protect the guns and keep them moving. Each gun had a five-man pioneer squad to clear obstacles and from 1917 each battery was assigned two heavy machine-gun squads.

Although the infantry battalion commander designated the targets of the Infantry Accompanying Batteries, the commander of a double-gun echelon could open fire on any suitable targets on his own initiative. There was a total of 53 Infantry Accompanying Batteries at the end of the war.

A War Ministry order of June 20, 1916, formed Infantry Gun Batteries 2 to 10.[8] Recruited from the Replacement Detachment of the Mountain Gun Detachments, they were armed with captured Russian 76.2mm Putilov M/13 fortress guns which were rebored to the German caliber of 77mm in order to avoid having to supply special ammunition. The Krupp archives show that 104 such guns were manufactured from 1916 to 1917. They were called the *7,62cm Infanteriekanone L/16,5;* the tubes were not shortened, being milled from the start at 16.5 calibers or 49.6 inches (1.26m) long. A shield, two seats, and a carriage were added to each gun, and Assault Battalion Rohr trained each six-man crew.

The 77mm Field Cannon 96, new pattern, of a Close Combat Battery (Nahkampfbatterie). This version of the gun was designated the 77mm Infantry Gun L/27 (7,7 cm Infanteriegeschütz L/27). Fifty Close Combat Batteries numbered 201-250 were formed on January 26, 1917, for antitank use. The Infantry Gun L/27 had small-diameter wheels, a crew of six, and a maximum range of 8530 yd. Each battery was composed of six guns.

On January 26, 1917, the War Ministry ordered the formation of 50 six-gun Close Combat Batteries *(Nahkampfbatterien),* numbered 201-250, which would be used against tanks.[9] They would be armed with a modification of the 77mm Field Gun 96, New Pattern, designated the 77mm Infantry Gun L/27 *(7,7 cm Infanteriegeschütz L/27).* Since machine guns with armor-piercing bullets were very successful in the antitank role at close range, and field and foot artillery were effective at longer ranges, Close Combat Batteries were withdrawn from service in May of 1917. Twenty-seven batteries were attached to field-artillery regiments as third batteries and used traditionally, while the remaining 23 became Infantry Gun Batteries 28 to 50. These were deployed in August of 1917, deemed unsatisfactory, and dissolved in November 1917. Only Infantry Gun Battery 28 remained, attached to Assault Battalion No.5 (Rohr) for instructional purposes.[10] Among the 18 assault units, only Assault Battalion No.5 (Rohr) always had a group or battery of artillery as a permanent part. This group or battery remained a "historic" unit owing to the fact that it was the first assault-artillery unit of the German army.

The *OHL* then acquired Skoda 75mm M.15 mountain guns *(7,5 cm Gebirgskanone M15)* from the Austro-Hungarian army and reformed the Infantry Gun Batteries, which were sent to the front in May of 1918. First Infantry Gun Batteries 29 to 36 were deployed, followed in June by Infantry Gun Batteries 37 to 51. Infantry-gun batteries were often attached to the assault battalions but never permanently. Several batteries could be attached to one battalion simultaneously, depending on the mission. By November

Three Kanoniere of a Guard Field Artillery Regiment serving in Close Combat Battery 210. The red shoulder straps of their M1915 blouses feature an exploding grenade, the letters "NG" (for "Nahkampfgeschütz") and the number "210" in yellow. They are equipped with knapsacks, Pickelhauben with the ball removed, M1911 cavalry-style ammunition pouches that hold 60 rounds, M1915 Gummimasken, and Kar 98AZ carbines.

of 1918 there was a total of 50 batteries, numbered 2 to 51; Bavarian batteries were not numbered separately. In 1917 Infantry Gun Platoons *(Infanteriegeschützzüge)* 701, 702, and 703 were formed in the *Asienkorps* on the Palestinian-Mesopotamian front.

Infantry Gun Batteries were comprised of six guns each and were assigned to individual infantry battalions as direct-fire weapons.[11] They followed directly behind the second line of the first assault wave and were hauled by hand. Each attack division received one battery, its guns distributed among the infantry battalions in the first wave. If the advance stalled, the guns were immediately withdrawn. Infantry guns did not fire in the artillery preparation or in the creeping barrage. They engaged targets usually at ranges of less than 1095 yards.

For the infantry gun to be successful, the deciding factor was not the number of rounds fired but the accuracy of each round and the speed in which the infantry could take advantage of the results obtained by the gun.[12] Machine guns, tanks, and snipers were nearly always the most important targets of infantry guns. The entire six-gun battery was rarely used as a whole. Instead, the infantry regimental commander assigned single pieces or sections to battalions. Mobility and bold decision-making generally avoided losses to the infantry guns. Infantry guns were often placed in the open to obtain quick results. Explosive shells *(Brisanzgranaten)* with delayed-action or instantaneous fuses were very effective; delayed-action fuses were used to fire ricochets against targets such as tanks and fortifications. The armor-piercing shell *(Panzerkopf)* was fired at hardened targets, while the Blue Cross explosive shell *(Blaukreuzbrisanzgeschoss)* was used to engage infantry with poison gas.

Battery squads *(Batterietrupps)* accompanied the advance infantry elements to conduct reconnaissance for the infantry guns. Like the crews of the Infantry Accompanying Guns they were trained as infantry shock troops. Assault Battalion No.5 (Rohr) trained battery troops and crews of the Infantry Accompanying Batteries and Infantry Gun Batteries, all of whom were recruited from the field artillery:

> The infantry-gun batteries that belonged to the assault battalions or were assigned to them (Assault Battalion Rohr had modern Krupp mountain howitzers, caliber 105mm, that could be broken down) were particularly suitable for suppressing the enemy at the break-through points and for gradually shooting ahead of the attacking assault troops. These could, thanks to the good training and excellent capabilities of the gun commanders and gunners, move to within 50-100 meters of their targets. Furthermore the batteries in proximity to the infantry line had to engage targets that were too close to their own positions to be detected by other artillery. In particular these targets were trenches, machine-gun positions, flanking installations, and so on. The mission of the howitzer battery and/or infantry guns was also to block the enemy approach routes in the immediate proximity to the sections of trench that were to be held. They had to unexpectedly open fire at the moment of the assault. Success had to be achieved through the rate of fire and the accuracy of the gun in the shortest time. In general only one position was to be taken per mission.[13]

Youthful Kanonier of an Infantry Gun Battery attached to an assault battalion. He wears a privately purchased M1907/10 field jacket with what appears to be a grenade badge on the upper left sleeve, and he is armed with a trench dagger to denote his role as an assault artilleryman.

Postwar photo of Austrian Skoda 75mm Mountain Gun M.15 (7,5 cm Gebirgskanone M.15), which replaced the Infantry Gun L/16.5 and Infantry Gun L/27 when the Infantry Gun Batteries were redeployed in May of 1918. With a crew of six, the 75mm Mountain Gun M.15 weighed 1359 lb when emplaced. It had a maximum range of 7655 yd.

Machine Guns

On August 10, 1915, the War Ministry ordered the creation of the 1st and 2nd Automatic Rifle Battalions *(1. and 2. Musketen-Bataillone)*.[14] An Automatic Rifle Battalion was comprised of three companies, each with a compliment of four officers and 160 NCOs and men.[15] Each company was armed with 30 Danish Madsen light machine guns, each of which was operated by a four-man squad.

The Automatic Rifle Battalions were first used at Champagne in September of 1915. They were placed in the second or third line in order to repel assaults. On March 10, 1916, they were renamed the 4th and 5th Battalions of Infantry Regiment No.117, but only a month later the War Ministry ordered that they be given their previous designation of Automatic Rifle Battalions 1 and 2.

Mountain troops training with the Danish Madsen M1904 light machine gun, April of 1918. Cockades and belt buckles are Prussian, Saxon, and Bavarian; one man is a pioneer, and two carry the Lange Pistole 08. The 8mm Madsen used a curved 25-, 30-, or 40-round magazine fitted to the top of the receiver. It fired 450 rounds per minute, weighed 16 lb, and had an effective range of about 656 yd.

During the Battle of the Somme the Automatic Rifle Battalions were placed in the second line and moved around to engage British troops at points of breakthrough. They suffered heavy casualties due to artillery. By the spring of 1917 the Madsen light machine guns of the Automatic Rifle Battalions had been replaced with British Lewis guns and German weapons. On April 22, 1918, the units were transformed into Machine Gun Marksman Detachments but retained their designation as Automatic Rifle Battalions.

Schütze of a machine-gun company, 4th Guard Grenadier Regiment. On his left sleeve he wears the M1916 Machine Gun Marksman badge (Maschinengewehr-Scharfschützen-Abzeichen) consisting of a brass MG08 surrounded by a cartridge belt, mounted on a field-gray cloth oval. The badge was issued to members of Machine Gun Marksman Detachments (Maschinengewehr-Scharfschützen-Abteilungen).

Machine Gun Marksman Detachments

The War Ministry order of January 17, 1916, created Machine Gun Marksman Sections *(Maschinengewehr-Scharfschützen-Truppes)* staffed by veteran machine gunners.[16] These 86-man sections would each be armed with six heavy machine guns and would be deployed at decisive points of the battle. Between February and May 200 such sections were raised.

On August 25, 1916, the Machine Gun Marksman Sections were organized into 83 Machine Gun Marksman Detachments *(Maschinengewehr-Scharfschützen-Abteilungen);* 1 to 79 were Prussian and 1 to 4 were Bavarian. Each Detachment would be comprised of three Machine Gun Marksman Sections, each of which would thereby be transformed into companies. The *OHL* determined the disposition of the Machine Gun Marksman Detachments, attaching them to individual armies, corps, and divisions.

Each Machine Gun Marksman Detachment was initially armed with 18 heavy weapons; on September 17, 1917, the number of guns per detachment was ordered doubled. The increase came in two installments that raised the number of guns in each detachment first to 27 and then to 36.

Light Machine Guns

On July 25, 1916, the War Ministry ordered the formation of autonomous Light Machine Gun Detachments *(leichtes-Maschinengewehr-Abteilungen)* 1 to 111.[17] Each Detachment was comprised of one officer and 44 NCOs and men and was armed with three Bergmann lMG *(leichte-Maschinengewehr)* 15 light machine guns.[18] The 111 Light Machine Gun Detachments were

Bergmann lMG (leichte Maschinengewehr) 15 light machine gun, new pattern, used to arm Light Machine Gun Detachments (Leichtes-Maschinengewehr-Abteilungen) 1 to 111 in July of 1916. The air-cooled, belt-fed Bergmann weighed 30 lb and had a firing rate of 600 rounds per minute. This gun has been fitted with the bipod of a Mauser antitank rifle.

Opposite
Top: Machine-gun course at Givry, April of 1918. Weapons include one MG08 heavy machine gun, two lMG08/15 light machine guns, and one British Lewis Light Machine Gun. The air-cooled Lewis was fed with 47-round drums; the Germans captured thousands of the weapons and rechambered them to accept German 7.92mm ammunition. Issued to assault troops, the Lewis weighed 26.5 lb, fired 600 rounds per minute, and had a maximum range of 3500 yd.

Bottom: The wheeled cart used to transport the lMG08/15 light machine gun, ammunition, and accessories. Note the rubber steam-condensation hose wrapped around the water jacket. The lMG08/15 weighed 43 lb with a full water jacket and 100-round drum (Trommel). It had a rate of fire of 450 rounds per minute and a maximum range of 1300 yd.

Two men of an Armored Vehicle Machine Gun Platoon in France, 1917. On the left is a Fahrer of the Motor Transport Troops whose M1915 blouse displays Guard lace and the light-gray shoulder straps mandated in September of 1915. His companion is an Unteroffizier recruited from a Machine Gun Marksman Detachment.

formed with infantrymen from the Döberitz Machine Gun School.[19] Although Bergmann lMG15 guns had a serious deficiency in that they could rapid-fire only 300 rounds before overheating, the barrels were easily changed. Most of the Light Machine Gun Detachments were used on the eastern front, where air-cooled weapons were more efficient in sub-zero temperatures. Bergmann light machine guns were mostly withdrawn from service when the lMG08/15 became available in early 1917.

From December 12, 1916, each company of infantry and *Jäger* was informally armed with three light machine guns.[20] The 111 autonomous light machine-gun detachments were dissolved in June of 1917, when the War Ministry officially established a light machine-gun detachment in each infantry and *Jäger* company. At the same time the number of weapons in each company light machine-gun detachment was doubled from three to six. This order applied to infantry assault battalions as well.

The number of heavy weapons in machine-gun companies and Machine Gun Marksman Sections was also doubled on September 17, 1917. Each company and Marksman Section had its guns increased first to nine and then to 12, giving each infantry battalion and Machine Gun Marksman Detachment a total of 36 weapons. The heavy machine gun was considered an arm of the battalion, while the light machine gun was an arm of the company.

In November of 1917 each artillery battery on the western front formed a machine-gun detachment to defend against aircraft and to engage in close-quarter combat against infantry. Each detachment – essentially a platoon – was armed with two heavy machine guns. This was not a new idea; in his report on lessons learned during the Battle of the Somme, dated January 30, 1917, *General* Fritz von Below had recommended that all forward artillery positions be issued machine guns and that the men of the field artillery be trained in how to use them.[21]

From August 20, 1918, each bicycle company was armed with three light machine guns and was equipped with specially designed bicycles to transport them.[22] In 1918 the Allies captured and translated the German document "Employment of Light Machine Guns in the Attack":

> The light machine gun groups (each of one NCO, one gunner, one loader, two carriers, and four reserve carriers, with one light machine gun), which are to be equipped for independent action (rifles, pistols, hand grenades, entrenching tools) form, owing to their great mobility and concentrated fire power, the framework of the infantry attack. They can carry on the fire fight, if necessary, without any groups of riflemen. There should be two of these machine gun groups in each infantry platoon, so that they may mutually support each other by fire.
>
> From the jumping-off trenches, the machine gun groups push as far forward as they can (if possible, before the end of the artillery and trench mortar preparatory bombardment) as "offensive points" ("offensive nests"). Their task is to secure the advance of their own infantry within the sectors allotted to them, by keeping down the fire of the enemy's front line and of any hostile machine guns which may remain intact. The fire of the advanced light machine guns will be opened suddenly, directly the artillery and trench mortar preparatory bombardment ceases; it will cease when the first wave penetrates into the enemy's position. These machine gun groups then follow the first wave.
>
> Other machine gun groups form part of the first wave. Their place is with the platoon commanders. During the advance, they open fire at

> close range; they take part in rolling up the enemy's trenches, and form the main fire power of the platoons which push right through as far as the initial objective of the assault. Here the machine gun groups will at once dig themselves in, will cover the reorganization of the attacking troops and will pursue the retreating enemy with fire. If bunching occurs in the line the machine gun groups which are following up will fill the resulting gaps either by occupying them or by fire. If the advanced machine gun groups encounter resistance, they will take up the fire fight, keep down the enemy's fire by their own fire, and thus enable the groups of riflemen and machine gun groups following them up to reach the enemy.[23]

By the end of the war most infantry and *Jäger* companies had six light machine guns (54 to 72 per regiment).[24] Each infantry battalion had 10 to 12 heavy machine guns. In 1914 a 12-battalion active division possessed 24 machine guns; in the winter of 1917-1918 a nine-battalion division had 216 light machine guns and 144 heavy, for a total of 360. There were enough machine guns that nearly all individual sections or squads could use them. In three and a half years the rifle strength of divisions had been halved, while the machine-gun strength had been multiplied 15 times. The ratio of firepower to men exposed was nearly tripled.

Armored Vehicle Machine Gun Units

Armored Vehicle Machine Gun Detachment 1 *(Panzer-Kraftwagen-Maschinengewehr-Abteilung 1)* was formed on November 16, 1916.[25] Armored cars were used in surprise assaults, appearing suddenly at the point of breakthrough and engaging the enemy with machine guns at close range. Since the cars had difficulty operating off road and were vulnerable

Erhardt/17, an improvement of the Erhardt/15. This vehicle belongs to Armored Vehicle Machine Gun Platoon 6, photographed on the eastern front. The radio mast has been extended, and the crewman on the right winds the wire onto a reel. Note the size of the car, which had a crew of eight or nine and was armed with three MG08 machine guns. Armored Vehicle Machine Gun Platoons 2-6 each included two Erhardt/17.

Heavy machine-gun squad of the 1st Machine Gun Company, II Landsturm Infantry Battalion "Gera" (XI/25), December of 1917. The MG08 has been fitted with the wheeled carriage of a captured Russian M1910 Maxim; it also includes barrel armor, an armored face shield, and a flash shield. Note the M1911 ammunition boxes (Patronenkasten 11) that each hold two 250-round belts. The wheeled carriage was an attempt to lighten the gun and make it more mobile for use by assault troops.

Opposite
Top: Unit squad (Einheitsgruppe) of Infantry Regiment No.95 (6. thüringisches Infanterie-Regiment Nr.95), 38th Infantry Division. Comprised of a light machine-gun squad and a rifleman-grenadier squad, the unit squad could number up to 16 men. By 1918 the unit squad was the smallest tactical unit. This squad is armed with an lMG08/15 and Kar 98AZ carbines.

Bottom: Light Machine Gun Detachment of an infantry company displaying its three lMG08/15. From December 12, 1916, each company of infantry and Jäger was unofficially armed with three Bergmann lMG15. In early 1917 the Bergmann was replaced with the lMG08/15, and in June the War Ministry officially established a light machine-gun detachment in each infantry and Jäger company, doubling the number of weapons from three to six.

to artillery, they were most effective when used in counterinsurgency operations, such as in the Ukraine and the Caucasus.

Armored Vehicle Machine Gun Platoons 2 to 6 were established in 1917, followed in 1918 by Armored Vehicle Machine Gun Platoons 7 to 11. Each Armored Vehicle Machine Gun Platoon was comprised of two officers, 33 NCOs and men, and two armored cars.

The first unit, Armored Vehicle Machine Gun Detachment 1, was equipped with three prototype armored cars – the Daimler/15, the Erhardt/15, and the Büssing/15 – as well as two improvised vehicles.[26] Each armored car was crewed by eight or nine men and armed with three heavy machine guns that could be fired from 10 alternative mountings in the body and turret.

Armored Vehicle Machine Gun Platoons 2 to 11 were each equipped with two Erhardt/17 armored cars and supporting vehicles. Like the prototype armored cars, the Erhardt/17 was crewed by eight or nine men and armed with three heavy machine guns which could be fired from 10 alternative mountings in the body and turret.

The Unit Squad

By late 1917, infantry platoons were no longer composed entirely of riflemen. The platoon could contain rifle squads, assault squads, grenade-launcher squads, rifle-grenade squads, and light machine-gun squads. Officially the light machine-gun squad consisted of eight men.[27] One gunner carried the weapon, while two or three others carried ammunition and water. Four or five more machine gunners followed the first squad, armed with carbines or rifles and hand grenades. This second squad often maneuvered as a rifle squad covered by the light machine gun.

This organization led to the creation of the "unit squad" *(Einheitsgruppe)* of a light machine-gun squad and a rifleman-grenadier squad of four to eight men. During the Spring Offensives of 1918, the unit squad was the smallest tactical unit.[28] It could both defend itself and go on the offensive. Although the unit squad was not officially adopted by the German army during the war, individual infantry regiments incorporated it in their own ways.[29] In 1918 one company of the Bavarian *Leib* Regiment, for example, was organized into five platoons:

Shock Troop IV, 3rd Platoon, 10th Company, Infantry Regiment No. 409, armed with M1916 stick grenades. Several appear to be older men. The regiment was raised in Hamburg in 1916 and assigned to the 203rd Infantry Division. It fought on both the eastern and western fronts, suffering heavy casualties.

a) three combat platoons, each composed of two unit squads and one assault squad;
b) one replacement platoon *(Erganzungszug)* of four NCOs, 16 men, and an armorer;
c) one reserve platoon *(Reservezug)* consisting of a reconnaissance squad and a grenade-launcher squad.

A second company of the Bavarian *Leib* Regiment had four platoons, three of which were combat platoons:

First combat platoon:
two rifle squads;
two light machine-gun squads;
one grenade-launcher squad.

Second combat platoon:
two rifle squads;
two light machine-gun squads.

Third combat platoon:
two rifle squads;
two light machine-gun squads;
one eight-man assault squad.

Company headquarters platoon:
one four-man assault squad;
one reconnaissance squad.

Endnotes

[1] The information on trench mortars is found in Cron, pp. 160-165, and *Oberleutnant* a. D. Biermann, "Die Entwicklung der deutschen Minenwerferwaffe, *Das Ehrenbuch der deutschen Pioniere,* pp. 489-492.

[2] Cron, p. 113.

[3] War Department, *Notes on the German Army in the War* (Washington, D.C.: Government Printing Office, 1917), p. 23.

[4] Kriegsministerium, *Ausbildungsvorschrift für die Fusstruppen im Kriege* (Berlin: Reichsdruckerei, 1918), pp. 113-119.

[5] Larcade, pp. 30-32.

[6] Zabecki, p. 43.

[7] "Accompanying and Infantry Batteries," *The Field Artillery Journal* Volume 8, January-March 1918, edited by Arthur F. Cassels (Philadelphia: J. B. Lippincott Company, 1918), p. 424.

[8] Larcade, p. 30.

[9] Cron, p. 140.

[10] Larcade, pp. 30, 32.

[11] Zabecki, p. 43-44.

[12] "German Artillery," *The Field Artillery Journal* Volume 8, pp. 579-585.

[13] Von Schwerin, p. 113.

[14] Cron, p. 120.

[15] Ian Drury and Gerry Embleton, *German Stormtrooper 1914-1918: Warrior Series No.12* (London: Osprey, 1995), p. 14.

[16] Cron, p. 122-123.

[17] Ibid.

[18] D. S. V. Fosten and R. J. Marrion, *The German Army 1914-18* (London: Osprey Publishing, 1978), p. 23.

[19] John Walter, *Central Powers' Small Arms of World War One* (Ramsbury, Marlborough, Wiltshire: The Crowood Press, 1999). p. 175.

[20] Cron, p. 122-123.

[21] *Experience of the German 1st Army,* p. 47.

[22] Cron, p. 124.

[23] War Department, *A Survey of German Tactics, 1918* (Washington, D.C.: Government Printing Office, 1918), pp. 24-25.

[24] Charles Francis Atkinson, "Army," *The Encyclopædia Britannica, the New Volumes,* Volume 30 (London and New York: The Enclyclopædia Britannica Company, Ltd., 1922). p. 236.

[25] Cron, pp. 124, 368.

[26] B. T. White, *Tanks and other Armored Fighting Vehicles 1900 to 1918* (New York: MacMillan Publishing Co., 1970), pp. 139-140, 165-166.

[27] Gudmundsson, pp. 100.

[28] John A. English, *A Perspective on Infantry* (New York: Praeger Publishers, 1981), p. 25.

[29] Gudmundsson, pp. 100.

CHAPTER 9

Short Training Courses in Assault Tactics

Füsilier of the 5th Company, Fusilier Regiment No.80 (Füsilier-Regiment von Gersdorf [kurhessiches] Nr.80). He wears a simplified field jacket with Guard lace in a style that dates back to the 18th century. In mid-November of 1916, shock troops of Fusilier Regiment No.80 were trained in the use of specialized weapons such as a single-shot "jet" flamethrower.

Shock-troop Training of Fusilier Regiment No.80

"The training of shock troops; revelations of a prisoner interrogated by French intelligence," December 7, 1916:

> The training course for shock troops of the 21st Infantry Division, Tenth Army, was provided in Charey during the time the XVIII Army Corps was in Saint-Mihiel. The 21st Infantry Division was transferred to Landrecies on or about November 15, 1916, along with its field recruit depot. The duration of the course seemed to be three weeks. The prisoner belonged to a group of 90 men of Fusilier Regiment No.80 who took the course under the direction of a Lieutenant VON TSUTY of Fusilier Regiment No.80, assisted by some noncommissioned officers.
>
> **Training Ground**
>
> The exercises took place in a group of trenches constructed using photographs of our lines taken by German aviators.
>
> At Charey the training trenches occupied a surface area of 2000 meters *[2187 sq. yd];* at Landrecies the surface area was less than half of that.
>
> **Program**
>
> The course program includes:
>
> 1. Throwing hand grenades for height, for length, and for height and length together.
> 2. The construction and destruction of trenches; the reconstruction of captured trenches.
> 3. Attacks on trenches.
> 4. Attacks on blockhouses.
> 5. Use of the jet flamethrower *[Flammenwerfer de jet]* and *Brandröhre* or fire tubes, the descriptions of which are given below.

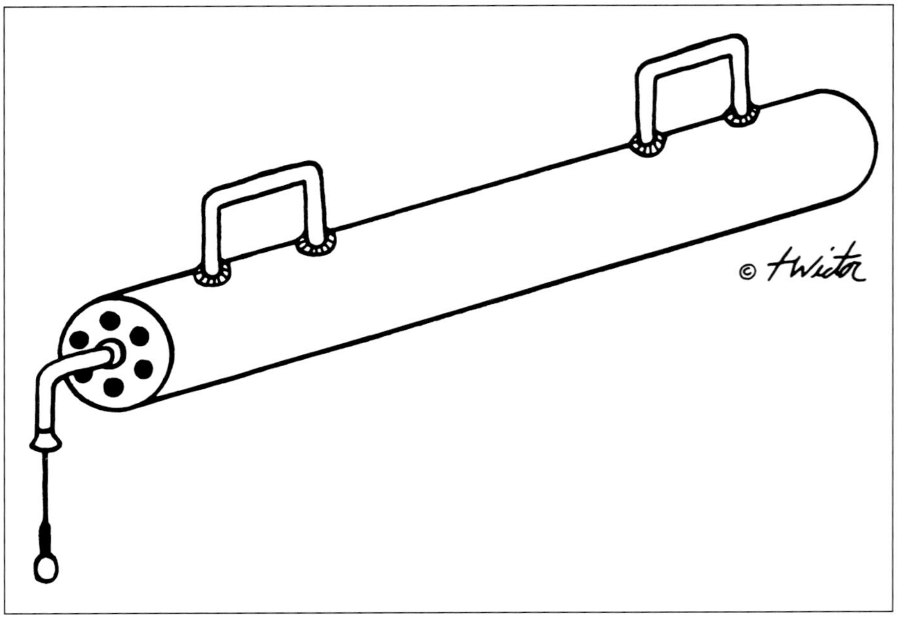

Provisional rendering of single-shot "jet" flamethrower created by the shock troops of Fusilier Regiment No.80 for use at Verdun, November of 1916. It consisted of an iron pipe 39-47 in long, fitted with two handles. The pipe was filled with oil that was ignited by a friction primer attached to the mouth of the device. Deployed against fortified positions such as bunkers, the "jet" flamethrower was discarded after one use.

Assault squad of an unidentified Landwehr infantry regiment. Weapons consist of stick grenades and Gew 98 rifles. The squad leader (second from left) is a Gefreiter who carries a binocular case on his belt. Shock troops omitted ammunition pouches during missions of short duration, such as identifying the unit in the opposing trench or capturing prisoners for interrogation.

Execution of Exercises

Every morning two hours are given over to the throwing of hand grenades from all positions, kneeling, prone, and while running. In addition, many more exercises are carried out, for the purpose of destroying wire barricades by means of concentrated grenade charges and cleaning out trenches.

Load of a Man of a Shock Troop

Each man must carry a minimum of 10 to 15 hand grenades:

- five stick grenades hung from the belt,
- five small defensive "egg" grenades,
- five large spherical defensive grenades.

In reality the majority of the men carried more than 20 grenades.

Additionally, each soldier must have a "geballte Ladung" (concentrated charge) attached to the belt and a box of powder (about 30 X 20 cm) *[11.8 X 7.8 in]*. During the attacks, the soldiers must deploy, in addition to the concentrated charge that is intended to clean out the trenches, an elongated charge that is used to breach barbed wire. One man can carry the elongated charge.

The men of the shock troops are equipped with a special helmet which is very light and protects well.

Above: Shock troops of Badener Grenadier Regiment No.110 in action. Taken with an unauthorized personal camera, the image shows the desolation of the typical battlefield and the minimal equipment of assault troops. The grenadier in the foreground carries only one grenade bag instead of the usual two.

Left: Assault troops pose with British Mark II tank No.799, knocked out at Arras on April 12, 1917. They wear white twill fatigue jackets over their tunics, likely to identify themselves to German snipers and forward artillery observers. The enlisted man (right) has also wrapped his marching boots in sandbags to keep out mud.

Jet Flamethrower

These small flamethrowers (between 1 and 1.2 meters *[3.3 to 3.9 ft]* long) are made of iron and equipped with two handles. They contain a flammable liquid and a wick inside, one end of which is ignited with a primer and the other of which leads into the liquid near the mouth of the apparatus:

> These flamethrowers are held to the openings of bunkers or shelters and are discarded afterward.

Brandröhre

This incendiary device consists of a tin tube one meter long *[39 in]* and 20 centimeters *[8 in]* in diameter .

It contains sulfur or a similar product. It is ignited by means of a match and brought into action, and then discarded as in the case of the jet flamethrower.[1]

To date no other account of the "jet flamethrower" have been located. If it existed, it may have been a weapon unique to Fusilier Regiment No.80.

Unteroffizier Reuder of Reserve Infantry Regiment No.15, equipped as a trench raider. He wears his M1915 Gummimaske in the "alert" position and is armed with two M1916 stick grenades and an Austrian 9mm Steyr M12 automatic pistol tucked into his belt. Due to shortages of the P08, German soldiers often purchased Austrian pistols.

German Infantry Divisions, January of 1917

The combat units of a German infantry division in January of 1917 were:

- one infantry brigade (three regiments);
- one to three assault companies (three 40-man platoons in each);
- two cavalry squadrons;
- one or two pioneer companies;
- one mortar company;
- one artillery regiment.[2]

Each infantry regiment was composed of three battalions.

A battalion was comprised of four infantry companies (180 rifles each) armed with three light machine guns each; one machine-gun company armed with six heavy weapons; one mortar platoon armed with four light trench mortars; and one grenade-launcher platoon armed with eight weapons.

Each pioneer company was armed with six smoothbore light trench mortars and two grenade launchers.

The mortar company was armed with two heavy, four medium, and 12 light weapons.

The artillery regiment was comprised of three detachments of three batteries each; three batteries were armed with four 105mm light howitzers each; six batteries were armed with four 77mm light field guns each.

Infantry Platoons and Light Machine Guns

"Proposed Regulation for Instruction of Infantry Troops in the Field," 1917:

I. Composition and Subdividing.

The company is composed of 3 platoons (sections). The platoon is commanded by an officer, or, in his absence, by a sergeant. It is subdivided into squads (groups).

The squad comprises 4 files of 2 men and is commanded by a sergeant or gefreiter (corporal). In war time it forms a squad commanded by a squad leader.

Assault squad of Badener Infantry Regiment No.111 (Infanterie-Regiment Markgraf Ludwig Wilhelm [3. badisches] Nr.111). Armed with P08 and C96 pistols and hand grenades, they wear the M1917 leather gas mask (Lederschutzmaske).

Opposite
Top: Shock troop, 2nd Machine Gun Company, Infantry Regiment No.168 (5. großherzolglich hessisches Infanterie-Regiment Nr.168), April of 1917. The Gefreiter third from the right is armed with a small automatic pistol – probably a Mauser 7.65mm M1914 – and a DEMAG dagger-bayonet. Note that the Schütze on the right wears an oval metal badge on his lower left sleeve; it appears to represent a helmeted head facing forward and is likely an unofficial shock-troop badge.

Bottom: Heavy machine-gun squad of a shock troop of Saxon Infantry Regiment No.183, armed with a captured British Vickers Mk I machine gun, hand grenades, and P08 pistols. This squad uses the gun without its tripod. The loader is second from the right, with boxes of ammunition over his shoulder, while the water carrier is on the right.

When the number of squads is over 3 the platoon is divided into two half platoons.

The organization of a fourth platoon depends upon the action demanded of the company, whether resistance of long duration or violent decisive action.

In the first instance (long drawn out combat) it is wise to form a fourth platoon comprising a certain number of noncommissioned officers (platoon and squad leaders), and specialists (detachments for assault or sturmtrupps), grenadiers, sharpshooters, automatic riflemen, and grenade throwers. This platoon, maintained in reserve, allows the company to conserve its fighting strength for the duration of the action.

In the second instance (violent, decisive action) noncommissioned officers and men, especially chosen, can be united in a *special platoon* and placed at the disposition of the company commander.

In addition to its three platoons the company includes a section of machine guns (infantry machine-gun trupp) for the automatic rifles, or a section of light machine guns, which are just now being issued.

To sum up, the German company remains at three platoons as before, but the eventual formation of a fourth platoon is provided for in case of long-drawn-out strain or particular violence of action.

Men using automatic rifles form a special unit belonging to the company but not bearing the title of fourth platoon.

II. *[Light]* Machine-gun Section (Inf. M. G. Trupp).

The section is commanded by an officer.

It comprises:

One experienced sergeant taking duties of armament sergeant. To each gun, one sergeant or gefreiter in charge of gun, four gunners, numbered 1 to 4 (No. 2 is the aiming gunner), six guns and one cart for the transport of guns and ammunition.

All the gunners should be trained in the service of aiming.

All in the section are armed with automatic pistols.

The section takes its place as a rule at the left of the company.

During marches the material is placed on the cart, which follows immediately behind the section.

If the march is known to be long, two to four horses are used.

In operation once the material is unloaded the carrying is done by summoning auxiliary carriers furnished by the company.

The number of carriers varies. As a rule a squad of seven carriers and a chief of squad is provided for each gun. They carry ammunition and the water jackets of the guns.

The guns being in position, the squad of carriers becomes a squad of combatants again.[3]

Opposite: Machine Gun Squad Sien (M.G.-Gruppe Sien) of Reserve Infantry Regiment No.15, August of 1917. Although the IMG08/15 officially had an eight-man squad, many reserve infantry regiments lacked machine gunners and were chronically under strength.

Shock troop of the 1st Company, 2nd Landsturm Infantry Battalion Hannover (X/8), 47th Reserve Division, February of 1917. They are equipped with rolled greatcoats and tent sections, grenade bags, pioneer shovels, and Gew 98 rifles. In Landsturm formations the younger, fitter men of the shock troops often carried out the bulk of the combat duties. Many Landsturm shock troops saw no action.

Assault Course Taught by Assault Battalion No.1
Order Ia/Ie No.25883, "Concerning: Assault Battalion and Flamethrower Battalion No.1," January 1, 1917.[4]

1. 1st Assault Battalion of the First Army is composed of:

three assault companies;
one machine-gun company;
one trench-mortar company.
Attached to this are:
three batteries of infantry guns;
one flamethrower platoon
(headquartered in Ghissignies).

Its mission is to serve as a training unit and to be committed to specific combat operations.

As a training unit it will be made available to the army to the furthest extent possible.

2. Every Thursday, from 1000 hours to 1300 hours, the battalion will organize on its training ground a demonstration of the special formations used by assault troops. These operations will conclude with an important live-ammunition exercise using all weapons of assault. On prior request the base commander at Le Quesnoy will arrange for the quartering of the officers or detachments wishing to take part.

If large detachments wish to assist, it is necessary for them to inform the assault battalion.

For ease of transporting officers of Le Quesnoy to the training ground the assault battalion will provide trucks when possible.

Grenadiers of Germano-Austrian Assault Battalion No.17 at Rohatyn, Galicia, spring or summer of 1917. They are throwing hand grenades from a kneeling position; an egg grenade inside a sock has been captured in midflight (top). A hole has been cut in the sock to allow the lanyard to protrude. The crowd of officers includes the commander of the Turkish XV Corps, Brigadier General Cevat Paşa (left).

Machine gunners undergoing assault training at Rohatyn. The MG08 has been fitted with a trench mount to reduce its weight so that it can be taken out into No Man's Land to provide support for assault troops. Firing from shell holes, machine gunners prevented the enemy from manning his parapets during the assault.

3. If the divisions intend to let their assault detachments train further with the assault battalion, a request must be made to the Commander of the First Army before the strength of the detachment can be determined. Training period 2-3 weeks.

4. Training in common for troops of the divisions behind the front, with the assault battalion and the 1st Battalion of the Guard Reserve Pioneer Regiment (Flamethrowers), can take place in Le Quesnoy by direct agreement at any time.

5. On each Friday some divisional officers and noncommissioned officers (also from recruit depots) may request one six-day training course – arrival and departures on Sundays – from the Commander of the First Army.

6. On each Friday the *[army]* groups may request that the Commander of the First Army provide assault-battalion training personnel for the coming week for the field recruit depots, the battalions at rest, or the divisions training behind the front.

Duration of these duty assignments is about three days per location.

7. At the same time flamethrower squads may be requested from the Commander of the First Army.

It must be considered that the 1st Battalion of the Guard Reserve Pioneer Regiment is at present weakened by its detached duties.

8. Accommodation and rations *[for the assault-battalion training personnel and flamethrower pioneers]* are in each case provided by the unit to which the duty assignment takes place.

Accordingly the assault battalion must come to an agreement with the Inspectorate of Lines of Communication.

This Unteroffizier of a Landwehr infantry regiment displays a cloth grenade badge on his upper left sleeve. Hand-grenade squads of infantry platoons wore such unofficial insignia; it had no standard configuration or color.

9. Every Sunday the commanders of the assault battalion and the 1st Battalion of the Guard Reserve Pioneer Regiment will contact the Commander of the First Army by telephone and convey the requirements of their respective battalions, in respect to Paragraphs 3 and 4; the Commander of the First Army will transmit to the two battalion commanders the requirements concerning Paragraphs 5 and 7.

10. *[Army]* groups can propose further utilization of the assault battalion each time such a requirement arises.

11. Employment of parts of the assault battalion and the 1st Battalion of the Guard Reserve Pioneer Regiment (Flamethrowers) is determined by the Commander of the First Army. Generally a decision will be made only after a personal investigation by the battalion commanders and a consultation with the First Army Commander. In discussions and preliminary training prior to the employment the battalion commanders must participate as personally as possible.

The 25-man Shock Platoon (Stosszug) of the 10th Company, Infantry Regiment No.20 (Infanterie-Regiment Graf Tauentzien von Wittenberg [3. Brandenburgisches] Nr.20), 5th Guard Infantry Division. Most are equipped with grenade bags, gas-mask containers, and Gew 98 rifles or pistols.

Opposite
Top: Shock troops attending an assault course taught by Jäger (Assault) Battalion No.3; the instructor stands on the right, identified by his all-green bayonet knot. These soldiers belong to units from all over the German empire.

Bottom: Austrian soldiers and Wehrmänner of Landwehr Infantry Regiment No.71 attend assault school (Sturm-Schule) in 1917. Part of the 215th Infantry Division, Landwehr Infantry Regiment No.71 spent most of the war on the eastern front and was extremely proficient in shock-troop tactics.

12. The First Army Commander's orders Ia No.1174 Secret of October 2, 1916, and Ia No.1722 Secret of November 21, 1916 (in the fundamental instructions T.15 and T.16) are annulled by the present order, which receives the number T.15.
(signed)VON BELOW.

Uniforms of the Assault Battalions

"War Ministry Order No.1/17 g. B3," February 6, 1917:

> Concerning the uniform and the insignia of the Prussian assault battalions and Assault Company No.13, the following prescriptions apply:

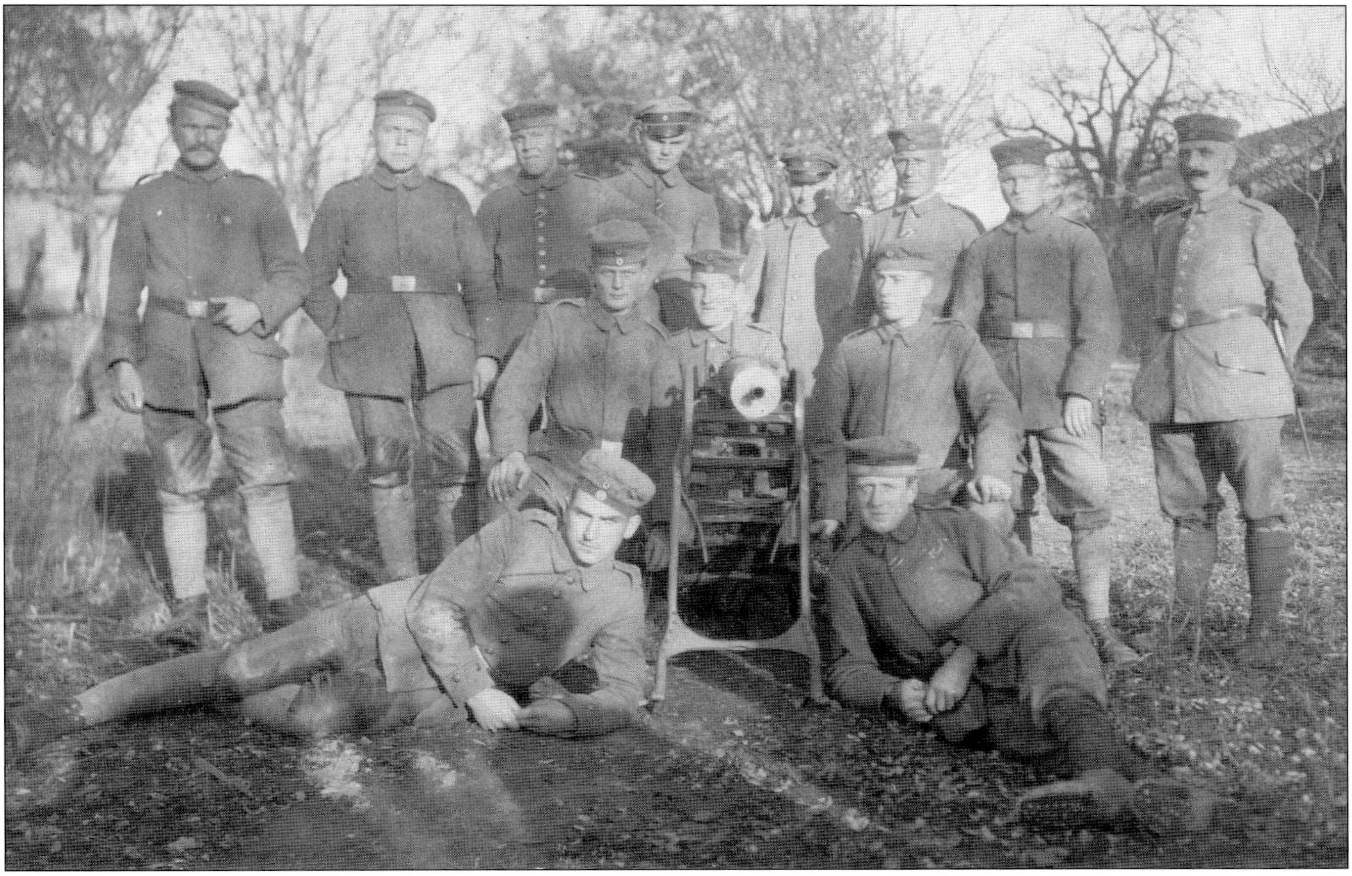

Sturm-Schule

Poor-quality but interesting photo of a Wehrmann of Landwehr Infantry Regiment No.99, taken during an assault course at Hucisco-Olesci, Galicia, June of 1917. He wears two improvised concentrated charges consisting of sand bags filled with hand-grenade heads. Courtesy Thierry Ehret.

1. The assault battalions – excluding No.3 and 5 – and Assault Company No.13 wear:
a) infantry uniforms for the assault companies and machine-gun companies (machine-gun squads, machine-gun platoons),
b) pioneer uniforms for the trench-mortar companies (trench-mortar platoons), with the battalion number (or company number in the case of Assault Company No.13) on the shoulder straps, along with the letters "MW."

2. *Jäger* (Assault) Battalion No.3 will retain the *Jäger* uniform.

3. Assault Battalion No.5 will wear:
a) pioneer uniform for the pioneer companies, pioneer park companies, flamethrower platoon, and machine-gun companies
b) field-artillery uniform for the cannon detachment, with the battalion number and the exploding grenade on the shoulder straps.

The patterns of January 20, 1917, IVa No.29037/28 are thus completed.[5]

Assault Battalion Rohr Trains the Infantry
"Training Plan for Assault Squads," June 1, 1916.[6]

Day 1
Morning - Explanation of German, French, and practice hand grenades. Throwing of dummy hand grenades in predetermined directions and at objectives, from standing and prone positions and out of a trench. Rapid forward advance from the trench (sortie steps, ladders), obstacle course.
Afternoon - Instruction: hand grenades, composition and equipment of assault squads.

Day 2
Morning - Throwing of dummy hand grenades on the run and in woods. Means of defense against hand grenades (lattices), obstacles of all types, overcoming of same.
Afternoon - Instruction: task, preparation, and procedure of assault squads.

Day 3
Morning - Throwing of dummy and half-live hand grenades from traverse to traverse and from sap to sap. Rapid reaching of the enemy position.
Afternoon - Instruction: types and development of assault positions and enemy defensive installations.

Day 4
Morning - Action of assault squads against occupied enemy trench with and without obstacles. Throwing of live hand grenades. Preparatory work in shell holes and the excavation of an assault position and protection.
Afternoon - Instruction: use of hand grenades in preparing elongated and concentrated charges.

Day 5
Morning - Throwing of hand grenades of all types. Elimination of obstacles, rolling up of trenches and approach trenches.

Assault squad of a Bavarian Landwehr infantry regiment wearing M1916 steel body armor. They are armed with Gew 98 rifles, Kar 98AZ carbines, and hand grenades. Although tested in combat, German body armor was too heavy, cumbersome, and noisy for assault troops.

Afternoon - Instruction: reconnaissance of own and enemy positions for the attack.

Day 6
Morning - Throwing of hand grenades. Fighting in a traverse set up for defense. Cleaning out and occupying an assault position during artillery preparation. Planting of bayonets. Breaking out of the assault squads from the assault position by the clock. Actions taken during gas attacks, forward assaulting while wearing gas masks.
Afternoon - Instruction: production of reconnaissance sketches and messaging of all forms.

Day 7
Morning - Conversion and clearing of taken positions. Actions taken in counterattacks. Activity of working and carrying squads. Throwing of hand grenades.
Afternoon - Instruction: production and use of attack sketches for assault squads.

Day 8
Morning - Use of steel shields in the attack. Establishment of relay runners. Use of telephones during the attack. Breaking out of infantry in three waves under the leadership of assault squads.
Afternoon - Instruction: preparation and implementation of an attack.

Left: Assault infantryman equipped with a metal device for priming and throwing ball and egg hand grenades with one hand. The wire pull ring of the grenade was slipped onto the metal spike; the soldier then yanked the grenade to prime it. Webbing straps were looped around the neck and attached to the belt. The strap slots in the edges of the chest plate allowed the device to be worn by either left- or right-handed grenadiers.

Right: Assault squad of Infantry Regiment No.381, 17th Landwehr Division, posing in a trench near the Russian town of Tveretch with what are identified as lachrymator grenades. The Germans tested several models of tear-gas grenade but did not use the weapon extensively. Some units on the eastern front wore the Pickelhaube well into 1918.

Day 9
Morning - Throwing of hand grenades. Explanation and use of flamethrowers, fire tubes, and smoke bombs. Fighting against and removal of blockhouses, infantry and machine-gun works, trench combat.
Afternoon - Instruction: use of machine guns, small trench mortars, grenade launchers, and infantry guns in the attack.

Day 10
Morning - Exercises in regular training works (quarry) with poles and ladders.
Afternoon -Instruction: experiences.

Day 11
Morning - Demonstration of machine guns, small trench mortars, grenade launchers, and infantry guns. Throwing of hand grenades.
Evening - Night exercises: Locating and digging an assault position with protection, cutting own and enemy wire obstacles.

Day 12
Morning - Carrying out an attack with all weapons.

Opposite
Top:Assault troops of Landwehr Infantry Regiment No.73, 5th Ersatz Division.They are armed with sharpened spades and dummy grenades consisting of wooden blocks mounted on handles. Most of the men wear the half-tunic called a Brustschöner, used to protect the uniform during training.

Bottom: Shock Troop 11 of the Guard Pioneer Battalion, 1917. Armed with Kar 98AZ carbines, they hold dummy hand grenades and wear the M1907/10 field jacket and simplified service jacket.As gas masks are not present, the setting would be a training field behind the lines.

Unteroffizier Maltus Kvamnet, a Norwegian serving in the Guard Reserve Pioneer Regiment. Photographed in 1917, he has adopted a pose that shows his death's-head sleeve badge to its best advantage.

The Military Passport *(Militärpass)* of a German Flamethrower Pioneer

Pionier Wilhelm Schübert was born on May 24, 1895, in Berlin. Listed in his military passport as a *Sekundarner,* a sixth- or seventh-year student of secondary school, he was 20 years old and 5 ft 8 in (1.72 m) tall when he began his service.

He was trained in the use of the *Gew 98* rifle, the *Kar 98AZ* carbine, and the flamethrower. His conduct was always rated "good," and he was given no punishments during his time in the army.

1915

May 26 - Entered service in the 3rd Recruit Depot *(3. Rekrut-Depot),* Guard Pioneer Replacement Battalion.
August 1 - Transferred to the 3rd Replacement Company *(3. Ersatz-Kompagnie),* Guard Pioneer Replacement Battalion.
September 4 - Transferred to the 1st Replacement Company, Guard Pioneer Replacement Battalion.
October 10 - Transferred to the Replacement Company, 3rd Guard Pioneer Battalion.
December 14 - Transferred to the Recruit Depot, 3rd Guard Pioneer Battalion.
December 19 - Transferred to the 11th Company, 3rd Guard Pioneer Battalion, in the field.
December 21, 1915, to January 1, 1916 - Fought in the mountains of the *Hartmannsweilerkopf* on the French-German border. Spent Christmas in combat.

1916

January 2 - Sent to hospital due to burns on the head caused by flaming oil.
February 22 - Took part in an assault on Bois de Ville in Verdun.
March 2 - Fought in Chauffour and Albain Wood.
March 2 - Fought at the village of Douaumont.
March 8 - Fought at the village of Douaumont.
March 18 to 19 - Fought at Fort Douaumont.
March 29 - Fought at Fort Douaumont.
March 29 - Wounded and sent to hospital.
April 15 - Transferred to the Garrison Company *(Garnison-Kompagnie),* 2nd Guard Pioneer Replacement Battalion.
May 11 - Transferred to the 3rd Replacement Company, 2nd Guard Pioneer Replacement Battalion.
July 26 - Transferred to the 3rd Company, Guard Reserve Pioneer Regiment.
July 26 - Attached as part of a flamethrower platoon to Reserve *Jäger* Battalion No.6, 12th Reserve Division, in the field.
August 2 to September 26 - Stationed in Flanders, near Armentières. Fought many times.
September 28 to November 3 - Fought at the Somme.
November 4 - Took part in an attack in the woods of St. Pierre Vaast, with Infantry Regiment No.116.
November 25 - In accordance with regimental orders he was assigned noncombat work in District Command *(Bezirkskommando)* Berlin-Schöneberg.
November 27 - Given leave to visit his parents in Wilmersdorf.
November 29 - Transferred to the Garrison Company, 2nd Guard Pioneer Replacement Battalion.

Kleif squad of Assault Battalion No.14. The flamethrower is a Kleif M.1917 missing the protective hinged lid, which has left the pressure gauge, oil-filler tube, and oil-pressurization valve exposed and vulnerable to damage. The 1.2m M1917 lance has been fitted with an igniter, indicating a live-fire exercise.

December 1 - By order of the Acting General Command of the Guard Corps *(stellvertretenden Generalkommando des Gardekorps),* Detachment II F. No.414354 *(Abteilung II F Nr.414354),* he was assigned to the Paul Mareus Company on Monumentstrasse in Schöneberg.
December 13 - Returned from leave, reported to the Paul Mareus Company.

1917
March 31 - Ordered back to armed service with the Garrison Company, 2nd Guard Pioneer Replacement Battalion.
June 1 - Transferred to the 1st Replacement Company, Pioneer Replacement Battalion No.2 *(Pionier-Ersatz-Bataillon Nr.2).*
June 21 - Transferred to the 1st Company, Württemberger Pioneer Field Recruit Depot 10 *(württembergisches-Pionier-Feld-Rekruit Depot 10),* Army Detachment C.
October 15 - Transferred to Pioneer Company 252 *(Pionier-Kompagnie 252),* 208th Infantry Division.
October 16 to November 26 - Fought in the heights of Lamorville, Spada, and St. Mihiel.
November 29 - Took part in antitank warfare in Cambrai.
November 30 to December 7 - Took part in offensive battles in Cambrai.
December 8 to 31 - Fought at the Siegfried Line.

1918
January1 to 31 - Fought at the Siegfried Line.
February 23 to 26 - Fought at the Siegfried Line.
February 26 to March 1 - In Field Hospital 78 *(Feld-Lazarrett 78)* due to ear infection.
March 1 to 9 - Fought at the Siegfried Line.
March 10 - By Order 208. J. D. II 2053, he was transferred into the Aviation Service *(Luftstreitkräfte),* joining Giant Aircraft Replacement Detachment Cologne *(Riesenflugzeug-Ersatz-Abteilung Köln),* which supplied parts, weapons, inspection, and personnel for R-class or "giant" bombers.

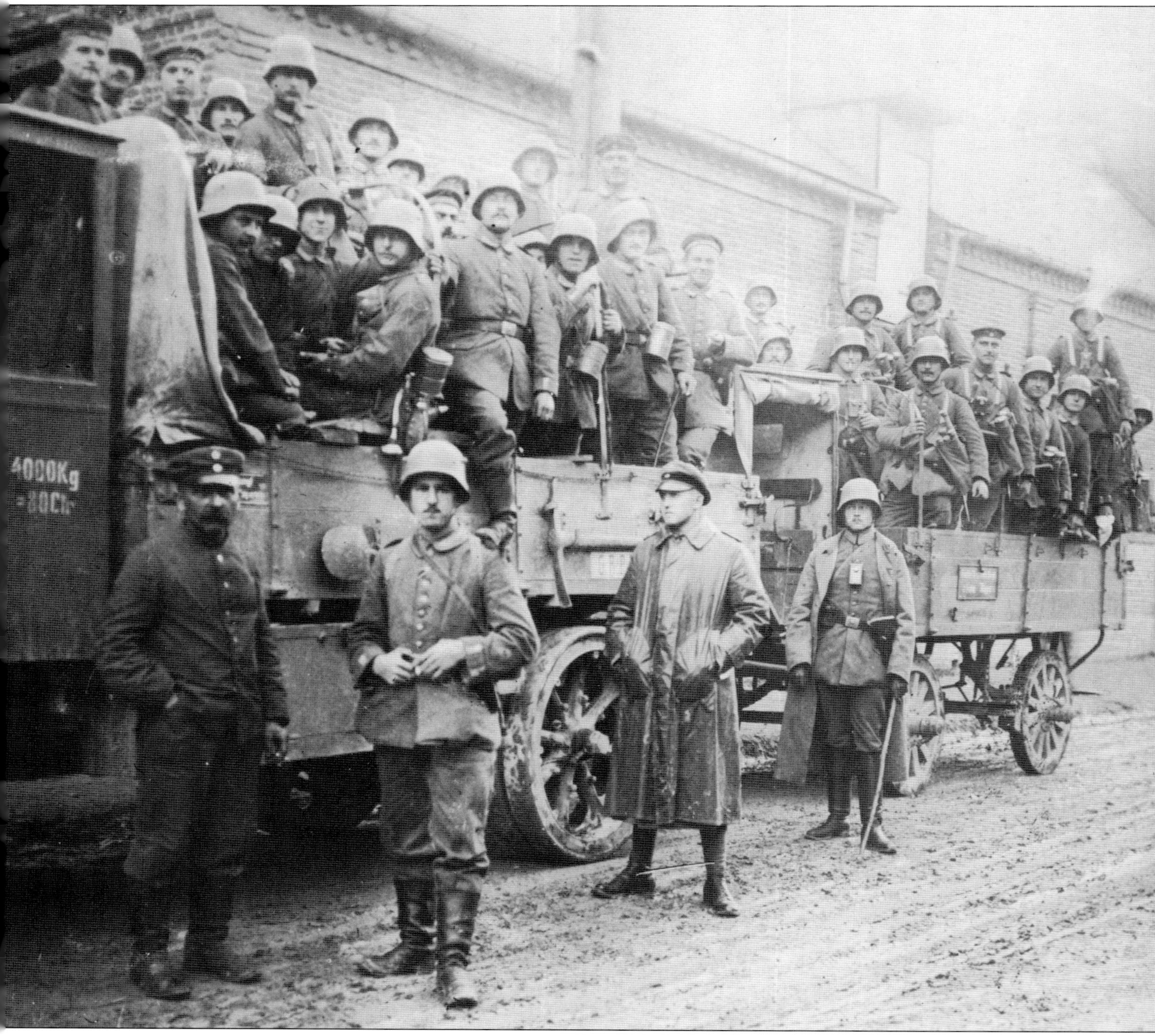

Assault troops of the 1st Platoon, 2nd Company, Guard Reserve Pioneer Regiment, about to be transported to their target. The men in the bed of the heavy truck are flamethrower operators, while those in the wagon attached to the rear of the vehicle are grenadiers. All appear to be armed with P08 pistols, while the grenadiers are also equipped with torches, cut-down shovels, and hand-grenade sacks. Two officers--one in a raincoat--are present.

March 11 - Reported to Giant Aircraft Replacement Detachment Cologne as a private *(Flieger)* of the Giant Aircraft Troops *(Riesenflugzeug-Truppe)*.
March 12 to November 22 - Stationed at Liegnitz, in Silesia. *[His passport includes an insert with a typewritten notation identifying him as a private of* Riesenflugzeug-Ersatz-Abteilung-Liegnitz, *a unit about which no information has yet been discovered, ed.]*
November 23 - Demobilized in District Command 5, Berlin.

Endnotes

[1] Larcade, p. 80, report of the French Second Army.

[2] Gudmundsson, pp. 95-97.

[3] War Department, *Notes on Recent Operations, No.2* (Washington: Government Printing Office, 1917), pp. 45-46.

[4] Larcade, p. 44.

[5] Ibid., p. 52.

[6] Gruss, pp. 163-168.

CHAPTER 10

Instructions for Shock Troops

"Instructions for the Training of Shock Troops," 1917.[1]

I. General.

Each shock troop is formed in the company through the selection of the most courageous and determined men, as well as by special training in a particularly conspicuous form of combat capability. Because of their equipment (hand grenades, etc.) and clothing (steel helmet, shield) the men already stand out in the Company.

A special badge on the sleeve or shoulder strap facilitates the recognition of shock troops and raises the self-confidence of the men.

The shock troops are generally used by their own companies. Their special training will first benefit themselves and later their companies. Even if initially the companies are able to train only around three shock troops each, the aim should nevertheless be to train all squad leaders and as many personnel as possible in the use of shock troops. Despite the systematic approach to training shock troops, the requirements of the fight often become a summary of local particulars, not the skills called for in trained groups such as shock troops. This is true particularly in the defense. The more noncommissioned officers and men of a company are given shock-troop training, however, the more easily they can facilitate a response. The shock-troop training should never influence the commitment of the company, meaning that the men should not believe that the shock troop will now accomplish everything by itself. Only the ruthless urge to advance every individual man of the attacking infantry in connection with the shock troops creates success.

Extremely unusual photo of the shock troop of a Bavarian foot-artillery regiment. They are armed as trench raiders with M1916 and M1917 stick grenades and the 9mm Lange Pistole 08. Although most wear puttees, one has retained his high leather boots. All except the officer have removed their shoulder straps.

This sage experience must always be remembered by the troops and remain common to all.

II. The Shock Troop in Attack.

The main task of the shock troop is to capture forward saps, flanking installations, detected blockhouses, machine guns, defended shelters, enemy defenses not previously detected, and to roll up trenches; that is, to facilitate the assault by removing the most difficult enemy installations.

For this they require particularly careful training of the leaders and each individual man in site assessment and corresponding use, in the reconnaissance of enemy positions, their strengths and likewise weaknesses, in the exploration of the points of penetration, in the preparation of attack sketches, in all kinds of trench warfare, in the throwing of hand grenades, in shooting with our own and French machine guns and in their use in battle (flanking).

The company shock-troop leaders in the front line must be in constant contact with each other; they must exchange the results of their reconnaissance of the area, the enemy positions, and flanking; and during the carrying out of operations they must meet specific agreements for mutual support – installing of flanking machine guns, use of flamethrowers, and so on.

Operations are carried out after a previous, exacting reconnaissance. Each individual must be completely familiar with the overall purpose and carry out his assigned role with the utmost skill, courage, and ruthlessness. Depending on the conditions of the area, the individual shock troops work completely independently, bypassing blockhouses and flanking installations, carrying out flanking attacks or attacks from behind, thereby mutually supporting each other.

When previously undetected enemy defenses suddenly appear, every man must dedicate himself immediately to the new task and work in common with the other men of the shock troop to remove the unforeseen obstacle.

Gefreiter Conrad Müller of the Assault Company, Bavarian 3rd Infantry Regiment (3. Infanterie-Regiment Prinz Karl von Bayern), Bavarian 11th Infantry Division. Photographed on leave in Mauregny-en-Haye, he wears the Bavarian M1916 blouse and M1910 field cap for officers.

Shock troops of an unidentified infantry regiment; a hand-written notation on the back of the postcard reads "Awarding of the Iron Cross, Gravelotte." The soldier standing in the second row on the right wears a badge on his lower left sleeve, directly above the cuff of his M1915 blouse. Apparently embroidered in field-gray thread, it depicts a wreath with an "S" in the center.

Landsturmmann Hans-Henning Vierordt, 4th Company of Badener Landsturm Infantry Battalion Mannheim (XIV/11), photographed in 1917. He is a member of a nine-man platoon assault squad; note the trench dagger on his left hip. The collar of his M1915 blouse displays metal numerals "XIV" above "11."

Placing the shock troops ahead of, within, or behind individual assault waves is to be arranged on a case-by-case basis according to the order of the company commander.

Their strength and the most appropriate composition are, depending on the task, one to three squads of infantry and if necessary one squad of pioneers, armed with one machine gun for flanking sweeps during the assault, one light trench mortar, and one or two flamethrowers.

The provision of support and equipment for each shock troop is to be considered in each case by the company commander and set correctly.

Purpose of the support squad *[Unterstützungstrupp]:* Immediate rapid response to traffic congestion. After removal of the enemy installations, support in the holding and transformation of the taken position.

Purpose of the equipment squad *[Gerätetrupp]:* Immediate transportation of the necessary devices (shields, hand grenades, spades, and pickaxes).

If permitted by the terrain, immediate construction of a communication trench to the rear.

Equipment.

Equipment of shock troops: without baggage.

Whether or not cartridge pouches are to be carried depends on the use of the shock troops after the assault. If after the pullout the shock troops are to stay behind and hold the position, cartridge pouches are taken. If the shock troops are to leave, cartridges are carried in jacket pockets or bread bag. Further equipment consists of two sandbags with three grenades in each slung around the neck and over both shoulders, wire cutters on the belt, rifle or carbine slung on the back (bayonet not fixed), steel helmet, pioneer tools (ax or hatchet) with medium-length handle in a carrying case fastened to the belt handle upwards, steel shield if the task requires it, gas mask, and small red or green (sandbag) badge for mutual recognition in the trench fight.

Equipment of the support squads: Bayonet fixed, otherwise as shock troop. The hand grenades carried by the support squads serve as the reserve for the shock troop.

Equipment squads: Rifle slung.

Rations: three iron portions, hard spirits, bread, plenty of drink.

III. The Shock Troop in Defense.

a) Just as important as use in the attack. Frequently practice under consistently new situations.

b) Task:

1. Drive the enemy from the penetrated position immediately after the breakthrough.

2. Dig nests after preparation.

The latter corresponds to procedure during the attack. An immediate counterattack is usually successful. Hesitation gives the enemy time to reinforce and create machine-gun nests.

c) Conditions for success: Rapid taking of the position leads to a rapid resolution; combine all the nearby men into a shock troop (previous unit affiliations have likely been destroyed by artillery fire). Divide the troop (since hand grenades are often scarce, designate the best men as throwers and the rest as carriers).

Opposite

Top: Assault squad of the Training Company, Infantry Regiment No.174 (Ausbildungskompagnie, 10. lothringisches Infanterie-Regiment Nr.174), 2nd Reserve Field Battalion. Photographed in August of 1917, the men are armed with Gew 98 rifles and M1916 stick grenades. Most wear camouflaged M1916 steel helmets.

Bottom: Machine gunners of Assault Battalion No.8 at Rohatyn, Galicia, summer of 1917. All three steel helmets and the MG08 have been painted with irregular lozenges of color as camouflage. The gunner is equipped with grenade bags, and the sled of the gun has been replaced with an improvised trench mount.

Half-platoon of Saxon Field Artillery Regiment No.77 (7. sächsisches Feldartillerie-Regiment Nr.77) attending a grenade-launcher course in Zeithain, May of 1917. Artillerymen of Infantry Accompanying Batteries received the same training as infantrymen. They were instructed in shock-troop tactics and the use of all infantry weapons.

d) Equipment: tightly buckled, ammunition pouches, as many hand grenades as possible.

e) Attack: Frontal, better yet flanking from trenches in accordance with "The Shock Troop in the Attack." The addition of machine guns and flamethrowers is desirable.

f) Exercises: As in "Attack." Note that lengthy reconnaissance is not possible, but an immediate counterattack is necessary. Otherwise the enemy may become too strong and make success questionable. Squad leaders and every man must be taught to achieve the utmost independence and make the most rapid decisions possible, as orders from the company and platoon leaders are often missing.

IV. Methods of Attack.

For the attack against fortified positions it is often recommended that the forces be broken down into several small assault columns used in advantageous positions previously reconnoitered. In order to surprise the enemy, the assault troops reach these points of penetration the moment that their own artillery fire moves on. Infantry units (squads, half-platoons, platoons) follow immediately behind the assault troops. More infantry and labor squads follow at short intervals and arrive at the breach in order to consolidate and fortify the positions taken. The strength of the units depends on the size and destination of the attack.

The principle is that to avoid unnecessary losses and mutual disability the individual assault columns are only as strong as necessary to achieve the task posed to them.

If heavy resistance from the enemy is not expected, the assault troops can also be initially held back and then used only if during the attack the infantry encounters obstacles which are difficult to take.

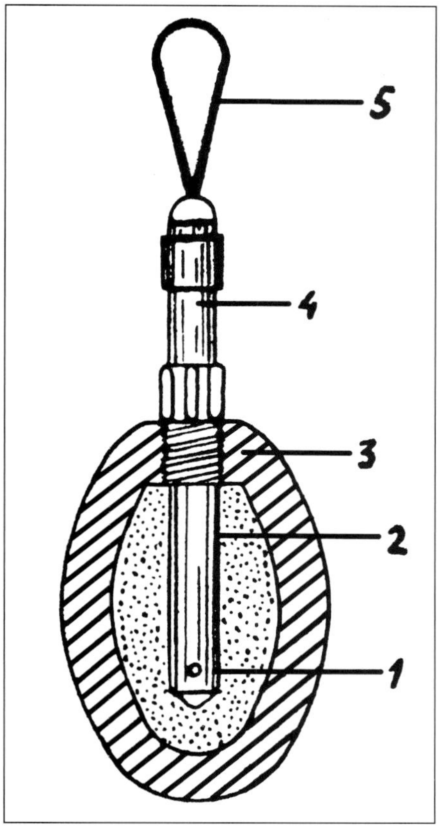

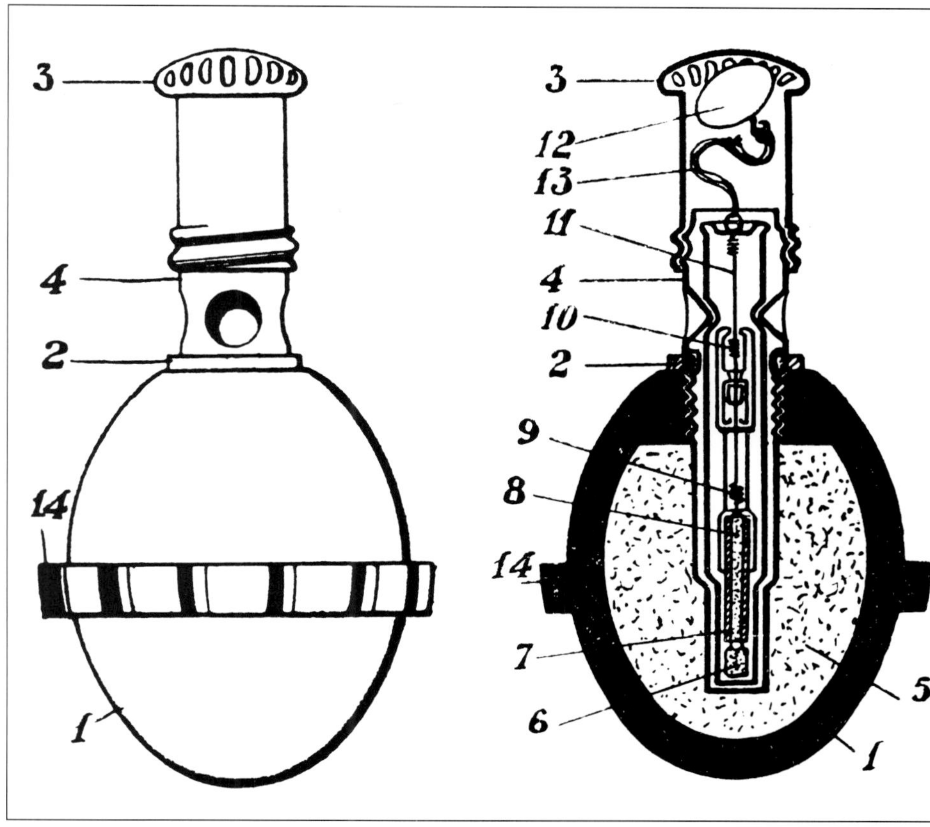

Left: M1917 egg grenade with early smooth body and M1915 friction fuse; the latter had a five- or eight-second delay. The egg grenade could be thrown further than the stick grenade, as it was smaller and lighter.

Right: Late-model M1917 egg grenade and M1917 fuse. The serrated band cast around the middle of the grenade improved the thrower's grip. To use the weapon the grenadier removed the safety cap (3) and pulled the porcelain ball (12) attached to the lanyard, which activated the 5-second time fuse.

Infantry guns can perform essential service during the assault.

Shortly before the attack small trench mortars and grenade launchers can keep the points of penetration under fire until the arrival of the assault troops. After carrying out this task, they follow the assault troops for use against other obstacles that may appear during the attack.

Attack in numerous small assault columns, not in a skirmish line; attack unexpectedly during a break of own artillery fire.

Ruthless advance of the first wave until the goal is achieved. A thorough cleaning up must be done by the second and third wave, because otherwise the first wave will be endangered from the rear.

Small flamethrowers must not be sent alone in advance; they require protection by assault troops.

Machine guns inserted on the flanks can support the attack well.

The telephone squads which follow the assault columns can rapidly inform the commander about the advance of the attack.

At the target position immediately dig in, insert the machine guns as rapidly as possible, and arrange occupation troops according to the depth.

Rifles are better defense against counterattacks than hand grenades.

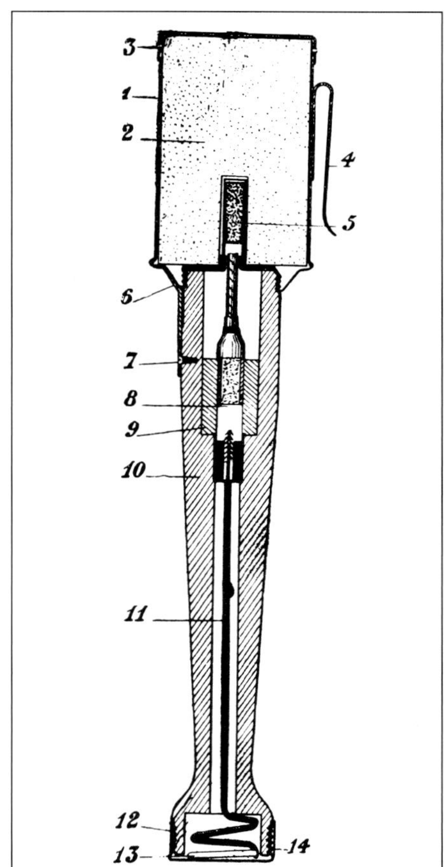

Right: M1916 stick grenade with time fuse. This was the first model of stick grenade with a safety cap on the end of the handle, which prevented the lanyard from being accidentally pulled. The fuse had either a five- or seven-second delay.

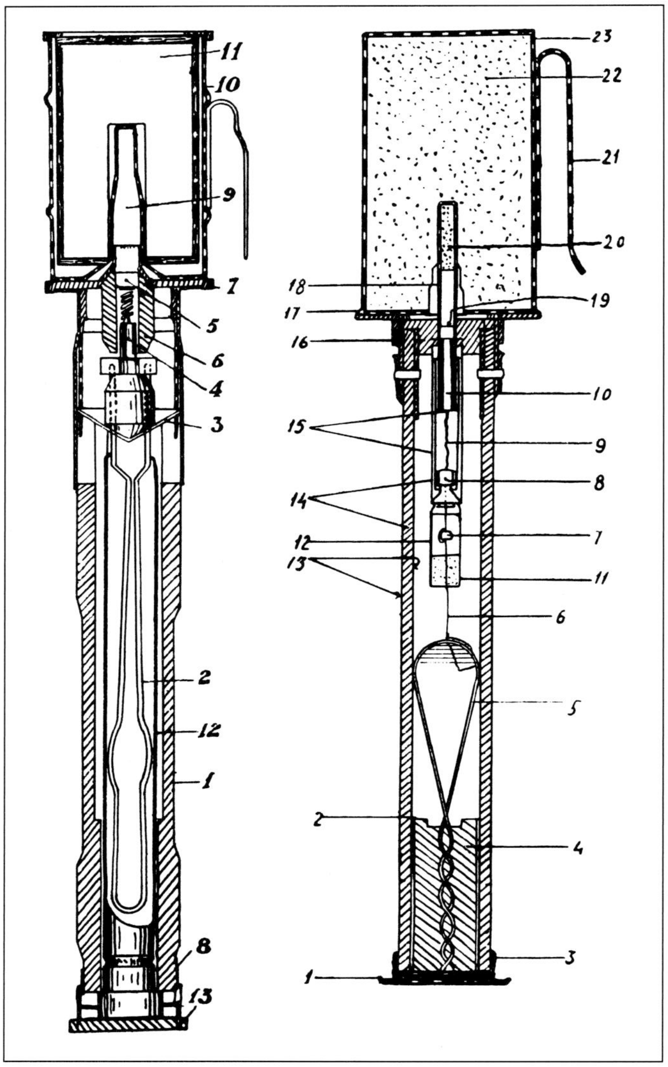

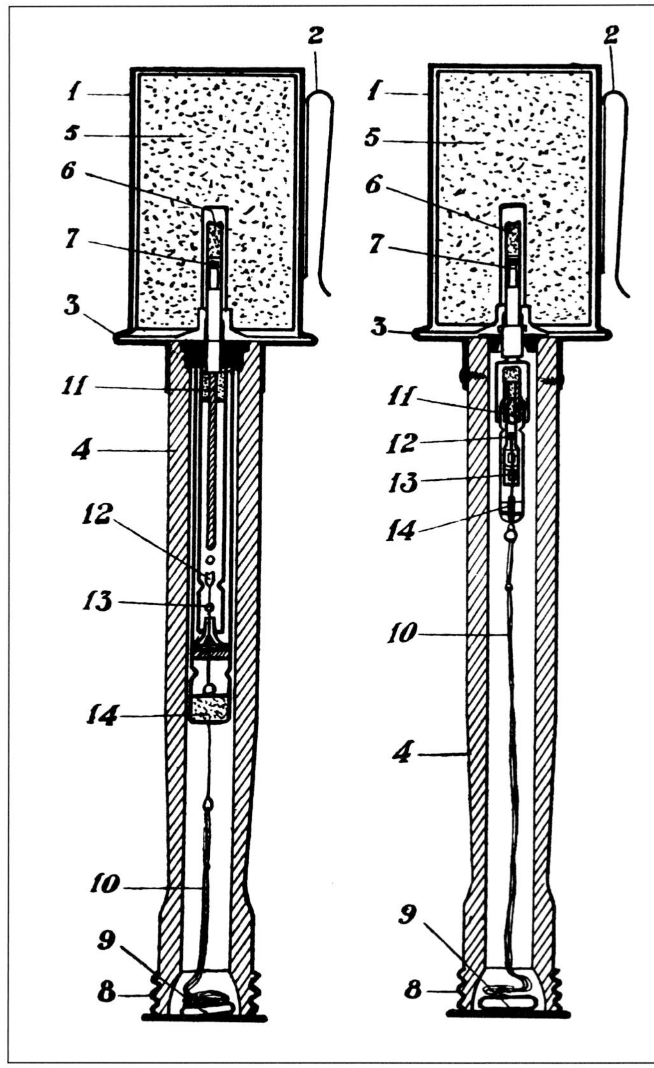

***Left:* M1916 percussion stick grenade (left) and M1916 stick grenade with metal handle and time fuse (right). Both models were automatically primed. When the safety cap was unscrewed and the grenade thrown, a weight fell out in flight. In the case of the percussion grenade a plunger was released, which allowed a firing pin to strike a primer when the grenade hit the target. The falling weight of the time-fuse grenade pulled the lanyard of a friction fuse, which detonated the grenade in five and a half seconds.**

***Right:* M1917 percussion stick grenade (left) and M1917 stick grenade with time fuse (right). Both were operated with lanyards that were freed after the safety cap was unscrewed. In the case of the percussion grenade pulling the lanyard released a firing pin that struck a primer when the grenade hit its target. Pulling the lanyard of the time-fuse grenade ignited a five-and-a-half-second friction fuse.**

V. Training.

The direction of training within the companies is led by an officer (shock-troop officer) under the supervision of the company commander. The shock-troop officers of the regiment are to be trained together in theoretical and practical relationships. They must be physically fit and qualified to immediately recognize and accordingly use each tactical circumstance.

The training of shock troops must change daily, in particular taking place as often as possible in wooded areas or otherwise difficult terrain and always within the context of the company. Training grounds already in existence are to be used.

New training grounds of various kinds are to be created by each company after receiving instruction from the regiment. They often need only be suggested: Trenches may be knee deep or made from piles of leaves; blockhouses may be made with stretched tarpaulins or shrubs and lines of leaves; flanking installations by collections of wooden stakes; barricades and machine-guns from fascines, etc. Within a regiment 12 changes of training grounds must be possible.

Along with the exercises the analysis of the setting and the assault of the shock troops must unambiguously take place. Immediately after a successful assault a further investigation at the front and flanks must begin.

The Inspection Stage (Inspektion-Etappen) for a squad of Infantry Regiment No.162 (Infanterie-Regiment Lübeck [3. hanseatisches] Nr.162), graduating from Close Combat Weapons School (Nahkampfmittelschule) at Lockstedt, 1917. Note the chalk drawings of egg and stick grenades on the signboard. The extreme youth of the soldiers underscores the massive losses that the Germans had suffered.

The enemy positions are represented by riflemen with blank cartridges and machine guns or mannequins overseen by referees, who are allowed to record the casualties and prevent all manner of unwarlike behavior by the reconnaissance patrols and shock troops.

VI. Blasting of Obstacles.
Obstacles are blasted with improvised elongated or concentrated charges as follows:

1. Elongated charge. Purpose: To create a channel through a barbed-wire obstacle. Preparation: On a slat the approximate length of the obstacle one binds the heads of hand grenades by means of wire in such a way that a distance of 15cm *[6 in]* remains between each head; the openings point in one direction. Into each opening of the heads one places a blasting cap, which is held in position with a small sliver of wood.

Two men crawl forward with the elongated charges and place them between the posts to which the barbed-wire obstacle is attached. In order to complete the charge, one screws a hand-grenade handle with a blasting cap

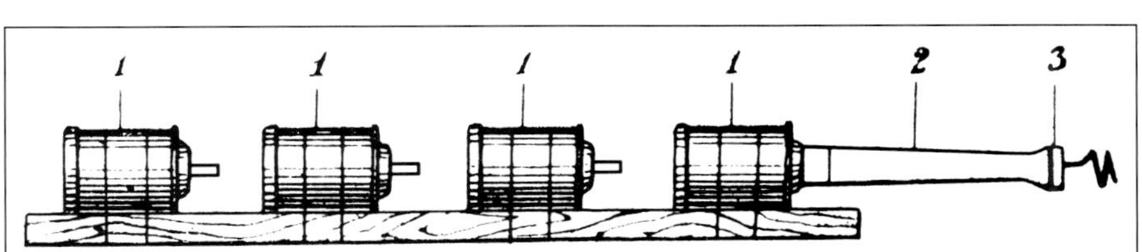

Elongated charge (gestreckte Ladung) consisting of several stick-grenade heads wired 6 in apart to a board. A detonator was fitted to each head, wedged in place with a sliver of wood. The final hand grenade retained its handle and served as the trigger; pulling the lanyard detonated all grenade heads. The elongated charge was used to blast openings in barbed wire.

inside it into the last head and attaches a long cord or length of telephone cable to the lanyard. The man who is to detonate the charge finds cover in a trench or shell hole and yanks the lanyard, setting off the explosion.

The charge explodes in 5 1/2 seconds and creates a wide lane in the obstacle.

Concentrated charge (geballte Ladung) consisting of six or nine extra hand-grenade heads wired to a grenade that retained its handle. Like the elongated charge, a detonator was fitted to each head, wedged in place with a sliver of wood. When the hand grenade in the center exploded, it detonated all the other heads simultaneously. The concentrated charge was used against barbed wire, trenches, sapheads, tanks, and fortified positions.

2. Concentrated charge. Preparation: Six or more grenade heads are bound with wire around a hand grenade, all of the openings facing one side. Detonators are clamped into the openings with small slivers of wood.

One man crawls near to the obstacle which must be destroyed and searches for a shell hole as cover. At this point he completes the charge (screwing in a hand-grenade handle with blasting cap in it), pulls the lanyard, and throws the charge into the middle of the obstacle. (Explodes in 5 1/2 seconds.) Several charges may be thrown simultaneously in order to create a wider and deeper pathway or to create in narrow obstacles several lanes in different places.

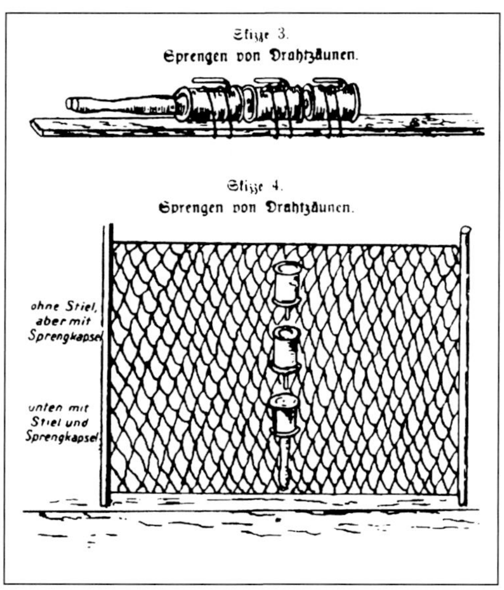

Shorter version of elongated charge (top) carried by one man. Sketch 4 shows how hand grenade heads without handles were hung by their belt hooks on wire screens; detonators were wedged in place with slivers of wood. The grenade at the bottom retained its handle so that the lanyard could be used to set off the time fuse, allowing the soldier five and a half seconds to take cover.

3. To create smaller passages through a wire-mesh obstacle, the explosion from a hand grenade hung from a height of 80cm *[31 in]* is sufficient.

To create larger gaps, one proceeds in accordance with Sketches 3 or 4. The blasting caps are lodged in the openings of the grenade heads with small slivers of wood.

A concentrated charge can also be prepared by filling a sandbag half or three-quarters full with hand-grenade heads and then inserting a hand grenade with the handle. The bag must be tied so that the handle visibly protrudes. Wrapping with wire or strips of sandbag increases the strength.

To destroy wire mesh by throwing hand grenades requires a fish-hook device. The fish-hook device is shown in Sketch 5, while a hand grenade with fish-hook devices is shown in Sketch 6. (A wire ring is wrapped around the grenade head; this wire is connected to the fish hooks.)

VII. Training Curriculum.

Fish-hook device (Angelvorrichtung) attached to hand grenades in order to destroy chicken-wire barriers. When the grenade was used against a wire barrier, it would become entangled by the hooks and remain precisely where the grenadier had thrown it.

1. Lessons.

1. Lesson on the purpose and use of shock troops.
2. Lesson on terrain analysis and reconnaissance of enemy positions on a training ground, in the field, and in the sandbox. (Type of ground, recognizing enemy lines, where the flanking installations are, where machine guns are, where blockhouses are, where trenches are. Recognizing specific places in the area where cover is found. Recognizing the most favorable point of attack. For the most part recognizing where one is not flanked and where one can roll up the enemy position.
3. Reading maps.
4. Making of area and panoramic sketches.
5. Lesson on the cooperation of support and equipment squads.
6. Use of own and enemy hand grenades.
7. Lesson in machine guns and French machine guns (loading, shooting, and eliminating inhibitions).
8. Lesson in the use of the small flamethrower during the attack.
9. Lesson in the use of the small trench mortar.

For officers and noncommissioned officers: Evaluating aerial photographs.

2. Practical Training.

A. Training in pairs (Principle: Two men work together constantly.)

1. Training in concealment and crawling with slung rifle and hand grenades, reconnaissance and making area and attack sketches, stalking blockhouses and flanking installations, creeping up on loopholes, etc.
2. Walking rapidly and silently from the assembly position to the assault position (rifle in hand, bayonet not fixed).
3. Rapid exiting of the assault position by ladders or sortie steps, taking up of the shield laid out in front of the trench. Rapid leaping and positioning with protective shields. Immediately opening fire (practice especially often on precipitous slopes).
4. Use of shields in the attack. Carrying and rapid setting up at a slant. Attack according to the area, particularly uphill. Walking, running, jumping with shield (rifle slung, steel shield carried diagonally in front of the chest so that it provides the largest possible coverage). Alternate crawling forward with shooting through shields (when crawling head is kept low, so that it is covered by the shield). Special exercises in: making short leaps with shields, shooting through shield loophole, then rapid slinging of the rifle and jumping. Constant mutual interaction with assault shields, a gap of one to two steps between each man (A slow, forward walk during the attack calls for close placement of the two shields to provide the most coverage).
5. Rapid leap back, in or out of blockhouses or flanking installations, and from that point fight on with hand grenades.
6. Removal of obstacles while crawling and from a prone position, with and without shields.
7. Rebuilding of taken positions.
8. Throwing live hand grenades daily, from and in trenches and behind shields. Throwing live hand grenades over traverses during the practice for rolling up trenches. Throwing with French grenades.
9. Live firing. Shooting against the loopholes of steel shields (shield mockups from wood to record the shots; loopholes painted with black lacquer). Live firing from behind steel shields, especially uphill. Shooting from trees. Live firing with machine guns and French machine guns.

10. Exercises in overcoming obstacles (improves skills and strengthens self-assurance).

Every obstacle in the area (ditches, hedges, thick woods, fences, sand pits, small stone quarries, cliff parts, walls, penetration in houses through the windows) is to be overcome as often as possible and is to be pursued as sport.

If obstacles are missing in the area, an obstacle course with many varied obstacles is to be erected. Unexpected obstacles with mannequins representing hidden enemies are especially valuable (wire mesh behind which is concealed a barrier of branches, dead ends under fire by flanking installations, etc.).

11. Physical exercises: Running quickly, training in the rifle leap (see Paragraph 12d, *Komp. Führ. Anleitung*), jogging, relay race with short military messages, many climbing exercises in trees. Also, a surprise appearance here of an enemy represented by mannequins serves to sharpen the determination.

Opposite: Musketiere of the shock troop, Infantry Regiment No.81 (Infanterie-Regiment Landgraf Friedrich I von Hessen-Cassel [1. kurhessisches] Nr.81). Note the Kar 98AZ carbine instead of the Gew 98 rifle. The threaded safety caps of the M1916 stick grenades have been removed so that the weapons may be used without delay.

Four Musketiere of the Assault Detachment, 26th Infantry Division, photographed in Cambrai, August of 1917. The 26th Infantry Division was comprised of Grenadier Regiment No.119, Infantry Regiment No.121, and Infantry Regiment No.125, all from Württemberg. In September of 1917 the division was trained in mountain warfare and sent to the Italian front.

B. Training in the Shock Troop.

1. The most careful training of the entire group, the same as done with pairs. (The shock-troop leader is always independent after receiving his orders and must never wait for special attack orders.)
2. Practice often: Quick, silent walking from the ready position to the assault position. Gun level in the hand, bayonet not fixed. As soon as the group arrives at its place, the group leader independently gives the sign for coming out (in particular practice in mountainous country where enemy positions are elevated, thus the intention of the assault can be easily recognized by the enemy, thereby shock troops could be prevented from coming out at other places).
3. Removal of obstacles while simultaneously fighting with grenades and firearms.
4. Long and short leaps into enemy trenches; immediate altering of the trenches.
5. Short leap into enemy trench with steel shields; hand-grenade combat by both sides with live hand grenades.
6. Rolling up an enemy trench from one side according to plan; the interaction of hand grenades and firearms (the latter outside of the trench).
7. Cordoning off of a taken enemy position.
8. Assault on flanking installation, etc., with and without shield.
9. Assault on a recognized blockhouse with and without shield.
10. Assault on a defensive installation not previously recognized, with and without shield.

Assaults are to be practiced daily, especially in mountainous, wooded, and difficult terrain.

Light machine-gun squad of an infantry shock troop; all five men wear a rectangular white "S" badge on their inner left elbows, and each is armed with a P08. The IMG08/15 is fed from an M1915 ammunition box; note the loaded Granatwerfer 16 in the left background.

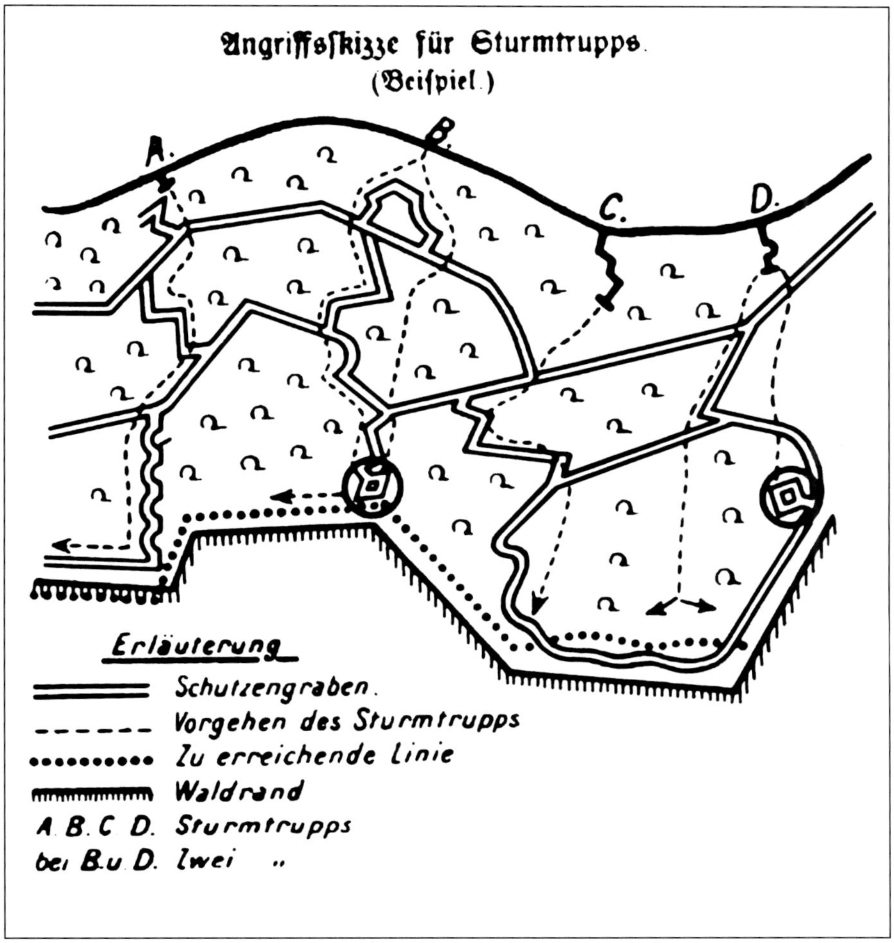

"Attack Sketch for Assault Squads (Example)." The key (Erläuterung) reads as follows: "Trench; Advance of Assault Squads; Line to be Reached; Edge of Forest; Assault Squads; Two Assault Squads." Shock-troop leaders prepared such sketches before an operation.

11. After penetration into hostile position immediate further investigation forward and on both flanks, regarding mission at hand; making sketches.
12. Assault exercise of several shock troops as a unified group. One or two attack, the others carry out fire support from another direction on recognized machine guns, blockhouses, or flanking installations.
13. Cooperation with support and equipment squads provided.
14. Cooperation of shock troops with their company, giving special consideration to own flanking protective fire and machine-gun fire.
15. Cooperation of shock troops with flamethrowers (represented by a stick as the lance and a backpack as the flamethrower) and machine guns, which fire from the other direction at the area to be assaulted for as long as possible; in addition, cooperation with light trench mortars.
16. Blasting of obstacles with improvised elongated and concentrated charges. Production of the same (See Segment VI.) See sketch at the back of the pamphlet.

Practicing Flamethrower Attacks

"Rehearsal of a Flame Attack with the Assault Infantry."[2]

A good preparation for a flame attack is to build an exercise work behind the front. The exercise work should be as much as possible a model of the enemy position where the actual attack will take place, in actual size based on aerial photos. If there is no time, trenches are used. Targets of the attack, etc., are represented by white tape or furrows in the earth made with a plow.

Unterstand.
Arras.
PFingsten 1917 im F

The entire flame attack is to be practiced at the exercise work with assault infantry and live-firing flamethrowers. At the exercise work each squad, each leader or man of the flamethrower pioneers and infantry must become thoroughly practiced at his task, including the throwing of live hand grenades.

The formation points of the flamethrower apparatuses, the locations of the lance operators who deliver the first flame jet (flame points *[Flammenpunkte]*), and the connecting routes to the front line must be specified in tables and numbered from right to left.

Flamethrower troops and infantry assault troops must know which approach and connecting trench they should use when inserting into the position, and to which point in the position they must locate themselves for the attack. This will prevent the troops from getting lost, piling up, or crowding together. Breach points must be exactly right.

The flamethrower shock troops have their individual orders at hand in the form of sketches that show enemy positions clearly drawn and described in detail. Each flamethrower shock troop must know exactly the point to which it must penetrate and the task it must carry out there. Every flamethrower shock troop should be given the orders of the adjacent shock troops.

The wing shock troops *(Flügelstosstrupps)* must do much work to protect the flanks. The flank shock troops *(Flankenstosstrupps)* must take care to protect the branches of the trench.

***Opposite:** Shock troops of the 12th Company, Guard Reserve Pioneer Regiment, photographed at Arras on the Christian feast day of Pentecost (Pfingsten), June 17, 1917. They are equipped with Kar 98AZ carbines, assault packs, hand grenades, wire cutters, and gas masks in M1916 metal canisters. Flamethrowers held only about 15 seconds' worth of oil and could not be refilled on the battlefield. The Death's Head Pioneers were therefore trained as assault infantrymen.*

***Below:** Shock troops of the 12th Company, Infantry Regiment No.74, 19th Infantry Division, attending assault school in July of 1917. Allied intelligence rated the 19th Infantry Division one of the best of the German army. Note the French Fusil Mitrailleur Modèle 1915 CSRG, the infamous Chauchat, held by the soldier lying on the right. All German shock troops were trained in the use of enemy machine guns.*

In the case of an enemy trench network with many branches, thorough rehearsal at the training work and careful preparation are particularly necessary.

Weapons and Equipment of Flamethrower Assault Troops

A. Means of Combat.[3]

Flame Jet.
The flame jet is the most effective weapon of the flamethrower in close combat. Full technical control is achieved only through a thorough individual training process. If the flamethrower pioneer wins absolute confidence in his fine flamethrower weapon through appropriate training and careful guidance, he will always use the flame jet, even if there exists only the potential of physical or moral success. Those who proceed against the enemy with the flame jet know the effectiveness of this close-combat technique and understand the fear of the enemy facing it.

Rifles and Carbines.
The flame jet is often superior to the rifle and carbine in man-to-man combat. Rifles and carbines can support the efficacy of the flame jet through targeted fire.

The shooting skill of the flamethrower pioneers should not be neglected in favor of other duties. Flamethrower pioneers themselves must use their shooting skill if for some reason they cannot depend on the overall effect of the flame jet.

Careful individual training in shooting educates the flamethrower pioneers in the determined and deliberate action required during close combat.

Shooting at close and the closest ranges. Shooting with live ammunition in groups under combat conditions. Folding targets that appear and disappear quickly are set up. Special work is done on training in rapid firing under combat conditions. Flamethrower pioneers must be transformed into shooters of swiftly completed single shots with machine guns, grenade launchers, rifles, and pistols.

Pistols, Bayonets, Spades.
Equipped with pistols, bayonets and sharpened spades for self-defense, the squad leader and flamethrower pioneers successfully enter into close combat if the flamethrowers are empty or disabled.

Machine Guns and Grenade Launchers.
Machine guns engaging enemies outside of the trenches and grenade launchers engaging enemies in the trenches provide valuable support for and protection of the flame jet during combat. Besides being used for the actual effect of their fire, both weapons are frequently inserted for diverting the attention of the enemy and affecting his morale. In special cases they make it possible for the flamethrower shock troops to penetrate to within firing

Top: Pioneers of Assault Battalion No.5 (Rohr), photographed at Malancourt in July of 1917. In the foreground are two members of the Flamethrower Platoon. They wear the Guard Pioneer uniform with a red number "5" on the shoulder straps. The camouflaged M1916 helmets are early models with square-dip visors.

Bottom: Oberleutnant Ludwig Charles Theune, commander of the 10th Company, Guard Reserve Pioneer Regiment, and author of the book "Sturmtruppen und Flammenwerfer".

Combined stationary and pouncing attack (vereinten stehenden und springenden Angriff) of large and small flamethrowers. At least two officers supervise the dangerous live-fire exercise.

range. The cooperation between machine guns, grenade launchers, and the flame jet requires very careful training. It is not enough that machine-gun and grenade-launcher personnel from the infantry join the flamethrower shock troops. An exercise in cooperation must always take place.

If in specific cases grenade launchers fire ahead along the route of the advancing flamethrower squads, or if our own machine guns begin to shoot over them, it is recommended that the machine guns and grenade launchers be operated by officers or older noncommissioned officers of the flamethrower troops.

Hand Grenades.

Hand grenades reinforce the effect of the flame jets. After a flame shock that reaches the enemy trench or is delivered in it, the enemy retreats and bunches up. Throw hand grenades into such accumulations of men!

The skillful throwing of hand grenades singly at fixed targets, then simultaneously in groups; throwing far and hit the target! The flamethrower pioneers must be able to throw hand grenades from every position of the body: standing, kneeling, and prone, also with full apparatuses on the

Officer of Infantry Regiment No.121 testing a flame-resistant cape for shock troops. As he stands in an open field, pioneers fire a flamethrower in his direction, directing the jet as close to his left side as possible. It is not known if such a dangerous testing method was standard practice.

back and while wearing gas masks. Throwing over obstacles, over sandbag barricades, traverses, and during assault attempts!

The main emphasis is to be put on the ability to throw hand grenades from trenches, sap heads, and shell holes. Sideways out of a trench or in the direction of the trench. Striking certain parts of trenches, sapheads, and shell holes. Through competitive throwing and the awarding of prizes, the enthusiasm the men have for this duty can be increased!

B. Equipment.

In addition to the field-marching pioneer equipment or the infantry assault uniform A.V.F. 160 will be equipment of the flamethrower pioneers and the special assault tasks they are ordered to carry out, which will change according to the enemy and the effects of hostile fire.

1. Equipment for Missions within a Larger Framework.

Squad leader for small, medium, and large flamethrowers.

For missions carried out with other weapons within a larger framework and which require the troops to remain in the newly taken position for a longer time, the following equipment for flamethrower pioneers has proven satisfactory:

Steel helmet; slung rifle; no back pack; belt with bayonet; no cartridge pouches; 30 cartridges in jacket pockets and bread bag; pickax or pioneer spade with shortened handle hung perpendicularly on belt; adhesive tape; mess kit rolled in overcoat and 10 empty sandbags (construction material) carried on back; bread bag; two water bottles; gas mask; rations. Screwdriver and small adjustable wrench in bread bag.

Opposite
Top: Platoon Leutnant Junger (Zug Lt. Junger), of the Guard Reserve Pioneer Regiment; Leutnant Junger stands in the third row, sixth from left. This 37-man platoon may have been detached in order to perform attacks with limited objectives. By late 1917 flamethrower pioneers had their own machine guns and grenade launchers, often performing as conventional assault troops.

Bottom: Grof squad in action. The lance operator and assistant wear steel helmets and light assault order; an officer directs the flame jet. Grof squads often connected the lance to 100 feet of hose and took the weapon into No Man's Land to spray enemy positions at point-blank range.

Below: Kleif squad armed with late-model Kleif M.1915. The men are uniformed for forcible operations and reconnaissance, wearing field caps, pistols, bayonets, and no packs. The flamethrower lances have been fitted with igniters and are ready for combat, but the carrying frames have been removed from the flamethrowers. Note the propellant tank on the left, labeled "Nitrogen" (Stickstoff).

Gefreiter of the 10th Company, Guard Reserve Pioneer Regiment, photographed in 1916 soon after receiving his death's head sleeve badge. He wears an M1916 steel helmet and M1907/10 service jacket and is armed with a P08 pistol and S98/05 bayonet.

Individual squad leaders: wire cutters; flare guns; white cloth (aircraft signs).

Small and medium flamethrower carriers.
Steel helmet; small or medium flamethrower; gas mask; pistol; bayonet; and no cartridge pouches.

Lance operator for small, medium, and large flamethrowers.
Steel helmet; pistol; bayonet; mess kit; overcoat; bread bag; two water bottles; gas mask; flamethrower lance and hose; three igniters in an igniter case on belt; spare igniter fork.

Assistants and large-flamethrower staff.
Steel helmet; pistol; bayonet; mess kit; overcoat; bread bag; two water bottles; gas mask; two igniters; tool bag worn around the neck or on the belt, containing:

One set of washers; one pair of pipe pliers; one spare igniter holder.

Provisions are as those of the hand-grenade throwers.

Hand-grenade throwers.
Steel helmet; slung rifle or carbine; bayonet; no cartridge pouches; 30 cartridges in jacket pockets and bread bag; hand-grenade sacks with hand grenades (about six stick grenades or 10 egg grenades in each).

One section of the grenade throwers issued pioneer shovels with shortened handles to be hung from the belt, the other section equipped with middle-sized wire cutters. Mess kit rolled in overcoat and 10 empty sandbags carried on back. Rolled sandbags tied with cord and attached to the back; two water bottles; gas mask.

Provisions in bread bag and mess kit:

one loaf of bread; two portions of meat; and two portions of dried fruit (each in a tin).

2. Equipment for Forcible Operations and Reconnaissance.
In the case of small combat missions, patrols, and reconnaissance in force, in which surprise and mobility are necessary for success, the equipment is limited to the bare minimum of what is required. One must consider the personal preferences of the flamethrower pioneers when determining the patrol equipment.

A flamethrower patrol without back packs, belts, bayonets, and ammunition pouches, with only:

field caps,

gas masks (without metal containers) tucked into field jackets,

pistols (without holsters) attached to bread-bag straps and carried in jacket pockets,

daggers carried in jacket pockets,

and laced shoes and puttees

is more mobile and therefore more successful at surprise and catching the enemy unawares than a patrol in steel helmets and with full assault equipment.

Endnotes

[1] *Anleitung für Kompagnieführer (K.F.U.).* Berlin: Reichsdruckerei, 1917.
[2] Theune, *Sturmtruppen und Flammenwerfer,* pp. 156-157.
[3] Ibid., pp. 219-225.

CHAPTER 11

Large-scale Attacks by Assault Troops

Opposite
Top: Kaiser Wilhelm II reviewing men of Naval Infantry Regiment No.1 after the assault on Nieuport. Naval Infantry Regiment No.1 and No.2 provided six infantry battalions for Operation Beach Party. The troops wear the simplified field jacket with Guard lace on the collar.

Bottom: Shock Troop 25 of the 1st Matrosen Regiment, 1st Marine Division, Naval Corps Flanders (Marinekorps Flandern). These seamen wear the field-gray M1915 naval blouse issued with no shoulder straps; the field-gray or dark-blue naval caps have "I. MATROSENREGIMENT" on the band in gold lettering. The two sailors fourth and eighth from the left are members of the 1st Matrosen Artillery Detachment, the shock troop's forward observers. Note that the IMG08/15 on the cart is fitted with a bipod near the muzzle, which improved the stability of the gun.

Operation Beach Party

On June 20, 1917, the British XV Corps took over French positions in Flanders near Nieuport and Lombartzyde, moving into a bridgehead on the eastern bank of the Yser Canal. This changeover was part of the preparations for the Third Battle of Ypres, more commonly called Passchendaele. The British plan was for the troops in Nieuport to link up with an amphibious invasion force that would land on the Belgian coast.

On the left flank of the bridgehead was a narrow belt of sand dunes about 1400 yards wide. In order to strengthen this position, four Australian tunneling companies were brought in.[1] They began offensive mining toward the German lines, built subways and dugouts, and sank wells for drinking water. The bridgehead was connected to the western bank of the canal by three wooden pontoon bridges, the only way reinforcements and supplies could be brought in.

While the British prepared for their large-scale offensive, the Germans devised a preemptive strike against the bridgehead, a plan dubbed Operation Beach Party *(Unternehmen Strandfest)*. A second, smaller mission within Strandfest was Operation Section Dunes *(Unternehmen Abschnitt Dünen)*.[2] The attacks were to be carried out by the Naval Corps Flanders *(Marinekorps Flandern)*, which would provide Naval Infantry Regiment No.1 and No.2 *(Marine-Infanterie-Regiment Nr.1* and *Nr.2)* – a total of six infantry battalions – as well as the 400-man Assault Detachment *(Sturmabteilung)*. In addition, four companies of pioneers, two flamethrower companies, three aircraft detachments, and 58 artillery batteries would take part. The assault was to begin at 8:00 P.M. on the evening of July 9 with a nine-hour preparatory barrage.[3] It was to be supported with gunfire from the destroyer and torpedo-boat flotillas; this support was canceled due to the weather.

The Pioneer Experimental Company was attached to the 3rd Naval Division during this period and took part in the assault, although the unit's role is unknown. It is likely that the company tested new weapons and infiltration tactics, as it did throughout the war.

It is not clear how many flamethrower pioneers took part in Operation Beach Party. According to the war diary of the Naval Corps Assault Detachment, five officers, nine NCOs, and 63 enlisted men from the 6th Company of the Guard Reserve Pioneer Regiment were assigned to the unit on July 3. They served as both flamethrower operators and field pioneers. Bernhard Reddemann, however, wrote that the entire 6th and 12th Companies – some 400 men – participated.[4] Regardless of their number, the Death's Head Pioneers provided shock troops for the Naval Corps Assault Detachment and flame-accompanying squads for Naval Infantry Regiment No.1 and No.2.

The mission called for the Naval Corps Assault Detachment to open the way for the naval infantry regiments, which would attack from the east on a front two miles wide and about 1000 yards deep. The Assault Detachment supplied five shock troops of 25 to 45 men each. On July 4 and 5 an unspecified number of shock troops trained with the 3rd Battalion of Naval Infantry Regiment No.2 for the smaller Operation Section Dunes, the precise objective of which is not known. The next day this training was repeated with the participation of flamethrowers. Also on July 6 the Germans began shelling the Nieuport sector in preparation for the assault.

A 48-man platoon of the Naval Corps Assault Detachment (Marinekorps Sturm-Abteilung). They wear the M1915 blouse in field gray and are equipped with grenade bags, Kar 98AZ carbines, and respirators in M1916 canisters. Standing on the left is an officer with a P04, while the man lying in the right front displays the arm chevron of an Able Seaman (Matrosen-Gefreiten).

Operation Beach Party was launched on July 10. Bernhard Reddemann devoted one paragraph to it:

> The 6th and 12th Companies under Battalion Commander *Hauptmann* Koch carried out a frontal attack on positions in the dunes and reclaimed land at Lombartzyde in Flanders. Four *Grof* and 26 small flamethrowers in shock troops were used on a front 2500 meters wide. Enemy positions were penetrated, trenches rolled up, machine guns silenced, and blockhouses and large company dugouts smoked out. The flamethrower troops advanced 800 to 1000 meters deep, capturing 1300 prisoners and much war material.[5]

It began at 5:30 A.M. with a sustained barrage from coastal batteries, howitzers, and heavy trench mortars. At 10:00 A.M. aircraft of Flying Detachment 231 and the 1st and 2nd Naval Flying Detachments bombed the bridges over the Yser River and strafed relentlessly at low levels. Mustard gas – which the Germans called Yellow Cross *(Gelbkreuz)* – was used for the first time. The British positions were pulverized and all three of the pontoon bridges were destroyed, isolating the bridgehead on the eastern bank of the Yser.

At 7:51 P.M. the German naval infantry advanced in a crescent formation between the ebb-tide sands in the west and the Lombartzyde position in the

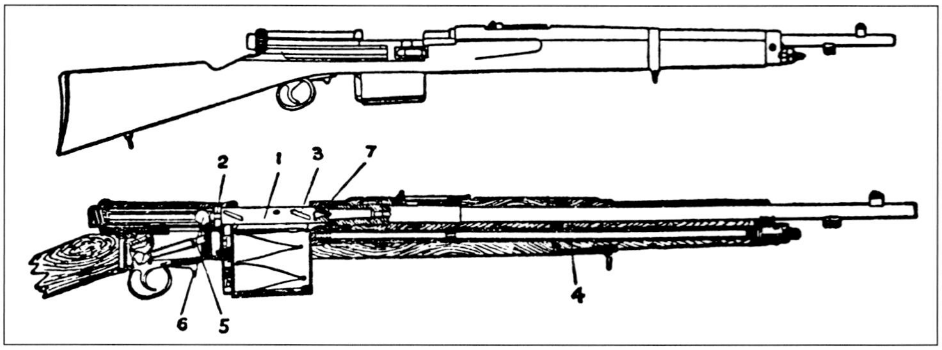

Mexican 7mm Mondragon M1908 semiautomatic rifle, used by the Naval Corps Assault Detachment. Weighing 9.5 lb, it was loaded with an 8-round clip and had a maximum range of 2197 yd. Though powerful, it was prone to jamming and fouling.

A combined stationary and pouncing attack in which Grof (left) lay down flame and smoke to cover the advance of shock troops armed with Wex M.1917. Four Grof and 26 Kleif or Wex were used during Operation Beach Party. U.S. National Archives 165-GB-6756.

east.[6] The use of the four *Grof* would indicate that a combined stationary and pouncing attack took place, a "shock" immediately prior to the infantry moving in. The assault was made in five waves:

> First wave: Shock troops who would attack the third line at the Yser River, ruthlessly destroying all enemy shelters in only 10 minutes.
> Second wave: Shock troops who would clean out the second line with hand grenades and flamethrowers and then move on to the third.
> Third wave: Regular infantry and light machine gunners, who were equipped with material to consolidate and hold the third line after the shock troops took it.
> Fourth wave: Regular infantry with pioneer equipment, who would clean out the first line and then proceed to the third.
> Fifth wave: Regular infantry who would take the second line and hold it.

When the British first line was pierced the attackers turned outward, splitting into two separate attacks. In the dunes on the far-left flank, the two battalions comprising the British 2nd Brigade, 1st Division, were virtually wiped out. Survivors took shelter in the dugouts and subways, but the Germans dropped hand grenades down the ventilation shafts and fired flamethrowers into the entrances.[7]

Shock Troop 1 of the Naval Corps Assault Detachment reported that since the British soldiers in two underground shelters refused an "energetic request" to emerge, they were killed with flamethrowers. Likewise, flamethrowers were sprayed at British machine-gun positions before they could fire a shot, whereupon the burning crews fell out on the ground. In the case of Shock Troop 4, however, some of the flamethrowers were damaged during the assault, and the rest were quickly emptied.[8]

Matrose of a naval infantry assault unit. He wears an M1915 blouse with the black wound badge (Verwundetenabzeichen) first issued on March 3, 1918, signifying one or two wounds. Weapons are a Gew 98 rifle, an S98/05 bayonet, and a 9mm P04 carried in a modified holster intended for the long-barreled artillery P08. Naval shock troops adopted this holster because it prevented the pistol from falling out.

One shock troop captured the British headquarters, attacked the regimental aid station with hand grenades, and machine gunned a Lewis-gun post in the rear, destroying the weapons and accepting the surrender of the few survivors.[9]

The fighting lasted until 8:30 P.M. When it was over, the Germans occupied a front on the bridgehead 1400 yards wide and 600 yards deep. Only four officers and 64 men of the British 2nd Brigade had managed to escape this position and swim across to the western bank of the Yser. South of Lombartzyde the Germans were driven back by a counterattack, but Operation Beach Party was deemed "a great and magnificent success" by Ludendorff.[10] German losses were five officers dead and four wounded; 29 enlisted men dead, 130 wounded, and eight missing.

Operation Summer Harvest

"German Attack by Gas Waves Which was to Have Taken Place in Champagne in September, 1917."[11]

I. Analysis of the Files of the First Bavarian Division Relating to the Attack by Gas Waves.

The operation was to have been carried out by the First Bavarian Division supported by two neighboring divisions. The front of the First Bavarian Division extended from the Saint-Hilaire-Saint-Souplet road to Souain Hill (6 kilometers).

Orders Nos. 1, 2, and 3 of the 12th, 13th, and 17th of August, 1917.

Operation Sommerernte *[Summer Harvest].*
General Instructions
The First Bavarian Division will make use of the powerful effect of gas in order to penetrate the enemy positions on the entire divisional front.

Troops employed. – Twelve shock troops of the First Bavarian Division, three shock troops of the Second Assault Battalion, twelve salvage squads, twelve destruction squads.

Attack on the flank. – The attack of the First Bavarian Division will be flanked by attacks of shock troops from the two neighboring divisions (the Thirtieth Division on the west and the Fifty-fourth Reserve Division on the east.)

Mission. – To destroy the enemy defenses on as wide a front as possible; to bring back the greatest possible quantity of war material of all kinds, as well as documents. In the orders the operation is called Sommerernte (summer harvest); to determine the losses of the enemy.

The occupation of the position. – The original plan provided for a wide outflanking attack to capture and occupy territory.

The menace of our attack on the Verdun front obliged the Germans to withdraw the Thirtieth Division and the Fifty-fourth Reserve Division. In replacing them the enemy could dispose only of divisions which had already suffered severely in Flanders, the Two Hundred and Twenty-first and the Fifty-second Reserve Divisions.

Under these conditions the German commander reduced the scope of his plan (order of the 17th of August). After the gas emission the extent of the effect was to be observed, the destruction completed, and the greatest possible quantity of booty brought back; but there was to be no question gaining territory.

Infanterist of a shock troop, Bavarian 2nd Infantry Regiment, Bavarian 1st Infantry Division. He wears the M1916 blouse with checkered blue-and-white lace on the leading edges of the collar; looped to his belt is a trench dagger with an elk-horn handle. This may be a postwar photo, as the imperial cockade is missing from the M1910 field cap.

Infanterist of the 3rd Company, Bavarian 1st Infantry Regiment, Bavarian 1st Infantry Division; his M1907 field jacket has Swedish cuffs, likely indicating that he was transferred into the regiment from the technical troops. Note the blue-and-white checkered collar lace that most Bavarians wore after 1916. All three regiments of the 1st Bavarian Division created four shock troops each for Operation Summer Harvest, August of 1917.

Front and objective. – The line to be attained formed an arc the chord of which was approximately 9 kilometers (from a point 2 kilometers east of Auberive to the Souain Hill) and 3 kilometers deep (1 kilometer west-southwest of Souain). The order of the 17th of August provided that three shock troops would push beyond the line originally fixed, and have for their respective objectives Saint-Hilaire, the Vacques farm, and Souain.

Prospective date. – The cylinders were to be in position by August 15.[†] The emission was to take place, at the earliest, during the night of the 17th to 18th, one hour before daylight (order of the 12th of August). Owing to prevailing contrary winds, the order of the 17th of August postponed the operation to the 1st of September (at the earliest).

Evacuation of the trenches. – The advanced trenches were to be evacuated for the attack, and only pioneer gassers (Thirty-fifth Regiment Pioneers), the sanitary personnel, and holding garrison were to remain in them.

Minute detailed instructions were given concerning the assembling of the shock troops and the different squads. All orders were given by code-conventional words.

Emission – Crossing the trenches. – The emission will last 15 minutes. Six companies of the Thirty-fifth Pioneer Regiment will be distributed along the emission sector. If it is dangerous for the shock troops to cross the emission trenches at the appointed hour, the commanders of pioneer companies will either detain them or point out a safe route for them.

Use of the artillery and trench mortars. – During the entire operation the enemy artillery will be neutralized by the fire of shell and gas shell. In each regimental sector a platoon of field artillery will advance as far forward as possible for the immediate support of the shock troops during the advance. The divisional artillery will hold itself in readiness to execute, on request from the shock troops, a barrage fire in front of the objective assigned. The trench mortars, medium and light, of the divisional company will be employed to support the attack and to reduce isolated points of resistance.

Aviation. – Three infantry aeroplanes and one or two artillery aeroplanes will be employed in the attack.

Opposite
***Top:** Grenadiers of Assault Battalion No.12 during an assault course for Austro-Hungarian officers and NCOs held at Nyárádszereda, Romania, May of 1917. Assault Battalion No.12 was established in Army Group Woyrsch in Poland and contained three assault companies.*

***Bottom:** Medium trench-mortar squad of a divisional trench-mortar company, during the assault course at Nyárádszereda. The weapon is the medium 170mm trench mortar, old pattern. In the left background Austrian and German officers gaze at half- and full-sized shells for a heavy 250mm mortar. An Austrian officer took this photo with an unauthorized camera.*

Two Pioniere of Pioneer Regiment No.35, which spent weeks preparing for Operation Summer Harvest. On the right is Pionier Rudolf Heintze, wearing the colored brassards of a trench raider on both sleeves of his M1907/10 field jacket. His companion – although a pioneer – is uniformed in an infantryman's field jacket. The two men belong to the 15th Reinforcement Squad (Armierungstrupp), 6th Company, 2nd Battalion.

Junkers gepanzertes Infanterieflugzeug aus dem Weltkrieg.

Junkers J.I; the caption reads "Junkers armored infantry aircraft from the world war." The J-class ("J" stood for "Infantry") of aircraft was used for infantry-contact patrols. It dropped messages and supplies to troops and strafed enemy ground forces. Three infantry aircraft were to be used in Operation Summer Harvest.

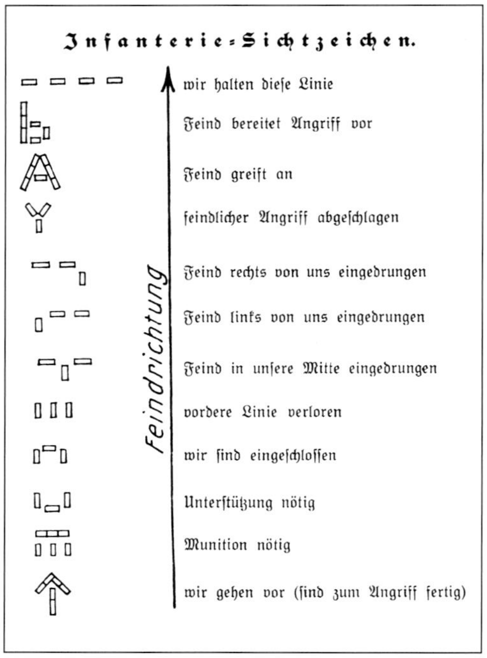

Infantry signs consisting of white cloth panels on the ground; the arrow points toward the enemy. From the top the signs are: 1. We are holding this line. 2. The enemy is preparing an attack ahead. 3. The enemy is attacking. 4. The enemy attack has been reduced. 5. The enemy has penetrated into our right. 6. The enemy has penetrated into our left. 7. The enemy has penetrated into our middle. 8. Our front line is lost. 9. We are surrounded. 10. Support is required. 11. Ammunition is required. 12. We are advancing (have finished the attack).

Preliminaries. – Special instructions to the shock troops and squads. Detailed reconnaissance. Special organization of liaison. Partial rehearsal of the operation during the night of the 16th to the 17th.

Composition of the Shock Troops and Detachments.
(a) *Shock troops.* – The First Bavarian Division will form 12 shock troops, Nos. 1-12 (four per infantry regiment), and the Second Assault Battalion will furnish three (A, B, C), making a total of 15 shock troops.

> *Shock Troops 1 to 12.*
> Furnished by the infantry:
> one officer,
> three noncommissioned officers,
> 16 men,
> one light machine gun (five men),
> two signalers.
> *[Bavarian]* First Battalion of Pioneers:
> one officer,
> four miners.
> Assault Battalion No.2:
> one corporal and three miners,
> one corporal and six grenade throwers,
> two stretcher bearers.
> Total, one officer and 47 noncommissioned officers and men *[in each shock troop].*

Shock troops Nos. 2, 7, and 10 will be known as the principal shock troops. They will have, in addition to the above, an artillery patrol (one officer and five men, including two telephone operators and two signalers), one detachment of infantry telephone operators (one noncommissioned officer and three men), one supplementary detachment of visual signalers (two men), and one pigeon tender, making an additional force of one officer and 12 noncommissioned officers and men.

> *Shock Troops A, B, C.*
> From Assault Battalion No.2:
> one officer,
> 30 men,
> one light machine gun (five men).
> From infantry trench-mortar detachments:
> two officers or warrant officers,
> 12 gunners and two light trench mortars,
> four telephone operators,
> two stretcher bearers.
> Total, three officers and 51 men *[in each shock troop].*

(b) *Destruction and salvage squads.* – The First Bavarian Division will form 12 salvage squads, Nos. 1 to 12 (four per infantry regiment), and the First Pioneer Battalion 12 destruction squads, 1 to 12.

Total strength of salvage and destruction squads.

> Infantry:
> one warrant officer,

Opposite
Top: Pioneers of the 3rd Company, Bavarian 1st Pioneer Battalion, Bavarian 1st Infantry Division. They wear light assault order consisting of rolled greatcoats slung across the body and gas masks in the "alert" position on the chest. The Bavarian 1st Pioneer Battalion formed destruction and salvage squads and provided men for the shock troops used by the Bavarian 1st Infantry Division for the aborted Operation Summer Harvest.

Bottom: Flamethrower squad of Assault Battalion No.12 demonstrating a late-model Kleif M.1915 at Nyárádszereda, May of 1917. The short range of the flame jet and the lance operator's one-handed grip indicate very low oil pressure.

Gun crew of a Bavarian Infantry Accompanying Battery attached to Bavarian 1st Landsturm Infantry Regiment on the western front. They pose in front of their wooden billet, "Villa-Kaln." Weapons include Kar 98AZ carbines, ersatz bayonets, and hand grenades. Artillerymen of Infantry Accompanying Batteries were trained as infantry assault troops and equipped accordingly. Several such batteries were to be used in Operation Summer Harvest.

three noncommissioned officers,
21 men.
Pioneers:
one noncommissioned officer,
four pioneers,
three pioneer gassers.

Total, one warrant officer and 32 noncommissioned officers and men *[in each squad]*.
Twelve men of each salvage squad will carry the ammunition for the light trench mortars of shock troops A, B, C.

(c) *Limber detachments (for removing enemy guns).* – Three limber detachments will be constituted, each comprising one officer, four six-horse teams, with the necessary drivers and gunners, and, in addition, one officer and 50 men of the pioneer battalion with entrenching material and explosives.

Details of Execution of the Operation.
The forces entrusted with the operation will be arranged for the attack in the following order:

(*a*) Shock troops 1 to 12 (first wave).
(*b*) Shock troops A, B, C (second wave).
(*c*) Salvage and destruction squads (third wave).

The principal shock troops (2, 7, and 10) will regulate the progress of the others.

The role of the shock troops will be to open a passage through the enemy's positions for the salvage and destruction squads, to break down the remaining resistance, to attain the objectives assigned them, and to protect the salvage and destruction squads during their operations.

If the shock troops attain their objectives and no enemy attacks occur during the day, the troops shall remain in the conquered lines until dark.

If the shock troops encounter a strong resistance, which they do not succeed in breaking down, they will hold out until the search for and seizure of the booty has been completed.

Before a superior enemy attack the shock troops will fall back slowly, protected by a barrage fire, which they will ask for.

The patrols of artillery officers marching with shock troops 2, 7, and 10 will support the advance by directing the fire of the advanced artillery platoons.

Shock troops A, B, and C, marching with the second wave, will support those who advanced with the first wave, breaking the enemy resistance as much as possible by flanking movements. They will put their trench mortars into action rapidly.

Shock troop of Landwehr Infantry Regiment No.386; a handwritten note on the back of the card reads, "In memory of the assault unit (Sturmtruppe)." All are equipped with two stick grenades, and all except two carry 7.65mm Mauser M1914 automatic pistols. Two riflemen in steel helmets round out the 16-man unit.

Soldat of a company shock troop, Saxon Infantry Regiment No.183. He is equipped with a gas mask and P08, and the bottoms of his trouser legs are folded over the tops of his boots in the Saxon and Württemberg style.

The salvage squads will explore the captured trenches. If the advance continues, they will organize a depot to which the companies in position will send their fatigue parties to transport important matériel to the rear.

All arms, appliances, telephones, listening apparatus, field glasses, searchlights, maps, orders, documents, equipment, and gas masks will be collected.

Enemies overcome by gas fumes will be brought into our lines.

The role of the sappers-gassers operating with the shock troops and squads is to point out the passages free from gas and to warn the men against the danger of being overcome.

The destruction squads, after removing the booty, will destroy the principal enemy defenses (command posts, observation stations, shelters, etc.).

Aviation. – The infantry aeroplanes will hold themselves in liaison with the shock troops and will keep the regimental commanders and the divisional commander informed of the advance of the shock troops.

Should a counter attack menace the shock troops, the aeroplanes will give warning by machine-gun fire.

Liaison. – The liaisons will be organized in every detail, in order that the regimental and brigade commanders and the divisional commander may be kept informed of the advance of the shock troops. Liaison on the flanks will be constantly maintained. Only the principal shock troops (2, 7, and 10) will communicate with the rear. The others will maintain lateral liaison only.

The principal shock troops will dispose of the following means:

Telephone. – Six kilometers of wire and three telephones.
Visual signaling. – Three groups of signalers (one for the rear, one for lateral liaison, and one for the artillery).
Pigeons. – Four pigeons.
Wireless. – Shock troop No.7 will be accompanied by a group of wireless operators.
Rockets will only be used in requesting barrage fire or extension of fire.

All the shock troops will designate runners for use in case the other means of communication should fail.

Order No.4 of the 25th of August, 1917.
By the 21st the Germans knew that we had discovered their plans. On the entire front in question our artillery began demolition fire (21st of August), and our infantry multiplied its surprise attacks, resulting each time in the capture of prisoners and matériel. In order to face our offensive at Verdun, the German commander was obliged to call upon his remaining available resources west of the Argonne.

Therefore an order dated August 25 modified the arrangement. "Under the present conditions a more energetic action on the part of the enemy must be expected than was at first anticipated." Consequently –

The shock troops of each regimental sector will be placed under the orders of a battalion commander, who, with his staff, will follow the movements of the principal shock troops. His duties will be: To determine what lines will be held, and for how long; to fix the moment of withdrawal, and to regulate the advance and the progressive withdrawal.

Machine gunners of Assault Battalion No.12 instruct Austrian officers in the use of a Russian Maxim M1910 (foreground) and Bergmann IMG15. All members of German assault battalions were trained in the use of enemy machine guns they were likely to encounter on the battlefield.

Each battalion commander will dispose of a platoon of at least 40 men, with two light machine guns, which will constitute a reserve to be called upon in case of need, particularly to support the shock troops in case of counter attacks.

The rear liaison installed by the three principal shock troops will be at the disposal of the three battalion commanders.

All the men of the attacking troops will have leather masks issued to them.

Each of the three battalion staffs will have a squad of six men furnished with Draeger apparatus.

Shortly before the sortie of the shock troops the trench mortars will direct an energetic fire on the breaches and on such machine guns as are still capable of operating.

Postponement of the Operation "Sine Die."

Finally, on the 29th of August a pioneer of the Thirty-fifth Regiment deserted, bringing us, in addition to the confirmation of a plan of attack, all the technical details to be desired. This desertion was noted, and the Germans became aware that they could no longer count on a surprise effect.

Moreover, they had taken some prisoners from us, who, in all probability, informed them of our counter preparations.

Under such conditions the operation threatened to lose a good part of its effectiveness. The intensity of our fire (increased since August 27) no longer permitted the enemy to attempt even a restricted infantry action, and the gas receptacles under our bombardment became a source of danger to the Germans,[††] a danger which would be increased by an unfavorable wind. It seemed certain that our very deadly and very depressing fire would not diminish, while our patrols continued to point out surviving installations.

There remained, then, but one solution to the situation – the postponement of the plan sine die and the removal of all the matériel as soon as possible, so that the enemy might be made aware of this through his patrols. On the 10th of September the Germans seem to have come to this decision.

To sum up, the "Sommerernte" seems to have gone through three phases:

Postponement of a very extensive plan because of atmospheric conditions and the menace of our attack along the Verdun front.

Reduction of the original plan owing to the Verdun attacks, while still maintaining a less comprehensive plan to be carried out as soon as the wind should permit.

Postponement sine die, if not definite abandonment, when all hope of surprise has been lost and the operation appeared more costly than profitable.

Opposite
***Top:** Crown Prince Wilhelm (right) inspects shock troops of the 1st Regiment of Foot Guards (1. Garde-Regiment zu Fuß). Note the unusual painted camouflage on the steel helmets, which takes the form of small, brightly colored lozenges.*

***Bottom:** Grenadiers of Assault Battalion No.12 and German infantry officers instruct Austrian officers (left) in the use of the grenade launcher 16. The weapon is placed on a sandbagged platform and fired by lanyard; the grenade-launcher squad will take cover in the trench when firing.*

II. Information Emanating from the Papers of a Deserter and the Declarations of Prisoners.

Nature of the Gas
The attack provided for two emissions, each of a different gas:

First. Irritant gas (Reizgas), probably sulphate of ethyl bichloride, white color, drug-store smell. Escapes under the form of a nontoxic vapor, accompanied by a little liquid, blue and turning brown in the air, very corrosive. This nontoxic gas penetrates the masks, and by irritating the skin compels their removal. Duration of the emission, four minutes.

Second. Toxic gas (Kampfgas), a gas already known, immediately following the preceding. It was expected that at this moment, our men having taken off their masks, will be without protection.

The officers captured from the Second Army indicated an analogous procedure for bombardment with poisonous shells.

Detailed Description of the Apparatus for Emitting Irritant Gas.

[Translation of a notebook taken on a deserter of the Thirty-fifth Regiment of Pioneers.]

Irritant Gas (Reizgas).

It is contained in a case consisting of two cylindrical tin containers 70 centimeters high, handle 15 centimeters, escape tube 10 centimeters, the reservoir proper therefore being only 50 centimeters high.

The reservoir proper consists of the handle fastened at the bottom; above the handle the priming powder, ignited by a fuse primer placed in the handle, igniting itself when the handle is pulled.

The interior of the receiver is constructed as follows: Two tin cylinders (concentric), the exterior cylinder containing a mass of sulphur and iron through which run fuses that are in contact with the priming powder.

Manipulation of the apparatus.
The gas box being placed in position, supposing that the gas is to be released at 11 o'clock, at five minutes to 11 the men put on gas masks, making sure that they are properly adjusted. Then the commander of the battery (20 or 25 cylinders) gives the signal to release the gas. Grasp between the first finger and thumb of the left hand the point where the priming-powder tube is screwed on and, having first unscrewed the stopper of the escape neck, pull the fuse primer. A light whistle will indicate that the priming powder has taken. On hearing this whistle, take some earth and cover the bottom of the box with it, the remainder of the box being already covered with earth except the neck.

Wait two or three minutes until the heavy vapors have escaped; now open the heavy gas cylinder (Beschwerungsflasche); a rag or any other sign distinguishes it from the irritant-gas cylinders. The reason for this proceeding is to make the irritant gas (lighter) trail nearer the level of the ground, as otherwise it would rise and do no harm to the enemy. At the end of four minutes the irritant-gas box is empty, and then is the time to release the real asphyxiating gas.

On releasing the irritant gas from the box, a liquid forms and settles on the rim of the neck. This liquid is very dangerous. When removing the boxes after the operation, if this liquid comes into contact with hands and faces, the box of chloride of lime carried by everyone should be immediately employed and the parts affected washed with this chloride of lime.

When the trench comprises a firing step, it is entirely removed. The toxic-gas cylinders are placed upright, buried at the bottom of the trench to a depth of 10 to 15 centimeters, and usually in two rows. They should be protected behind and on top with sandbags – two rows of sandbags behind the cylinders and at least four, preferably six, layers above. Between each

Opposite
Top: *A second shot of the same grenade-launcher position as in the previous image. On the left, a grenadier of Assault Battalion No.12 holds open a box of aerial grenades, while the launcher is prepared for another shot. After completion of the assault course, the Austrian officers would have trained their own men in German shock-troop tactics.*

Bottom: *Heavy machine-gun squad of Assault Battalion No.8, photographed on the eastern front. On the left is an officer wearing spectacles; the remaining six are enlisted men. All carry pistols, and three wear grenade bags. Field jackets include the M1907/10, the simplified jacket, and the M1915 blouse. Shoulder straps have been removed for security.*

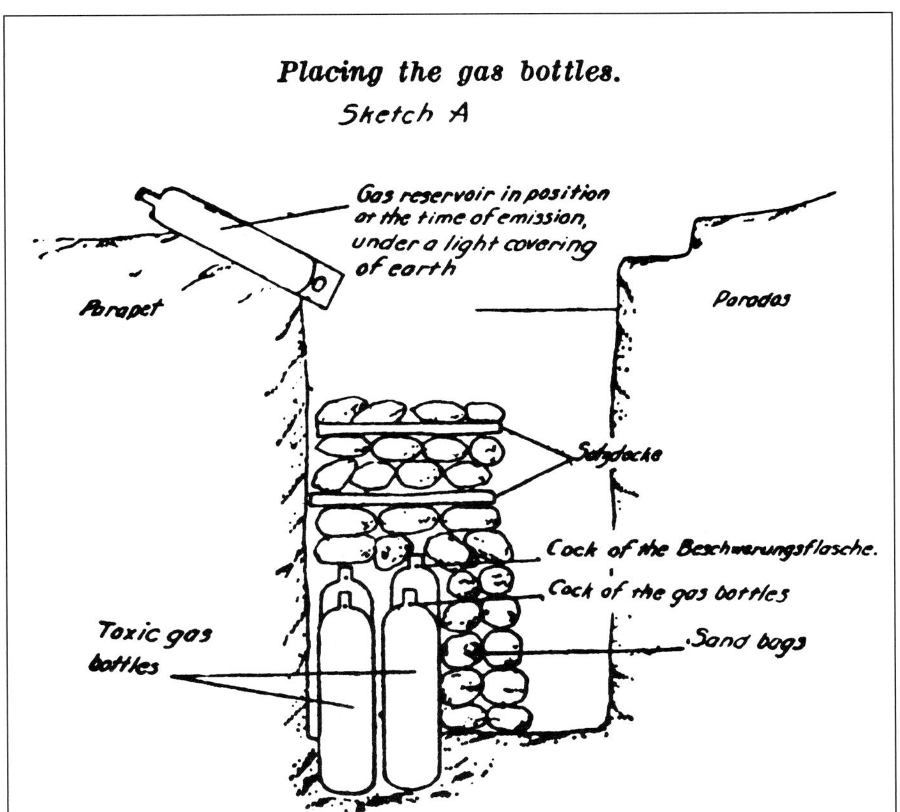

Arrangement of gas cylinders for Operation Summer Harvest, August of 1917. Cylinders of irritant gas (Reizgas) are laid on the parapet of the trench, while toxic gas (Kampfgas) is contained in cylinders (Beschwerungsflaschen) on the trench floor. Layers of sand bags and a salt-impregnated cloth (Salsdecke) would absorb any gas accidentally emitted into the German trench. The flexible lead gas pipes attached to the cylinders are not depicted.

Assault troops training for a gas attack. They wear heavy assault order, steel helmets, M1915 Gummimasken, and rifles with fixed bayonets. After the cancellation of Operation Summer Harvest, the Germans did not launch any more cylinder attacks on the western front, employing projectors and shells instead.

pair of layers of sandbags on top of the cylinders there must be a sort of covering called by the prisoner "Salsdecke," impregnated with a salt intended to absorb the gas, which would otherwise escape into the trench at the time of the emission. A spare Salsdecke is always kept in a corner of the trench section where the cylinders are. Should one of the cylinders explode as the result of a bombardment, the Salsdecke is at once thrown over the bottle and absorbs the gas. The Salsdecke is brownish in color, like wet earth.

At the time of the emission the sandbags covering the bottles are removed, the lead tubes are screwed to the neck; they are bound together in sheaves and thrown out onto the parapet of the trench. At the same time the irritant-gas cylinders are laid on the parapet. The whole arrangement before the emission resembles a firing platform made of sandbags. Only the ends of the keys of the cylinders can be distinguished, barely protruding behind the bags. One of the keys is marked with a distinguishing sign (a rag, for instance). It is the one to be opened at the same time as the irritant-gas bottles in order to weight the latter down. This is the "Beschwerungsflasche."

But in the future it is ordered that the bottles be placed in a sort of niche in the actual trench wall. Only the sandbags behind the bottles will project into the trench.

German infantrymen posing with a 76.2mm Infantry Gun L/16.5. Some of the men belong to Infantry Regiment No. 51, while at least two are Guard Jäger. The Jäger standing on the far right wears a small, dark-bordered "S" badge on his inner left elbow, denoting his membership in a shock troop.

Probable duration of the attack.
Four minutes for the irritant gas and 20 minutes for the toxic gas. The effect of the toxic gas may be felt for a depth of 6 to 7 kilometers.

Instruction.
In the rear depots the new irritant gas is not yet known, and the men only know how to handle the old poisonous gas.

Masks.
The irritant gas will penetrate the new leather masks. When handling irritant gas, carry in addition individual oxygen bottles.

Notes.
† The Thirty-fifth and Thirty-sixth Regiments of Pioneers seem to have arrived on the sector the beginning of July.

††According to the declarations of prisoners captured on the 29th of August, our artillery fire caused the explosion of numerous cylinders and this resulted in casualties. After the fire of the night of the 1st-2nd *[of September]* all the cylinders which had been placed in the first trench were brought back to the second.

Endnotes

[1] W. Grant Grieve and Bernhard Newman, *Tunnelers* (London, 1936), p. 200.

[2] Much of the information on Operation Beach Party is found in the War Diary of Sturmabteilung Marinekorps, Bundesarchiv-Militärarchiv RM 120/324.

[3] Mark D. Karau, *Wielding the Dagger: The MarineKorps Flandern and the German War Effort, 1914-1918* (Westport, Connecticut: Praeger Publishers, 2003), p. 150.

[4] Reddemann, *Geschichte,* pp. 34-35.

[5] Ibid.

[6] Edward Wright, "The British Offensive at Ypres and the Battle of Lens," in *The Great War,* Volume 10, edited by H. W. Wilson and J. A. Hammerton (London: The Amalgamated Press, 1915-1918), p. 436.

[7] Grieve and Newman, p. 200.

[8] War Diary of Sturmabteilung Marinekorps.

[9] Northamptonshire Regimental History Committee. *The Northamptonshire Regiment 1914-1918*. Aldershot: Gale & Polden, 1932. pp. 192-200.

[10] Wright, "The British Offensive at Ypres," p. 436.

[11] War Department, *German Notes on Minor Tactics* (Washington, D.C.: Government Printing Office, 1918), pp. 35-46.

CHAPTER 12

Infantrymen Transformed into Assault Troops

The Assault on Riga

Artillery played a pivotal role in the assault on Riga, Latvia. The commander of artillery was *Oberstleutnant* Georg Bruchmüller, who had been brought out of retirement at the start of the war.[1] By the end of October 1914 he was on the eastern front serving as artillery commander of Division von Wernitz, later redesignated the 86th Infantry Division. Bruchmüller shifted control of fire planning from individual attacking divisions to a centralized command; he also advocated that a rolling barrage cover the attacking troops for the entire operation. The result was much more violent, concentrated fire. After successful German attacks at Lake Narotch, Zarzeize Bridgehead, Korytnica-Swiniuchy, Witonitz, and the Toboly Bridgehead, during which Bruchmüller was given command of larger and larger batteries, he was awarded the prestigious *Pour le Mérite* or Blue Max, one of only four higher-level artillery commanders to receive the distinction in the war. For a retired colonel on temporary active duty it was an impressive achievement.

German troops on the eastern front felt that if Bruchmüller conducted the artillery preparation, the attack was guaranteed to be successful.[2] He was nicknamed Breakthrough Müller *(Durchbruch Müller)*, and the key to his tactics was to have the infantry follow the rolling barrage as closely as possible. This required a high level of coordination among the batteries to ensure that the artillerymen adhered to the predetermined schedule and did not fire short rounds. Signal rockets, liaison officers, and forward observers would facilitate the cooperation between artillery and infantry.

The rolling barrage that protected the infantry was created by light field guns, light field howitzers, and trench mortars. Larger guns in the rear fired high explosive, shrapnel, and gas shells to prevent the enemy from manning his artillery and machine guns. They also created box barrages that prevented the enemy from bringing up his reserves and retreating. Heavy trench mortars were the only weapons assigned specific targets such as command posts or bunkers.

For the assault on Riga, 100 heavy, 130 medium, and 320 light trench mortars were set up in the woods behind the Germans trenches. They were organized into a Trench Mortar Brigade under a commander who reported directly to Bruchmüller.

The reinforced Eighth Army, under the command of *General der Infanterie* Oskar von Hutier, attacked at Riga. The order of battle was:

Assault Company No.18;
Guard *Ersatz* Division;
1st Guard Infantry Division;
1st Reserve Infantry Division;
2nd Guard Infantry Division;
2nd Bavarian *Landwehr* Division;
14th Bavarian Infantry Division;
19th Reserve Infantry Division;
20th Infantry Division;
22nd *Landwehr* Division;
29th *Landwehr* Division;
42nd Infantry Division;
75th Reserve Infantry Division;
105th Infantry Division;

Grenadier Albert Schumacher of the 2nd Regiment of Foot Guards (2. Garde-Regiment zu Fuss), 1st Guard Infantry Division, which assaulted Riga on September 1, 1917. The Allies considered the 1st Guard Infantry Division one of the best German formations. Schumacher wears the M1097/10 field jacket with white Guard lace on the collar and plain shoulder straps piped in red.

This confident-looking Wehrmann is a member of the Bavarian 2nd Landwehr Infantry Regiment, 2nd Bavarian Landwehr Division, another assault unit at Riga. He wears the Bavarian M1915 simplified tunic, an S98/05 bayonet, and cleated mountain boots.

203rd Infantry Division;
205th Infantry Division;
1st Cavalry Division;
Cavalry Division North (Composite);
Reinforced *Leib* Hussar Brigade.

On August 31, 1917, about 40 German bombers and fighters carried out a series of attacks on islands in the Gulf of Riga and at the entrance to the Gulf of Finland in preparation for the assault.[3] The artillery bombardment began at 4:00 A.M. on September 1, the Germans firing 20,650 Blue Cross and Green Cross gas shells over two hours.[4] This was followed by a bombardment with high-explosive and shrapnel shells along a front 75 miles wide.

The three divisions that led the attack at 9:10 in the morning were the 2nd Guard Infantry Division on the left, the 14th Bavarian Infantry Division in the center, and the 19th Reserve Division on the right, covering a front 9900 yards wide.[5] They crossed the Dvina River in wooden pontoon boats, rowing 380 yards to the Üxküll Peninsula. Once ashore, infantry commanders fired green rockets, the signal for the barrage to begin rolling forward.[6] After taking the first Russian line, the assault troops moved ahead to the second. Behind them, pioneers built three pontoon bridges, one in each sector of the assaulting divisions, so that three more divisions could cross. By the night of September 1, the Germans had six divisions on the Russian side, creating a bridgehead 8 miles wide. Riga fell three days later, although the Russian Twelfth Army was able for the most part to escape encirclement and destruction.

After Riga, German shock-troop tactics became known among the Allies as "Hutier tactics," even though Hutier had nothing to do with their development. In a memo dated June 16, 1918, Marshal Ferdinand Foch described the tactics:

Assault troops row across the Dvina River at Riga on September 1, 1917. In the background a German artillery barrage strikes the Üxküll Peninsula.

***Above:** Kaiser Wilhelm II and General der Infanterie Oskar von Hutier (the tall officer in the Pickelhaube) inspect infantry and pioneer assault troops. The men in the first row are armed with MP18/I submachine guns and trench daggers. It appears that they carry spare 32-round ammunition drums in their jacket pockets.*

***Below:** Pioneers on the eastern front in a pontoon boat of the type used to ferry troops across the Dvina River during the assault on Riga. The men in the boat and a few on the shore wear mosquito veils lifted off their faces.*

The German method of attack is characterized by surprise, violence, rapidity of execution, manœuvre, and the extreme depth of penetration sought.

I. The surprise is obtained by the brevity of the artillery preparation (three to four hours) and by the transport to the place of attack of units to be engaged at the very last moment, the marches to the front of the troops to be used being made at night and on foot.

Up to the night which precedes the attack there is not the slightest change in the customary appearance of the front; quiet reigns and the usual formations are in line.

The attack always takes place just at daybreak, the infantry being preceded by a barrage consisting of a strong proportion of smoke shells. As a result of the cloud effect thus produced, our infantry and our artillery only perceive the enemy when he is within a few metres of him.

II. The violence is achieved by the intensity of the bombardment, all calibres and every sort of shell being employed simultaneously on a depth of four or five kilometers *[between two and a half and three miles]* and by the attack of masses of infantry which, during the artillery preparation, assemble at from 700 to a thousand feet before the first lines to be taken.

After the first lines are taken *[the mass of infantry]* lengthens out and spreads out, the units in advance aiming as quickly as possible at successive objectives, which have been indicated for them in advance, without having any preoccupation for their own flanks or for cleaning up in their rear, to which task other units are assigned.

The designation of these successive objectives does not imply any halt at any of them, but merely provides landmarks showing the direction to be followed.

III. During the forward movement the infantry is protected by a rolling barrage of artillery, then by the light artillery and *minnenwerfer[sic],*

Unteroffiziere of the 3rd and 7th Companies, Guard Reserve Pioneer Regiment, in a postcard sent from Vilna, Lithuania, on November 27, 1917. Note the many styles of Guard and NCO lace on the collars. The flag is a trophy with a Cyrillic inscription that reads "United Socialists Horse Army."

which accompany it. It also makes free use of its own rifle fire and of its own machine guns.

If an infantry unit encounters an obstacle which it cannot take by its own strength, it halts and is immediately passed by units which support it, and these are charged with the task of taking the strong point which remains by enveloping it.

IV. The Germans generally employ the best troops in the centre of the attacking front in such a fashion as to give themselves every chance of obtaining a rapid and profound advance in the centre.

The manœuvre consists, first, in enlarging rapidly the breach thus opened, and then in attacking on the flanks of the breach.

V. The penetration in depth is obtained by the rapid and resolute march of the troops upon predetermined objectives situated far within the enemy's lines. It has for its consequence a prompt disorganization of any defence not completely organized by taking from it the essential points of organization, which are its predetermined objectives.[7]

Three Schützen of the 3rd Company, Bicycle Battalion No.5. The 5300-man Bicycle Brigade No.2 played a pivotal role in Operation Albion, its speed and firepower preventing the Russians from escaping. Two of these bicyclists wear the Jäger gray-green M1915 blouse, while one may be uniformed in field gray.

Bernhard Reddemann wrote that the 3rd and 7th Companies of the Guard Reserve Pioneer Regiment under Battalion Commander *Hauptmann* Beck attacked at Riga with 84 *Kleif*.[8] After the troops were ferried across the Dvina River by pontoon boat, flamethrower shock troops achieved breakthrough by using the Knife Tactic, advancing in long, snakelike formations behind a rolling barrage. Machine guns were silenced and dugouts and farm houses were captured. Eight thousand prisoners, 180 cannons, 200 machine guns, and much war material were taken.

The flamethrower pioneers were "half-*Kleif* squads" *(Halbkleiftrupps)*, their flamethrowers only half-filled with oil to reduce weight and increase speed and mobility.

Operation Albion

From 1915 the Germans held most of Courland Province.[9] At the mouth of the gulf the islands of Ösel, Dagö, and Moon sat between the Irbe Straits to the west and Moon Sound to the east. The Russians had built several fortifications and batteries of coastal artillery on the islands to cover these two narrow passageways. In order to fully control the Gulf of Riga, the Germans had to take Ösel, Dagö, and Moon. The plan for a massive amphibious landing was dubbed Operation Albion *(Unternehmen Albion)* and would be organized by *General* Oskar von Hutier, commander of the Eighth Army.

The most heavily defended positions were on the Sworbe Peninsula in the southwest of Ösel. These included artillery batteries at Zerel aimed at the Irbe Straits. Tagga Bay on the northwest coast of Ösel was defended by batteries of 120mm guns at Hundsort and 150mm guns at Ninnast, each on either side of the bay. In the northeast, batteries at Pamerort on Ösel and Toffri on Dagö covered the Soela Sound between Ösel and Dagö. The causeway at Orrisar, which connected Ösel Island and Moon Island, was guarded at both ends by Russian troops. Altogether there was about one division of Russians on Ösel.

Operation Albion was carried out by the German XXIII Reserve Corps. The assault troops were:

the 65th Infantry Brigade of the 42nd Infantry Division, consisting of:

Assault detachment of Infantry Regiment No.255, which reinforced the 42nd Infantry Division during Operation Albion. They wear full knapsacks and gas masks in the "alert" position and are armed with stick grenades and Gew 98 rifles.

Men of Infantry Regiment No.138, 42nd Infantry Division, posing with a Lanz 91.5mm light trench mortar. Leather-reinforced trousers indicate that these are likely members of the regimental assault company.

a) Infantry Regiment No.17,
b) Infantry Regiment No.131,
c) Infantry Regiment No.138;
Infantry Regiment No.255;
Bicycle Brigade No.2;
Assault Battalion No.10;
Assault Company No.18.

The Landing Corps would include about 23,000 men, 5000 horses, 1400 vehicles, 150 machine guns, 54 artillery pieces, 12 mortars, and munitions and provisions for 30 days.[10] Nineteen steamers would bring the assault echelons from their concentration at Libau to Tagga Bay on Ösel's western shore. Learning from the British disaster at Gallipoli and Russian successes in the Black Sea, the Germans had their transports "assault loaded," meaning the troops and weapons needed to establish a beachhead were on deck or easily accessible while equipment or supplies to be unloaded later were placed deeper in the ships' holds.

Eight dreadnoughts plus the light cruiser *Emden* were assigned to suppress the coast defense artillery; all were brought to their pre-assigned places without incident. The only fire support allotted directly to the landing troops were the torpedo boats' light guns, since the sophisticated fire support offered by the U.S. Navy during World War II was still more than 25 years in the future. At Ösel the Germans had no procedure by which the troops ashore could request fire from the ships. The big ships would fire according to pre-arranged bombardment plans, while the torpedo-boat gunnery officers would observe the shoreline and fire on targets they determined themselves.

Minesweepers went in 24 hours ahead of the invasion, accompanied by three small steamers carrying 1600 bicycle troops and 150 soldiers and sailors who would land at Pamerort. Bicycle Brigade No.2, brought in from Flanders, was comprised of 144 officers, 5199 soldiers, 734 horses, 4597 bicycles, 215 wagons, 51 automobiles, 111 trucks, and 32 machine guns. The soldiers landed at Pamerort were signalmen and artillerymen trained in using captured Russian guns, while the sailors were armed with 10 heavy machine guns.

Assault Company No.18 aboard torpedo boat B110 during Operation Albion, October 12, 1917. The torpedo boat flotilla transported assault troops into Tagga Bay on the Island of Ösel. Note the life vests draped over the rail.

The 2nd Torpedo Boat Flotilla, a tender, and two steamers carried the 3600-man assault force of Infantry Regiment Nos. 131 and 138. This was followed by two battleship squadrons, a light-cruiser flotilla to provide security for the 14-ship transport fleet, and then the ammunition ships, cargo carriers, water tenders, two hospital ships, two oilers, and a seaplane tender. Cruisers, destroyers, minesweepers, and zeppelins watched for submarines. Altogether the German fleet numbered 363 vessels.

At dawn the 3600 assault troops would land at Tagga Bay, led by regimental assault companies. They would arrive in torpedo boats, the motor launches of the battleship squadrons, and the steamers. Darkness and the element of surprise would allow the assault force to make its way past the forts at the mouth of the bay. The troop carriers preceded the battleships, which would steam in circles to keep the forts under continuous fire. Once the troop carriers made it past the forts, they were safe from gunfire, as the Russian guns were fixed seaward.

The German torpedo boats would use their 105mm guns to suppress the Russian batteries firing from the woods on either side of the bay. Before the troop carriers landed in Tagga Bay, two assault detachments from Assault Battalion No.10 would attack the two Russian forts at Hundsort and Ninast, which sat on opposite sides of the bay. Two battalions of Infantry Regiment

Assault troops landing on Ösel during Operation Albion, October 12, 1917. Two of the tramp steamers used as troop carriers can be seen in the background, along with an inflatable raft and lifeboats that shuttled soldiers ashore.

No.131 would land at Ranna (Veere) on the west bank, while two battalions of Infantry Regiment No.138 would take the east bank. The assault units were given the mission of securing the beach and forming a defensible perimeter. Only then would the rest of the troops steam into Tagga Bay and land. Ships would bombard the batteries at the mouth and sides of the bay, as well as the seaplane station at Papensholm. Most of the 42nd Infantry Division would capture Arensburg to prevent the Russian from retreating to the Island of Moon in the northeast; simultaneously Infantry Regiment No.131 would march from Tagga Bay to the Sworbe Peninsula in the south to take Fort Zerel.

At the Cape of Pamerort the secondary landing of bicycle troops was intended to confuse the Russians and place the troops 18 miles closer to their target, the bridgehead to the causeway at Orrisar. The sailors armed with heavy machine guns would hold the cape, allowing the two battalions of bicycle troops to advance inland. One would ride toward Arensburg and the other toward Orrisar.

A ship's lifeboat serves as a landing craft during Operation Albion, October 12, 1917. In the foreground a steel-helmeted cyclist wades toward the camera, leading a horse and pushing his heavily laden bicycle.

Naval feints and bombardments of Dagö Island in the north and Zerel in the south would distract from the main landings in Tagga Bay. After the assault force went ashore, the fleet would enter the Gulf of Riga through the Irbe Straits and use its guns to support the 107th Infantry Division at Arensburg and Infantry Regiment No.131 on the Sworbe Peninsula. Once the Germans had taken Arensburg, the fleet would use the city as its base of operations, providing support for ground troops assaulting Orrisar and Moon.

The amphibious assaults were rehearsed on the beaches at Libau, while at night the men attended lectures by intelligence officers which included magic-lantern shows that depicted the Russian fortifications. To increase the speed of the invasion, the Pioneer Landing Company *(Pionier Landungskompagnie)* was transferred in from Romania to serve as stevedores, and Pioneer Battalion No.9 arrived from the Elbe River to build the floating docks, pontoon bridges, and gangways for unloading cargo.

Airships were active during the preparations for Operation Albion.[11] In addition to reconnaissance missions they also conducted bombing raids. During the night of September 24-25 *LZ120* dropped over four tons of bombs on the Zerel battery at about 2:45 A.M., which was followed by *LZ113* with 400 pounds of bombs. On the evening of October 1 *L30, L37,* and *LZ120* attacked Salis and Salismunde and their environs, dropping a combined total of nearly nine tons of bombs. Since the area was poorly defended, *L30* attacked from only 4000 feet.

The rain and fog were heavy on the morning of October 12, 1917.[12] At around 5:44 A.M. the German fleet opened fire on Ösel. A short time later two launches landed men from Assault Battalion No.10. The torpedo boats offshore used their guns to support the assault force; the laborious, time-consuming process was to put naval officers ashore who found the units in question and asked them where they wanted the fire. The officers then returned to their ships and identified the visible targets. It could take as long as two hours to complete one fire-support mission.

During the assault German seaplanes launched from a tender performed vital reconnaissance flights.[13] The heaviest fighting took place at Orrisar, where one bicycle battalion and Assault Company No.18 took the Ösel side of the causeway leading to Moon and the second bicycle battalion covered the road from Arensburg to Orrisar. Naval forces in the Kassar Inlet in the north served as artillery support, bombarding the Russians incessantly. The trapped Russians tried for two days to break through the bicyclist battalion at Orrisar, but surrendered when the 42nd Infantry Division arrived on the scene after a forced march in pouring rain from Arensburg.

By October 16 the battle for Ösel was over; the Germans then launched several assaults across the causeway into Moon. The Assault Company of Infantry Regiment No.138 finally succeeded in crossing and taking the fortifications guarding the causeway. The remainder of the regiment joined the assault company and secured Moon by October 17. On October 19 Infantry Regiment No.17 was ferried across Soela Sound to Dagö Island, where it faced weak resistance. The land battles had ended.

At a tactical level, Operation Albion was an unqualified success.[14] The Germans took the islands and captured 20,130 Russians, 141 cannons, 130 machine guns, 2000 horses, two armored cars, 28 automobiles and trucks, and 10 aircraft. German casualties were three officers and 51 soldiers killed and six officers and 135 soldiers wounded; four naval officers and 152 were sailors killed, and 60 sailors were wounded. Seven small German ships were

Infantry assault troops on the march. Along with their knapsacks they carry empty sandbags and gas masks in cloth bags. Many have slipped waterproof covers over the muzzles of their Gew 98 rifles. The success of Operation Albion was due in part to the assault troops' ability to quickly undertake long marches across the islands.

Bavarian Infanterist of the Alpine Corps in walking-out dress consisting of Bavarian M1915 simplified field jacket, black trousers, and lace-up shoes. The band of his M1910 officers' service cap displays the Edelweiss badge of the Alpine Corps as well as two Austrian unit or campaign badges.

sunk before and during the operation, and another two that ran aground were later scuttled.

The Battle of Caporetto

For the Battle of Caporetto the central powers created the Austro-German Fourteenth Army, 15 divisions that were used as assault troops.

Group Krauss (I Corps):
a) Austrian *Edelweiss* Division;
b) Austrian 22nd *Schützen* Division;
c) Austrian 55th Infantry Division;
d) German *Jäger* Division.

Group Stein (III Corps):
a) Austrian 50th Infantry Division;
b) German 12th Infantry Division;
c) German Alpine Corps;
d) German 117th Infantry Division.

Group Berrer (LI Corps):
a) German 21st Infantry Division;
b) German 200th Infantry Division.

Group Scotti (XV Corps):
a) Austrian 1st Infantry Division;
b) German 5th Infantry Division.

Fourteenth Army Reserves:
a) Austrian 4th Infantry Division;
b) Austrian 13th *Schützen* Division;
c) Austrian 33rd Infantry Division.[15]

The Fourteenth Army had 1076 guns, 174 heavy mortars, 31 pioneer and sapper companies, and nine aviation detachments. *Jäger* (Assault) Battalion No.3 – less the 1st and 2nd Assault Companies – was attached to the German *Jäger* Division for the battle, while the Württemberg Mountain Battalion was attached to the Alpine Corps.[16] At this time the Württemberg Mountain Battalion was comprised of 11 companies; *Oberleutnant* Erwin Rommel led a detachment of two mountain companies and one machine-gun company.

In February of 1917 the Austrian Supreme Army Command (*Armee-Oberkommando* or *AOK)* had ordered that assault battalions be formed on the German model. An Army Assault Battalion *(Armeesturmbataillon)* consisted of four infantry companies, each of which had two nine-man Assault Patrols; one or two machine-gun companies; one mountain-artillery battery with four guns; one infantry-gun battery with four pieces; one trench-mortar platoon with four grenade launchers and four medium trench mortars; one flamethrower platoon with six portable devices; and one construction company.[17]

On June 30, 1917, the *AOK* ordered a reorganization of the assault battalions. Army Assault Battalions were transformed into Divisional Assault Battalions *(Divisionsturmbataillone)*. Every infantry division would now have an assault battalion consisting of one assault company from each regiment in the division; one machine-gun company; one infantry-gun battery; one sapper platoon; one ordnance platoon; one flamethrower platoon armed with six portable devices; and one telephone detachment.[18]

Above: Gas pioneers of Pioneer Regiment 35 or 36 lay lead wire for the projectors in the background. The Battle of Caporetto opened at 2:00 A.M. on October 24, 1917, when the Germans fired 894 gas projectors. Five to six tons of phosgene were dropped on the Italians, whose gas masks failed to protect them.

Below: A 46-man platoon of an Austro-Hungarian assault battalion in Italy during the Battle of Caporetto. They wear the M1915 service jacket and M1916 duty blouse, both in field gray. Equipment includes very large hand-grenade bags, 8mm Mannlicher M95 rifles, German M1916 steel helmets, wire cutters, bayonets, and pioneer tools. The absence of gas masks would indicate that they are far from the front.

At Caporetto the German and Austrian forces were moved into position in great secrecy.[19] Troops undertook arduous night marches, at the rate of one or two battalions per division, and artillery was moved only at night. Italian guns were spotted and photographed by Austrian aviators, who passed the information to German and Austrian artillery commanders. The guns of the Fourteenth Army were registered on their targets over a period of weeks, the shots disguised as daily harassing fire.

At 2:00 A.M. on October 24, the Germans fired 894 gas projectors, dropping five to six tons of phosgene on the Italians.[20] Austrian artillery fired gas shells for two and a half hours, followed by high-explosive shells and mortar barrages. Italian gas masks were useless against the phosgene and chlorine; by the time the masked German and Austrian assault troops moved in behind a rolling barrage, hundreds of Italians had already died from gas poisoning.

The Italians apparently believed that bad weather would delay the Austro-German attack; as a result they were surprised by the assault and did not adequately prepare a defense in depth.[21] Too many men were concentrated in the front lines, preventing effective counterattacks when the Germans and Austrians broke through. In addition, the Italians failed to provide artillery support for two of their corps due to poor communication and commanders not complying with their orders.

Detachment Rommel served as the advance guard for the Württemberg Mountain Battalion.[22] At 8:00 A.M. Rommel's men began climbing the narrow mountain footpath up the Kolovat ridge, in intervals of 150 yards between subunits. Elements of the 1st Mountain Company formed the point, followed by a platoon from the 1st Machine Gun Company, the detachment staff, the remainder of the 1st Mountain Company, the 2nd Mountain Company, and the remainder of the 1st Machine Gun Company. The machine gunners each carried 90 pounds of weapons, ammunition, and equipment.

Although Rommel and his men would soon face the heavy combat for which they were trained as assault troops, their first engagement relied on surprise rather than firepower. In pouring rain, Detachment Rommel took the second Italian position near Lehize Peak. Rommel first deployed a heavy

Half-company of German assault troops, including a 16-man flamethrower detachment of the Guard Reserve Pioneer Regiment (left), photographed on the Italian front. All are armed with P08 pistols, and most carry grenade bags and trench daggers. Several display Italian trophies, including a helmet, rifle, ammunition pouches, and an officer's cap. On the left is a Wex M.1917 flamethrower painted in camouflage colors.

German assault troops pause beside a disabled Italian truck during the Battle of Caporetto. They wear light assault order, including M1916 gas mask canisters in the "alert" position; the soldier standing on the left is equipped with a machine gunner's dragging strap. Note the fire-breathing dragon badge painted on the truck tarpaulin.

machine-gun platoon to respond to potential resistance. He then sent a nine-man assault patrol armed with hand grenades and rifles to begin taking the Italian dugouts. Rommel chose a man of enormous physical size to lead the patrol, in order to intimidate the Italians into surrender. The assault patrol's orders were to use a minimum of violence, but they would be supported by machine guns and the entire detachment if necessary.

Word came back that the assault patrol was succeeding in taking the Italians without a fight; Rommel therefore ordered the entire detachment of two mountain companies and one machine-gun company into the position, followed by a second detachment of two more mountain companies and one machine-gun company. Assault squads created a breach in the barbed wire 100 yards wide. Since resistance was minimal, Rommel did not try to protect his flanks, concentrating instead on penetration. German shells fell too closely to the Württembergers, but Rommel realized that firing Very lights to request that the barrage be shifted forward would alert the remaining Italian garrisons to their presence and cost the Germans the element of surprise. Detachment Rommel reached the peak of the ridge at 11:00 A.M.

After only a few hours of rest, Detachment Rommel continued across the Kolovat, taking over 1500 prisoners by October 25.[23] Rommel's men then captured the village of Luico, again using stealth and surprise. After rounding up another 150 prisoners, Detachment Rommel surprised the 4th Bersaglieri Regiment outside Luico. The entire regiment of 2000 surrendered after Rommel's men surrounded them.

Defying his commander's order to halt and wait for reinforcements, Rommel departed for Matajur with one mountain company. He and his advance force of 100 men armed with six heavy machine guns captured the

1365

entire Salerno Brigade, some 2700 men, who either gave up immediately or fought back only a short time. Many of the Italians shouted, "Long live Germany!" as they ran into their captors' arms.

On October 26 Rommel reached the base of Matajur. The Italian garrison on the summit fought back with rifles and machine guns.[24] Rommel's six heavy machine-gun squads responded from the south slope, their fire forcing the Italians to duck for cover. The streams of bullets broke off splinters of rock that were deadly projectiles in their own right. Rommel and a few of his men took the opportunity to move eastward and then double back west along a ridge. They surprised the garrison in the summit guardhouse; the Italians, still pinned down by Rommel's machine gunners, surrendered.

At 11:40 Rommel fired three green flares and one white to signal that he'd taken the Matajur. In 52 hours, Rommel had captured 9000 Italians and suffered only 20 casualties.[25] He was awarded the *Pour le Mérite* and promoted to *Hauptmann*.

The Battle of Caporetto may have cost the Italians as many as 800,000 killed, wounded, captured, or deserted, while the Germans and Austrians suffered about 5000 casualties.[26]

The Battle of Cambrai

The German counterattack during the Battle of Cambrai (November 20-December 7, 1917) was improvised. There was no careful reconnaissance, nor were there the usual lengthy rehearsals.[27] Instead, the operation was quickly devised after the British achieved breakthrough with their tanks. As part of the hurried preparations for the counterattack, *Jäger* (Assault) Battalion No.3 was divided: The 1st Assault Company, two flamethrower squads, and the 2nd Machine Gun Company were attached to the 34th Infantry Division, while the 2nd Assault Company and two flamethrower squads were attached to the 28th Infantry Division. The 28th Division assaulted the environs of Banteux, while the 34th Division attacked south of the village.

The 1st Assault Company provided the 34th Division with three assault squads and two light machine-gun squads attached to the 3rd Battalion of Infantry Regiment No.67; two assault squads and two light machine-gun squads attached to the 2nd Battalion of Infantry Regiment No.67; and three assault squads attached to the 2nd Battalion of Infantry Regiment No.25. Two assault squads under the assault-company commander remained behind at the center of Infantry Regiment No.67. The disposition of the two flamethrower squads is not clear, but they were sent forward with the assault squads.

After an exhausting march throughout the night of November 29, the infantry and *Jäger* assault troops reached their jumping-off points at dawn. An enormous artillery barrage began at 8:50; the assault was launched an hour later, supported by "an extraordinary number" of aircraft flying low strafing runs.[28] The assault troops followed behind the first wave of infantry, with orders to deal with points of resistance and thereafter act on their own initiative. Attacking in the form of triangular wedges, the assault troops quickly overcame the first and second British lines. The *Jäger* fought at the forward points of the triangles, while at the sides and bases the infantry engaged in further close combat, cleaning out the trenches and gullies. Soon the two *Jäger* assault squads kept in reserve were brought up to engage the British. The attack achieved a forward depth of three to four miles past Villers-Guislain, into the area of Gouzeaucourt and nearly reaching the road to Epehy.

Opposite
Top: General der Infanterie Friedrich von Gerok reviewing men of the Württemberg Mountain Battalion after their taking of Monte Matajur, October 26, 1917. The officer standing second from the left in full profile is Hauptmann Erwin Rommel, soon to receive the Pour le Mérite. All the mountain Jäger wear the M1914 ski Litewka and are armed with Kar 98AZ carbines or P08 pistols.

Bottom: German assault troops armed with hand grenades engage British tanks during the counterattack at Cambrai, November 30, 1917. The improvised counterattack was so successful that the Germans recovered all the territory lost to the British.

Grenadier of Badener Leib Grenadier Regiment No.109. On the inner elbow of his left sleeve he wears the stylized cloth "S" badge of a shock troop. This young veteran has clearly seen plenty of combat, as evidenced by the ribbons of the EKII and Baden War Merit Cross on his heavily patched M1907/10 field jacket.

Assault squad wearing the M1917 snow overcoat (Schneemantel) with hood. It was cut loosely enough to fit over a soldier's equipment, including knapsack, and was closed with four ties in front. Prior to the adoption of this garment troops wore white overcoats or capes of no specific design, generally made locally.

Opposite: Gefreitere of a dismounted dragoon regiment serving as assault troops in the Vosges Mountains. They are armed with Kar 98AZ carbines and M1917 stick grenades. The M1911 cavalry ammunition pouches hold two five-round clips each, for a total of 60 rounds instead of the 120 carried in infantry pouches. Courtesy Maurice Sublet.

The operation was deemed successful, and the 1st Assault Company of *Jäger* (Assault) Battalion No.3 was slowly pulled out. On its march to the rear, it cleared the remaining British centers of resistance. Several hundred prisoners were taken, and numerous cannon, machine guns, and rifles were captured, much of which were then used on the British. The *Jäger* assault troops were said to have contributed substantially to the success of the operation. Seventeen *Jäger* of the 1st Assault Company were killed in action, and 26 were wounded.

Assault Blocks

Simultaneously with the attack by the 1st Assault Company, the 2nd Assault Company of *Jäger* (Assault) Battalion No.3 was tasked to lead Baden *Leib* Grenadier Regiment No.109 through two British trench systems:

> A differently constituted task was assigned to the 2nd Company under *Leutnant der Reserves* Vensky with I.R. 109. It would go in ahead of the infantry, together with some assigned infantry groups, to take and clean the English first and second position to a depth of approximately 1700 meters. It would be divided into two Assault Blocks and one Security Block, each block advancing in three waves.
>
> Assault Block Right (Leader: *Leutnant der Reserve* Vensky, with *Vizefeldwebel* Klaus) consisted of four assault squads, one light machine-gun squad, two grenade-launcher squads, and one flamethrower squad (squad leaders were *Oberjägers* Schmidt II, Käding, Liebsch, Kohler,

Die ersten gefangenen Amerikaner

> Görsdorf, *Gefreitere* Stobbe, Schliebener); Assault Block Left (Leader: *Leutnant der Reserve* Lindner) consisted of three assault squads, two light-machine gun squads, one grenade-launcher squad, and one flamethrower squad (squad leaders were *Oberjägers* Wiemann, Lehmann, Müller, Rolke, Sydow, *Gefreiter* Liesicke); Security Block (Leader: *Vizefeldwebel* Demmin) consisted of three assault squads (squad leaders *Oberjäger* Preutzer and *Gefreitere* Kaiser, Sawatzki).
>
> The three Blocks were used on three different trench systems. The British offered the most violent resistance. Again and again they held out in small spur trenches from which they were extremely difficult to dislodge, but eventually they had to yield and all three detachments finally reached the objectives assigned to them. In doing so they opened up the hardest way forward for the attacking infantry. The troops remained in position at the further disposal of the commander of I.R. 109. They were, however, not used again and were pulled back to Maurois on December 2.
>
> Losses: one officer (*Leutnant der Reserve* Vensky) and nine *Jäger*, including one *Grefreiter* serving as squad leader, were killed; four *Oberjäger* and 24 *Jäger* were wounded.[29]

Opposite
Top: *Assault troops of Bavarian Landwehr Infantry Regiment No.7 display the first American prisoners taken in the war, men of Company F, 16th Infantry Regiment, 1st Division. The doughboys were captured during a night attack on the Rhine-Marne Canal, November 3, 1917, carried out by a 200-man shock troop. Booty includes French Lebel rifles and Chauchat machine rifles, half-moon clips for the Chauchat, and M1917 Enfield rifles.*

Bottom: *Saxon shock troops armed with an IMG08/15. The Gefreiter standing third from right has a dark "S" badge on his upper left arm, while the Unteroffizier in the center wears a light-colored "S" badge on his left elbow, visible beside his P08 holster. Officially the light machine-gun squad consisted of eight men. In practice a squad of five was often used instead.*

Each attacking regiment of regular infantry received a battery of four horse-drawn 77mm light field guns that served as infantry accompanying batteries.[30] They were used for direct fire against strong points such as machine-gun nests. Pioneers and light machine-gun squads often reinforced infantry accompanying batteries at Cambrai.

One division organized its infantry into larger versions of the assault blocks used by *Jäger* (Assault) Battalion No.3. Company-sized assault blocks were comprised of three to five infantry platoons, four light trench mortars, and three or four heavy machine guns. Battalion-sized assault blocks were made up of four infantry companies, four to eight light trench mortars, one machine-gun company armed with 12 heavy weapons, and an infantry accompanying battery. Both kinds of assault blocks were carefully kept in reserve and only used to overcome stubborn points of resistance.

An unforeseen circumstance for the Germans was the massive supply dumps abandoned by the retreating British. German assault troops slowed their advance in order to gorge themselves on food and rum. By December 7 the German counteroffensive had petered out and the British had strengthened their line.

Endnotes

[1] Zabecki, pp. 28-29.

[2] Gudmundsson, p. 113-114, 116.

[3] *The New York Times Current History, the European War,* Volume 13, October-December, 1917 (New York: the New York Times Company, 1917), p. 70.

[4] Gudmundsson, p. 117.

[5] Zabecki, pp. 22-23.

[6] Gudmundsson, p. 117.

[7] Frank H. Simonds, *History of the World War, Volume 5: The Victory of Armistice* (Garden City, New York: Doubleday, Page and Company, 1920), pp. 30-31.

[8] Reddemann, *Geschichte,* p. 36.

[9] Spenser C. Tucker and Priscilla Mary Roberts (eds.), *World War I: A Student Encyclopedia* (Santa Barbara: ABC-CLIO, Inc., 2006), pp. 119-121.

[10] Michael B. Barrett, *Operation Albion: The German Conquest of the Baltic Islands* (Bloomington and Indianapolis: Indiana University Press, 2008), pp. 105-107, 259.

[11] Gary Staff, "Operation Albion: The Attack On The Baltic Islands," http://www.gwpda.org/naval/albion1.htm (accessed August 16, 2010).

[12] Barrett, pp. 107, 158-159.

[13] Tucker and Roberts, pp. 120-121.

[14] Barrett, pp. 228-229.

[15] Mario Morselli, *Caporetto 1917: Victory or Defeat?* (London: Frank Cass Publishers, 2001), p. 21.

[16] Rommel, p. 202.

[17] Ortner, p. 24.

[18] Ibid., pp. 32-34.

[19] John R. Schindler, *Isonzo: The Forgotten Sacrifice of the Great War* (Westport, Connecticut: Praeger, 2001), pp. 248-253.

[20] Simon Jones, *World War I Gas Warfare: Tactics and Equipment* (Botley, Oxford: Osprey Publishing, 2007), p. 45.

[21] Maurice C. Bigelow, "A Critical Analysis of the Battle of Caporetto," individual research paper (U.S. Army Command and General Staff School, 1932), pp. 5-7.

[22] Rommel, pp. 210, 213-214.

[23] Schindler, pp. 255-256.

[24] Anthony Livesey, *Great Battles of World War I* (New York: Macmillan Publishing, 1989), pp. 158-159.

[25] Schindler, p. 256.

[26] Livesey, p. 161.

[27] Friedrich Müller, *Brandenburgerisches Jäger-Bataillon Nr.3* (Oldenburg, Germany: Verlag Gerhard Stalling, 1922), pp. 85-87.

[28] Edward Wright, "The Cambrai of Surprises: II. – From the Capture of Bourlon Ridge to the Retirement of Flesquières," *The Great War,* Volume 11, p. 254.

[29] Müller, p. 87-88.

[30] Gudmundsson, pp. 142-143.

CHAPTER 13

The Spring Offensives

Preparation for the Spring Offensives

The second edition of the *Training Manual for Foot Troops in War (Ausbildungsvorschrift für die Fusstruppen im Krieg)* was published on January 1, 1918.[1] It was the first official document to articulate Ludendorff's order that all German infantrymen be trained as assault troops. Shock tactics would be vital to the Spring Offensives, also called the Kaiser's Battle *(Kaiserschlacht)*. The manual contained exercises similar to those used by the assault battalions and did not mention specialized assault units within the infantry platoon, company, or battalion. Instead, all infantrymen were now to be considered shock troops.

According to the manual the infantry squad was now the smallest tactical unit, discrete and capable of independent action. Six of the 18 squads in an infantry company were light machine-gun squads, and heavy machine guns were to be used as offensive weapons.

Shock-troop Tactics in the German Army of 1918

In the manual, the specialized tactics of Willy Rohr and Bernhard Reddemann were codified and officially adopted by the German army:

> Shock-troop Training: All noncommissioned officers and men are to be trained for use in shock troops. For special operations, especially in position warfare (raiding posts, taking out a saphead, blockhouses, etc.), however, on a case-by-case basis it may be advisable to put together shock troops composed of particularly suitable men.

Shock troop of Infantry Regiment No.185, 208th Infantry Division, one of the attack divisions (Angriffsdivisionen) of the Kaiser's Battle. They wear light assault order of rifle, grenades, and gas masks. Note the badge on the lower left sleeve, consisting of a white "X" above a white horizontal line. The 208th was known as the "Line Division" (Querstrich Division) for the sleeve badges it adopted in place of numbered shoulder straps.

Two Unteroffiziere and a Sergeant (center) of Assault Battalion No.5 (Rohr), photographed after being awarded the Iron Cross, Second Class, and two Baden Silver Merit Medals. The man on the right displays the unofficial sleeve badge adopted by the battalion on February 18, 1918. Worn on the left sleeve directly above the cuff, it consisted of a crown above a "W," mounted on a field-gray cloth oval. Some examples were made of white metal, while others appear to have been embroidered in silver bullion.

Depending on the scope and nature of the task, it can be assigned to shock-troop pioneers, machine gunners, grenade-launcher squads, and flamethrowers...

The mission of assault battalions was to support infantry attacks in position warfare. They were to use the experience they had garnered in order to perfect new means and ways of close combat. They were also trainers and were to make their experiences available to all troops in training courses. Shock troops of assault battalions were to be familiar with all German and enemy close-combat techniques.

Trench fighting and the cooperation of all weapons in the attack are to be practiced to perfection. The army command is to make its request for shock troops early, and it is to consult the shock troops according to an agreement with the commander of the assault battalion to carry out preliminary training with the infantry used in the attack.

The officers and shock troops of the assault battalions are subordinate to the leader of the infantry attack. The officers of the assault battalions make preliminary investigations with shock-troop leaders before the attack and discuss the results with the leader of the infantry attack. The officers of the assault battalions and the leader of the infantry attack cooperate in preparing the operation.

During the attack the shock troops are intended for the support and guidance of the infantry in difficult circumstances. They form the first assault wave, each shock troop strengthened by two or three infantry squads. These are tasked with supplying the shock troops with hand grenades and ammunition, as well as occupying and mopping up the sections of enemy trench taken. The use of shock troops without attached infantry squads is not recommended.

Machine-gun squad of the Howitzer Battery, Assault Battalion No.5 (Rohr), armed with an MG08 on an improvised trench mount. The Kanonier at left wears the unofficial battalion badge on his upper right sleeve. It is possible that artillerymen and assault pioneers were required to display the insignia on opposite sleeves.

Infantrymen attending a trench-mortar course (Minenwerferkursus) in the Vosges Mountains, 1918. At least two wear the Jäger gray-green M1915 blouse, and two are veterans of the Alpine Corps. The soldiers surround a 76mm light trench mortar, new pattern.

The officers of the assault battalion are responsible for the appropriate execution of the attack by shock troops.

In principle the machine guns, grenade launchers, flamethrowers, light machine guns, and infantry guns of the assault battalion are to be used in cooperation with the shock troops of the assault battalion.

After accomplishing their tasks all elements of the assault battalion are withdrawn so that they remain fresh and ready for combat. The leader of the infantry attack gives the order for this to take place.[2]

The Attack in Position Warfare

The Attack in Position Warfare (Der Angriff im Stellungskreig), published by the *OHL,* was the manual for the Spring Offensives.[3] Strategic breakthrough was the goal of the attack, which was achieved through penetration and the close tactical connection between the offensive and counterattacks. It was not possible to totally destroy the enemy with this attack. Instead, the Germans would do everything possible to keep the enemy off balance. They would disrupt his communications, strike specific units, continuously press the attack, and maintain the initiative.

Similarly, artillery could not destroy all enemy forces. Preparatory fire, rolling barrages, and isolation of the objective were used to disrupt enemy artillery operations. For this purpose gas shells were to be used. In addition, large numbers of low-flying aircraft would strafe in support of the advancing infantry.

An attack in position warfare required that the infantry rely on speed and depth. Speed would prevent the enemy from organizing a counterattack, while deployment in depth would provide enough units to overcome the isolated pockets of resistance and strong points bypassed by assault troops:

Right: Halberstadt CLII ground-attack fighters strafe enemy trenches during the Spring Offensives. Note the colored flares in the background used as signals for artillery, aircraft, or assault troops. Battle Flights (Schlachtstaffeln) of CL- and J-class aircraft carried out infantry-contact patrols and ground-attack missions.

Below: Troops of Bavarian 15th Landwehr Infantry Regiment, Bavarian 30th Reserve Infantry Division, photographed in the Vosges. Although a position formation of mediocre offensive value, the division formed a shock detachment in each battalion, as well as one divisional assault company. The average age of the shock troops was 24, while most of the remaining men were over 35.

Squad of Prussian telegraphers undergoing shock-troop training in 1918. Note that the NCO in the center is armed with a close-combat dagger on the left side of his belt. Some wartime Prussian telegraph detachments wore Brandenburg cuffs rather than the Swedish cuffs usually worn by technical troops. Weapons are the P08 pistol and Kar 98AZ carbine.

> The first penetration is comparatively easy. The difficulty lies in maintaining the vigor of the attack. The enemy must not be allowed to recover from his surprise. His countermeasures must be rendered useless by the rapid progress of the attack. *It is a question of taking rapid action with the consciousness that protection of flanks and rear, as well as support from artillery, will be provided from behind.*
>
> The danger of slackening in the force of attack is great. The dead center must be overcome by the energy of commanders well forward in the line and by fresh effectives.[4]

Following the assault troops were the "combat units" *(Kampfeinheiten)* and reserves.[5] The combat units were comprised of infantry, machine gunners, trench-mortar squads, pioneers, horse-drawn field artillery, and ammunition carriers. Their mission was to destroy strong points and pockets of resistance and defeat counterattacks. The combat units were to follow as closely behind the assault troops as possible; therefore, they would not spend much time on individual obstacles, leaving them for the reserves.

Officially the smallest tactical unit during the Spring Offensives was the nine-man infantry squad, but in practice the smallest unit capable of offensive and defensive action was the unit squad, the eight-man light machine-gun squad paired with the four- to eight-man assault squad.

Musketier of Württemberg Infantry Regiment No.120 (Infanterie-Regiment Kaiser Wilhelm, König von Preussen [2. württembergisches] Nr.120), of the 27th Infantry Division. Designated an attack division, the 27th was rated a "first-class shock unit" by the Allies, one of the best divisions to take part in the Spring Offensives. Note the red monogram on the shoulder strap of the M1915 blouse.

Attack Divisions

Prior of the Spring Offensives a significant number of German infantry divisions were designated attack divisions *(Angriffsdivisionen),*[6] also called "shock divisions" by the Allies. They were given the best supplies, weapons, and replacements and spent most of the winter of 1917-1918 training in shock-troop tactics. The remaining divisions held the line and were designated "position divisions" *(Stellungsdivisionen);* Allied intelligence often translated the German term as "sector divisions."

Some attack divisions dissolved their assault units, deeming them superfluous now that every man in the division was trained in assault tactics. Although the men of the attack divisions were considered shock troops, many of them were simply too old and war weary to function at peak performance. While the cutoff age in assault battalions was around 25, attack divisions accepted men aged up to 35. Young, energetic men were no longer available in significant numbers; many of the divisions were therefore comprised of older veterans who did not meet the physical, mental, and psychological standards of the assault battalions.[7]

With the formation of attack divisions, the term *Stosstrupp* now referred specifically to those whose job it was to spearhead attacks rather than perform other functions, such as protecting crew-served weapons. Although position divisions were not used offensively, many maintained divisional assault companies as well as battalion or regimental shock troops.

Between 56[8] and 58 of 192 German divisions were designated attack divisions, having undergone a four-week course in assault training by February 10, 1918.[9]

The combat units of an attack division were:

one infantry brigade (three regiments);
one to three assault companies (three 40-man platoons in each);
one Machine Gun Marksman Detachment;

Part of the howitzer battery of West Prussian Field Artillery Regiment No.35 (1. westpreußisches Feldartillerie-Regiment Nr.35) photographed on the western front in 1918. The field piece is the 105mm light field howitzer 98/09 (10,5 cm leichte Feldhaubitze 98/09). In the foreground is MG08 No.1 of the battery Machine Gun Detachment. The weapon has been fitted with an improvised trench mount of the type used by infantry assault troops.

two cavalry squadrons;
one or two pioneer companies;
one trench-mortar company;
one field-artillery regiment
one battalion of foot artillery;
40-45 artillery batteries attached for the purposes of a particular battle.

Infantrymen and heavy machine-gun squads of a Machine Gun Marksman Detachment train in the use of assault ladders. On the right is one of the infantry regiment's IMG08/15 light machine guns. The soldiers are equipped with assault packs, gas masks, and grenade bags; infantrymen carry Gew 98 rifles while machine gunners are armed with P08 pistols or Kar 98AZ carbines.

Each infantry regiment was comprised of three battalions, for a total of nine.

A battalion was comprised of four infantry companies (180 rifles each), one machine-gun company armed with 12 heavy weapons, one trench-mortar platoon armed with four light weapons, and one grenade-launcher platoon armed with eight weapons. Each infantry company contained six light machine-gun squads.

The Machine Gun Marksman Detachment was comprised of three companies, each armed with 12 heavy machine guns for a total of 36.

The trench-mortar company was armed with two heavy, four medium, and 12 light weapons.

Musketier of Württemberger Infantry Regiment No.180, 26th Reserve Infantry Division. An attack division rated "first-class" by Allied intelligence, the 26th Reserve suffered heavy losses in the Spring Offensives. This soldier's uniform is a mystery in that he wears a field jacket with Swedish cuffs and his bayonet knot is the all-green Jäger version. Note the M1915 service cap with field-gray peak.

Opposite

Top: Mixed assault squad of Württemberger Landsturm Infantry Battalion Eßlingen (XIII/18) and men of the Bavarian 39th Reserve Division, to which the Württembergers were attached. A crate of 25 M1917 egg grenades leans against the spool of barbed wire, and stick grenades are hung on belts for immediate use.

Bottom: Postwar image of a Reichswehr Wex squad consisting of two Wex M.1917 served by a carrier and lance operator each, two assistant-grenadiers, and a squad leader (right). During the Spring Offensives the Guard Reserve Pioneer Regiment reinforced its Wex squads to this configuration. The M1918 steel helmets feature cutouts for the ears, intended to improve the soldiers' hearing.

Each pioneer company was armed with six smoothbore light trench mortars and two grenade launchers.

The field-artillery regiment was comprised of three detachments of three batteries each; three batteries were armed with four 105mm light howitzers each; six batteries were armed with four 77mm light field guns each. In addition each detachment was armed with six heavy machine guns for close combat.

The foot artillery battalion was comprised of three batteries, each armed with four 150mm guns. In addition, the battalion was armed with six heavy machine guns for close combat.

On September 17, 1918, the divisional trench-mortar companies were dissolved due to the continuing shortage of pioneers to man the weapons. Battalion light trench-mortar detachments were consolidated into regimental trench-mortar companies;[10] medium trench mortars were assigned to the new regimental trench-mortar companies, and heavy trench mortars to the 13 battalions of the Army Trench Mortar Reserve. Each regimental trench-mortar company was to be armed with nine light and three medium trench mortars. The purpose of the reorganization was to obtain a better utilization of the existing means of antitank defense. As a result, regimental trench-mortar companies were especially trained and equipped as antitank formations. They were divided into three detachments of three light trench mortars and three trench-mortar wagons each, with a reserve of two or three medium trench mortars with their limbers. This reorganization was still in the process of being carried out when the war ended.

As part of the preparations for the Spring Offensives *Hauptmann* Pulkowski of the artillery devised a means of delivering accurate artillery fire without registering the guns.[11] Each piece was test fired and its specific idiosyncrasies were recorded and tabulated. The effects of the weather and powder temperature were tabulated as well, and target data was plotted using maps. After extensive testing the Pulkowski Method was adopted for use in the Spring Offensives. Firing without registering would add to the surprise factor.

Flamethrower March Companies

Prior to the Spring Offensives the 12 field companies of the Guard Reserve Pioneer Regiment were reorganized as March Companies *(Marsch-Kompagnien)*, each composed of three March Platoons *(Marschzüge)* and one Ordnance Platoon *(Gerätzug)*.[12] Each March Platoon consisted of a combat platoon, a replacement squad *(Ersatztrupp)*, and a maintenance section *(Gefechtstross)*. The combat platoon was comprised of four *Wex* squads *(Wextrupps)*, one light machine-gun squad, and one grenade-launcher squad; each *Wex* squad was armed with two flamethrowers and reinforced with extra men. If necessary, the personnel of the grenade-launcher squad could be equipped as a fifth *Wex* squad armed with two reserve devices, bringing the total number of flamethrowers in the platoon to 10.

Once the Guard Reserve Pioneer Regiment had completed its reorganization, the 1st, 6th, 8th, 9th, 10th, 11th, and 12th March Companies were transferred to attack divisions on the western front, which distributed them by platoon to their infantry regiments.[13] There was a total of 21 flamethrower March Platoons for the attack divisions of the Second, Seventeenth, and Eighteenth Armies. As later breakthroughs were attempted in other sectors on the western front, the March Companies were shifted around. Beginning on May 27 the 3rd, 5th, and 7th March Companies were also brought into the western front for single engagements.

Small-flamethrower attack, late 1918. The soldier on the lower left appears to be armed with a captured French P_4 flamethrower, a weapon that weighed 42 lb. In comparison the German Wex weighed 55 lb, and the Kleif weighed 70 lb. It is doubtful that the Germans used this flamethrower in combat, as the French manufactured only 320 of the devices during the war.

Jäger of Jäger (Assault) Battalion No.3, armed with a P08 and Kar 98AZ. The contrast between the gray-green M1907/10 field jacket and field-gray or stone-gray trousers is apparent. During the Spring Offensives three assault companies of Jäger (Assault) Battalion No.3 were assigned to three different infantry divisions, while the Second Army kept the fourth assault company in reserve.

"Organization of a *Wex* March Platoon *(Wex Marschzug).*"[14]

Strength:
one officer (platoon leader),
nine NCOs (squad leaders),
33 men, one runner.

Composition:
Five *Wex* squads *[one was a grenade-launcher squad, ed.]*, each comprised of one NCO, one lance operator, two *Wex* carriers, one assistant.
One machine-gun squad, comprised of one NCO, four machine gunners.
One replacement troop, comprised of three NCOs, nine men.
Each *Wex* squad was armed with two apparatuses, for a total of 10 per platoon; each platoon was also armed with one light machine gun and one grenade launcher.

Side arms:
Enlisted men armed with pistols; NCOs leading the *Wex* squads armed with carbines.

Tools equipping a *Wex* squad:
three spades, two wire cutters, one wrench, one tool kit.

Platoon march formation, in four columns:
platoon leader;
four NCOs (squad leaders);
four lance operators;
four *Wex* carriers;
four *Wex* carriers;
four assistants;
one runner, three NCOs;
two replacements, one machine gunner, one lance operator;
two replacements, one machine gunner, one *Wex* carrier;
two replacements, one machine gunner, one *Wex* carrier;
two replacements, one machine gunner, one assistant;
one NCO, one replacement, one NCO.

Youthful Pionier of the 2nd Assault Company, Assault Battalion No. 5 (Rohr). He wears an M1915 blouse with black shoulder straps, a trench dagger and bayonet knot, and the M1915 NCO's cap with field-gray brim. His white-red-white state cockade represents the Free City of Bremen.

Task Organization of an Assault Battalion

"Task organization of *Jäger* (Assault) Battalion No.3," March 21, 1918.[15]

1st Assault Company:
three assault platoons,
10 flamethrowers of 1st March Platoon, Guard Reserve Pioneer Regiment,
two infantry guns.
Assigned to 79th Reserve Infantry Division.

2nd Assault Company:
three assault platoons,
four light mortars.
Kept in Second Army reserve.

3rd Assault Company:
three assault platoons,
one machine-gun company,
seven flamethrowers of *Jäger* (Assault) Battalion No.3,
two light mortars,
two infantry guns.
Assigned to 50th Reserve Infantry Division.

4th Assault Company:
three assault platoons,
one machine-gun company,
10 flamethrowers of 1st March Company, Guard Reserve Pioneer Regiment,
two light mortars,
two infantry guns.
Assigned to 18th Infantry Division.

The Spring Offensives Begin

Ludendorff launched five offensives on the western front between March 21 and July 17. The morning of March 21 was unusually misty, which hid the assault troops' movements.[16] Operation Michael began with a violent artillery bombardment that included thousands of gas shells. After two hours the shelling became a rolling barrage that screened the advance of the shock troops. Initially the Germans were spectacularly successful; four enormous offensives netted them well over 130,000 prisoners and had brought them to within heavy artillery range of Paris. Nearly four months of fighting had

Shock troops of Badener Infantry Regiment No. 113, 1918. Three of the men are armed with rifles and one with a P08. The stick grenades – including the pile at the feet of the soldier second from the right – are a mixture of M1916 and M1917. Note the assault ladders in the foreground, used to aid troops in leaving the trench.

Shock troops carry out a mock assault in the Argonne, 1918. Behind a rolling barrage, columns of steel-helmeted soldiers race up the slope throwing hand grenades that produce clouds of gray smoke. A flamethrower fires a jet of burning oil on the crest of the hill (top center) and a horse-drawn light trench mortar is brought forward on the lower right.

smashed the Allied line and forced the French and British to deploy all of their reserves.

In his memoirs Chief of the General Staff Paul von Hindenburg provided a detailed description of Operation Georgette, known by the Allies as the Battle of the Lys. It deftly presents the arc of fortune and misfortune experienced by the Germans during the Spring Offensives:

> On April 9th, the anniversary of the great crisis at Arras, our storm troops rose from their muddy trenches on the Lys front from Armentières to La Bassée. Of course they were not disposed in great waves, but mostly in small detachments and diminutive columns which waded through the morass which had been upheaved by shells and mines, and either picked their way toward the enemy lines between deep shell holes filled with water or took the few firm causeways. Under the protection of our artillery and trench-mortar fire, they succeeded in getting forward quickly in spite of all the natural and artificial obstacles, although apparently

Opposite
***Top:** Two Bavarian officers and an Infanterist with a Portuguese prisoner captured during Operation Georgette, or the Battle of the Lys (April 7-29, 1918). The two divisions of the Portuguese Expeditionary Corps broke and ran when subjected to the violence of a German combined-arms assault. Note the prisoner's unraveling puttees and shell-shocked expression.*

***Bottom:** Shock troop of Reserve Infantry Regiment No.149 with three French prisoners (center) captured in a trench raid carried out at 4:00 A.M. on March 24, 1918. The Reservist kneeling in the second row, his cap tipped back on his head, wears a shock-troop arm badge consisting of a rectangle divided diagonally into two colors.*

neither the English nor the Portuguese, who had been sandwiched in among them, believed it possible. Most of the Portuguese troops left the battlefield in wild flight, and once and for all retired from fighting in favor of their allies. It must be admitted that our exploitation of the surprise and the Portuguese failure met with the most serious obstacles in the nature of the ground. It was only with the greatest difficulty that a few ammunition wagons were brought forward behind the infantry. Yet the Lys was reached by the evening and even crossed at one point. Here again the decision was to be expected only in the course of the next few days. Our prospects seemed favorable. On April 10 Estaires fell into our hands and we gained more ground northwest of Armentières. On the same day our front of attack was extended to the region of Wytschaete, We again stormed the battered ruins of the much-fought-for Messines.

The next day brought us more successes and fresh hopes. Armentières was evacuated by the enemy and we captured Merville. From the south we approached the first terrace of the great group of hills from which our opponent could see our whole attack and command it with his artillery. From now on progress became slower. It soon came to a stop on our left wing, while our attack in the direction of Hazebrouck was slowly becoming paralyzed. In our center we captured Bailleul and set foot on the hills from the south. Wytschaete fell into our hands, but then this first blow was exhausted.

The difficulties of communication across the Lys Valley which had to be overcome by our troops attacking from the south had been like a chain round our necks. Ammunition could only be brought up in quite inadequate quantities, and it was only thanks to the booty the enemy had left behind on the battlefield that we were able to keep our troops properly fed.

Our infantry had suffered extremely heavily in their fight with the enemy machine-gun nests, and their complete exhaustion threatened unless we paused in our attack for a time. On the other hand, the situation urgently exacted an early decision. We had arrived at one of those crises in which the continuation of the attack is extremely difficult, but when the defense seems to be wavering. The release from such a situation can only come from a further attack and not by merely holding on.

We had to capture Mount Kemmel. It had lain like a great hump before our eyes for years. It was only to be expected that the enemy had made it the key to his positions in Flanders. The photographs of our airmen revealed but a portion of the complicated enemy defense system at this point. We might hope, however, that the external appearance of the hill was more impressive than its real tactical value. We had had experiences of this kind before with other tactical objectives. Picked troops which had displayed their resolution and revealed their powers at the Roten-Turm Pass, and in the fighting in the mountains of Transylvania, Serbian Albania, and the Alps of upper Italy, might once more make possible the seemingly impossible. A condition precedent to the success of our further attacks in Flanders was that the French High Command should be compelled to leave the burden of the defense in that region to their English allies. We therefore first renewed our attacks at Villers-Brétonneaux on April 24th, hoping that the French commander's anxiety about Amiens would take precedence of the necessity to help the hard-pressed English friends in Flanders. Unfortunately, this new attack failed. On the other hand, on April 25th the English defense on Mount Kemmel collapsed at the first blow. The loss of this pillar of the

R T

defense shook the whole enemy front in Flanders. Our adversary began to withdraw from the Ypres salient which he had pushed out in months of fighting in 1917. Yet to the last Flemish city he clung to as if to a jewel which he was unwilling to lose for political reasons.

But the decision in Flanders was not to be sought at Ypres, but by attacking in the direction of Cassel. If we managed to make progress in that quarter, the whole Anglo-Belgian front in Flanders would have to be withdrawn to the west. Just as our thoughts had soared beyond Amiens in the previous month, our hopes now soared to the Channel coast. I seemed to feel how all England followed the course of the battle in Flanders with baited breath. After that giant bastion, Mount Kemmel, had fallen, we had no further reason to flinch from the difficulties of further attacks. It is true that we had received reports about the failure of certain of our units. Mistakes and omissions had occurred on the battlefield. Yet such mistakes and omissions are inherent in human nature. He who makes the fewest will remain master of the battlefield. We were now the master and intended to remain so. Victories such as we had gained at Kemmel not only elate the troops who actually win them, but revitalize the spirits of whole armies.

***Opposite:** Soldiers of an attack division march through Armentières during the Spring Offensives. They wear heavy assault order and carry Kar 98AZ carbines instead of rifles. Note the cloth covers for the steel helmets worn by the two men on the left. Their companion clutches a bag of provisions along with his carbine.*

***Below:** Trench raiders of the 5th Company, Landwehr Infantry Regiment No.25. All four carry P08 pistols; the Wehrmann on the left also has a DEMAG trench dagger-bayonet on his belt. Two of the greatcoats are peacetime models with collar patches, while the others are M1915 universal greatcoat for troops.*

21.

Therefore on! We must have Cassel at least! From that vantage point the long-range fire of our heaviest guns could reach Boulogne and Calais. Both towns were crammed full with English supplies, and were also the principal points of debarkation of the English armies. The English army had failed in the most surprising fashion in the fight for Kemmel. If we succeeded in getting it to ourselves at this point, we should have a certain prospect of a great victory. If no French help arrived, England would probably be lost in Flanders. Yet in England's dire need this help was once more at hand. French troops came up with bitter anger against the friend who had surrendered Kemmel, and attempted to recover this key position from us. It was in vain. But our own last great onslaught on the new Anglo-French line at the end of April made no headway.

On May 1st we adopted the defensive in Flanders, or rather, as we then hoped, passed to the defensive for the time being.[17]

By late June the German armies were nearly spent. The speed of the advance had exhausted the men, many of whom were ill and hungry. Supply lines and discipline were breaking down, and casualties were mounting. The German offensive of July 15, from the Château Thierry salient, was repulsed and then answered with a Franco-American counterattack that robbed the Germans of their momentum and put them on the defensive. Ultimately the Spring Offensives cost the Germans their best assault troops and devastated their morale. Losses and difficulties in recruitment forced the *OHL* to issue an order on August 18, 1918, that all divisions with an average battalion combat strength of less than 650 men would divide their battalions into three rather than four companies.[18] Most divisions in the Army of the West had to implement this measure.

Flamethrowers in the Spring Offensive

Although the Spring Offensives failed, one would never know from reading Bernhard Reddemann's history of German flamethrower troops. The irrepressible Prince of Hades referred to the offensives as the Breakthrough Battles *(Durchbruchsschlachten),* omitting all reference to their outcome. His writing was nearly incandescent with optimism:

> The special joy of attack pulsed through all, down to the last man, as they went into these battles. The prospect of the coming of a final victory and the end of the war appeared for all to see. The advance of the flamethrowers in all of the different combat sectors during these battles was once again excellent. Resolute in the face of death, the men stormed forward with the infantry.[19]

Reddemann cited one action as the model of what he called the even more courageous way that the men of the flamethrower regiment discharged their duties during the Breakthrough Battles.[20]

On March 21 the advancing Germans encountered a British machine-gun post east of Croisilles, in a sector that had been heavily shelled and mostly evacuated. Almost impervious in their concrete pillbox, the British put up a remarkably stiff resistance with seven strongly built-in weapons. Since artillery could not destroy the position, infantry assault troops were sent against it, but each attempt was repulsed with heavy casualties to the

Opposite
***Top:** Shock Troop 21 of an unidentified infantry regiment, photographed on March 21, 1918. They display captured French rifles and equipment including caps, packs, and respirators. Note the white brassards worn by several of the men. All appear to be armed with pistols, trench daggers and hand grenades instead of rifles or carbines.*

***Bottom:** Bavarian assault infantryman escorting British prisoners through a German trench; in the background a flamethrower squad is visible against the skyline. Although the Bavarian wears a steel helmet and grenade bags and carries a Kar 98AZ carbine, the flamethrower pioneers are dressed in the lightest possible assault order of field caps and almost no equipment. This ensured mobility and silence, increasing the element of surprise.*

Diminutive young assault infantryman, 1918. He uses the strap of his haversack to support his M1909 ammunition pouches, and he wears his pocket watch on his wrist in a special leather holder. The Gew 98 rifle has been fitted with a brass muzzle cover.

Germans. One of the infantry battalions had attached to it a flamethrower half-platoon *(Halbzug)* from the 10th March Company of the Guard Reserve Pioneer Regiment, armed with six small flamethrowers and under the command of *Unteroffizier* Grund. This unit was given the order to silence the machine-gun nest, which lay more than 1000 yards ahead.

Unteroffizier Grund divided his half-platoon into two flame shock troops of 10 men and three flamethrowers each. They immediately launched into Indian-style Forward Stalking in wide arcs, while the infantry assault troops concealed themselves and tried to distract the British machine-gun position with heavy fire. The two flamethrower shock troops were able to advance for a short distance in a shallow communication ditch, then they had to cross open terrain individually, sprinting from cover to cover. They came under machine-gun fire from a tank on their left; instead of retreating, they turned and attacked the tank. Two flamethrower pioneers were killed, but the rest slowly approached the tank diagonally in a flanking maneuver

Grenadier of Bavarian Assault Battalion No.16 attacking a machine-gun nest; in the background is a plume of smoke from a flamethrower. He carries two concentrated charges consisting of sand bags filled with hand-grenade heads.

Cannoneers of Infantry Gun Battery 7 carry a dismantled 76.2mm Infantry Gun L/16.5 during maneuvers. Most wear an unidentified shield painted on the side of their camouflaged steel helmets. Personal equipment has been reduced to bayonets and M1916 gas-mask containers.

until they were close enough to fire two streams through a pistol port, which silenced the machine gun.

The bright jets of burning oil apparently alerted the garrison of the British machine-gun position; several weapons opened fire, killing one member of the right-hand shock troop and wounding another. The survivors were pinned down in a shell hole while *Unteroffizier* Grund and the other shock troop crept up on the machine-gun post from the left. As Grund's troop reached a battered section of trench behind the position, they were spotted and fired upon by British infantry. The Germans responded with a flame jet, killing the riflemen. Grund's shock troop then sprayed a covering jet, which allowed one or more flamethrower squads to approach the machine-gun post and fire through the loopholes.

"One could hear the enemy screaming and moaning loudly," noted Reddemann. "They ran out of the exits wailing painfully with arms held high, some of them burned."[21]

Three British officers, 72 men, and seven machine guns were captured by nine flamethrower pioneers. More importantly, a stubborn obstacle was removed from the German advance. For his bravery *Unteroffizier* Grund was promoted to *Vizefeldwebel.*

Endnotes

[1] Gudmundsson, pp. 147-148.

[2] Kriegsministerium, *Ausbildungsvorschrift für die Fusstruppen im Krieg* (Berlin: Reichsdruckerei, 1918), pp. 97, 175-177.

[3] Lupfer, pp. 41-42.

[4] Meyer, p. 60.

[5] English, pp. 23-25.

[6] Gudmundsson, pp. 151-152.

[7] Patrick T. Stackpole, "German Tactics in the 'Michael' Offensive, March 1918," Master of Military Art and Science thesis (U. S. Army Command and General Staff College, 1993), pp. 6-7.

[8] Lupfer, p. 48.

[9] *A Survey of German Tactics 1918,* p. 14.

[10] Second Section, General Staff, American Expeditionary Forces, Summary of Information No.155, September 3, 1918, pp. 1042-1043.

[11] Lupfer, p, 45.

[12] Reddemann, *Geschichte,* pp. 38-39.

[13] Ibid., pp. 39-40.

[14] Ministère de la Guerre, Section technique des Etudes et Expériences chimiques. *Conférences de l'Ecole des gaz de combat: Les Lance-flammes. 3ème Conférence. Lance-flammes portatifs étrangers.* Paris, 1920, p. 18.

[15] Müller, p. 94, and Gudmundsson, p. 159.

[16] Livesey, pp. 180-184.

[17] Paul von Hindenburg, *Out of my Life,* Volume II (New York and London: Harper and Brothers Publishers, 1921), pp. 165-170.

[18] Cron, p. 112.

[19] Reddemann, *Geschichte,* p. 39.

[20] Ibid., pp. 44-45.

[21] Ibid., p. 45.

CHAPTER 14

Tanks and Antitank Warfare

Organization of Assault Armored Vehicle Detachments

Tanks or armored vehicles *(Panzerkraftwagen)* were initially under the control of the Head of Field Motorized Transport (*Chef des Feldkraftfahrwesen* or *Chefkraft*).[1] On September 29, 1917, the War Ministry ordered the organization of Assault Armored Vehicle Detachments *(Sturmpanzerkraftwagen-Abteilungen)* 1 and 2. Each would consist of five A7V tanks, five officers, and 109 NCOs and men. Four tanks would each be armed with six machine guns and two flamethrowers, and one tank would be armed with one main gun and four machine guns. The flamethrowers were never carried in the tanks.

German infantry swarm over a stalled Mark I tank at the Somme, July of 1916. At this point in the war the Germans had no effective antitank tactics. Some of the soldiers have inserted their rifles into the pistol port in the sponson door, while another does the same with the vision port in the cab. The fallen man in the foreground is equipped with a pole for fire tubes, theoretically a very effective antitank weapon provided the user survived his approach to the tank.

On November 6, 1917, the War Ministry decreed the establishment of Assault Armored Vehicle Detachment 3 along the same lines as Detachments 1 and 2.

Detachment 3 was followed on January 8, 1918, by Assault Armored Vehicle Detachments 4 to 7. Each was to be organized with five A7V tanks, eight officers, and 118 NCOs and men. Each tank was armed with one Belgian 57mm main gun and four machine guns. Crews were also equipped with pioneer tools, *Kar 98AZ* carbines, P08 pistols, and hand grenades.

Shock-troop Training of Tank Crews

After an inspection by Crown Prince Wilhelm, Assault Armored Vehicle Detachment 1 was shipped at his suggestion to the training grounds of Assault Battalion No.5 (Rohr).[2] The tanks arrived at the assault battalion on January 1, 1918, and were then sent to Pierrepont. Training was based on "Instructions for the Use of Assault Armored Vehicle Detachments" by the *OHL,* carried out in collaboration with the assault battalions. Assault Armored Vehicle Detachment 1 participated in exercises devised by Assault Battalion No.5 (Rohr); in the process the tankers gradually familiarized themselves with driving and shooting techniques.

Tanks were primarily a weapon of attack and an auxiliary weapon of the infantry. Their mission resembled that of the Infantry Accompanying Batteries. It consisted of joining with shock troops to overcome enemy

Postcard issued by Bavarian Infantry Gun Battery 10, attached to Assault Battalion No.2; the cannon is the Austrian Skoda 75mm Mountain Gun M.15. Although used in an antitank role, the gun was ineffective due to the relatively low velocity (383 yd per second) and correspondingly low penetrative power of the shell.

Gefreiter of an Infantry Gun Battery. He wears a simplified field jacket with covers on the shoulder straps that conceal the letters "IG" and the battery number. The "2" embroidered in dark thread on his upper left sleeve is his gun number.

positions, machine-gun nests, and other pockets of resistance in order to clear the way for the main waves of infantry. During combat tanks would facilitate the advance of the attacking troops by destroying inanimate obstacles and breaking enemy opposition on the battlefield. The closest cooperation between the tanks and troops, through a progressive series of movements, was necessary for the fulfillment of these tasks.

The tank crews completed a six-week course taught by Assault Battalion No.5 (Rohr) that trained the men how to function as dismounted shock troops when they encountered difficult strong points or if their vehicle broke down or was put out of action.[3] They learned how to clear trenches with hand grenades and fire captured enemy machine guns, and the pioneers among them learned how to use flamethrowers to roll up enemy positions.

On February 23, 1918, Assault Battalion No.5 (Rohr) launched a major exercise at Doncourt to demonstrate the use of tanks against fixed positions in conjunction with infantry, a circumstance which would occur often in the coming offensive.[4] In addition to the German A7V tank, captured British tanks were also used. *General* Ludendorff visited a captured-tank detachment and watched it train with shock troops. After the inspection he was very skeptical of the British tank's utility. *Major* Rohr agreed, stating that captured British tanks were too slow to cooperate with the infantry.[5]

By July 7, 1918, each Assault Armored Vehicle Detachment was to consist of seven officers and 172 NCOs and men, including:

five officers and 86 men of the motor-transport troops;
one officer and 49 men of the machine-gun troops;
one officer and 23 men of the field artillery;
12 men of the signals troops;
two stretcher bearers.

Each Assault Armored Vehicle Detachment (Captured) *(Sturmpanzerkraftwagen-Abteilung [Beute]),* equipped with captured British Mark IV tanks, was to consist of seven officers and 136 men, including:

Left: Fahrer of the Motor Transport Troops (Kraftfahrtruppe); men of the Assault Armored Vehicle Detachments (Sturm-Panzerkraftwagen-Abteilungen) wore the same uniform. The green collar of the M1915 blouse displays gray Guard lace with white center lines (Litzenspiegel), and the shoulder straps are light gray with a red "K."

Right: Pionier of Assault Battalion No.5 (Rohr) photographed at Beuville in February of 1918. In late January Assault Armored Vehicle Detachment I was sent to Beuville for a six-week course in shock tactics. Instructors of Assault Battalion No.5 (Rohr) taught the tank crews how to reduce strong points and roll up trenches.

five officers and 86 men of the motor-transport troops;
one officer and 21 men of the machine-gun troops;
one officer and 15 men of the field artillery;
12 men of the signals troops;
two stretcher bearers.[6]

Regulations for the Employment of Assault Armored Vehicle Detachments

I. General[7]

1. The Assault Armored Vehicle Detachments are placed under direct command of the Supreme Army Command and are allocated to the armies for combat action. The detachments are part of the motor-transport branch and during assignment to an army disciplinarily and technically are placed under the responsible commanders of the motor-transport branch.

II. Tasks.

2. During the **attack,** the **main task** of the tanks is to support the advance of the infantry by

a. demolishing enemy **obstacles** by rolling over them,
b. silencing enemy troops, above all those manning strong points and machine guns,
c. repulsing enemy counterattacks.

Appearing unexpectedly at a thinly occupied sector, they are to pave the way for the infantry breakthrough by pushing ruthlessly through and turning the enemy's flank.
At **sectors of major combat** where strong enemy artillery fire is to be expected the use of tanks will only be possible in extremely favorable circumstances.

3. In **defense** the tanks serve as a **mobile reserve** under the command of the local leaders for
a. repulsing enemy breakthroughs,
b. supporting the counterattacks of the enemy,
c. silencing enemy tanks.

III. Preparatory Measures
4. Most stringent concealment is necessary is necessary to ensure an unexpected appearance of the tanks as basic requirements of success. This means:

A7V 501 and tank crewmen of Assault Armored Vehicle Detachment 1, photographed at Beuville in March 1918. Tankers were trained in shock tactics so that they could dismount and fight with hand grenades, carbines, machine guns, and flamethrowers. The tall soldier standing third from the right is equipped with grenade bags, while the crewman sitting in the center front row displays an "S" badge on his upper left arm.

British Mark IV male "Fritz," Tank No.5 of Assault Armored Vehicle Detachment (Captured) 14, May of 1918. In the foreground is a Wex squad of Assault Battalion No.7. British armored vehicles were too slow to be integrated into assault battalions and were therefore used in antitank exercises.

a. Total concealment of the tanks until they come into action in front of their own troops' positions and concealment against enemy air observation, therefore:
b. All movement by night only, covered assembly in dense forests, at farmyards, etc., or under camouflage, obscuring the track marks before dawn with rakes and harrows, avoiding all unnecessary noise while on the move, i.e. exhaust valves, gaskets not tight, unlocking compressor taps when inspecting the engines, covering all unavoidable noises by artillery or machine guns.

5. Exact terrain reconnaissance by the commander of the detachment and thorough briefing of the vehicle commanders on the terrain has to precede each action. Inconspicuous behavior to cause no attention. Doubts on practicality of action such as unsuitable terrain will be announced by the commander to the local command as soon as possible.

6. Lanes of advance have to be ordered and marked avoiding surfaced roads. All obstacles in these lanes must be cleared away.

7. Preparatory exercises of the infantry assigned for the attack with the tanks must be executed far behind the lines in order to not jeopardize concealment.

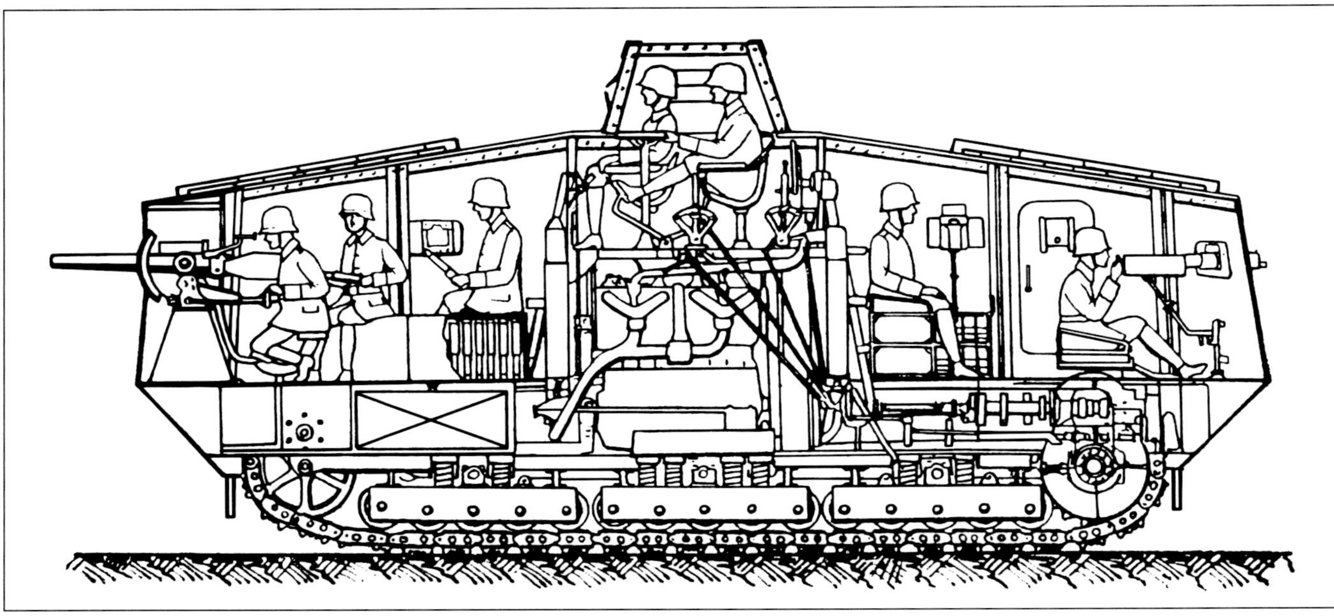

Interior of an A7V male armed with a Maxim-Nordenfelt 57mm cannon (left) and four MG08 machine guns. Only seven of the 18-24 crewmen are pictured. The conditions inside the fighting compartment were harsh from the extreme heat, noise, smoke, and rough ride. Tanks crews quickly became exhausted and ill, requiring frequent halts to recover.

The 11-man crew of British Mark IV male "Heinz," Tank 207 of Assault Armored Vehicle Detachment (Captured) 14, May of 1918. Leutnant Heinrich Köhler, the tank commander, stands in the center wearing a leather crash helmet. Most of the men are outfitted in the linen coverall to protect their uniforms. The tanker on the right is missing his left eye, almost certainly as a result of spall created when a projectile hit the armor plate. "Heinz" was lost on June 1, 1918, near Fort de la Pompelle.

IV. Details of Employment
Attack.
8. Conduct is determined by the **order for the attack.** This must contain:
Mission,
Starting position,
Time of departure,
Lane of advance (map),
Order of march,
Deployment to combat formations,
Distances between tanks.
Cooperation and communication with infantry.
Conduct in case of counterattack and after mission accomplished.
Technical directions,
Place of commanding officer,
Place of assembly for crews of disabled tanks (cf Paragraph 11).

9. Permanent close contact with the infantry is of the highest importance. The tank may be able achieve a break-in, but it is not able to hold the ground. For this the infantry is needed and for this reason it must follow closely behind the tanks. During the advance, the **place of the tanks** depends on the type of mission. In most cases the tanks will be close behind the first wave of assault troops. On difficult or heavily shelled terrain, **sections of engineers** must be assigned to them in order to overcome particularly difficult spots or to mark tank traps. In order to not disrupt the lanes of advance unnecessarily, it may be appropriate to omit the tank lanes during the preparatory shelling. The **distance** between the vehicles depends on the terrain giving due regard to cover from enemy shelling.

By skillful employment of **smoke bombs** and **smoke shells,** the tanks must be concealed from the enemy for as long as possible, even during the advance.

A7V 506 and her crew, with eight British prisoners at St. Quentin, March 21, 1918. Writing on the back of the photo indicates that the tankers dismounted and fought as shock troops. Weapons include Kar 98AZ carbines, P08 pistols, grenades, a Lewis gun with the stock removed (right) and a flamethrower with a cloth cover (left). This device may have been a special model manufactured by the L. von Bremen Company.

Opposite
Top: British Mark IV female "Hedda," Tank No.5 of Assault Armored Vehicle Detachment (Captured) 11, lost near Fort de la Pompelle on June 1, 1918. The tank broke through the French first line, silenced resistance in the second, and was advancing toward the Aisne-Marne Canal when a shell destroyed her starboard track. "Hedda" was then attacked by a French aircraft, which her crew drove off with machine-gun fire before abandoning the vehicle without destroying it.

Bottom: Pioneers of Assault Battalion No.5 (Rohr) examine a destroyed British Mark II at Cambrai, December of 1917. The tank has taken at least one direct hit from artillery, as evidenced by the gaping hole in the starboard side. At Cambrai the Germans were able to stop British tanks with Infantry Accompanying Batteries, infantry guns, mortars, concentrated charges, and flamethrowers.

10. Special arrangements for the speedy detection and silencing of the enemy's antitank guns by the artillery **must be made.**

11. After the **mission has been accomplished** the tanks drive back to cover in order to avoid destruction by unnecessary exposure to the artillery. If this is impossible during daylight, the vehicles must be hidden in folds of the ground and be camouflaged with branches and soil. The tanks try to avoid **heavy enemy shelling** under cover of smoke bombs; also, playing "dead" may be temporarily useful.

Immobilized vehicles must be thoroughly demolished if their recovery is impossible. Weapons and serviceable components are to be removed. **Crews** of immobilized tanks join the infantry action. According to the situation, they either join the advance as an assault party or they form strong points with their machine guns in order to repulse enemy counterattacks. Staying close to the tank is to be avoided as it will draw enemy fire.

Defenses

12. The tasks of the tanks in **defensive action** are laid down in Paragraph 3. Here also total concealment until commitment is of special importance. The conduct of **counterattacks** is regulated according to Paragraph 9.

Place of the Commander

13. The commander of the detachment takes part in the **attack** in one of the tanks and directs the movement of the detachment by signals. In **defense,** he chooses his place in such a way that he can survey the course of the action and direct his vehicles by signals.

Independent action of the tank commanders will often be necessary in both cases because of the difficulties of communication.

Communications

14. Communication between vehicles and commander, between vehicles and infantry, and between vehicles takes place according to special orders by light signal, colored signal disks, and carrier pigeons, and if necessary by special liaison teams of the assault infantry.
(signed) Ludendorff.

The Spring Offensives

On March 20, 1918, Assault Battalion No.5 (Rohr) was made available to the Assault Armored Vehicle Detachments.[8]

Two assault companies, one machine-gun company, and the howitzer battery were assigned to the 50th Infantry Division.

One assault company, one-half of the machine-gun company, and the howitzer battery were attached to Infantry Regiment No.158, while one assault company and the other half of the machine-gun company were attached to Infantry Regiment No.53 to cooperate with Assault Armored Vehicle Detachment 11 (Captured). One officer and 20 men of Assault Battalion No.5 (Rohr) served as a tank patrol.

Two assault companies, one machine-gun company, the trench-mortar company, and part of the flamethrower platoon were assigned to the 36th Infantry Division to cooperate with Assault Armored Vehicle Detachment 1. One officer and 20 men of Assault Battalion No.5 (Rohr) served as a tank patrol.

One assault company and the rest of the flamethrower platoon were kept in reserve at St. Quentin.

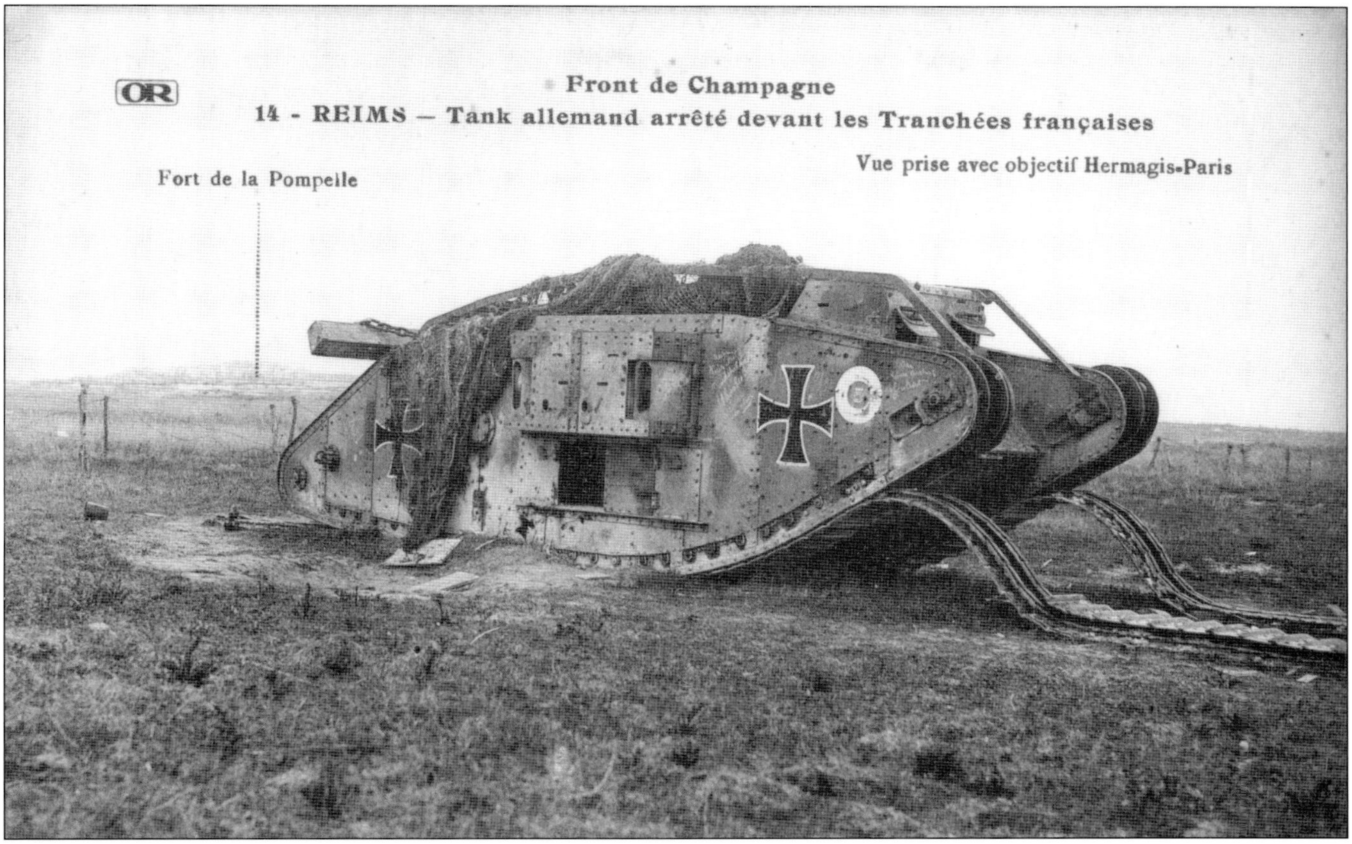
OR
Front de Champagne
14 - REIMS – Tank allemand arrêté devant les Tranchées françaises
Fort de la Pompeile
Vue prise avec objectif Hermagis-Paris

Part of the order for the attack for the 36th Infantry Division stated that Assault Armored Vehicle Detachment 1 would attack the northeast edge of the "Entente Position," joined by the 4th and 5th Assault Companies and 2nd Machine Gun Company of Assault Battalion No.5 (Rohr), one light mortar platoon of Infantry Regiment No.128, the 2nd Detachment of Field Artillery Regiment No.36, and a flamethrower platoon of the 9th Company of the Guard Reserve Pioneer Regiment.

Assault Armored Vehicle Detachment 1 and five patrols from the 5th Company of Assault Battalion No.5 (Rohr) would enter combat at 9:25 A.M., supporting the Flank Clearing Detail of the 2nd Company of Infantry Regiment No.128. The combined force of Assault Armored Vehicle Detachment 1 and Assault Battalion No.5 (Rohr) would attack the northwestern part of Urvillers or bypass the village and attack west of it.

Kanonier in assault order, including knapsack, M1915 field cap, and M1916 gas-mask canister in the "alert" position. Note the lack of ammunition pouches for the Kar 98AZ carbine, which identifies this Kanonier a member of an infantry-gun or Infantry Accompanying Battery. He would carry only about 30 rounds of ammunition in his tunic pockets, as his battery would be pulled out immediately after the end of the mission.

The shock-troop training of the tank crews paid off on March 21, 1918, when Assault Tank Detachment No.1 saw action in St. Quentin. Tanks 501 and 506 launched a flanking attack on a British position that pinned down the German advance with its heavy machine-gun fire, mortars, and rifle grenades. Men of Infantry Regiment No.28, assault pioneers and machine gunners of Assault Battalion No.5 (Rohr), and a flamethrower platoon of the Guard Reserve Pioneer Regiment accompanied the tanks. After the tanks successfully enfiladed the position with machine-gun and cannon fire,[9] the dismounted crews of the disabled Tanks 505 and 507 fought as shock troops, using hand grenades and flamethrowers to roll up the trenches from the flank.[10] The position was completely overrun and the British fled. Thirteen machine guns and much equipment were captured.

Assault Armored Vehicle Detachments (Captured)

On January 8, 1918, the War Ministry ordered the formation of Assault Armored Vehicle Detachments 4 to 7, which were to be equipped with the A7V.[11] Since the tanks were not available, *Chefkraft* assigned the men in these detachments to captured British tanks. Assault Armored Vehicle Detachments 11 and 12 were organized at Charleroi and equipped with the 10 serviceable Mark IVs held by the Germans.

Assault Armored Vehicle Detachment 11 was ready for battle on March 8, 1918. It was equipped with five captured female Mark IV tanks armed only with machine guns, since the Belgian 57mm main guns were not yet ready. Detachment 11 assembled at St. Quentin for Operation Michael and was attached to the 50th Infantry Division along with Half-battalion Hoffmann of Assault Battalion No.5 (Rohr). The Detachment was to attack British position northwest of St. Quentin.

The tanks of Assault Armored Vehicle Detachment 11 began their advance at 9:40 A.M. on March 21. The fog was so heavy that all elements of the force had to move slowly, allowing the tanks to keep up with the assault troops. As soon as the fog lifted, the assault troops outpaced the tanks, which crawled along at four miles per hour. Assault troops were under standing orders to execute their missions as rapidly as possible without regard for the progress of the tanks; they were not to stop or slow down if the tanks could not keep up.[12] The tanks, without infantry protection, were able to destroy enemy trenches and machine-gun nests bypassed by the assault troops in the first wave.

Two tanks were put out of action by British shellfire, and the other three eventually ran out of fuel. Total casualties were four men killed and one officer and four men wounded.

Mark IV used in Berlin by the government-loyal Kommand der Kraftwagenabteilungen, or Kokampf, during the German civil war of 1918-1923. In the background is an Erhardt/17 armored car and a flamethrower shock troop. Although too slow for the rapid advances achieved by the Germans in the Spring Offensives, the Mark IV was an effective psychological weapon in postwar urban combat.

An American newspaper article, dated April 13, 1918, provided details of the German divisional organization during the battle:

> The division advances in two regimental groups progressing side by side. The first line of each group consists, first, of one regiment of three battalions of infantry, whose task is to advance straight upon their objectives, regardless of losses, leaving the work of reducing our centers of resistance to specialist detachments following them.
>
> These consist, first, of one company of storm troops, one and one-half machine gun company, a half company of sappers, one detachment of liquid flame throwers, half a heavy trench mortar company, one battery of light trench mortars, and two batteries of what is called infantry guns.

French Schneider CA1 destroyed at Juvincourt on April 16, 1917. Originally claimed by Bavarian Close Combat Battery 218, the tank now sports a chalked message reading "Knocked out in close combat on April 16, 1917, 4th Company, Infantry Regiment No.54." Beneath it is written "2nd Machine Gun Company, 19th Squad." Passing units clearly felt no compunction about erasing other claims and substituting their own, likely for the purpose of photos.

In reserve come the third infantry regiment and a division of five tanks of British origin and an independent group consisting of two cyclist companies and one company of storm troops.

This division is supported by twelve batteries of field guns and six of heavy artillery, including a battery of 8-inch howitzers.

According to prisoners, a number of enemy battalions have now got special light trench mortar detachments, known as infantry artillery, equipt with two light trench mortars of a new model, mounted on high wheels, supposed to be capable of firing twenty rounds a minute against tanks or other obstacles. The personnel of each detachment comprises two officers and forty men.[13]

Tank Detachments are Renamed

On September 27, 1918, the designation Assault Armored Vehicle Detachment was changed to Heavy Fighting Vehicle Detachment *(Schwere Kampfwagen-Abteilung)*.[14] The designation Assault Armored Vehicle Detachment (Captured) was changed to Heavy Fighting Vehicle Detachment (Captured) *(Schwere Kampfwagen-Abteilung [Beute])*. Finally, *Panzerkraftwagen (A7V)* was changed to *Schwerer Kampfwagen (A7V)*, and *Panzerkraftwagen (Beute)* was changed to *Schwerer Kampfwagen (Beute)*.

Allied Summary of German Antitank Tactics

Anti-Tank Defense. – Tanks are dangerous for the infantry only at very close range (less than 100 meters), on account of the inaccuracy of their fire.[15] Beyond this distance excellent results can be obtained with anti-tank rifles, machine guns and concentrated charges.

The infantry will withdraw to permit the fire of the artillery and trench mortars and engage in combat against the enemy infantry which generally follows at a considerable distance.

Anti-Tank Instruction. – Courses of 8 days were held in January. A large number took part as spectators. Wooden tanks were used, at which machine guns and trench mortars fired until the tanks had penetrated beyond the second line, when the defense was taken over by the artillery. Instruction in the vulnerable parts of the tank was given.

Pioneers train in moving a 77mm gun of an Infantry Accompanying Battery. Such field pieces were also supplied with armor-piercing shells for antitank duty. Five pioneers were assigned to each gun of an Infantry Accompanying Battery to clear obstacles.

A 77mm truck-mounted cannon (7,7 cm Krupp Kraftwagengeschütz), originally an antiaircraft gun but also used in an antitank role. When engaging tanks, it fired an armor-piercing shell. K.Flak Detachments (Kraftwagen-Flugabwehrkanone-Abteilungen) often supported assault infantry in antitank warfare.

Anti-Tank Rifle. – A single shot Mauser model, very strong and simple in construction. The caliber is 13.4 mm., the weight 17 kg., and the length 1.69 meters. It is mounted on a fixed bipod 29.5 mm. in height. It is sighted up to 500 meters and fires a non-explosive bullet which pierces a 21 mm. steel plate at 200 meters.

The allotment is 2 per regiment. They are placed on the main line of resistance or just behind it. Each is served by two men, a rifleman and an ammunition carrier who is the reserve rifleman. Due to an excessive recoil and barrel heating, only 20 shots per minute can be fired. This slow rate of fire, its weight and size prevent its being formidable.

Anti-Tank Ammunition. – Each soldier is issued 10 steel cased bullets. The two best bombers out of every nine are designated to attack tanks with bunches of five grenades, wired together, which are thrown on top of the tanks.

Anti-Tank Machine Guns. – Heavy machine guns are supplied with armor-piercing cartridges. Each must combat tanks which penetrate into its zone. These, which are placed at points especially liable to tank penetration, are designated "anti-tank machine guns."

Tank Vulnerability. – "Tanks are best attacked from the rear."

Tank Barriers. – "Tank Sperren," erected in village streets, consist of a palisade of small iron girders set to a depth of three meters below the ground, in concrete. The girders rise to a height of 2 meters and are inclined at an angle of 70 degrees towards the enemy. There is a gap in the middle large enough for a limber to pass.

Anti-Tank Mines. – Anti-tank mines complete the action of the other arms in anti-tank defense. They consist of wooden boxes 8 x 10 x 2 inches, painted and camouflaged to suit the ground where they are to be laid. They are best placed in the outpost zone and secondly in strong points of the intermediate zone and in the supporting positions. A heavy weight passing over explodes them.

Infantryman armed with two M1917 stick grenades that have a band of color painted around the base of the head, likely indicating a shorter time fuse. The two best hand-grenade throwers of every infantry squad were designated antitank specialists and equipped with concentrated charges to throw on the tops of enemy armored vehicles.

Anti-Tank Groups. – "In the forward battle zone anti-tank groups, under especially energetic leaders, are to be formed. These will consist of anti-tank guns, machine guns, anti-tank rifles and trench mortars. The various weapons of these groups need not be close together, but they must be able to render mutual support within their group, except in the case of anti-tank rifles, which must be in groups of four to six. Groups are to be distributed in depth in the battle zone."

Anti-Tank Forts. – Localities called "tank forts" have been organized for anti-tank defense. They are equipped with field guns, mortars, anti-tank rifles, machine guns, and searchlights. All weapons in each are mutually supporting. The area of the forts varies with local conditions up to several hundred square yards. They are located from just behind the main line of resistance to 1,000 meters back.

Anti-Tank and Close Combat Pieces. – In front of the line of artillery protection were stationed various batteries with special missions, anti-tank and close-combat flanking pieces in, or immediately in rear of, the principal line of resistance and surveillance batteries distributed through the main combat zone. To each of the latter was assigned the protection of a sector of the advance zone.

Increased Materiel. – Early in the winter anti-tank batteries were being disposed of, field and heavy artillery was considered sufficient to engage tanks, but since the operations of the spring and summer began much emphasis has been laid, in many German orders, on the importance of anti-tank defense. Special anti-tank materiel was increased. On August 22, the two hundred and fourteenth division received 16 additional anti-tank guns, raising the total to 28 permanent anti-tank guns. A corps order, of June 23, requires that the greatest possible number of guns should participate in anti-tank combat. In addition to the special anti-tank guns, in the forward zone, each division was to designate a section from the field artillery to be held in readiness outside the line for "urgent" alarm when tanks break through. Heavy batteries, with good opportunity for observation, were considered especially efficient against the tanks.

Position of Anti-Tank Guns. – "In each regimental sector a field gun, with armor-piercing shell, is placed in the outpost zone to fire on tanks. These anti-tank guns, which should have a large lateral field of fire, use direct fire. In addition, an anti-tank surveillance battery is placed on both flanks of the division." The armament of an anti-tank fort included one or two field guns.

Mobility. – An order of the Crown Prince's army group, of August 12, states that tanks have frequently broken through the fronts of the second and eighteenth armies and attacked batteries and division H. Q. and that it was impossible to organize the defense in time, because the artillery lacked sufficient mobility. The guns were too deeply dug in and were not able to fire in time against the tanks attacking from any direction. To attain mobility for anti-tank defense it was recommended that observation facilities should be increased and guns arranged with a view to admitting of quick withdrawal from their positions and of fire in all directions. Mobile anti-tank sections should be increased.

Opposite
Top: Heavy machine-gun squad in light assault order. They wear M1916 steel helmets, rolled packs, dragging straps, cloth gas-mask bags, and machine-gunners' spades with short handles. The squad leader on the right holds the rubber condensation hose and water can shaped like an ammunition box; the ammunition carrier on the left is equipped with two M1915 single-belt ammunition boxes (Patronenkasten 15) that each hold 250 rounds. Armor-piercing bullets were used by heavy machine guns assigned antitank duties.

Bottom: The 20mm Becker aircraft machine cannon (2 cm Flugzeugmaschinenkanone) used in an antiaircraft role. It was slightly modified for antitank work and designated the M11 (2 cm Tankabwehrkanone Becker M.11). Only about 200 were used in combat, as the recoil was considered too great and the penetrative power of the shell too low. The gun on its tripod weighed 66 lb, had a maximum range of 3200 ft, and a firing rate of 500-700 rounds per minute.

Machine Gun Nests. – Concealed machine-gun nests, manned by special detachments of picked machine gunners, were often established near field batteries for protection of the batteries against tanks. In April these detachments were being provided with 20 mm. anti-tank guns.

German Antitank Combat at Juvigny

On August 29, 1918, the American 32nd Division attacked Juvigny, supported by French Tank Companies 311 and 312 of the XXX Army Corps:

> In the early morning, after a short but violent artillery preparation, the Americans began an attack with only infantry, clearly to take our forward positions to prepare the way for the subsequent tank attack. The attack came under fire from our main line of resistance, which caused heavy casualties among the enemy. The actual main attack followed shortly thereafter, again after heavy artillery preparation. This time several squads of tanks – the feared armored fighting vehicles – accompanied the enemy infantry attack. About six squads of five to six tanks each advanced against the sector held by the regiment. The enemy infantry followed close behind like a swarm of bees, especially in the immediate vicinity of the attacking modern-day war elephants moving in dense herds. Everything took place in the way described to us during the instruction time for tank defense. It may be said without exaggeration that the tanks made a very small impression on our men. After the destructive artillery fire which preceded the attack, the appearance of the enemy – even if he sat behind a tank – was almost a relief. Exactly as was so often impressed on them, the companies on the main line of resistance opened fire on the infantry following the tanks, which soon lay down under the onslaught and suffered heavy losses. The heavy weapons of the regiment – the heavy machine guns and tank rifles – then opened fire on the tanks themselves. The trench mortars, which had laid down defensive fire until the appearance of the tanks, were concealed and took part in the fire upon the tanks. Particularly successful defensive work was carried out by an antitank cannon of Field Artillery Regiment 40 behind the south wing of the sector, in the proximity of the Combat Troops Commander (*Kampftruppenkommandeur* or *K.T.K.*). The excellent, very dashing cannoneers undoubtedly destroyed many tanks.
>
> *Leutnant der Reserve* Sauer shot two tanks with the antitank rifle, while *Unteroffizier* Stockhaus of the Trench Mortar Company took out a tank at 300 meters with a flat-trajectory shot from his trench mortar. *Unteroffizier* Dudler of the 3rd Machine Gun Company shot up four tanks with his machine gun, while *Leutnant* Wuttke used a concentrated charge to settle a tank driving along the railway line. On the whole after the attack there were over 20 disabled tanks – all of which were the small, fast Renault type – along the front of the regiment. Nevertheless some of the attacking tanks managed to break through the main line of resistance. Some of them drove on against Juvigny and others pivoted to the south, in order to roll up the main line of resistance from the rear. While most of the tanks attacking Juvigny turned back or were destroyed, the tanks emerging in the rear of the main line of resistance forced the garrison of the main line of resistance to retreat to the road running westward to Juvigny. The retreat was carried out in quite good order, hardly disturbed by the enemy. The deep ravines crossing the terrain allowed a concealed retreat. Under fire from the junction the tanks soon retreated behind the hill west of the railway embankment, while the

Opposite

***Top:** The 76mm light trench mortar, new pattern, with the flat-trajectory carriage (Flachfeuerlafette) that allowed the weapon to be used in direct-fire mode against tanks and other fortified targets. Weighing 550 lb with the carriage, the flat-trajectory mortar fired a 10-lb shell with an effective range of 957 yd. A five-man squad of two gunners, two loaders, and one NCO served the weapon.*

***Middle:** Squad moving the 76mm light trench mortar, new pattern, with flat-trajectory carriage. The barrel is in the position adopted when transporting and loading the weapon. Four men could drag the mortar with straps, as shown, while six were required to manhandle it without straps.*

***Bottom:** The 37mm Rheinmetall antitank gun on a more rigid wheeled carriage (3.7 cm TAK [Tankabwehrkanone] Rheinmetall in starrer Räderlafette), which used the tube of a captured French 37mm revolving canon and the carriage of the German 76mm light trench mortar. With an emplaced weight of 385 lb, it fired solid 1-lb armor-piercing shells that could defeat .6 in of armor at 547 yd.*

Mauser 13mm T-Gewehr (Tankgewehr) displayed by a French sapper. Introduced in January of 1918, the antitank rifle was served by a two-man squad of gunner and assistant who carried 112 rounds of ammunition. At 67 in long, the antitank rifle weighed 41 lb with bipod. The 13.2 x 92mm (.525 caliber) round had an effective range of 547 yd; after 20 rounds the gun barrel overheated. Another shortcoming was the massive recoil. Initially two rifles were issued per regiment, later increased to two per company.

Line pioneers train in the use of Wex flamethrowers as antitank weapons. On September 28, 1918, the War Ministry ordered that all pioneer companies on the western front form a flamethrower platoon armed with six portable devices. In this photo a wooden mockup of a Renault FT-17 sits in the background. Strangely, the individual standing fifth from the right is a young boy in knee pants. His presence at a dangerous live-fire exercise is inexplicable.

enemy infantry occupied the railway embankment. Thus the attack was successful in pushing back the regiment a few hundred meters, but only at a tremendous cost of material and supplies. In addition this modest success was bought with much blood.[16]

Flamethrowers as Antitank Weapons

War Ministry Order No.1672. 18. G. A6, dated September 28, 1918, decreed that all pioneer companies on the western front would each receive six portable flamethrowers, the number of devices that armed a platoon.[17] The weapons would be used in antitank warfare. Pioneer companies attached to infantry divisions would be equipped with flamethrowers first. As the initial installment the companies were given two flamethrowers each, to be used by a "special unit" under the command of an officer. The Guard Reserve Pioneer Regiment was not affected by this order. It retained its function as a combat formation that undertook difficult missions, a training school for the army, and the authority responsible for the further development of the weapon.

Pioneers armed with portable flamethrowers attacked the tank only from the front, where the hatches, pistol ports, and vision slits could not be closed tightly enough to keep out the burning oil.[18] The closer the flamethrower was to the tank, the greater the destructive effect; an ideal range was 11-16 yards.

On February 12, 1918, at the Beuville training ground of Assault Battalion No.5 (Rohr), Bernhard Reddemann volunteered to sit inside a captured British Mark IV tank that was sprayed with a flamethrower. The reason he undertook this potentially deadly experiment was that he wanted to see for himself how effective the weapon would be. When the flamethrower was ignited the oxygen inside the tank was immediately consumed and the vehicle's oil supply caught fire. Reddemann and the other occupants hastily bailed out with only seconds to spare.[19]

According to Charles Theune, "When defending against tanks and undertaking flame defense, the daring spirit of attack generally remains the best guarantee for the success of the flamethrower. The flame attack is the best flame defense."[20]

Endnotes

[1] Maxwell Hundleby and Rainer Strasheim, *The German A7V Tank: And the Captured British Mark IV Tanks of World War I* (Sparkford, Nr Yeovil, Somerset: Hayes Publishing Group, 1990), pp. 34-39.

[2] Gruss, pp. 101-102.

[3] Hundleby and Strasheim, pp. 98-100.

[4] Gruss, p. 102.

[5] Ibid.

[6] Hundleby and Strasheim, pp. 232-233.

[7] Ibid., pp. 41-42.

[8] Ibid., p. 102.

[9] Ibid., pp. 107-108.

[10] Walter Greiff, "Durchbruchschlacht," in *Kreuz-Zeitung* No.71 (March 24, 1935): 18.

[11] Hundleby and Strasheim, pp. 156-157.

[12] Second Section, General Staff, American Expeditionary Forces, Summary of Information No.151, August 30, 1918, pp. 1020-1021.

[13] "How the Battle Goes," *The Independent,* Volume 94 (April, May, June 1918) (New York: Independent Corporation, 1918), p. 81.

[14] Hundleby and Strasheim, p. 234.

[15] *A Survey of German Tactics, 1918,* pp. 38-40, 49, 51-52.

[16] Otto Fliess, *5. hannoversches Infanterie-Regiment Nr.165 im Weltkriege* (Oldenburg i.O.: Verlag Gerhard Stalling, 1927), p. 203.

[17] Hermann Cron, *Geschichte des deutschen Heeres im Weltkriege 1914-1918* (Berlin: K. Siegismund, 1937), p. 174.

[18] Theune, *Sturmtruppen und Flammenwerfer,* p. 187.

[19] War Diary of Sturmpanzerkraftwagen-Abteilung 1, Bundesarchiv-Militärarchiv N 89/5, entry for February 12.

[20] Theune, *Sturmtruppen und Flammenwerfer,* p. 187.

CHAPTER 15

Expeditionary Forces and the Final Assaults

Postcard dated September 4, 1917, depicting Grenadier Finking of the 3rd Company, R.N.A.G., Asia Corps. The unit has not yet been identified. Grenadier Finking wears the M1901 pith helmet with a mosquito veil and neck flap, khaki field jacket and trousers, and M1909 ammunition pouches.

The Asia Corps

In March of 1916 the Germans sent Expedition Pascha to Turkey in preparation for the Suez campaign.[1] Troops sent to assist the Ottoman Empire were designated the Asia Corps *(Asienkorps)* or the Levant Corps *(Levantkorps)*.

The armed units of Pascha included Machine Gun Companies 601-608, Foot Artillery Battalion 60, Balloon Defense Platoons 133-136, Trench Mortar Battalions 350-352, and Aviation Detachment 300.

In March of 1917 the Turks organized Army Group Yilderim (Thunderbolt) to recover Baghdad from the British. To assist Turkey in this mission the Germans sent a second expedition, Pascha II, in August. The firepower of this force was impressive.

Pascha II.

Infantry Battalion 701:
1st, 2nd, 3rd Companies (18 Bergmann light machine guns in total);
Machine Gun Company 701 (six heavy weapons);
Cavalry Detachment 701 (two heavy machine guns);
Infantry Gun Platoon 701 (two 105mm howitzers);
Trench Mortar Section 701 (four 76mm weapons);
one grenade-launcher platoon (six *Granatwerfer 16*).

Infantry Battalion 702:
1st, 2nd, 3rd Companies (18 Bergmann light machine guns in total);
Machine Gun Company 702 (six heavy weapons);
Cavalry Detachment 702 (two heavy machine guns);
Infantry Gun Platoon 702 (two 105mm howitzers);
Trench Mortar Section 702 (four 76mm weapons);
one grenade-launcher platoon (six *Granatwerfer 16*).

Infantry Battalion 703:
1st, 2nd, 3rd Companies (18 Bergmann light machine guns in total);
Machine Gun Company 703 (six heavy weapons);
Cavalry Detachment 703 (two heavy machine guns);
Infantry Gun Platoon 703 (two 105mm howitzers);
Trench Mortar Section 703 (four 76mm weapons);
one grenade-launcher platoon (six *Granatwerfer 16*).

Machine Gun Detachment 701 "Hentig" (six heavy weapons);

Artillery Detachment 701 (three howitzer batteries with four guns each);

Pioneer Company 701 (six smoothbore light trench mortars, two grenade launchers);

Flak Battery 15 (two 177mm guns).

Pascha II Reinforcements.

Two Gefreitere of an Infantry Gun Platoon, Asia Corps, pose with women and a puppy in 1918. Both men have been awarded the Ottoman War Medal, which the Germans called the Iron Crescent (Eiserner Halbmond) and the Allies nicknamed the Gallipoli Star. Uniforms are the field-gray M1915 blouse and khaki M1915 field cap. The artilleryman on the right wears the black wound badge and unidentified light-colored bands on his collar.

Masurian Infantry Regiment No.146 (three battalions, each with one machine-gun company armed with six heavy weapons; each battalion also included 24 light machine-gun squads, one trench-mortar platoon armed with four 76mm weapons, and one grenade-launcher platoon armed with eight weapons);

Pioneer Company 205 (six smooth-bore light trench mortars, two grenade launchers);

Reserve *Jäger* Battalion No.11 (two machine-gun companies armed with 24 heavy weapons, 24 light machine-gun squads, one trench-mortar company armed with eight 76mm weapons, one grenade-launcher platoon armed with eight weapons);

Mountain Artillery Detachment 1 (three batteries of four 77mm guns each);

Mountain Machine Gun Detachments 201, 203, 207, 208 (nine heavy weapons each);

Musketier of the 1st Company, Masurian Infantry Regiment No. 146 (1. masurisches Infanterie-Regiment Nr. 146). Photographed in Constantinople in the fall of 1917, he wears the field-gray simplified tunic, M1907 trousers, and M1910 service cap. Late in the Middle Eastern campaign German troops often retained their field-gray uniforms to avoid being mistaken for British troops.

Austrian artilleryman of the Mountain Gun Detachment in Turkey (k.u.k. Gebirgskanonenabteilung in der Türkei) of the Orient Corps (k.u.k. Orientkorps). The detachment joined the Pascha II Expedition of the Asia Corps in June of 1918. This Kanonier wears the cotton khaki tropical uniform, pith helmet with neck flap, leather artillery gaiters, and a 9mm Steyr M12 automatic pistol. His collar displays scarlet patches (Paroli) of the artillery, which by this date were reduced to narrow strips.

Fahrer of a motor-transport battalion, Pascha II Expedition, Asia Corps, wearing assault order that includes Kar 98AZ carbine, M1887/88 ammunition pouches, M1916 gas-mask canister, and S98/05 bayonet. His cotton khaki uniform is topped by the M1908 troops' peaked service cap with a neck flap and goggles.

Soldat of Ersatz Infantry Regiment No.32, 19th Ersatz Division, in full marching order. His rifle is a Gew 88 with an ersatz bayonet. Although rated a third-class formation by the Allies, the 19th Ersatz Division devised an elaborate shock-troop attack named Operation Rheingold, to be carried out against the French at Bezonvaux on April 16, 1918.

7th Battalion, Foot Artillery Regiment No.2 (one battery of four guns);

7th Battalion, Foot Artillery Regiment No.9 (one battery of four guns);

Flak Platoon 120 (one battery of two guns).[2]

Under the administrative control of the 201st Infantry Brigade and commanded by *Generalmajor* Werner von Frankenberg zu Proschlitz, Pascha II fought in the Battle of Beersheba (October 31, 1917) and the Third Battle of Gaza (October 31-November 7, 1917), significant Turkish defeats. Following the British capture of Jerusalem in December, the Germans sent further reinforcements for Pascha II. From the summer of 1916 the Austro-Hungarians also contributed Motor Mortar Battery No.9, Howitzer Battery No.36, and Mountain Artillery Regiment Nos. 4 and 6.

The Battle of Megiddo (September 19-25, 1918) saw the destruction of the Turkish Seventh and Eighth Armies and the full retreat of the Fourth Army. After advancing nearly 300 miles, the British had taken more than 75,000 prisoners, 360 guns, and all of the Turks' transport equipment, for a loss of 5720 men.[3] The Germans and Austrians of Pascha II tried to conduct a fighting retreat to Damascus but were cut off. Most were captured or killed.

Operation Rheingold

"Order Ia No.176; Divisional Order No.2, Royal Saxon 19th *Ersatz* Division."[4]

1. Operation "Rheingold" will probably take place during the night of April 16-17, 1918.[5] Time of beginning of operation designated "X."

This infantryman late in the war displays the ideal shock-troop kit conceptualized by Willy Rohr three years earlier: Kar 98AZ carbine, two hand-grenade bags, size 3 respirator in cloth bag, pioneer ax, haversack, water bottle, wire cutters, cavalry-style "Y" braces, and steel helmet.

2. <u>Target of attack:</u> The enemy's shelter constructions at $97r_{1-4}$, 97_t, 97_r *[at Bezonvaux, a destroyed village about five miles northeast of Verdun, ed.]*

3. <u>Purpose of operation:</u> Determine enemy's tactical distribution; take prisoners and spoils of war; destroy enemy's buildings within area of attack.

4. <u>Management of infantry attack:</u> Lieutenant-Colonel v. SEYDLITZ, commander of E.I.R. 32 *[Ersatz Infantry Regiment No.32],* at regimental observation point. He will lead Trench Mortar Company No.164 with Captain SCHULZE.

In charge of artillery tactics: Artillery Commander 137.

5. <u>Assault Party:</u>
<u>Leader:</u> Captain SCHMIDT, Battalion Commander of II/E.I.R. 32, in Battle Force Commander [*Kampftruppenkommandeur* or K.T.K.] observation point.

<u>Combat Group:</u>
five details of II/E.I.R. 32, a total of six officers, six sergeant-majors, 25 noncommissioned officers, 168 men, and three machine guns;

one raiding party of the divisional assault school, comprised of one sergeant-major, one NCO, and 12 men;

four pioneer detachments of Reserve Pioneer Company No.22, a total of one sergeant-major, three NCOs, and 24 men.
Also: two flamethrowers.

6. <u>Machine gun 08:</u> Operational action according to regimental setting-up.
<u>Task:</u> To suppress enemy's machine guns and trench garrisons.

7. <u>Artillery:</u> It will be supplied:
a) for preparation and defensive barrages;
b) for artillery duels.

8. <u>Trench Mortars:</u>
All men appointed for the operation, the 19th *Ersatz* Division, and the neighboring divisions will come under the uniform leadership of Trench Mortar Company 164 and the commander of E.I.R. 32.

Commander of the Trench Mortar Company: the most senior officer.

Commander of the trench mortars will be at the regimental observation point from X minus 2 hours.

Postwar image of a submachine gunner of II. Marine Brigade Erhardt, armed with a 9mm MP18/I. By the end of the war every officer, NCO, and 10 percent of enlisted men of infantry companies were to be issued the MP18/I. A special machine-pistol detachment was also to be created in each company, consisting of six gunners, six ammunition carriers, and three ammunition carts.

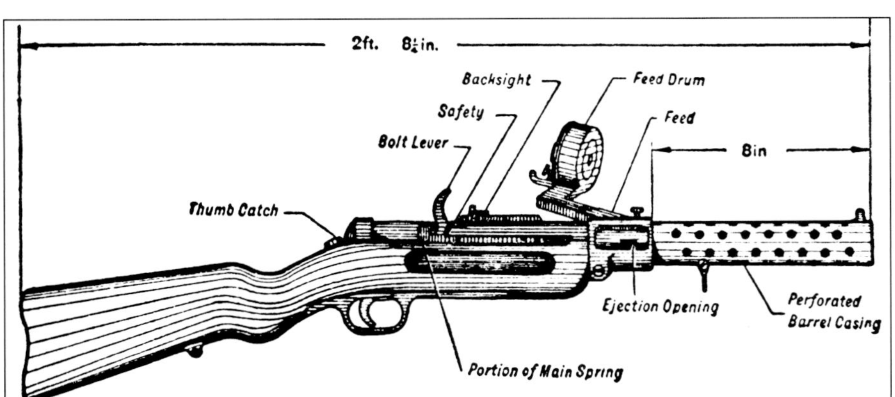

The 9mm MP18/I, the first practical submachine gun. Weighing 11.6 lb when fitted with the loaded 32-round drum, it had a rate of fire of 400 rounds per minute and a maximum range of 328 yd. German troops called it the "bullet sprayer" (Kugelspritz).

A 12-man flamethrower shock troop of the 9th Company, Guard Reserve Pioneer Regiment, after a successful assault. The officer in the center is the company commander, Hauptmann Karl Walter, the Brandinspektor (Fire Inspector) of Bremerhaven from 1908 to 1919. Note the torn trouser knees, camouflaged helmets, P08 pistols, and Kar 98AZ carbine.

The most exact shooting must be observed, and the artillery correction group will supply statements on the day's wind direction every two hours.

9. Practice shooting of artillery and machine guns: To be unobtrusive and to inform the machine-gun groups through the artillery liaison officer; practice shooting must cease on the evening of April 15. Notice given to Division through Artillery Commander 137 and Commander E.I.R. 32.

10. Time for the beginning of the operation (X hours) decided by the Commander of E.I.R. 32 is to be given to the Division in writing by the morning of April 16 and then forwarded to the artillery commander and neighboring divisions.

The day of the operation is to be kept from the raiding parties for as long as possible.

11. Progress of the operation:
X minus 90 minutes to about X minus 70 minutes: First destruction of enemy's batteries in wind-corrected shooting according to artillery commander's advice (only in good weather).

X minus five minutes: Readying of assault troops in jumping-off positions.

X minus one minute: Beginning of artillery and mortar fire; beginning of machine-gun fire.

In favorable winds the second destruction of enemy's curtain-fire batteries (same as above until X plus 19 minutes). In bad weather harassing fire with high-explosive or Blue Cross high-explosive munitions during the entire operation.

Lining up of assault troops so that they can break into the enemy's trenches after the last trench-mortar salvo.

X hour: Final strike on enemy's K2 and K3 trenches, machine guns, and batteries.

Shortly afterward the assault troops break through into enemy's trenches.

Laying of artillery and machine-gun fire according to Enclosures 3 and 4. (II. Moment).

X plus three minutes: Final strike of medium and heavy machine guns and batteries on enemy's K4 trench and observation points.

Laying of fire according to Enclosures 3 and 4 (III. Moment).

X plus 6 minutes: Final strike of light machine guns on enemy's k4 trench and observation points, and laying of fire according to Enclosure 4 (IV. Moment).

For artillery the laying of fire in III. and IV. Moments is the same.

The assault troops reach their targets in one strike after the laying of our own fire. If necessary the attached pioneer groups will carry out the demolition of obstacles with elongated charges.

Trench mortars will unobtrusively continue to expand the lanes they already created through enemy obstacles.

After completion of his tasks the leader of Assault Group II will give the signal for retreat through rockets and several firings of Very light "green-red double star." The signals will be repeated by the other assault groups. This will be followed by the withdrawal of the assault groups with prisoners and spoils of war, via the shortest way and according to the circumstances of

The youthful shock troop of the 10th Company, Landwehr Infantry Regiment 133, in a postcard sent January 31, 1918. Although ostensibly men of a second-line formation, they display up-to-the-minute equipment including Gew 98 rifles, small grenade bags, and camouflaged helmets.

enemy fire. Security groups in trenches $91m_1$ and $91m_2$ will cover the retreat. They will leave only by special order of the assault group leader.

After the return of all assault groups to our own K1 trench, the leader of Assault Group II will give the signal "yellow with floating balls" – cease machine-gun fire. Machine-gun and artillery fire will taper off according to Enclosures 3 and 4 (II. Moment). Ten minutes after the observation of light signals all fire will cease.

12. Directions for assault troops:
The way through our own obstacles is shown with white panels of cloth. In addition, Pioneer Battalion No.519 will erect two searchlights on Marien Hill for the benefit of retreating assault troops, in accordance with the following from E.I.R. 32:

With the appearance of the Very signal "green-red double star" blinking lights will begin (about three seconds of light and 20 seconds' pause) aimed vertically to the sky and continuing until the order to stop has been given.

13. Clock time:
An officer of the signals troops will be appointed; on both April 15 and 16 he will state the exact clock time of 1000 hours and 1600 hours to E.I.R. 32 in the regimental observation post.

On April 15 and 16, at 1200 hours and 1800 hours, accurate watches will be supplied to those who have ordered them.

The exact time for all participating formations and neighboring divisions will be supplied by E.I.R. 32 to the infantry, machine guns, and trench mortars, as well as Artillery Commander 137.

It should be noted that April 15 is daylight saving time.

14. Communication equipment:
All divisional communication equipment is alarm ready at X minus 30 minutes. The observation post will be manned by an officer of the Division.

Signal-lamp stations will show V_1 and W_1 with green; K.T.K. V and W with white; V_3 and W_2 with red light. Ground telephone station in V_1 must continue sending from X minus 30 to the cessation of the operation, and K.T.K. V must remain in place for the same time in order to receive the messages. For W_1 to contact K.T.K. a K-Funk device will be supplied.

Radio and ground telephone will be supervised at K.T.K. by an officer of the Division.

E.I.R. 32 must initiate the Very signals "green-red double star" and "yellow with floating balls" through each of the signal posts on Grenadier Hill, Marien Hill, and Hill 310.

15. Again it is emphasized that all identification signals will be promptly stopped when ordered.

16. Collection point for prisoners and spoils of war: BERGQUELLE.

17. All troop dressing stations to be occupied according to 45th Reserve Brigade:
a) company leader tunnel in W_3
b) troop dressing station: ORNES
c) Preussenlager

Opposite: Two Unteroffiziere of the Bavarian 6th Infantry Regiment (6. Infanterie-Regiment Kaiser Wilhelm König von Preußen), Bavarian 6th Infantry Division, one of the German army's best formations according to Allied intelligence. They are armed with M1917 stick grenades and British Short Magazine Lee-Enfield (SMLE) Mk.III rifles. The .303 caliber SMLE was used by assault troops on an extremely limited basis.

Kanonier of an infantry accompanying battery. He wears a Wurttemberg cockade on his M1908 field cap, but his belt buckle is Saxon. A small, embroidered badge in the form of a "G" can be seen on his left inner elbow. This unofficial insignia stands for "Grenade-launcher Squad" (Granatwerfertrupp).

Opposite
***Top:** Men of Bavarian 29th Infantry (Jäger) Regiment, which provided the bulk of the Caucasus Expedition in June of 1918. Most wear the Bavarian M1907 field jacket with Swedish cuffs. The grenade bags are the small version that held only three or four hand grenades each.*

***Bottom:** Russian Austin armored car used by the Kokampf during the German civil war of 1918-1923. Armored Car Machine Gun Detachment 1 may have used two captured Austins during the Caucasus Expedition. The original Vickers machine guns have been replaced with the German MG08.*

18. The submitted recommendations of artillery commanders, the leaders of trench-mortar and machine-gun groups, and E.I.R. 32 are endorsed, unless changed in the above.

19. The Division is to be updated constantly with all available information about the progress of the operation.
(signed) v. d. DECKEN

The Caucasus Expedition
On May 28, 1918, the Democratic Republic of Georgia signed the Treaty of Poti with Germany and requested German protection from the chaos of the Russian revolution and Ottoman military threats. Germany therefore sent the 3000-man Caucasus Expedition *(Kaukasusexpedition)*, which would also secure oil supplies. The Expedition consisted mostly of Bavarian troops:[6]

Bavarian 29th Infantry *(Jäger)* Regiment:
Bavarian 7th Reserve *Jäger* Battalion;
Bavarian 9th Reserve *Jäger* Battalion.

Bavarian 15th Reserve *Jäger* Regiment:
Bavarian 1st Reserve *Jäger* Battalion, taken from Bavarian 29th Infantry *(Jäger)* Regiment;
Caucasian Railway Protection Battalion, raised from German former prisoners of war.

Assault Battalion No.10:
one assault company;
one machine-gun company;
one trench-mortar company;
one garrison company, raised from German former prisoners of war.

Trench Mortar Company 176.

2nd Detachment, Reserve Field Artillery Regiment No.65.

Armored Car Machine Gun Detachment 1.

7th Bavarian Cavalry Brigade:
Bavarian 5th *Chevauleger* Regiment Erzherzog Friedrich von Österreich;
Bavarian 4th *Chevauleger* Regiment König.

Aviation Detachment 28.

Signal Section 1750.
The Caucasus Expedition arrived at the Georgian capital of Tiflis (Tbilisi after 1936) on June 10, 1918. Soon its ranks were expanded with German former prisoners of war freed by the Russians and Württemberg colonists who had settled in Georgia. On August 27 the Germans made an agreement with Soviet Russia to stop the Ottoman Army of Islam in exchange for 25 percent of the oil produced in Baku. However, the Army of Islam began its assault on Baku the next day and took the city by September 14, ejecting the Soviet, British, and Armenian defenders.

On October 21 Germany ordered the withdrawal of all troops from Georgia. The Caucasus Expedition departed from Poti in December and

251. 11.9.18.

arrived in Germany in April of 1919. It was the last German formation to return from active service during the war.

Assaults on the Vesle

After the failed offensive of July 17, 1918, the Germans were on the defensive until the end of the war. However, they were still able to inflict significant casualties on their enemies, as the Americans discovered when the German 29th Infantry Division carried out two major attacks on the Vesle.[7]

The first, launched on August 22, was called either Operation America *(Unternehmen Amerika)* or Operation Border Guard *(Unternehmen Grenzschutz). Hauptmann* Petersson led 10 shock troops composed of men from:

the 1st Battalion of Badener Infantry Regiment No.112;
the 9th and 10th Companies of Badener Infantry Regiment No.113;
the 1st Company of Pioneer Battalion No.14.
the 9th Company of the Guard Reserve Pioneer Regiment.

The mission of the shock troops was to destroy the bridges over the Vesle; six of the 10 shock troops contained one flamethrower squad each. After an artillery barrage at dawn, the shock troops attacked Companies I and K of the American 308th Infantry Regiment, 77th Division. Fierce close-quarter fighting took place before the Germans were driven off:

> The solitary German who got through K Company's fire of rifles, chauchats, and hand grenades, was killed by Private Spinella, who, it is said, first used the butt of his own chauchat and then finished with the enemy's bayonet. Company I, as was later learned from prisoners, was attacked by four companies of Baden troops accompanied by a detachment of pioneers with flame-throwers. These *flamenwerfer* did considerable damage, though it is supposed that all belonging to this command were killed by the men of I Company with the exception of those who were burned to death by their own hands through getting the nozzles of their machines entangled in the heavy underbrush of the swamp.[8]

The Germans captured two officers and 31 men of the 308th Regiment, but the Americans took their own prisoners. A lieutenant and five men of K Company accepted the surrender of shock troops from Baden Infantry Regiment No.112 in the woods behind company headquarters. The *Feldwebel* in command disclosed his orders, which had been to drive the Americans out of their outposts on the Vesle before 4:45 A.M:

> It was a regular raiding party, equipped with light machine guns, hand grenades, and flame-throwers. All the prisoners had been told that capture by the Americans meant instant death, and in their gratitude at being spared, they turned out their pockets, furnishing an abundance of souvenirs, among which was a large package of British cigarettes.[9]

The second assault carried out by the German 29th Infantry Division took place on August 27. Operation Baden *(Unternehmen Baden)* called for 13 shock troops to be organized from:

the 1st Battalion of Badener Infantry Regiment No.113;
the 3rd Battalion of Badener Infantry Regiment No.142;
the 9th Company of the Guard Reserve Pioneer Regiment.

Opposite
***Top:** Bavarian Chevauleger in full marching order, September of 1918. The Caucasus Expedition included the 4th Chevauleger Regiment König and the 5th Chevauleger Regiment Erzherzog Friedrich von Österreich. These cavalrymen wear the M1909 tunic, M1908 riding breeches, and high boots. Dismounted cavalrymen served as assault troops on most fronts. Note that at this late date the men retain the Pickelhaube.*

***Bottom:** Kaiser Karl I of Austria inspects Turkish assault troops in Constantinople, 1918. The men wear the M1917 steel helmet manufactured locally; it has a rolled rim instead of the sharp edge seen on Turkish helmets cut down from the German version. Weapons and equipment include Gew 98 rifles, German ersatz bayonets, and wire cutters. Note the woolen mountaineering socks and trousers with leather-reinforced knees. These shock troops would be headed for the eastern front rather than Palestine.*

Infanterist Pfiligg, Bavarian 12th Infantry Regiment (kgl. bayer. 12. Infanterie-Regiment Prinz Arnulf), of the Bavarian 2nd Infantry Division. Rated by Allied intelligence as "one of the very best German shock divisions," the Bavarian 2nd Infantry Division fought on the western front for the entire war, suffering heavy casualties. Infanterist Pfiligg's face appears to show the strain of unrelenting combat.

Heavy machine-gun detachment of a dismounted cavalry formation serving as shock troops in 1918. The men are armed with P08 pistols and hand grenades; the MG08 on its sled is transported on a horse-drawn wagon that also carries ammunition. Note the camouflaged steel helmets and machine-gun dragging straps.

Under the command of a *Major* Grohe, the shock troops were to take Fismette. Eight of the 13 shock troops contained one flamethrower squad each. The Germans gained control of Fismette on August 28, capturing three American officers and 254 men, mostly form the 307th Infantry Regiment. In addition G and H Companies of the 112th Regiment, holding Fismette at the time of the attack, lost 165 of their 206 men.

The official U.S. Army history of the III Corps reached several conclusions about the disaster at Fismette:[10]

1. The attack, which followed immediately after G and H Companies of the 112th Regiment relieved the previous garrison, caught the American troops before they had become familiar with the positions they occupied.

2. The Americans were vulnerable to demoralization caused by enemies in American uniforms or cowardly soldiers of their own creating panic.

3. American troops apparently assumed that the bombardment was routine and consequently were not on the alert to repel an attack.

4. There was culpable negligence on the part of the American commanders in not requesting artillery support.

5. The garrison holding the west and north of the town lacked the spirit to fight to the last man.

6. The Americans were demoralized by attacking German aircraft.

7. American organization was faulty, as no provision was made for the defense of the village in case flank attacks should occur. Additionally no provision was made to properly use machine-gun and rifle fire for the protection of the rear and flanks of the platoons in position.

Shock troop conducting a night attack with flamethrowers. The infantrymen in the trench wear steel helmets, while the flamethrower pioneers on the right are outfitted in field caps and a minimum of equipment. Night photography was nearly nonexistent during the First World War.

Battery squad (Batterietrupp), the reconnaissance personnel of a field battery. Battery squads were equipped with telescopes, flags, directors, telephones, and hand grenades. Trained as infantry assault troops, their mission was observation.

Shock troops of Assault Battalion No.8 advance behind a rolling barrage during training at Buczacz, Galicia. Two waves of assault troops are present, the first only about 30 yd behind the artillery strikes. Such realistic training often resulted in fatalities.

This weary looking young Leutnant of Assault Battalion No.2 has been awarded the EKI. He is uniformed in an officers' M1915 blouse and M1910 service cap with wire stiffener removed. Assault Battalion No.2 carried out the unsuccessful attacks on the American Lost Battalion in the Argonne, October 7-8, 1918.

The Lost Battalion

In the Argonne shock troops were used against the Lost Battalion, a mixed formation from the American 77th Division comprised of K Company, 307th Infantry Regiment; A, B, C, E, G, and H Companies, 308th Infantry Regiment; and F and D Companies, 306th Machine Gun Battalion; about 554 men in all.[11] On the German side were units of the 76th Reserve Division, including Reserve Infantry Regiment No.254, a battalion of dismounted Uhlans, *Landwehr* Infantry Regiment No.122, Pioneer Battalion No.376, and Pioneer Companies 76 and 77.

Although the Germans surrounded the Americans, cut them off from the rest of their division, and subjected them to mortars, artillery, machine guns, snipers, and hand grenades for four days, the Lost Battalion stubbornly held out. The period literature claimed that a very large body of shock troops – an entire battalion, according to one source – was finally sent in, but German records show that the actual force was quite small. In total, Assault Battalion No.2 dispatched two NCOs, a 16-man shock troop, eight rifle grenadiers, and a flamethrower platoon of 15 pioneers armed with five small devices.[12] Forty-one men were to clear out the *Amerikanernest* that had withstood four days of almost everything the Germans could bring to bear.

The shock troops used their flamethrowers first, no doubt hoping to break the morale of the Americans:

> A long pennon of sissing, smoking black slashed through the leaves and among the brown trunks, a hundred feet or more, its drops shedding into little fiery pools whenever they touched anything – liquid fire sure enough, the most dreaded, though actually one of the least dangerous German methods of attack. All around on the flank where it had come men were swearing and sobbing, letting off their guns blindly in a kind of wild fury over this final barbarity. Another slash of it and another, half a dozen of them, and arching above it the potato mashers with their violent shock.[13]

The Germans succeeded only in capturing nine badly wounded doughboys, who were not expected to survive. On October 7, after sending a note to the Americans appealing to their "humane sentiments" and requesting their surrender, the Germans launched a final attack. They opened fire with trench mortars and machine guns, the shock troops flinging volleys of hand grenades as they led the charge. The Americans responded with rifles and shouted obscenities:

> The German's humane sentiments now changed. He attacked with flame throwers on the right flank where there was the one remaining Hotchkiss gunner, who fired pointblank on the assault teams, kindling the *Flamenwerfer* men into human torches.[14]

Like the attack of the day before, this one also failed. Later that night the Lost Battalion was relieved. Of the original 554, only 194 were able to walk out unassisted. Casualties for Assault Battalion No.2 were two dead and one wounded.

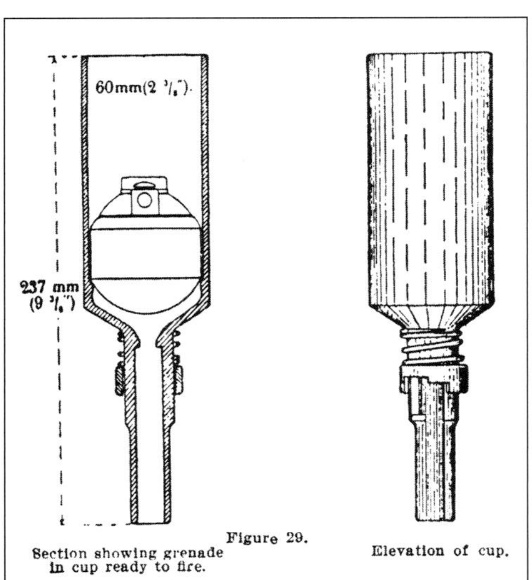

M1917 rifle grenade, a copy of the French VB (Vivien-Bessières) grenade. Fired with a standard cartridge, it was launched about 200 yd by the muzzle blast. The bullet passed through a channel in the grenade body and struck a plate that ignited a primer, lighting the eight-second delay fuse. On detonation the grenade scattered shrapnel for a radius of about 75 yd.

Wex squad in Berlin, during the postwar fighting of late 1918. The steel-helmeted pioneer with the carbine (third from right) wears a death's-head sleeve badge below his left elbow, the position used by the flamethrower platoon of Assault Battalion No.5 (Rohr). A medic and an NCO round out the reinforced Wex squad.

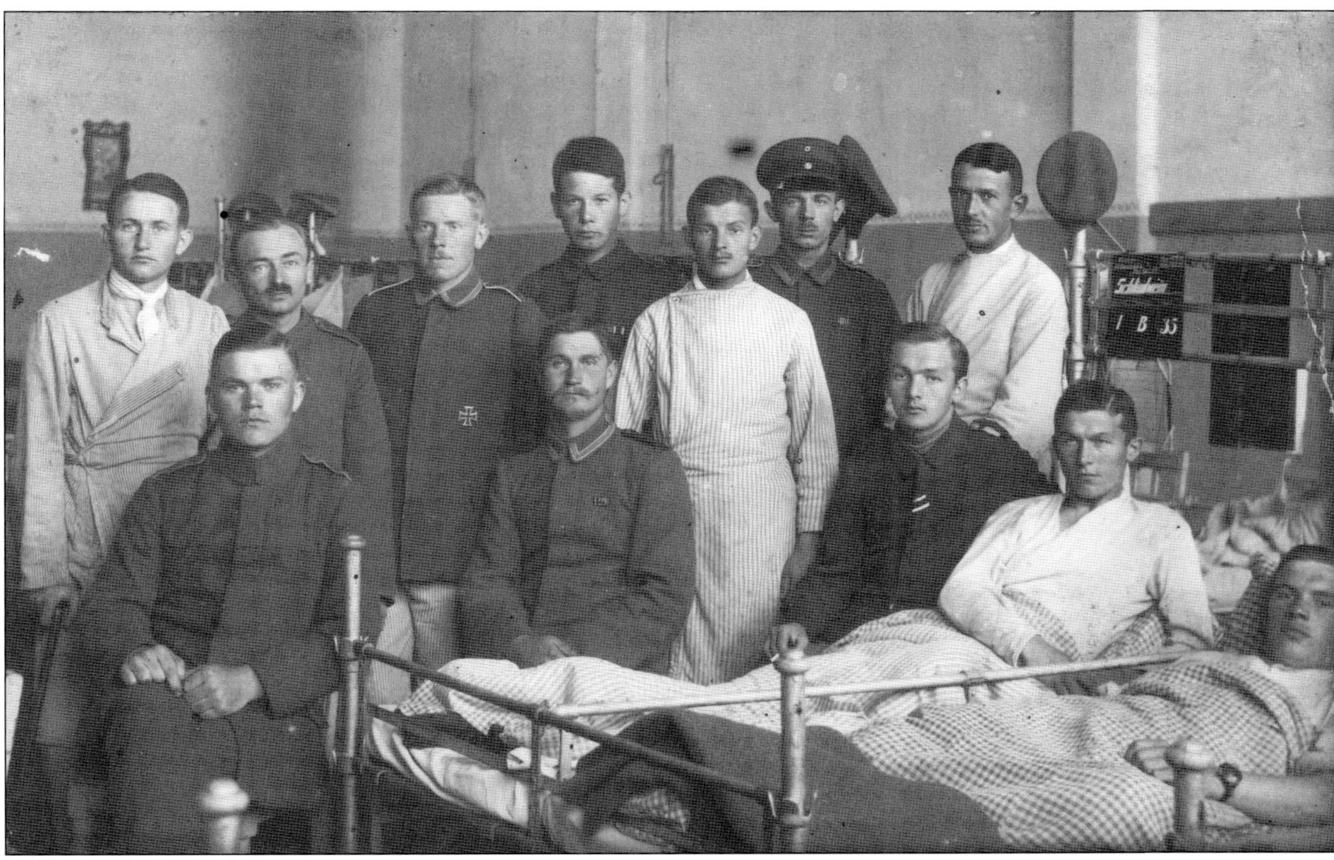

Military hospital in Bremen, October 29, 1918. Young, physically fit, and highly trained in assault tactics, these soldiers have survived the war.

Postwar photo of a Reichswehr 76mm light trench mortar, new pattern, mounted on a flat-trajectory carriage. The Unteroffizier in the background is armed with a trench dagger and decorated with Freikorps insignia. He wears collar badges of the Guard Cavalry Schützen Division and the sleeve badge of Minenwerfer Detachment Heuschkel. On his left cuff is a white death's head, showing that he is also a veteran of the flamethrower regiment.

The Last Major Assault of the War

On October 25, 1918, the Germans assaulted Verdun:

> Alarmed by the pressure of our troops, the Germans yesterday put in 800 Prussian shock troops, who gained only a temporary success, being driven back within an hour. On this front the Germans put in a fresh division against the American divisions.
>
> The fighting is no less severe west of the Meuse, where the Germans are contesting bitterly every foot of ground we gain and hurling frequent attacks against us. For the last twenty-four hours there has been almost constant fighting for possession of Belle Joyeuse Farm, which we have captured twice and as many times have lost.
>
> We have had Grand Pré free from Germans three times. Twice they have come back, but now they are out and we hold a handsome margin north of the ruins of this once pretty Aire Valley town.[15]

The Germans had already asked for an armistice on October 5. It was signed at 5:00 A.M. on November 11, 1918, and took effect at 11:00 A.M., ending combat operations.

Endnotes

[1] Cron, *Imperial Germany Army 1914-18,* p. 61.

[2] http://www.asienkorps.de/kriegsgliederung.htm (accessed August 23, 2010).

[3] Livesey, p. 170.

[4] Rated a third-class division by Allied intelligence. War Department, *Histories of Two Hundred and Fifty-one Divisions of the German Army which Participated in the War (1914-1918)* (Washington, D.C.: Government Printing Office, 1920), p. 305.

[5] A typewritten, English-language translation of this order was found in the papers of an anonymous Australian army officer.

[6] Cron, *Imperial Germany Army 1914-18,* pp. 61, 366; and http://www.sacktrick.com/igu/germancolonialuniforms/hist%20ottoman.htm.

[7] War Diary of *Infanterie-Division Nr.29,* Bundesarchiv-Militärarchiv PH 8-I/205, 206, and 374.

[8] L. Wardlaw Miles, *History of the 308th Infantry 1917-1919* (New York and London: G. P. Putnam's Sons, 1927), pp. 85-86.

[9] Ibid., p. 88.

[10] "Setback at Fismette: Study of a Fiasco," http://www.worldwar1.com/dbc/fismette.htm (accessed November 3, 2010).

[11] Thomas M. Johnson and Fletcher Pratt, *The Lost Battalion* (Lincoln, Nebraska, and London: University of Nebraska Press, 2000), pp. 58-59.

[12] War Diary of *Reserve-Division Nr.76*. Bundesarchiv-Militärarchiv PH 8-II/86 and PH 8-II/87.

[13] Fletcher and Pratt, p. 206.

[14] Laurence Stallings, *The Doughboys: The Story of the AEF, 1917-1918* (New York: Harper and Row, 1963), p. 275.

[15] "The Battle that Won Sedan," by Edwin L. James, in *The New York Times Current History: The European War,* Volume XVII (New York: The New York Times Company, 1919), p. 470.

Conclusion

On mobilization in August of 1914 the combat units of a German infantry division on the western front consisted of:

two infantry brigades (two regiments each);
four regimental machine-gun companies (six heavy weapons each, 24 in total);
one cavalry regiment (three or four squadrons);
one or two pioneer companies;
one field-artillery brigade (two regiments of two detachments each; three six-gun batteries per detachment, for a total of 72 guns).

Each infantry regiment was comprised of three battalions, for a total of 12.

A battalion contained four infantry companies of 240 rifles each. One division in each Corps was also assigned one *Jäger* battalion with one machine-gun company and one bicycle company.

Four years later the German army had evolved into shock-troop specialists. In November of 1918 the theoretical combat units of a German division on the western front were:

one infantry brigade (three regiments);
one to three assault companies (three 40-man platoons in each);

Left:* *The idealized image of the assault infantryman. German, Austrian, Bulgarian and Turkish soldiers strike heroic poses; the caption reads, "Ready for the final blow." In the background Allied forces advance.

Right:* *From a "war chronicle" (Kriegs-Chronik) certificate awarded a German infantryman in 1919 to commemorate his service. The transformation from 19th century foot soldier to modern assault specialist is striking.

one Machine Gun Marksman Detachment;
two cavalry squadrons;
one or two pioneer companies;
three trench-mortar companies;
one field-artillery regiment;
one battalion of foot artillery;
40-45 artillery batteries attached for the purposes of a particular battle.

Each infantry regiment was comprised of three battalions, for a total of nine.

A battalion was comprised of three infantry companies (180 rifles each), one machine-gun company armed with 12 heavy weapons, and one grenade-launcher platoon armed with eight weapons. In addition to riflemen each infantry company contained six light machine-gun squads, two antitank-rifle squads, and one machine-pistol detachment armed with six weapons.

The Machine Gun Marksman Detachment was comprised of three companies, each armed with 12 heavy machine guns for a total of 36.

Each cavalry squadron was armed with two heavy and three light machine guns.

Each pioneer company had one trench-mortar detachment armed with six light smoothbore weapons; one grenade-launcher detachment armed with two weapons; and one antitank flamethrower detachment armed with six small weapons.

Each regimental trench-mortar company was armed with nine light and three medium weapons.

The field-artillery regiment was comprised of three detachments of three batteries each; three batteries were armed with four 105mm light howitzers each; six batteries were armed with four 77mm light field guns each. In addition, each detachment was armed with six heavy machine guns for close combat.

The foot-artillery battalion was comprised of three batteries, each armed with four 150mm guns. In addition, the battalion was armed with six heavy machine guns for close combat.

One division in each Corps also had one *Jäger* battalion of four companies that included six light machine-gun squads each; two machine-gun companies armed with 12 heavy weapons each, for a total of 24; one grenade-launcher platoon armed with eight weapons; one trench-mortar detachment armed with eight light weapons; and often a mountain-gun battery.

The two original assault formations ended their careers somewhat ingloriously. In 1918 Assault Battalion No.5 (Rohr) experienced continuous combat, suffering its heaviest casualties of the war. By mid-October the battalion had been withdrawn to the rear area of the Fifth Army and remained there as a reserve. In the final days of the war Rohr's men served as the honor guard of the Kaiser's Supreme Headquarters at Spa. Forty-eight hours after the Kaiser abdicated and fled to Holland, the *OHL* delegated command of the battalion to the Soldiers' Councils, apparently fearing that Rohr's men were experiencing a breakdown in discipline. *Major* Rohr demanded and was granted the right to march his men back to Germany, but only after the *OHL* removed a company's worth of the best troops to serve as the headquarters' bodyguards.

On the way home, the reduced assault battalion undertook its final mission and cleared the Herbestal train station of mutinous troops. After this, desertions became so commonplace that by the time Rohr reached

Freikorps and Reichswehr troops gather to confront communists during the general strikes, March of 1919. In the foreground is a heavy machine-gun limber of the former Assault Battalion No.5 (Rohr); the soldiers in the background are a mixture of Rohr's assault pioneers and men of a Guard formation.

As both a flamethrower pioneer and a member of Assault Battalion Nr. 5 (Rohr), this sad-faced young man would have received the best possible training in shock tactics during the war. Photographed in April of 1918, he still faced seven months of extremely heavy fighting ahead.

Preparing for the next war. This photo of a Reichswehr assault platoon was taken August 18, 1919. Note the Wex M.1917 flamethrower, grenade bags, and M1918 steel helmets with cutouts over the ears.

Schwelm the only men remaining were the grooms who cared for the horses of the howitzer battery and the machine-gun and trench-mortar companies. The horses were sold and the proceeds given to the Workers' and Soldiers' Council of Schwelm. Assault Battalion No.5 (Rohr) was then dissolved. The volunteer company that remained in Spa to guard the *OHL* travelled to Colberg, where it formed the core of *Freikorps* Hindenburg.

Major Rohr served with the *Reichswehr* Guard *Schützen* Battalion in Lichterfelde and then became a staff officer in charge of supply in Flensberg. After leaving the army he died in 1929. During the war 624 men of Assault Battalion No.5 (Rohr) were killed in action, died of wounds, accident, or disease, or went missing.

Following the Armistice of November 11, the Guard Reserve Pioneer Regiment destroyed most of its flamethrowers and retreated to Germany. It was disbanded in Berlin in January of 1919. During the war Reddemann's men carried out 653 flamethrower attacks, of which 535 were successful. A total of 890 flamethrower pioneers were killed in action or died from accident or disease.

After the war Reddemann became Technical Director of Minimax A.G. in Berlin, which produced firefighting equipment and had manufactured flamethrowers during the war. Reddemann also patented several firefighting inventions, including fire-extinguisher nozzles and devices for introducing foam into tanks of flammable liquids. He died in 1938 at the age of 69.

Only a year later the world discovered how far the Germans had taken the tactics Rohr and Reddemann developed.

Appendices

Appendix 1
Instructions for the Employment of Flame Projectors

From a captured German document dated December 12, 1915.[1] Although the instructions were written specifically for the use of flamethrowers, they also provide a detailed summary of the infantry shock-troop tactics created by Willy Rohr and Bernhard Reddemann.

A. – Troops and Equipment.

1. Flame projectors *(Flammenwerfer)* are a new weapon for trench warfare. The 3rd Guard Pioneer Battalion (6 Coys.) has been equipped with them and trained in their use. They are under the command of General Headquarters, and will be placed at the disposal, as a unit or by sections, of particular formations for a particular purpose, when they will, for the time being, be entirely under the orders of the responsible Commander, who, after consulting with the Flame Projector Commander and taking the limitations of the weapon into consideration, will give the tactical orders for the assault. The responsibility for their technical employment rests entirely with the Flame Projector Commander.

2. Each company of the 3rd Guard Pioneer Battalion is equipped with 20 to 22 large flame projectors (range of jet 33-44 yards). They will be built into sapheads, advanced galleries, or the front line position. In addition, each company has 18 small flame projectors (range of jet 16-19 yards). These are easily portable and will be carried on the back.

B. – Capabilities of Flame Projectors.

3. During a flame attack each large flame projector (built in at about 27 yards distance from the enemy's trench), will cover the enemy's foremost trenches with flames on a front of about 55 yards. The enemy in these trenches will either be destroyed or driven off, or if he happens to be in deep dugouts will have his morale so shaken that he will allow himself to be captured without resistance. Machine guns, even if provided with overhead cover or in blockhouses, are put out of action by directing the flames against the loopholes. The flame attack lasts about one minute.

4. The front covered by a company of the 3rd Guard Pioneer Battalion is about 1,100 to 1,640 yards. The effect, physical and moral, of such a flame attack on the enemy is very great.

5. The assault will be made by infantry and pioneers immediately after the flame attack. Detachments with small flame projectors will accompany the assaulting troops in order to overcome any resistance which may be offered by blockhouses, etc., and also to spread the fear of the flames to the enemy's rearward positions. Many successive positions can often be taken by assault at the same time.

6. The small portable flame projectors may also often be employed with advantage in combination with bombers in making progress in the enemy's trenches, and for flank attacks on portions of trench, etc.

C. – Necessary Conditions for Flame Attacks.

7. *For large flame projectors,* trenches, sapheads and galleries must have been pushed forward to within 27 yards at least of the enemy's position at several points, or there must be a prospect that they will be able to approach so near within the next few days.

8. *For small flame projectors,* the portions of trench referred to in para. 6 must be approached under the cover of trenches or saps.

9. In both cases (paras. 7 and 8) an accurate previous reconnaissance of the points at which the flame projectors are to be employed, and of the approaches to them, is absolutely essential. This must be made by the officers of the Flame Projector Battalion. The reconnaissance, transport of the apparatus and other preparations take, as a rule, several days. The building in of the large flame projectors requires 12 hours and can be done without the enemy becoming aware of it.

10. The direction of the wind has very little influence on the effect of a flame attack. A postponement of an attack will become necessary only if there is a very strong head wind.

D. – Tactical Employment of the Flame Projector Detachment.

11. Flame projectors must be used offensively. It is forbidden to build flame projectors in as defensive weapons in the foremost lines. Small flame projectors may be used, however, to drive off counter-attacks against positions, the capture of which has been facilitated by a flame attack, until such positions have been consolidated. For technical reasons they cease to be effective after about 48 hours. In other special, and quite exceptional, cases when it is proposed to use them defensively, the Commander of the Flame Projector Detachment should be consulted beforehand.

12. Flame attacks proper (*i.e.* sudden attacks with a number of large flame projectors, without any special preparation by artillery and trench mortars) should be the usual method of employment. The assaulting troops (infantry, pioneers, and the small flame projectors) must advance at once (*i.e.* 1 minute after the large flame projectors have come into action) and take every advantage of the panic caused in the enemy's ranks by the flame attack, with a view to capturing the 2nd and 3rd Line Positions. For the action of the artillery and trench mortars see para. 35.

13. If the Commander of the Flame Projector Detachment considers it safe to do so, one or more sections of the front to be attacked may be left untouched by the flames, between the areas covered by the individual large flame projectors which have been built in. The length of such sections may be 100 yards or even more.

14. The fact that the enemy is taken by surprise by the flame attack has much to do with making it a complete success. It is, therefore, of the highest importance that the enemy should not obtain information of the arrival of a Flame Projector Detachment in the Division, etc., or of the sector in which it is intended to employ it. It is consequently necessary that the word "*Flammenwerfer*" should never be mentioned during a conversation, when speaking over the telephone or in orders. A code word is to be used, such as "Neue Minenwerfer" or something similar. *The Detachment will not be* *spoken of as "Flammenwerfer" Company, but as – th Company, 3rd Guard Pioneer Battalion.*

E. – General Tactical Instructions.
15. When giving orders for an attack in which large flame projectors are to be employed, the following points based on previous experience should be considered:

(i.) – Objective.
16. Exact instructions must be given how far the attack is to be *pushed* under the most favorable conditions. It has happened that our troops, taking advantage of the panic of the enemy, have carried the advance too far, thereby coming under our own artillery barrage.

17. In order to ensure secrecy as much as possible, it is advisable that the intended operation should be denominated by a code word (in writing or when using the telephone), such as "*Vortrag,*" "*Vorführung,*" "*Verhandlung*" (Lecture, production, negotiation).

(ii.) – Time of Attack.
18. As a rule, half an hour, or on dull days one hour *before sunset* is the most suitable time. Only in exceptional cases, when, in the course of the day, the destruction, by artillery or trench mortars, of the large flame projectors which are built in, appears to be fairly certain, may the attack be carried out in the early morning.

19. It is sometimes advisable that the day and hour should not be mentioned in the orders for the attack, but should temporarily be *kept secret,* and should be referred to as "X" and "Y." In later orders, which will be issued in writing only to Battalion, Artillery, and Group Commanders, and the Commanders of independent Companies, inclusive, the time should then be indicated, for instance, as follows: "X" equals 27th Nov. "Y" equals 3.20 p.m.

(iii.) – Assaulting Troops.
20. The carrying out of the preparations for the attack is often better done if the assault is not made by the troops occupying the trenches, but by a detachment which *has been kept in rest billets.* All troops which up to that time have been in the trenches will then retire to the 2nd Position shortly before the assault, and as soon as the attack by the assaulting party has begun, again move forward into the foremost trenches previously held by them, in order to hold a possible counter-stroke.

21. *The size of the assaulting force must not be too great. The calculation should be one (man?) of the assaulting party to each meter of front. Each party must have a good Second in Command in addition to the Commander.*

22. The individual assaulting columns will be distributed in four successive waves, as follows:
(*a*) **Assaulting Party,** which advances immediately after the flame attack and occupies the enemy's positions. In this party are included bombers, engineers (for the demolition of obstacles) and small flame projectors.
(*b*) **Consolidating Party** for the consolidation of the enemy's trenches.

(*c*) **Communication Trench Construction Party,** to construct communication trenches from the captured trenches to our previous foremost position.
(*d*) **Carrying Party,** which will take forward material for obstacles, especially knife-rests, sandbags, hand grenades and ammunition.
The attacking parties on the flanks will have *several* bombing parties and Small Flame Projector Detachments attached to them to assist them in clearing the trenches from the flanks.

23. Assaulting Detachments and Consolidating Parties will take up positions in the saps or in the front line trenches; Communication Trench and Carrier Parties will be ready behind them in the communication trenches. The stationing of troops in readiness will of course depend upon the existing system of saps, and will sometimes necessitate previous reconstruction of this system.

24. *The division* of the assaulting columns into these parties is best carried out well behind the front. If no other troops are to be employed except those manning the trenches, it is advisable to relieve them, for a short period at least, from the foremost trenches for the purpose of preparation and organization. The troops will march up to their positions in the line in the order detailed for the assault.

(iv.) – Preparations for the Assault.

25. Special preparations must be made in order that the assaulting troops can mount the parapet rapidly. *Short ladders* with one pole about 1 metre *[1.1 yards]* longer than the other are the most useful means. These should be made previously in the Engineer Parks. One ladder is required for every 3-4 men of the Assaulting Party. When being taken up to the front line they must be carried horizontally. They must not be placed in position in the trenches until the commencement of the flame attack.

26. All necessary *matériel,* such as hand grenades, loophole plates, sandbags, knife-rests, barbed wire, entrenching tools, and light-pistols with ammunition must be kept in readiness either in the communication trench depots or with the assaulting columns.

27. *Communication trenches and approaches* must be divided up and *allotted* to the assaulting columns and reserves. Communication trenches, saps, etc., will be distinctly marked with numbers, letters, or names.

28. Should other troops than those holding the trenches be employed for the assault, their officers and N.C.O.s must carry out a thorough *reconnaissance* of their trenches in the early dawn and during the day. No unusual movement, however, must take place in the trenches and there must be no loud talking.

29. The advance of the assaulting troops into the front line trenches and the relief of the troops in the trenches must be carried out in *complete silence.* No talking is to be allowed. Unnecessary crowding together should be avoided. Bayonets will be fixed behind the lines and not in the front line. Rifles must be carried at the trail as far as possible.

(v.) – The Assault in Conjunction with a Flame Attack.

30. Charges (long or concentrated), to create gaps in our own *obstacles,* will be exploded by the engineers at the earliest 15 minutes *before* the flame attack, and this work must be completed 10 minutes before the flame attack. It will often be found sufficient if, on the night previous to the attack, the engineers cut the wire which connects the knife-rests in front of the foremost trenches. This must be done without attracting attention, the knife-rests being left in the original position until the troops are ready to attack, *i.e.*, immediately after the flame attack, when the engineers will precede the assaulting force, swinging the knife-rests round lengthways at right angles to the parapet.

Engineers will also hurry forward and make gaps in the *enemy's wire* should these not have been made previously by trench mortars or engineer detachments. Obstacles which are not too strong can very often be easily crossed by the assaulting troops, as after a flame attack the enemy fires very little or not at all.

31. The duration of the *flame attack* is only one minute. The signal for it is given by a siren whistle, or at a given time, watches having been previously synchronized. The *assaulting troops* must be *instructed* that they have nothing to fear from the flames and smoke, nor need they fear that they may themselves be caught by the fire jet, as this is cut off by simply turning a tap previous to their advance. They must understand that they can advance immediately after the cessation of the spray without danger, as small bursts of flame on the ground or in the enemy's trenches will burn out at once, and a little fire on the ground is at once extinguished when trodden upon. It is most important to impress upon the troops that the assault is much facilitated by the use of the flame projector, as it has been proved by experience that the enemy fires very little or not at all after a flame attack.

32. The *assault* is made immediately after the flame attack. The *Assaulting Party* charges, followed closely by the *Consolidating Party*. The small flame projectors allotted to the Assaulting Party attack any machine guns that are still in action, blockhouses that are still being defended, etc., with short spurts of fire. They are at the disposal of the Commander of the Assaulting Party for this purpose.

It is of the highest importance to drive out the enemy simultaneously to a considerable distance on both flanks by means of bombing and flame projector detachments (*see* para. 22), and to construct sandbag barricades at these points. Communication trenches which lead into the captured position must also be cleared for a certain distance and blocked by constructing sandbag barricades about 27 yards forward of the position won.

The action of the *Communication Trench Construction Party* will commence immediately after the nearest enemy position had been taken. Material is brought up as soon as possible by the *Carrier Party,* which will continue to bring up fresh material from the rear as required. Carrier Parties can at times on their return journey also take charge of prisoners as far as the point at which the reserves are situated in rear.

It is especially important to bring up and dig in machine guns immediately.

33. It may be of advantage to order a password for our attacking troops, especially if several successive positions are to be taken, and in the twilight of dull days. Words which the enemy would find it difficult to pronounce are particularly suitable, such as "*Schweineschmalz,*" "*Stiefelwinsche,*" etc.

(vi.) – Action of the Artillery and Trench Mortars.

34. In a *flame attack pure and simple,* which is generally to be preferred (*see* para. 12), the action of the artillery and trench mortars will not commence until about one minute after the projection of the flames, when the more retired positions, which it is not intended to take, should be shelled. Barrage fire will be opened on the ground behind these positions and on the communication trenches, etc.

35. Should it be impossible, in exceptional circumstances, to dispense with previous *preparation by the artillery and trench mortars,* only the enemy's rear positions and not his foremost position are to be shelled. It does not matter if this results in the enemy pressing forward into the positions nearest to us in order to obtain shelter, thereby reinforcing the garrison. It must, however, always be borne in mind that by artillery and trench mortar preparation the enemy is warned of an imminent attack, and is thus enabled to take precautionary measures.

36. In most cases, however, it is advisable to request the *Divisions on the right and left* to open with artillery on the enemy's rear positions behind the front which it is intended to capture. Registration must be carried out so as not to attract attention.

37. As a rule it is advisable to detail a *special Artillery Group* to repulse hostile counter-attacks. Its commander must take up his position with the Commander of the attacking force and must arrange for special telephonic communication.

(vii.) – Forces on the Flanks of the Front of Attack.

38. The effect of a flame attack is sometimes felt to the right and left of the front which is covered with flame. Our troops which are posted on the flanks of the actual front of an attack can sometimes, therefore, gain ground by a prompt advance in force. It is, consequently, necessary to keep under close observation the enemy's troops on the flanks of the front of attack, and, according to circumstances, either subject them to a heavy fire or attack them as well. Engineer detachments are to be posted in readiness for forming gaps through the obstacles, should this be necessary.

(viii.) – Equipment, Ammunition, and Rations.

The *assaulting troops* will wear "assault order." Each man will take his greatcoat, tent square, mess tin, full water bottle, 4 days' rations in his haversack, and, in addition, at least 200 rounds, 2 hand grenades and rifle with fixed bayonet.

The Consolidating Parties are similarly equipped, except that they sling their rifles (bayonets not fixed). Each man will carry a loophole plate, 50 sandbags and heavy entrenching tool.

Communication Trench and Carrier Parties will appear in their usual order of dress. Only the N.C.O.s will carry rifles. The men of the Communication Trench Party will each carry a heavy entrenching tool, 50 sandbags and at least 2 hand grenades.

(ix.) – Telephone Communications.

40. A number of infantry telephone lines will be laid from the captured position to the rear, immediately after the assault.

41. All lines leading to the Commander of the attacking force are to be used solely for service messages which concern the attack, so that he can bring his personal influence to bear upon every part of the front.

Notes

[1] *The Infantry Journal* Volume 14. Number 9 (March 1918). pp. 692-698.

Appendix 2
Badges of Assault Units

1. Shoulder strap of Bavarian 1st Reserve Infantry Regiment; the "H" may stand for hand-grenade squad *(Handgranatentrupp).*

2. Unidentified shoulder-strap badge of Bavarian 4th Reserve Infantry Regiment.

3. Cloth badge worn by hand-grenade squads on upper or lower left sleeve. Many units adopted this badge in dark or light colors, often mounted on circular field-gray patches.

4. Embroidered chevron worn on upper left sleeve by shock troop of Bavarian 1st Reserve Infantry Regiment. Dark-colored thread.

5. Cloth badge worn on upper left sleeve by hand-grenade squads of several infantry regiments. Dark-colored grenade on field-gray oval patch.

6. Cloth badge worn by Assault Battalion No.2 on lower left sleeve, above cuff. Black on field-gray circular patch.

7. Badge worn on lower left sleeve by shock troops of unidentified infantry regiment on western front. Embroidered in field-gray thread.

8. Cloth badge worn on upper left sleeve by assault detachment of West Prussian Reserve Infantry Regiment No.149. Likely green on top, red on bottom.

9. Cloth badge worn on upper left sleeve by shock troops of unidentified Saxon infantry regiment. Red "S" in the shape of a snake on a field-gray oval.

10. Flamethrower badge awarded by the Kaiser on July 28, 1916. Cut from gray cloth for enlisted men, embroidered in silver bullion for officers. Both were mounted on field-gray oval patch. Worn on lower left sleeve by men of Guard Reserve Pioneer Regiment, left inner elbow by flamethrower platoon of Assault Battalion No.5 (Rohr).

11. Official variant of flamethrower badge, cut from white cloth and mounted on field-gray oval patch. Worn on lower left sleeve by men of Guard Reserve Pioneer Regiment, left inner elbow by flamethrower platoon of Assault Battalion Rohr.

12. Badge worn on lower left sleeve by assault troops of 4th Hannoverian Infantry Regiment No.164. Cut from white and dark-gray cloth.

13. Badge worn on left inner elbow by shock troop of unidentified infantry regiment on western front. Cut from white cloth.

14. Badge worn on lower left sleeve by Assault Company of 38th Infantry Division. Cut from black, white, and field-gray cloth.

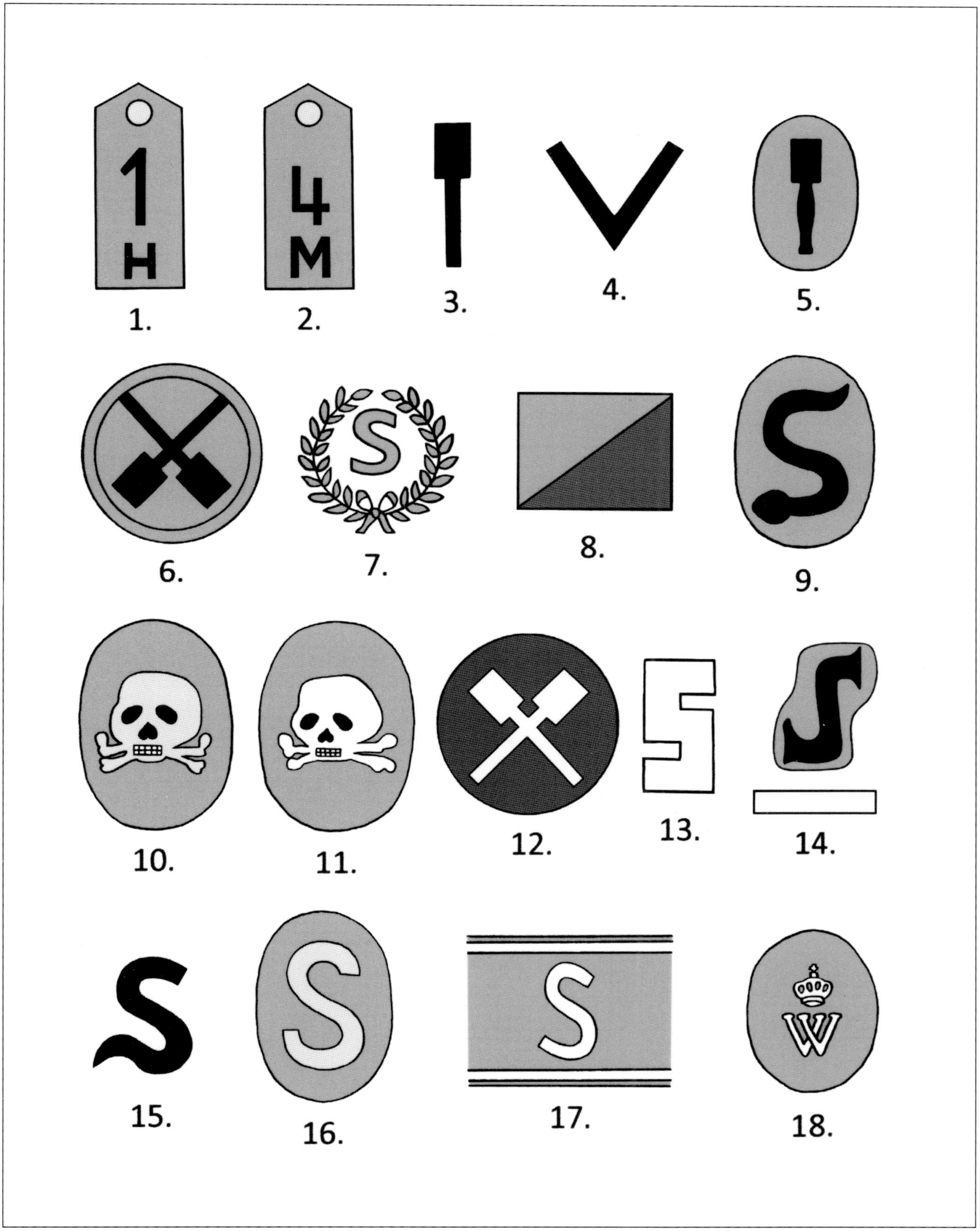
1
H
4
M
1.
2.
3.
4.
5.
S
S
6.
7.
8.
9.
10.
11.
12.
13.
14.
S
S
S
W
15.
16.
17.
18.

15. Badge worn on upper left sleeve by shock troop of unidentified Saxon infantry regiment. Embroidered in dark thread.

16. Badge worn on inner left elbow by shock troop of the same unidentified Saxon infantry regiment. Cut from light-colored cloth, mounted on field-gray oval patch.

17. Brassard worn on upper left sleeve by Assault Company of Saxon 24th Reserve Division. Green with white horizontal lines above and below white "S."

18. Badge unofficially adopted by Assault Battalion No.5 (Rohr) on February 18, 1918. White-metal crown and "W" on field-gray oval patch, worn on lower left sleeve.

Bibliography

Primary Sources

Government Documents and Public Records

Engineer School, United States Army. *Experience of the German 1st Army in the Somme Battle, by General von Bülow. Occasional Papers Number 56.* Washington Barracks, D.C.: Press of the Engineer School, 1917.

Generallandessrchiv Karlsruhe 456 EV 142/1.

Headquarters Fort Niagra Training Camp, *Memorandum No.15: Gases and Flame.* New York: Fort Niagra, 1917.

Historical Section, U.S. General Staff. *A Survey of German Tactics 1918: Tactical Studies No.1.* Base Printing Plant, 29th Engineers, U.S. Army, 1918.

Kriegsgeschichtlichen Abteilung I des Grossen Generalstabes. *Die Kämpfe der deutschen Truppen in Südwestafrika,* Volumes I and II. Berlin: Ernst Siegfried Mittler und Sohn, 1906.

Kriegsministerium. *Anleitung für den Kampf um Festungen (K. u. F.).* Berlin: Ernst Siegfried Mittler und Sohn, 1910.

—. *Anleitung für Kompagnieführer (K.F.U.).* Berlin: Reichsdruckerei, 1917.

—. *Ausbildungsvorschrift für die Fusstruppen im Krieg.* Berlin: Reichsdruckerei, 1918.

—. Nr.355.10.15 A6II, October 17, 1915, Generallandesarchiv Karlsruhe 456 F3/966.

—. *Pionier-Sturmanleitung (P. St.) vom 10 Marz 1904.* Berlin: Reichdruckerie, 1904.

Ministère de la Guerre, Section technique des Etudes et Expériences chimiques. *Conférences de l'Ecole des gaz de combat: Les Lance-flammes. 3ème Conférence. Lance-flammes portatifs étrangers.* Paris, 1920.

Ministère des Affaires Étrangères. *Les Violations des Lois de la Guerre par l'Allemagne.* Paris/Nancy: Librairie Berger-Levrault, 1915.

Petter, Erich. *Kampfwagenabwehr im Weltkriege 1914-1918.* Unpublished typewritten study, Berlin: 1932. Bundesarchiv-Militärarchiv Freiburg W10/50769.

Records of the Chief, Chemical Warfare Service, Record Group 175, U.S. National Archives.

Records of *Pionier-Regiment 23,* Bundesarchiv-Militärarchiv PH 14/218.

Records of *Wüttembergisches Pionier-Bataillon Nr.13,* Hauptstaatarchiv Stuttgart M 200 Bü. 80; M 209 Bü. 17.

Second Section, General Staff, American Expeditionary Forces, Summary of Information Nos. 151, 153, and 155, August-September, 1918.

"Verwendung der Flammenwerfer." Bundesarchiv-Militärarchiv W10/51589.

War Department. *Histories of Two Hundred and Fifty-one Divisions of the German Army which Participated in the War (1914-1918).* Washington, D.C.: Government Printing Office, 1920.

—. *German and Austrian Tactical Studies: Translations of Captured German and Austrian Documents and Information Obtained from German and Austrian Prisoners from the British, French and Italian Staffs.* Washington, D.C.: Government Printing Office, 1918.

—. *German Military Dictionary.* Washington, D.C.: Government Printing Office, 1944.

—. *German Notes on Minor Tactics.* Washington, D.C.: Government Printing Office, 1918.

—. *Notes on the German Army in the War.* Washington, D.C.: Government Printing Office, 1917.

—. *Notes on Recent Operations, No.2.* Washington, D.C.: Government Printing Office, 1917.

—. *A Survey of German Tactics, 1918.* Washington. D.C. Government Printing Office, 1918.

War Diary of *General der Pioniere der Armee-Abteilung Gaede,* Genrerallandesarchiv Karlsruhe 456 EV 105/57.

War Diary of *Kommando der Pioniere der Landwehr Division Nr.12,* Genrerallandesarchiv Karlsruhe 456 EV 105/69.

War Diary of *1. Landwehr-Pionier-Kompagnie XIV. Armee Korps,* Generallandesarchiv Karlsruhe 456 EV 105/98.

War Diary of *Infanterie-Division Nr.29,* Bundesarchiv-Militärarchiv PH 8-I/205, 206, and 374.

War Diary of *Reserve-Division Nr.76,* Bundesarchiv-Militärarchiv PH 8-II/86 and PH 8-II/87.

War Diary of *Sturmabteilung Marinekorps,* Bundesarchiv-Militärarchiv RM 120/324.

Books

Dem Andenken unserer gefallenen Kameraden: Garde-Reserve-Pionier-Regiment (Flammenwerfer). Berlin: Kameradschaft der Flammenwerfer im NS.-Reichskriegerbund, 1931.

Dion, S. A. *Tanks, Gas, Bombing, Liquid Fire.* New York: George U. Harvey Publishing Company, 1917.

Dose, Wolf Jan. *Die 187er im Felde.* Hamburg: Eigenverlag, 1922.

Elliott, F. Haws. *Trench Fighting.* Boston and New York: Houghton Mifflin Company, 1917.

Fries, Amos A., and Clarence J. West. *Chemical Warfare.* New York: McGraw-Hill Book Company, Inc., 1921.

Gay, Adrien. *Grenade Warfare.* Atlanta: E. W. Allen and Company, 1918. Von Hindenburg, Paul. *Out of my Life,* Volume I and II. New York and London: Harper and Brothers Publishers, 1921.

The Independent, Volume 94 (April, May, June 1918). New York: Independent Corporation, 1918.

The Infantry Journal, Volume 13, Part 2 (November 1916-June 1917). Washington, D.C.: The United States Infantry Association, 1917.

Kellermann, Bernhard. *Der Krieg im Argonnerwald.* Berlin: Verlag Julius Bard, 1916.

Laffargue, André. *The Attack in Trench Warfare.* New York: D. Van Nostrand Company, 1917.

Ludendorf, Erich. *Ludendorff's Own Story,* Volumes 1 and 2. New York and London: Harper and Brothers Publishers, 1919.

Oskar Charles Gustavus Adolphus, *Die Winterschlacht in der Champagne (16. Februar bis 18. Marz 1915).* Oldenberg, Germany: Druck und Verlag von Gerhard Stalling, 1915.

Raynal, Colonel Sylvain-Eugène. *Le Drame du Fort de Vaux.* Frémont, Verdun: Éditions Lorraines, 1949.

Reddemann, Bernhard. *Geschichte der deutschen Flammenwerfer-Truppe.* Berlin: Verein ehem. Angehöriger der Garde-Reserve-Pionier-Regiments, 1933.

Theune, Charles. *Sturmtruppen und Flammenwerfer.* Berlin: Landes-Verlag, 1921.

Articles

"Instructions for the Employment of Flame Projectors." *The Infantry Journal* Volume 14. Number 9 (March 1918).

"Sweeping Out Captured Dugouts with a Broom of Fire." *Scientific American,* September 8, 1917.

Newspapers

"Germans Use Liquid Fire in Attack on Russians." *The Syracuse Herald* (March 10, 1915), p. 2, col. 6.

"Germans Using Gas." *Fairbanks Daily Times* (June 8, 1915), p. 1, col. 2.

Communications with the Author

Gramatski, Ventsislav. E-mails to the author, May 27-31, 2008. Interview conducted by Mr. Gramatski with Dobrin Todorov Dobrinov, staff member of National Museum of Military History, Sofia, on May 26, 2008.

Hans Schmidt. E-mail to the author, June 15, 2006. Information about the combat experience of Pioneer Hermann Schmidt, of the Pioneer Experimental Company.

Secondary Sources

Books

The Americans in the Great War, Volume II: The Battle of St. Mihiel. Clermont-Ferrand, France: Michelin and Cie., 1920.

Balck, Wilhelm. *Development of Tactics – World War.* Fort Leavenworth, Kansas: The General Service School Press, 1922.

—. *Entwickelung der Taktik im Weltkriege.* Berlin: R. Eisenschmidt, 1920.

Barrett, Michael B. *Operation Albion: The German Conquest of the Baltic Islands.* Bloomington and Indianapolis: Indiana University Press, 2008.

Barron, Elwyn (ed.) *Deeds of Heroism and Daring.* London/New York: Harper and Brothers, 1920.

Bordeaux, Henry. *The Last Days of Fort Vaux.* Paris: Thomas Nelson and Sons, 1919.

Bull, Stephen. *German Assault Troops of the First World War. Stosstrupptaktik: The First Stormtroopers.* Stroud, Gloucestershire: Spellmount Publishers, Ltd, 2007.

—. *World War One German Army.* London: Brassey's, 2000.

—. *World War I Trench Warfare (1).* Botley, Oxford: Osprey Publishing, 2002.

Arthur F. Cassels, ed. *The Field Artillery Journal* Volume 8, January-March 1918. Philadelphia: J. B. Lippincott Company, 1918.

Clausius, Oberstleutnant. *Erinnerungsblätter deutscher Regimenter, Band 176: Infanterie-Regiment von Wittich (3. kurhessiches) Nr.83.* Oldenburg iO/Berlin: Verlag Georg Stalling, 1926.

Cron, Hermann. *Geschichte des deutschen Heeres im Weltkriege 1914-1918.* Berlin: K. Siegismund, 1937.

—. *Imperial Germany Army 1914-18: Organisation, Structure, Orders-of-Battle.* Solihull, West Midlands, England: Helion and Company, 2002.

De-Lazari, Aleksandr Nikolaevich. *Khimicheskoe Oruzhie na Frontakh Mirovoĭ Voĭny 1914-1918 gg.* Editing and commentary by Dr. Mikhail Vasilyevich Supotnitskiy. Moscow: Vuzovskaya Kniga, 2008.

Drury, Ian, and Gerry Embleton. *German Stormtrooper 1914-1918: Warrior Series No.12.* London: Osprey, 1995.

The Encyclopædia Britannica, 12th Edition. The New Volumes, Volumes 30, 31, 32. London: The Encyclopædia Britannica Company, Ltd., 1922.

English, John A. *A Perspective on Infantry.* New York: Praeger Publishers, 1981.

Fliess, Otto. *5. hannoversches Infanterie-Regiment Nr.165 im Weltkriege.* Oldenburg i.O.: Verlag Gerhard Stalling, 1927.

Ganoe, William A. *The English of Military Communications.* Menasha, Wisconsin: George Banta Publishing Co., 1918.

Goes, Gustav. *Hartmannsweiler Kopf: das Schicksal eines Berges im Weltkriege.* Berlin: Traditionsverlag Kolk, 1930.

—. *Hartmannswillerkopf.* French translation by P. Waechter. Paris: Payot, 1934.

Gollwitzer, Fritz, and Karl Bruno Hock. *"Jäger vor!" Erinnerungs- und Gedenkbuch der Aschaffenburger Jäger (2. Bayr. Jäger-Batl., bayr. Res. Jäger Batl. Nr.2, Radfahrer und Ersatz Radfahrer-Komp.)* Münchberg: A Dreschler, 1936.

Gruss, Hellmuth. *Aufbau und Verwendung der Deutschen Sturmbataillone im Weltkrieg.* Berlin: Junker und Dunnhaupt, 1938.

Gudmundsson, Bruce. *Stormtroop Tactics: Innovation in the German Army, 1914-1918.* Westport, Connecticut: Praeger, 1989.

Hartenstein, Prof. Dr. *Das kurhessische Pionier-Bataillon Nr.11 im Weltkriege 1914-1918.* Zeulenroda in Thüringen, Germany: Verlag Bernhard Sporn, 1936.

Heinrici, Paul, ed. *Das Ehrenbuch der deutschen Pioniere.* Berlin: Verlag Tradition Wilhelm Rolf, 1931.

Horne, Alistair. *The Price of Glory: Verdun 1916.* London: Penguin Books, 1993.

Hundleby, Maxwell, and Rainer Strasheim. *The German A7V Tank and the Captured British Mark IV Tanks of World War I.* Sparkford, Nr Yeovil, Somerset: Hayes Publishing Group, 1990.

Johnson, Thomas M, and Fletcher Pratt. *The Lost Battalion.* Lincoln, Nebraska, and London: University of Nebraska Press, 2000.

Jones, Simon. *World War I Gas Warfare: Tactics and Equipment.* Botley, Oxford: Osprey Publishing, 2007.

Karau, Mark D. *Wielding the Dagger: The MarineKorps Flandern and the German War Effort, 1914-1918*. Westport, Connecticut: Praeger Publishers, 2003.

Koch, Fred. *Beutepanzer im Ersten Weltkrieg: britische, französische und russische Kampf- und Panzerwagen im deutschen Heer*. Freiburg: Podzun-Pallas Verlag, 1994.

Krapchanski, V. N.; D. D. Vazel; G. R. Hristov; and I. K. Skachokov. *Kratak Obzor na boynia sastav, organizatsiyata, popalvaneto i mobilizatsiyata na balgarskata armia ot 1878 do 1944g*. Sofia: Darzhavno voenno izdatelstvo, 1961.

Kraus, Jürgen. *The German Army in the First World War: Uniforms and Equipment 1914-1918*. Vienna: Verlag Militaria, 2004.

Lacoste, Werner. *Deutsche Sturmbataillone 1915-1918: Der Kaiserstul und das Markgräflerland als Geburtsstätte und Standort deutscher Sturmbataillone des Ersten Weltkrieges*. Aachen, Germany: Helios-Verlag, 2009.

Larcade, Jean-Louis. *Deutsche Sturmtruppen: Troupes d'assaut allemandes (1914-1918)*. Les Jonquerets de Livet, France: Editions des Argonautes, 2002.

Laparra, Jean-Claude. *Les "Gladiateurs": Les Formations Offensives dans l'Armée Allemande 1914-1918*. Louviers Cedex, France: Ysec Éditions, 2007.

Livesey, Anthony. *Great Battles of World War I*. New York: Macmillan Publishing, 1989.

Lupfer, Timothy T. *The Dynamics of Doctrine: The Changes in German Tactical Doctrine During the First World War*. Leavenworth Papers No.4. Fort Leavenworth, Kansas: Combat Studies Institute, U.S. Army Command and General Staff College, 1981.

Miles, L. Wardlaw. *History of the 308th Infantry 1917-1919*. New York and London: G. P. Putnam's Sons, 1927.

Morselli, Mario. *Caporetto 1917: Victory or Defeat?* London: Frank Cass Publishers, 2001.

Müller, Friedrich. *Brandenburgerisches Jäger-Bataillon Nr.3*. Oldenburg, Germany: Verlag Gerhard Stalling, 1922.

The New York Times Current History: The European War, Volumes 13 and 17. New York: The New York Times Company, 1917, 1919.

Northamptonshire Regimental History Committee. *The Northamptonshire Regiment 1914-1918*. Aldershot: Gale & Polden, 1932.

Ortner, M.C. *Die K.u.K. Sturmtruppen 1916-1918: Elitesoldaten der Monarchie: Österreichische Militärgeschichte 1998*, Volume 6. Vienna: Verlagsbuchhandlung Stöhr, 1998.

Riebicke, Otto (ed.). *Unsere Pioniere im Weltkriege*. Berlin: Kyffhäuser Verlag, 1925.

Richter, Oliver. *Sturmtruppen: The Kaiser's Elite Stormtroopers*. Erlangen, Germany: Verlag Jochen Vollert-Tankograd Publishing, 2010.

Rommel, Erwin. *Attacks*. Provo, Utah: Athena Press, 1979.

Rouquerol, Jean-Joseph. *La Guerre en Argonne*. Paris: Payot, 1937.

Samuels, Martin. *Command or Control? Command, Training and Tactics in the German and British Armies, 1888-1918*. London: Frank Cass, 1995.

Saunders, Anthony. *Weapons of the Trench War 1914-1918*. Phoenix Mill, Stroud, Gloustershire: Sutton Publishing, 1999.

Schindler, John R. *Isonzo: The Forgotten Sacrifice of the Great War*. Westport, Connecticut: Praeger, 2001.

Schwencke, Alexander, and Martin Reymann. *Die Tragödie von Verdun 1916. II. Teil: Das Ringen um Fort Vaux Reichsarchiv Band 14*. Oldenburg, Germany: Drud und Verlag von Gerhard Stalling, 1928.

Von Schwerin, Eberhard Graf. *Königliches preussisches Sturm-Bataillon Nr.5 (Rohr)*. Zeulenroda in Thüringen, Germany: Drud und Verlag von Bernhard Sporn, 1939.

Simonds, Frank H. *History of the World War, Volume 5: The Victory of Armistice*. Garden City, New York: Doubleday, Page and Company, 1920.

Stallings, Laurence. *The Doughboys: The Story of the AEF, 1917-1918*. New York: Harper and Row, 1963.

Taylor, Emerson Gifford. *New England in France, 1917-1919. A History of the Twenty-sixth Division U.S.A.* Boston and New York: Houghton Mifflin Company, 1920.

Thomas, Nigel, and Dusan Babac. *Armies in the Balkans 1914-18*. Botley, Oxford: Osprey Publishing, 2001.

Thomas, Nigel, and Ramiro Bujeiro. *The German Army in World War I: 1917-18*, Volume 3. Botley, Oxford: Osprey Publishing, 2004.

Tröbst, Hans, and Artur Leipold. *Das posensche Pionier-Bataillon Nr.29 und seine Kriegsformationen.* Berlin: Kolk, 1932.

Tubbs, Floyd R., and Robert W. Clawson. *Stahlhelm: Evolution of the German Steel Helmet: Revised and Expanded Edition.* Kent, Ohio: Kent State University Press, 2000.

Tucker, Spenser C., and Priscilla Mary Roberts (eds.). *World War I: A Student Encyclopedia.* Santa Barbara: ABC-CLIO, Inc., 2006.

Walter, John. *Central Powers' Small Arms of World War One.* Ramsbury, Marlborough, Wiltshire: The Crowood Press, 1999.

White, B. T. *Tanks and other Armored Fighting Vehicles 1900 to 1918.* New York: MacMillan Publishing Co., 1970.

Wilson, H. W., and J. A. Hammerton (eds.). *The Great War.* London: The Amalgamated Press, 1915-1918.

Windrow, Martin. *Tank and AFV Crew Uniforms Since 1916.* Carrollton, Texas: Squadron/Signal Publications, 1979.

Woolley, Charles. *Uniforms and Equipment of the Imperial German Army 1900-1918,* Volumes 1 and 2. Atglen, Pennsylvania: Schiffer Publishing, 1999, 2000.

Wynne, G. C. *If Germany Attacks: The Battle in Depth in the West.* Westport, Connecticut: Greenwood Press, 1976.

Zabecki, David T. *Steel Wind: Colonel Georg Bruchmüller and the Birth of Modern Artillery.* Westport, Connecticut: Praeger, 1994.

Zaloga, Stephen. *German Panzers 1914-1918.* Botley, Oxford: Osprey Publishing, 2006.

Articles

Alfoldi, Lazlo M. "The Hutier Legend." *Parameters* 5 (1976).

Greiff, Walter. "Durchbruchschlacht." *Kreuz-Zeitung* No.71 (March 24, 1935).

Scholarly Works

Bigelow, Maurice C. "A Critical Analysis of the Battle of Caporetto." Individual research paper, U.S. Army Command and General Staff School, 1932.

Meyer, Bradley J. "Innovation and Expertise: Some Changes in German Tactical Doctrine during World War I," Master of Art thesis, Ohio State University, 1981.

Stackpole, Patrick T. "German Tactics in the 'Michael' Offensive, March 1918." Master of Military Art and Science thesis, U. S. Army Command and General Staff College, 1993.

Online Resources

http://www.asienkorps.de
http://www.denkmalprojekt.org
http://www.militaerpass.net
http://www.pickelhauben.net
http://www.supotnitskiy.ru/
http://www.worldwar1.com/

Glossary

Angriffsdivision - attack division, all members of which were trained as shock troops. Called "shock division" by the Allies.

Angriffstrupp - attack squad.

Aufraumungswelle - clearing out wave; second assault wave.

Aufrollen - rolling up a trench with grenades and often flamethrowers. Conceived by Leutnant Walter Beumelberg of *Pionier-Bataillon Nr.30.*

Batterietrupp - battery squad; reconnaissance squad of artillery battery.

Bautrupp - consolidation squad; used to convert a captured trench.

Brandröhre - fire tube. Incendiary device consisting of sheet-metal tube filled with fusing compound. Used by pioneers and assault troops.

Brandröhrentrupp - fire tube squad. Consisted of one NCO (as needed) and five pioneers. Two carried a guide pole and three carried armed fire tubes.

Eingreifdivision - counterattack division, used in elastic defense.

Einheitsgruppe - unit squad; light machine-gun squad and rifleman-grenadier squad, up to 16 men in total.

Erkundungstrupp - scouting or reconnaissance squad.

Erkungdungspatrouille - reconnaissance patrol; often performed as a raiding party.

Fang - (abbr.) flame attack. See *Flammenangriff.*

Fert - (abbr.) flame defense. See *Flammenverteidigung.*

Feuerwaltz - rolling barrage.

Fl.W. - (abbr.) flamethrower. See *Flammenwerfer.*

Flammenangriff - flame attack. See Fang.

Flammenbegleittrupp - flame accompanying squad. Flamethrower squad attached to an infantry assault unit.

Flammenstoss - flame shock or flame attack; also flame burst.

Flammenstosstrupp - flame shock troop. Assault unit consisting of small-flamethrower squads and infantrymen armed with grenades, rifles, and light machine guns.

Flammenverteidigung - flame defense. See Fert.

Flammenwerfer - flamethrower.

Flammenwerferstosstrupp - flamethrower shock troop. Consisted of:
shock-troop leader *(Stosstruppführer),*
two flamethrower squads (*Kleiftrupps* or *Wextrupps*),
four hand-grenade throwers *(Handgranatenwerfern).*
See *Flammenstosstrupp, Flammenwerfertrupp, Stosstrupp.*

Flammenwerfertrupp - small-flamethrower squad of four men.

Flankenstosstrupp, Flankensturmtrupp - flank shock or assault squad; guarded the branches of the occupied trench.

Flügelstosstrupp, Flügelsturmtrupp - wing shock or assault squad; protected the flanks of the raiding party.

Gebirgsjäger - mountain *Jäger* or light infantryman.

Gebirgskanone - mountain gun.

Gerätetrupp - equipment squad; transported shields, hand grenades, spades, and pickaxes of shock troops.

Grabenkanone - trench cannon; 37mm gun.

Granatenwerfer, Granatwerfer - grenade launcher.

Greifzug - intervention platoon; assault platoon.

Handgranatentrupp - hand-grenade squad of six to nine men.

indianermässigen Vorpirschen - Indian-style Forward Stalking. A method of moving forward indirectly, in small leaps and bounds, while taking advantage of the natural cover provided by the terrain.

Infanteriebegleitbatterie - infantry accompanying battery; 77mm artillery pieces that accompanied the infantry to engage in direct fire.

Infanteriebegleitgeschütz - infantry accompanying gun; infantry gun.

Infanteriekanone - infantry cannon; infantry gun.

Infanteriegeschütz - infantry gun; artillery piece used by assault troops to engage in direct fire.

Infanteriegeschützbatterie - infantry gun battery.

Jagdkommando - hunting command; a temporary assault formation.

Kampfzug - combat platoon.

Kleif - (abbr.) small or medium flamethrower.

Kleifstosstrupp - small/medium-flamethrower shock troop. Consisted of:
shock-troop leader *(Stosstruppführer)*,
two four-man *Kleif* squads *(Kleiftrupps)*,
four hand-grenade throwers *(Handgranatenwerfern)*.
See *Kleif, Kleiftrupp*.

Kleiftrupp - small-flamethrower squad of four men.

kleine Flammenwerfer - small flamethrower.

Ladungswerfer - charge thrower.

leichtes-Maschinengewehr-Abteilung - Light Machine Gun Detachment.

Maschinengewehr-Scharfschützen-Abteilung - Machine Gun Marksman Detachment.

Messertaktik - Knife Tactic. A tactic in which long, narrow formations of flamethrower shock troops attacked the enemy line perpendicularly.

Minenwerfer - trench mortar.

mittlere Flammenwerfer - medium flamethrower.

Musketen-Bataillon - automatic-rifle battalion.

Nahkampfbatterie - close-combat battery of 77mm guns used in an antitank role.

Offizierspatrouille - officer patrol; reconnaissance patrol composed of officers and NCOs.

Panzerkraftwagen-Maschinengewehr-Abteilung - Armored Vehicle Machine Gun Detachment; armored-car detachment.

Patrouille - patrol; raiding party.

Patrouillenkommando - patrol command.

Patrouillentrupp - patrol squad.

Priesterwerfer, Priestwerfer - grenade launcher invented by Hungarian priest named Vecer.

Scherentrupp - wire-cutting squad.

Schwarmlinie - swarm line; a line of skirmishers.

Schwere Kampfwagen-Abteilung - Heavy Fighting Vehicle Detachment; tank detachment.

Spähtrupp - observation squad.

springenden Angriff - pouncing attack. An assault using only small portable flamethrowers. See *vereinten stehenden und springenden Angriff.*

stehenden Angriff - stationary attack. An assault using only large emplaced flamethrowers. See *vereinten stehenden und springenden Angriff.*

Stellungsdivision - position division, assigned to hold a position. Also called "defensive division" by the Allies.

Stossbatterie - shock battery; artillery that accompanied infantry to engage in direct fire.

Stosseinheit - shock unit of any size.

Stosseinheit in Form eines Angriffskeils - shock unit in the form of an attacking wedge. Consisted of:
two flamethrower shock troops,
three light machine-gun squads,
three grenade-launcher squads,
two infantry squads,
one squad of pioneers with explosives,
one infantry half-squad as machine-gun ammunition carriers,
one infantry squad as grenade-launcher ammunition carriers,
one infantry half-squad as hand-grenade throwers.

Stosseinheit in Form zum Aufrollen eines Schutzengrabens - shock unit for rolling up a trench. Consisted of:
two flamethrower shock troops,
two light machine-gun squads,
one grenade-launcher squad,
one infantry squad.

Stosskolonne - shock column.

Stosslinie - shock line, or line of attack.

Stosstrupp (pl. Stosstrupps) - shock troop. Varied in size from a squad up to a company.

Stosstruppen - members of a shock troop.

Stosszug - shock platoon.

Streifpatrouille - campaign patrol.

Streiftrupp - campaign squad.

Sturmabteilung - assault detachment. Varied in size from a squad up to a company.

Sturmabwehr - repelling of an assault.

Sturmabwehrgeschütz - assault defense gun; infantry gun used to repel an assault.

Sturmanzug - assault order.

Sturmbataillon - assault battalion.

Sturmbatterie - assault battery.

Sturmbegleitbatterie - assault accompanying battery.

Sturmbegleitkanone - assault accompanying cannon.

Sturmgasse - passage through wire for the assault.

Sturmgruppe - assault squad of eight to 16 men.

Sturmkolonne - assault column.

Sturmkompagnie - assault company.

Sturmleiter - assault ladder.

Sturmleitertrupp - assault-ladder squad.

Sturmmarsch - quickened step for the assault.

Sturmpanzerkraftwagen-Abteilung - assault armored vehicle detachment; tank detachment.

Sturmreifmachen - to prepare for the assault.

Sturmreifschiessen - to bombard in preparation for the assault.

Sturmstellung - position from which the assault is made.

Sturmtrupp - (**pl. Sturmtrupps**) - assault squad or troop.

Sturmtruppe - (**pl. Sturmtruppen**) - assault unit.

Sturmtruppen - assault troops; members of a *Sturmtruppe.*

Sturmvorbereitungsfeuer - preparatory bombardment.

Sturmwelle - assault wave; first wave of an assault.

Trägertrupp - carrying squad for supplies and ammunition.

Trupp - (**pl. Trupps**) - squad or troop.

Truppe - (**pl. Truppen**) unit, troops, corps.

Unterstützungstrupp - support squad; prevented traffic congestion among assault troops and helped convert captured trench.

Verbindungstrupp - construction squad; used to improve captured trenches.

vereinten stehenden und springenden Angriff - combined stationary and pouncing attack. An assault using large emplaced flamethrowers and small mobile flamethrowers. See *springenden Angriff; stehenden Angriff.*

verstärkter Flammenwerferstosstrupp - reinforced small/medium-flamethrower shock troop. Consisted of:
two shock-troop leaders *(Stosstruppführern),*
three flamethrower squads (*Kleiftrupps* or *Wextrupps*),
six hand-grenade throwers *(Handgranatenwerfern).*

Verstärkungswelle - strengthening wave; third assault wave.

Wechselapparat - interchangeable flamethrower. Small, ring-shaped flamethrower introduced in 1917. See *kleine Flammenwerfer, Wex.*

Weiderstandnest - nest of resistance comprised of mutually supporting pillboxes, strong points, and machine-gun bunkers.

Wex - (abbr.) small, ring-shaped flamethrower. See *kleine Flammenwerfer, Wechselapparat.*

Wexbegleittrupp - *Wex* accompanying squad, attached to an infantry unit. See *Wechselapparat, Wex.*

Wextrupp - small-flamethrower squad of four men.

Zangen-Taktik - Pincers Tactic. Squeezing the target between machine-gun and grenade-launcher fire and a flamethrower assault.

Index